Lobbying America

POLITICS AND SOCIETY IN TWENTIETH-CENTURY AMERICA

SERIES EDITORS

William Chafe, Gary Gerstle, Linda Gordon, and Julian Zelizer

A list of titles

in this series appears

at the back of

the book

.

Lobbying America

THE POLITICS OF BUSINESS FROM NIXON TO NAFTA

Benjamin C. Waterhouse

PRINCETON UNIVERSITY PRESS

PRINCETON AND OXFORD

Copyright © 2014 by Princeton University Press
Published by Princeton University Press, 41 William Street, Princeton, New Jersey 08540
In the United Kingdom: Princeton University Press, 6 Oxford Street, Woodstock,
Oxfordshire OX20 1TW

press.princeton.edu
Jacket photograph: Pennsylvania Avenue, 1962. Courtesy of the District Department of
Transportation (DDOT), Washington, DC

Library of Congress Cataloging-in-Publication Data

Waterhouse, Benjamin C., 1978–
  Lobbying America : the politics of business from Nixon to NAFTA /
Benjamin C. Waterhouse.
      pages cm. — (Politics and society in twentieth-century America)
  Includes bibliographical references and index.
  ISBN 978-0-691-14916-5 (hardcover)
  1. Lobbying—United States—History—20th century. 2. Pressure groups—United
States—History—20th century. 3. Political action committees—United States—
History—20th century. 4. Corporations—Political activity—United States—History—
20th century. 5. Business and politics—United States—History—20th century. I. Title.
  JK1118.W36 2013
  324'.4097309045—dc23

                                                                    2013018172

British Library Cataloging-in-Publication Data is available

This book has been composed in Sabon

Printed on acid-free paper. ∞

Printed in the United States of America

10 9 8 7 6 5 4 3 2 1

Para Daniela, por amor
and for my father, who's read every word

Contents

Acknowledgments

ALTHOUGH THE DEBTS I have accumulated in the ten years I spent on this book are innumerable, I will try my best to enumerate them here. This study is based on work done at Harvard University under the direction of Professor Lizabeth Cohen. My debt to Professor Cohen is very great for her unfailing encouragement, for her critical reading of the manuscript at various stages, and, most of all, for her influence—often subtle but always profound—on my thinking. The inquiry began life as a seminar paper when Sven Beckert off-handedly advised a confused first-year graduate student to look into something called the Business Roundtable. His wise counsel on the study of business elites as social actors as well as his enthusiasm for the history of capitalism have left a clear mark on this book. In the last four years, I have found a wonderful professional home in the history department of the University of North Carolina at Chapel Hill and am thankful for the support of the staff, especially Joy Jones, Joyce Loftin, and Adam Kent, as well as the graduate students, undergraduates, and faculty.

Several scholars deserve effusive thanks for reading all or significant parts of the manuscript along the way: Julian Zelizer, Kim Phillips-Fein, Ed Balleisen, Lisa McGirr, Louis Hyman, Jennifer Delton, Mark Wilson, Bethany Moreton, Zaragosa Vargas, Ajay Mehrotra, Kathleen DuVal, and my go-to economist Marc Levinson. Kim McQuaid, a model of scholarly citizenship, not only commented on early drafts of several chapters but graciously shared his now thirty-year-old notes on the creation of the Business Roundtable. My gratitude also goes to Chuck Myers and the staff at Princeton University Press for their faithful stewardship of the book, and to Jenn Backer for astute copyediting. Several extremely helpful research assistants devoted many hours at crucial points in this process. I sincerely thank Scott Krause, Summer Shafer, and Xaris Martínez, who checked every note.

A number of participants in or witnesses to the events described in this book agreed to speak or correspond with me, either formally or off the record, and thus shaped my analysis in important ways. For their time and insight, I am very grateful to Bernadette Budde, James A. Baker III, John Post, Dr. Carl Grant, Mark Green, Ralph Nader, John Richard, Victor Kamber, Jules Bernstein, and Dan Fenn. Golf blogger John Sabino graciously allowed me to cite his description of the Links Club. Former Business Roundtable president John Castellani twice granted me permission to consult that group's privately held papers, a privilege for which I am extremely grateful.

Even historians of the relatively recent past find untold treasures in the archives, where skilled, patient, and talented reference librarians and archivists play a vital role in scholarly work. For their kindness, wisdom, and professionalism, I would like to thank: Barbara Burg at Widener Library; Marge McNinch, Lucas Clawson, Jon Williams, Carol Lockman, and Lynn Catanese at the Hagley Library; Stacy Davis, Josh Cochran, and Mary Lukens at the Ford Library; Keith Shuler at the Carter Library; Terri Goldich at the University of Connecticut's Dodd Center; Christopher Pendleton at the Bush Library; Lisa Jones at the Reagan Library; and Sahr Conway-Lanz at the National Archives. Amie Brennan and Joe Crea at the Business Roundtable aided my research there and fielded subsequent inquiries.

I have benefited from the opportunity to present aspects of this work in a number of academic settings, where participants' comments, critiques, and questions greatly influenced my arguments and presentation. I thank members of the Market Cultures Workshop in New York City (h/t Julia Ott), the Rethinking Regulation Working Group at Duke University, and the Triangle Legal History Seminar; audiences at the Business History Conference, Power and the History of Capitalism, the American Historical Association, the Organization of American Historians, and the Policy History Conference; and participants in faculty lunch colloquia in the history departments at UNC and Duke. Parts of chapter 4 were previously published in the *Journal of American History* as "Mobilizing for the Market: Organized Business, Wage-Price Controls, and the Politics of Inflation, 1971–1974" (September 2013). Finally, I gratefully acknowledge the financial support I received from: Harvard University's history department, Graduate School of Arts and Sciences, Charles Warren Center for Studies in American History, Center for American Political Studies, and Weatherhead Center for International Affairs; the Harvard Business School's Chandler Travel Grant; the Hagley Museum and Library; the Gerald R. Ford Library; the O'Donnell Grant Program at the George Bush Presidential Library Foundation; the Newcomen Society of the United States; and UNC's history department, Dickson Fund, and College of Arts and Sciences.

Many other scholars, friends, and colleagues have had a hand in shaping this book by providing commentary, suggesting relevant sources, and otherwise supporting my inquiry. With deep gratitude, I thank especially: Noam Maggor, Ann Wilson, Betsy More, Miles Fletcher, Konrad Jarausch, Peter Coclanis, Lee Vinsel, Dominique Tobbell, Paula Gajewski, Mark Rose, Christine Desan, James Kloppenberg, Bruce Schulman, Meg Jacobs, Gerald Davis, William Becker, James Livingston, Judith Stein,

Elizabeth Sanders, Ed Berkowitz, Jonathan Weiner, Lawrence Baxter, Jeff Fear, and John A. Ruddiman (the elder). For nearly a century of intellectual stimulation (combined), I thank Jeffrey F. Haynes, Curtis A. T. Wright, and Vilas K. Sridharan.

Professor Jake Ruddiman has been a source of wisdom and encouragement since college. From the muggy July evening in Paris when he talked me into going to graduate school through the travails of doctoral work and our good fortune to land jobs in the same state, he has been a superb friend and counselor. Finally, I wish to acknowledge years of support from Professor Walter Jean of Georgetown University, whose "soap box" thesis has proved invaluable to my career so far.

My family has always been my first and most important source of strength. In their individual ways, my parents, Claudia and Bill Waterhouse, have opened many doors for me throughout my life. More important, their love and support have given me the confidence to open many more. I can never thank them enough. My sister and brother-in-law Molly and Mark bring humor and spirit to my life. Finally, in the brief years I was blessed to know them, my parents-in-law, Damião and Maria Leite of João Pessoa, Brazil, inspired and taught me in ways I was never able to express but which I hope they knew. They left this world too soon and too suddenly, and their loss has left a hole in the hearts of all who knew them. I am proud to be their *genro*.

Daniela Leite Waterhouse makes me who I am. This brilliant and beautiful woman has the perfect ability to lift me up, nudge me along, or push me back into my place, depending on what I need at the moment. She imbues my life with purpose and inspires my heart. She is my compass, my coach, my teacher, and my best friend. Finally, she is my steady and unfailing partner in the most important work of my life, raising our amazing children, Luna and Gabriel, who are the source of my perspective on what matters most. *À la tienne, mon ange.*

Lobbying America

American Business, American Politics

IN THE SUMMER OF 2011, the front-runner for the Republican presidential nomination stumped for votes in Iowa. A founder of the private equity firm Bain Capital, Mitt Romney was one of the wealthiest men ever to seek the nation's highest office, and he campaigned vigorously on the strength of his private sector know-how. Boasting only limited experience in electoral politics—a four-year stint as governor of Massachusetts that followed a failed run for Senate—Romney embodied a longstanding hope in American politics: that a businessman turned statesman could cut through the morass of ideology and infighting to restore prosperity to a beleaguered economy. Yet like Wendell Willkie, Steve Forbes, and countless others before him, Romney discovered that running as the "business candidate" brought substantial challenges, even from within his own party. In a telling exchange at the Iowa State Fair, for example, Romney awkwardly confronted the persistent anticorporate populism that has long marked American political discourse. As he proclaimed the perils of the national budget deficit, some in the crowd shouted that Congress should raise taxes to fund social programs like Medicare. No, Romney insisted, he would never "raise taxes on people." But the hecklers weren't finished. Not people, they countered: "Corporations!" Rather than back off, the candidate engaged the critique, intoning an instantly famous phrase that succinctly captured one of the most protracted and important debates in modern American politics. Tax corporations instead of people? The Republican hopeful would do no such thing. "Corporations *are* people, my friend," he said.[1]

In a narrow sense, Romney was completely correct. Any new corporate expense, like a tax, would change the way a company allocated its funds and affect the distribution of money to actual human beings. Moreover, business historians largely agree that "legal corporate personhood," such as the right to own property or sue in court, proved instrumental to the development of modern capitalism. Yet by stressing the *distinctions* between corporations and the people who manage them, Romney ironically proved himself wrong in the larger sense: corporations cannot pay taxes because only people can pay taxes, he said. Corporations, therefore, are not people.

Yet the rhetorical firestorm that Romney's comment provoked, both among his Republican rivals and in liberal circles, extended far beyond legal notions of corporate personhood and the semantics of taxation.

Rather, Romney's entire campaign, from his successful quest for the Republican nomination to his loss to President Barack Obama in November 2012, reflected persistent and contentious debates over the role of business and business leaders in national politics. Corporations may not be people, but people do run corporations, and many achieve great wealth in the process. But how should that economic power operate politically, and in whose interests? Do corporate leaders' values enhance or detract from the public good and the general welfare? In a political democracy, what is the appropriate role for business?

Americans have grappled with such questions throughout their history. Business has tangled with the state since the earliest days of the republic, and the interests of capital have frequently clashed with the demands of democracy. Industrialization and the expansion of modern administrative government brought ever louder complaints, as entrepreneurs and executives from J. P. Morgan to Ross Perot opined that "politicians just don't get it" or that only businesspeople "know what it takes" to run the country right. At times, particularly amid economic unrest, American voters have felt drawn to the notion that a captain of industry might hold the secrets to renewed prosperity. Yet just as often, such appeals have faltered in the face of longstanding concerns over unchecked corporate power and the unseemly pursuit of profit. The mix of admiration and skepticism with which the American public views corporations and their leaders has deeply shaped the nation's political values and traditions.

Although the business community has always played an important role in national politics, American corporate leaders came to wield a historically unprecedented degree of influence over both political debate and policymaking in the late twentieth century. As this book argues, this new phase of the politics of business dovetailed with the rise of an increasingly powerful conservative critique of New Deal–style liberalism that came to fruition during the economic crisis of the 1970s. That organized opposition, which both grew from and fed off of popular distrust of government, reshaped American politics into an ideological contest over the role of the state. In the wake of liberalism's apparent failures, conservatives promoted "business" and its abstract partner, "free enterprise," as alternatives. Indeed, although Americans had long debated the public role of private enterprise, only in the last three decades of the twentieth century did the now common dichotomy between "business" and "government," or the idea that devotion to "state" and "market" entailed mutually exclusive social visions, come to dominate national politics.[2]

This book contends that the decline of liberal and progressive politics and the ascent of a business-oriented, neoliberal political culture did not emerge naturally from the exigencies of economic crisis or the inexorable logic of political traditions but rather as the result of specific efforts by a diverse set of conservative activists. In the chapters that follow, I examine one such group—the executives, managers, public affairs experts, and trade association directors who claimed to speak for the collective interests of the American business community. Through their mobilization in the 1970s, I argue, these business leaders catalyzed and shaped the process that historians have labeled the "right turn" toward conservatism in American politics. To the extent that corporations are people, in other words, this book is about those people.

In the 1970s and 1980s, as the global economic landscape shifted beneath their feet, a coalition of business leaders worked to halt the expansion of the regulatory state, decrease the power of labor unions, liberalize market mechanisms, and shift the tax burden. Their "movement," to use the term loosely, united corporate executives and free-market ideologues, association directors and small shop owners, presidential staff members and think-tank scribblers. *Lobbying America* tells the story of that movement, focusing chiefly on the country's three most significant business associations—the U.S. Chamber of Commerce, the National Association of Manufacturers, and, after 1972, the Business Roundtable—which united corporate leaders from across industries and regions and formed the backbone of a powerful political coalition. Although business's critique of modern liberalism developed over decades, if not generations, it achieved a new level of political effectiveness by the mid-1970s. Organized through these business associations, corporate activists played a vital role in stopping the tide of liberal reform legislation and took much, but not all, of the wind from the sails of organized labor and the public interest movement. Tapping into Americans' longstanding ambivalence toward state power, these champions of market-based economic policies fundamentally reshaped public debates on regulation, taxation, and fiscal policy by the 1980s.

Yet business's triumph was far from absolute, notwithstanding frantic cries from certain corners that the capitalist class naturally rules politics with an iron fist. Indeed, the story told in this book highlights the limitations of business activism in addition to its successes. Progressive liberals, despite suffering fracture and a loss of cohesion in the 1970s and 1980s, remained a significant political foil. More important, disagreements both parochial and philosophical frequently strained business activists' unity, and internal divisions at times prevented them from achieving their stated goals. Those struggles exacerbated tensions within conservatism, especially between businesspeople and populist skeptics of corporate power (like Romney's hecklers). Divisions over regulatory and fiscal policy in the 1980s, for example, presaged later schisms, including the rise of the Wall Street–bashing Tea Party movement in 2009. Moreover, the institutional and ideological glue that held the business coalition together proved weak and fleeting. In the face of economic globalization, ideological fracture, and the financialization of the American economy, the broad-based campaign for a "pro-business" agenda ultimately waned. Although business leaders continued to wield substantial political power as individuals, the coalition that emerged from the economic crisis of the 1970s did not survive the 1980s with nearly as much collective clout.

Although their organizational cohesion did not endure, organized American business leaders nonetheless established a vital legacy that continues to shape politics into the twenty-first century. Through their political mobilization, these workhorses of the industrial economy helped establish the political preconditions for the success of conservative politics, electorally and in policymaking. Through their sustained intellectual and lobbying offensive, these corporate leaders helped redefine the way Americans discussed issues like regulation, labor, and the role of government in the economy and loudly defended the assertion, captured so fully in Mitt Romney's presidential campaign, that business leaders naturally know best how to govern a modern, diverse democracy. By successfully parlaying their economic clout into a broad-reaching movement with real policy consequences, they cemented a conservative and market-oriented political vision whose legacy lingers today.

WHO AND WHAT IS BUSINESS?

The story of business's political mobilization is deeply entwined with the history of conservative politics, but it also departs in important ways from the trajectory that historians, journalists, and political insiders often describe. In the last twenty years, scholars have explored modern conservatism from all sides and have analyzed in great detail the often fraught intellectual, philosophical, and organizational connections among self-identified conservatives. This scholarship analyzes a broad array of grassroots social activists, Burkean intellectuals, religious and moral crusaders, racist reactionaries, economic libertarians, and ardent Cold Warriors, as well as the politicians who organized their activities, courted their votes, and relied on their financial and political support. While scholars debate this diverse group's goals, coherence, and ultimate successes, few doubt that it mounted a sustained and penetrating critique of New Deal–style liberalism and became the defining political story of the late twentieth century. Moreover, most accounts agree that conservative politics proved sufficiently expansive to include within its ranks the powerful corporate interests that mobilized through national business associations in the 1970s. Business leaders, in other words, emerged as a standard constituency of conservative politics.[3]

Yet the executives and business association leaders who populate this book were distinct from those people often described as "movement conservatives"—politicians like Barry Goldwater and Ronald Reagan as well as policy entrepreneurs like Richard Viguerie and Jude Wanniski. The people whose lobbying campaigns I analyze embraced a unique role and specific policy agenda on issues that directly affected their companies and industries. Most were career managers, not self-made entrepreneurs, during a period of American capitalism in which managerial values— professionalism, pragmatism, consistency—dominated business culture. Although the majority shared conservative perspectives on economic is- sues, many identified as liberals, or at least modern Democrats, on ques- tions like race, immigration, and feminism. Indeed, most politically active executives and association leaders kept their distance from hot-button issues like Vietnam, Watergate, and civil rights. More important, rela- tively few saw themselves as a part of a "conservative movement." Although ideology played an important organizing and proselytizing role, these men were not ideological foot soldiers in Ronald Reagan's army. Rather, they were "business conservatives" who focused on labor, regulation, eco- nomic planning, and taxation with minimal interest in most social issues. Throughout this book, therefore, I employ terms like "liberalism" and "conservatism" in the context of business and economic debates, leaving other aspects of modern American politics to other scholars.[4]

By incorporating the politics of business leaders into the broader history of conservatism, this book expands beyond recent scholarship that places a high explanatory premium on intellectuals, politicians, and right-wing policy entrepreneurs. One result is that the story told here ex- poses the failures of the left in addition to the triumphs of the right. In the second half of the twentieth century, American liberalism splintered mightily, not from an outside attack but under the weight of its own internal contradictions. As a philosophy of government simultaneously committed to the collective good and to the rights of individuals, liber- alism faced challenges when those two imperatives came into conflict. Labor-liberals and public interest reformers in particular clashed over such contests of rights—a union member's right to a well-paid factory job versus a citizen's right to clean air achieved by closing down that fac- tory, for example. The "pocketbook politics" of the stagflationary 1970s exacerbated those tensions as one person's pay raise became another's price hike. As several chapters of this book demonstrate, business conser- vatives skillfully positioned themselves to take advantage, and postwar liberalism's failure to reconcile its competing impulses created intellec- tual and political space for antiliberal policies.

At the same time, business leaders likewise suffered the sting of inter- nal contradictions that hampered their political activism. Historically, a critical fault line has divided big business from small business, or, in today's parlance, the interests of "Wall Street" from the interests of "Main Street." Prior to the Great Depression and the rise of New Deal–style liberalism, distinctions according to size dominated the politics of business. Yet as historians like Alan Brinkley have argued, the antimonopolist spirit that so shaped the Progressive Era declined sharply in the postwar period.[5] Although the populist impulse that valorized small over large enterprise certainly persisted in many quarters, Americans' general acceptance of bigness—from government bureaucracies to corporate organizations—helped blur those distinctions in policy debates. Indeed, just as the liberal coalition assembled by Franklin Roosevelt and the New Dealers managed to unite disparate constituencies, so too did business leaders and conservative activists achieve common cause between big and small firms. Although the alliances they formed were far from airtight, the politics of business that this book explores encompassed the interests of everyone from the CEO of the United States Steel Corporation to the self-employed accountant; from defense contractors at Lockheed to the owners of a photography studio in Chapel Hill, North Carolina.

As a political category, business has a clearly discernible identity, and anyone who reads the news understands the journalist who writes that "Business opposed the legislation" or "the president sought support from business." But this identity is both slippery and historically contingent. "Business" does not entail a constant set of values or preferences across different industries, sectors, and regions, or across time. In this book, I employ the concepts of "business" and "business leader" primarily to describe people who self-identified as representatives of concerns that extended beyond their specific corporate affiliation. In the 1960s and 1970s, as myriad speeches, letters, and media reports attest, "business" was frequently synonymous with "industry": the extractive, construction, chemical, energy, and automotive corporations that typified "big business." The managers and executives from those firms—almost exclusively college-educated white men—claimed to represent all of American business, whether acting individually or through organizations like the Business Roundtable or government advisory boards. As the early chapters of this book argue, large national employers' groups performed a vital homogenizing function by distilling the various parochial interests and preferences of their thousands of members into a coherent policy platform. Moreover, although such organizations counted many small enterprises alongside industrial giants on their membership rolls, their political lobbying positions in the 1970s collapsed those size-based distinctions. Even when they spoke for small business owners, the directors of national employers' associations nonetheless operated as "big business."

But the mobilization of American business, and thus the category of "business leader," extended beyond employers' associations. In the second half of the twentieth century, wealthy businesspeople increasingly found ways to influence politics with their checkbooks by bankrolling business-oriented policy institutes. Buoyed by corporate cash, these "think tanks" led an intellectual assault on liberalism and institutionalized conservative and libertarian economic policy ideas. Older organizations like the American Enterprise Institute (established 1938) underwent revivals in the 1960s and 1970s, while new outfits like the Heritage Foundation, the Cato Institute, and the American Legislative Exchange Council all burst onto the scene. Finally, individual companies also ramped up their political presence. Large firms retained growing numbers of in-house lobbyists, while small and midsized companies leaned more heavily on a growing army of industry-specific trade associations. Owners of small firms had their pick between two ideologically divergent national associations that represented their "class" interests, the conservative National Federation of Independent Business (NFIB) and the more liberal National Small Business Association, each of which expanded its scope and operations in the 1970s.[6]

The nation's three largest employers' associations, however, most clearly embodied the spirit of business's political mobilization. During the 1970s, the U.S. Chamber of Commerce, the National Association of Manufacturers (NAM), and the Business Roundtable distinguished themselves as the "Big Three" of business activism and the preeminent voice of the collective business community. Though institutionally and historically distinct, together they represented the belief that a united corporate class could and should defend the common interests of all business. Moreover, their public relations campaigns and direct advocacy with policymakers pioneered lobbying campaigns that recast political debates and policy options. As a result of their national prominence, the Chamber, the NAM, and the Roundtable form the empirical and analytic focus of this book.

The politics of business in an era of economic upheaval and dramatic change in the operation of American capitalism unfolded primarily on the national stage. Based in Washington, D.C., the organizations and leaders who populate this book dedicated the bulk of their political energies to national policymaking on such issues as environmental and consumer product regulation, labor law, economic planning, and taxation. Ironically, in an era in which Americans came to trust their government less and less and conservative politicians preached the virtues of antistatism, the federal government in the second half of the twentieth century became the fundamental battleground for organized business groups. To be sure, such a focus should not minimize business leaders' abiding concern with policy issues that extended beyond the nation's shores. Although this book primarily considers domestic economic policy and its implications for national politics, global economic transformations, from the liberalization of capital flows to the increasingly multinational nature of major producers, provide essential context for those debates. If I appear to downplay the international in favor of the national, such omissions stem from my desire to reflect the paramount concerns of my subjects.

Likewise, I can only hint in these pages at the numerous ways corporate leaders and business associations shaped American political culture outside Washington, D.C. As business and labor historians have shown, individual firms played vital roles in reshaping American capitalism during the second half of the twentieth century by deliberately relocating their factories, interceding in local politics, and partnering with local boosters. Moreover, the powerful dynamics of industrial relations likewise played out on state, municipal, and workplace levels. But the politics of business, as understood by the men who identified as its chief advocates, revolved around federal policy, so this book generally retains a focus on national politics. Thus I concentrate on organized labor's campaigns for specific legislation rather than its shop-floor operations, and I track regulatory politics in the U.S. Congress rather than in state houses. Business's issues were national issues, and its story is a national story.[7]

What Is Lobbying?

Lobbying is not the world's oldest profession, but it's close. For as long as human beings have selected some among their number to make decisions for the rest, people have found ways to promote their personal interests. At its heart, lobbying is the process by which an interested person or group petitions a society's leaders for some favor, benefit, or privilege. In the United States, every citizen's right to petition the government is enshrined in the First Amendment, alongside the freedoms of speech, religion, and the press. As any number of sordid tales confirm, the process has historically appeared messy and unseemly—from gunmaker Samuel Colt bribing congressmen to extend his patent to Tommy "The Cork" Corcoran using his New Dealer credibility to procure government contracts for clients. However, although businesspeople have lobbied government since the early days of the republic, the second half of the twentieth century witnessed a historic boom in the sheer quantity of paid representation. The mobilization of American business and the burgeoning strength of conservative critiques of liberalism arrived right along with this explosion in lobbying.[8]

For many people, in the 1970s no less than today, the very word "lobbying" provokes loud protests about corruption, influence peddling, and the underhanded subversion of democratic principles, and corporate lobbyists face the brunt of this public ire. Yet for all its pejorative implications, lobbying remains a protected constitutional right and, in the view of most policymakers, an indispensable element of modern governance. In the years after World War II, the federal bureaucracy grew ever more expansive and complex. The 535 voting members of Congress and the staffs of myriad regulatory and administrative agencies could never hope to remain abreast of the tremendous flow of information, analysis, and interpretation relevant to their daily decisions. Lobbyists fill that gap, as political scientist Lewis Dexter wrote in 1969, "by supplying information, feeding useful questions, writing speeches, making analyses of reports, finding out who is lined up how on any matter of concern." Indeed, from a social science perspective, lobbying's key function is to facilitate what business and legal scholar John de Figueiredo describes as "information transfer between interest groups and policymakers."[9]

The popular belief persists, however, that lobbying is dirty; information provided to a policymaker by an interested party is, by definition, self-serving and cannot make any claim to objectivity. For as long as there has been a government to lobby, therefore, reformers have advocated regulation. In the early years of industrialization, the United States took the lead over other democratically governed nations by attempting to reign in professional influence peddlers. In the 1870s, Congress responded to outrage over the machinations of railroad industry representatives by attempting to require lobbyists to register with the government, but those efforts fared poorly, beset by weak enforcement provisions. Beginning around the turn of the twentieth century, progressive political activists helped develop state-level regulations, such as the prohibition on giving gifts to lawmakers, and by the 1950s, nearly forty states regulated lobbying in some way. But at the federal level, only with the arrival of the modern administrative state during the New Deal did Congress make real strides. The first significant lobbying regulation occurred in 1935 and 1936 through the Public Utilities Holding Company Act and the Merchant Marine Act, which required employees of certain types of firms (registered holding companies and shipping companies, respectively) to file reports with the government before lobbying legislators or regulators. In 1938, fears of fascism spawned the Foreign Agents Registration Act, which regulated lobbying by representatives of foreign governments. Finally, in 1946, the Federal Regulation of Lobbying Act mandated that any person hired to lobby Congress on behalf of someone else had to register and submit reports of her or his expenses related to that lobbying. The legislation placed no limitations on the constitutionally protected act of lobbying itself, and even its calls for greater transparency and disclosure were, in the words of one lobbying expert, "widely ignored." That 1946 law was ultimately superseded by the Lobbying Disclosure Act of 1995, which broadened the definition of a lobbyist beyond those in the pay of third parties and increased the registration and reporting rules. During the entire period discussed in this book, therefore, the 1946 act was the law of the land.[10]

But the classical notion of lobbying represents only one avenue by which corporate leaders influenced the political process. Yet another essential component to business's political mobilization involved the dramatic increase in campaign donations to candidates who supported business groups' agenda. Although policymakers initially hesitated to restrict lobbying for fear of breaching the First Amendment right to petition, no such ambivalence applied to limiting campaign spending. The flagship regulations, the Tillman Act of 1907 and the Foreign Corrupt Practice Act of 1911, barred corporations and banks from giving money to candidates for federal office and established formal spending limits for certain federal campaigns.[11] Not until 1976, in *Buckley v. Valeo*, did the Supreme Court declare that political donations constituted constitutionally protected political speech (a logic upheld and extended in *Citizens United v. FEC* in 2010). As chapter 1 describes, a series of congressional reforms to campaign finance law, particularly after Watergate, paved the way for a dramatic explosion in corporate-funded political action committees (PACs), dramatically recasting the landscape of campaign financing.

By the end of the twentieth century, the concepts of campaign finance and corporate lobbying had become deeply intertwined in the national political imagination. The arrest, trial, and imprisonment of conservative lobbyist Jack Abramoff in 2006 revived the public's interest in big-money lobbyists with tight connections to fund-raising PACs. Lobbyists like Abramoff doubled as "bundlers," major campaign donors who used their influence and networks to encourage others to contribute the maximum amounts allowed. The *Citizens United* ruling in 2010, which overturned restrictions on corporate and union campaign donations on the grounds that such giving constituted constitutionally protected speech, likewise brought increased scrutiny on the intersection between influence and campaign finance. Furthermore, recent social science has demonstrated the degree to which modern lobbyists use campaign donations as a means to gain and maintain access to lawmakers. Although a minority of organized pressure groups devote resources to both lobbying and campaign finance—most choose one or the other—those who pursue both strategies account for a striking majority of the money spent on either one.[12]

Although this strategic combination of lobbying and campaign finance may appear commonplace in the post-Abramoff, post-*Citizens United* world, it represents a relatively recent historical development. In fact, during the years treated in this book, campaign finance and lobbying largely operated in separate spheres. Most interest groups, including major corporations and business associations, believed that influencing incumbent lawmakers through lobbying was far more important than donating to campaigns. Through the 1980s, in fact, many large corporations and trade associations kept their campaign contributions separate from their lobbying activities. Corporations, for example, would direct PAC money to local and state politicians where parochial decisions could have a major effect on their immediate balance sheets but did not give as much to national candidates. Instead they would send their lobbyists to Washington.[13]

Moreover, the practice of lobbying—a distinct strategy from campaign finance—can itself be divided into two distinct forms: direct and indirect. Direct lobbying, probably the more familiar form, occurs when a firm, union, or other interest group hires a specific person to represent its interests on a given piece of legislation or regulatory rule making. Such lobbyists might be permanent employees of a company or group, or they might be hired professionals from independent lobbying firms who represent clients but have no institutional commitment to any issues or causes. In the 1960s and 1970s, American companies hired greater numbers of in-house lobbyists and public affairs specialists, known euphemistically as "Washington Representatives," or sometimes just "WashReps." In 1961, for example, only 130 firms were represented by registered lobbyists, and only 50 of those were based in the nation's capital; by 1979, 650 firms boasted such representation, and 247 had staffs in Washington. As lobbyists' numbers grew, moreover, their character shifted. In the early 1960s, most Washington Representatives focused on sales and marketing and worked for companies that did significant business with the federal government, such as defense contractors. By the end of the 1970s, most full-time Washington Representatives were lawyers, public affairs executives, and former government officials whose daily work centered far more on legislative issues. Although the lobbyists' jobs and backgrounds changed, such in-house representation remained the dominant model for most large companies until the 1980s, when the proliferation of private lobbying firms offered companies the opportunity to outsource their Washington representation.[14] The growth of this second model created the much-reviled "revolving door" culture by which former government officials—elected and otherwise—routinely leave public service to leverage their insider contacts into lucrative paychecks.

Business's political mobilization in the 1970s—that brief moment of unity and intra-industry cohesion that so deeply shaped modern American politics—overlapped both the rise in direct lobbying by Washington Representatives and the rapid expansion of business-oriented PACs. Nonetheless, national employers' associations profited most from a different strategic option: indirect, sometimes called "grassroots," lobbying. Indirect lobbying meant that rather than hire professional influence peddlers, groups like the NAM, the Chamber, and the Business Roundtable organized constituents themselves to contact and pressure lawmakers on specific issues. Their chief organizational strategy thus involved rallying support among business owners, trade association members, and, in the case of the Business Roundtable, high-powered chief executive officers from major industrial corporations. As several chapters in this book illustrate, Washington-based associations used massive public relations campaigns to generate broad-based enthusiasm for or against certain policies. They then used their national networks to coordinate a common vocabulary—"talking points," to the cynics—and consistent message, which constituents from across the country communicated back to their representatives. Finally, paid lobbyists, association directors, and corporate executives relied on evidence of that grassroots support as they took their cases directly to lawmakers.

Indirect lobbying emerged as the most effective and most common strategy for national employers' associations because it provided a mechanism for overcoming the collective action problem at the heart of pan-business mobilization. Political campaign donations and direct lobbying represented firm- and industry-specific approaches to gaining preferential treatment, such as a subsidy or government contract, but they proved less effective vehicles for targeting larger policy issues whose effects touched different types of firms and industries. Why would a company devote scarce resources to a political battle where its competitors—who hadn't contributed—would also benefit? Employers' associations overcame these free-rider problems through the mechanisms of indirect lobbying, which involved less commitment of financial and political capital by individual companies. Because the issues they focused on most had the broadest appeal, these associations were able to develop vast networks to generate grassroots lobbying, rooted in broad ideological claims about free enterprise and the stifling effect of government regulation. As a result, this type of engagement cemented a shared political consciousness among disparate businesspeople and deepened their sense of commitment to a common political project. In the process, united and organized business groups honed their two-pronged attack on a variety of economic policy issues, targeting specific legislators as well as the general public's attitudes toward business, regulation, labor, and taxation. Their movement ultimately coalesced at the confluence of these tactics: on one hand, lobbying Congress; on the other, lobbying America.

***

Placing the politics of business in the context of a rapidly shifting economic and cultural landscape between the late 1960s and the early 1990s, *Lobbying America* tells the story of how businesspeople got themselves mobilized and what their mobilization created. The book follows a loose chronological format, although the thematic chapters in the middle overlap in time as they explore the variety of policies around which business groups mobilized. While certain issues, such as consumerism and taxes, receive sustained treatment in specific chapters, I spread the analysis of other themes, such as environmental regulation, inflation, and labor power, throughout the book. Overall, the narrative traces the politics of American business from a sense of foreboding and crisis in the late 1960s through its period of cohesion and political power in the mid- to late 1970s and finally to its fragmentation in the 1980s and 1990s. For in the end, the unity that distinguished business lobbying during the 1970s dissolved, fractured both by changes in the nature of American capitalism and by the shifting political climate. Yet even once that historical moment passed, the experience of the pan-business political movement left a profound legacy. By lobbying America, organized corporate leaders ultimately shaped both the policy options available to lawmakers and the framework through which Americans—liberals, conservatives, and all others—debated and considered the central problems of capitalism and democracy.

CHAPTER 1

From Consensus to a Crisis of Confidence

> The whole business community is going to have to get involved in
> political activities if our American way of life and our enterprise
> system, the free economy of this country, [are] going to survive.
> —Joseph Coors, executive vice president,
>   Adolph Coors Company, 1975

BUSINESSPEOPLE SHOULD HAVE BEEN HAPPY. The American economy
soared during the 1960s, and in 1969 a Republican named Richard Nixon
assumed the presidency, promising peace, prosperity, and a retreat from
his predecessors' "big government" policies. Yet despite that apparently
sunny forecast, a collective sense of woe descended across the American
business community as the 1970s dawned. Subdued in nervous whispers
at first, the ominous refrain grew louder, echoing through boardrooms
and conference centers, across golf courses and country clubs. By the
middle of the decade, the once-low grumbling reached a fevered pitch,
and despondent business leaders let loose a cacophonous scream:

"The American economic system is under broad attack," cried a jurist.[1]

"The American capitalist system is confronting its darkest hour," bemoaned an executive.[2]

"The existence of those free institutions which together make up the
very fabric of the free society is in jeopardy," proclaimed a think-tank
director.[3]

"Yet those institutions are under attack, and the captains of industry
stand helplessly by," complained a senator.[4]

To myriad business owners, executives, and conservative politicians
and intellectuals, the stakes could not have been higher. "The issue is
survival!" they cried. Survival of capitalism. Survival of free enterprise.
Survival of America.

But who was spearheading this dreaded attack? For conservative businesspeople, the culprit was neither the Soviet Union nor its secret agents
hiding under every bed. Rather, this perilous attack on liberty and prosperity took root among the most American of institutions. The assault
flowed, as one of the most publicized Cassandras put it, "from the college
campus, the pulpit, the media, the intellectual and literary journals, the
arts and sciences, and from politicians."[5] This sickness grew from a debilitating antibusiness bias that coursed through the veins of the American

body politic, infecting national policy. Heavy-handed, hyper-regulatory government, abetted by a public deeply hostile to business, increasingly saddled American companies with resource-sapping regulations, devastating taxes, and crippling labor policies. For the self-styled defenders of American business, the stakes far exceeded narrow concerns like profits and productivity. This totalizing attack stood poised to undo the very fabric of the "free enterprise system" itself.[6]

To appreciate the depth of this fear and loathing, consider the first-hand accounts by a team of social scientists retained by the Conference Board, a nonadvocacy business association. Founded in 1916, the Conference Board had long endeavored, in the words of its founder, Magnus Alexander (an executive at General Electric), to serve as "a clearinghouse of [business and economic] information" that would "promote a clearer understanding between the employer . . . and the public."[7] Reaffirming that mission in 1974 and 1975, Conference Board president Alexander Trowbridge (former commerce secretary under Lyndon Johnson and future president of the National Association of Manufacturers) arranged a series of three-day meetings for business leaders from across industrial sectors to gather informally and discuss the topic of corporate social responsibility. To document the pervasiveness of business's anxiety, Trowbridge invited two scholars: Leonard Silk, an academic economist and business columnist for the *New York Times*, and David Vogel, a young political scientist fresh out of graduate school at Princeton.

Like anthropologists in the bush, Silk and Vogel observed the Conference Board proceedings and conducted anonymous interviews with some 360 business leaders at eight weekend conferences over the course of a year. The interviews ranged widely, covering the executives' views on government, politics, the media, and liberal reform, and provided the backbone for *Ethics and Profits*, a searing psychological study of business leaders' troubled mind-set that Silk and Vogel published in 1976. According to the authors, the "Crisis of Confidence in American Business" (the book's subtitle) unfolded along two planes. On one hand, opinion polls demonstrated conclusively that between the mid-1960s and mid-1970s, Americans lost faith that business leaders would "do the right thing" or "serve the public interest." But just as important, Silk and Vogel showed that business leaders had also lost confidence in themselves. Though they retained a strong faith in the business system in general and remained convinced of their ability to successfully manage their firms, they believed they had lost the ability to communicate that success to the country. "Public acceptance of business has reached its lowest ebb in many a generation," one executive complained. Added another: "We have been inept in the communication of ideas and the information that creates understanding among people."[8] In a decade marked by numerous "crises of confidence"—capped famously by President Jimmy Carter's invocation of that phrase in his 1979 "malaise" speech—business leaders joined the chorus, protesting their impotence, voicelessness, and deep fear for the future.

The intense anger and pessimism that Silk and Vogel documented lay at the heart of the nearly paranoid declarations about an "attack on free enterprise." Business leaders firmly believed that the public's growing distrust, combined with their collective inability to defend themselves and promote the virtues of the capitalist system, had led directly to debilitating policy measures—including stiffer regulations and higher taxes. Such policies, they maintained, depressed profitability and caused economic stagnation, further decreasing the public's confidence in the private sector. In this devastating vicious cycle, rising unemployment fueled the heavy hand of government, so business leaders' sense of besiegement grew worse as economic performance slackened. As the robust growth of the 1960s gave way to rising inflation and declining productivity growth by 1970, trade association meetings and Rotary Club speeches hummed with despair over the future. After 1973, as the country suffered recession, severe price instability, energy crisis, and double-digit unemployment, these panicked warnings about the future of capitalism reached a fever pitch.

But such gnashing of teeth about existential threats to free enterprise was hardly new in the 1970s. Businesspeople have *always* complained about the government, particularly at moments of state expansion. The Conference Board itself formed in 1916 amid Progressive Era labor battles, when executives at large industrial corporations like General Electric bemoaned their low public approval and claimed that they risked losing control over their companies' operations.[9] Similarly, in the 1930s, Irénée du Pont rallied fellow industrialists to join his anti-Roosevelt American Liberty League by accosting the New Deal as "the Socialistic doctrine called by another name."[10] According to business historians like Alfred Chandler and Sanford Jacoby, American business leaders condemned government regulation in particularly fierce terms because of the peculiar birth order of managerial capitalism and the administrative state in the United States. Because big business developed in the late nineteenth century in the virtual absence of muscular bureaucratic regulation, employers developed a strong tradition of resisting state intrusion on their operations, and the persistence of such arguments after World War II reflected their long institutional memory.[11] And ironically, despite this tradition of vehement protests, scholars have also demonstrated the degree to which business has historically prospered under the stabilizing influence of growth- and competition-oriented regulatory policies.[12] Complaints about an assault on capitalism, in other words, have proved far from unusual and we should take them with a grain of salt.

Although couched in old-fashioned rhetoric, the crisis many business leaders articulated in the 1970s proved historically distinctive both in its causes and in its effects. To be sure, corporate executives and conservative politicians grossly exaggerated the threats business faced, just as du Pont had far overstated the "Socialistic" tendencies of the New Deal. Nonetheless, their feelings were genuine, largely because their anxiety stemmed directly from very real changes to the political and economic landscape in which business leaders operated. These broader transformations certainly did not augur the end of capitalism, but they did fundamentally unsettle the business world and fuel business leaders' antistatist hysteria. On a policy level, the restructuring of the administrative state through the proliferation of social regulations altered the landscape of interest group politics and increased compliance costs and disclosure requirements for more heavily regulated firms. Politically, the shifting composition of Congress—from the disintegration of the Solid South to the arrival of liberal "Watergate babies" in 1975—upset longstanding alliances between corporate leaders and representatives. On a cultural level, a palpable wave of hostility toward *all* established institutions swept American politics in the wake of the counterculture, Vietnam, and later Watergate, compounding business's crisis of confidence. Finally, very real shifts in global capitalism compounded business leaders' angst as foreign competition threatened profits and inflationary supply shocks sapped capital.

The powerful and sincere notions, however hyperbolic, that these changes provoked had real and profound consequences because business leaders' sense of panic directly sparked overt political action by an increasingly unified capitalist class. For most of the postwar period, business leaders had been loath to engage too directly in the political process. Some considered politics unseemly; others believed lobbying was a job best reserved for public relations specialists. In the early 1970s, however, longstanding political grievances reached a tipping point, as frenzied declarations of the "attack on free enterprise" drove many executives to overcome their reticence and inject themselves more forcefully into politics. At the Conference Board meetings that Silk and Vogel attended, one executive declared: "If you don't know your senator on a first-name basis, you are not doing an adequate job for your shareholders."[13] During the 1970s, in response, individual firms dramatically escalated their direct lobbying, corporate PACs multiplied, and libertarian and conservative think tanks blossomed across the political landscape, funded largely through donations by successful businesspeople. In addition, as chapters 2 and 3 explore in greater detail, industry-specific and pan-business trade associations responded to the sense of an external threat to business by greatly expanding their memberships, budgets, lobbying prowess, and influence. Ultimately, this pan-industry mobilization formed an integral part of a conservative intellectual and political project to undermine the political ethos and institutional structures of the New Deal state. What made the politics of business in the 1970s unique, therefore, was not the substance of business leaders' critiques but their effectiveness in mobilizing around them.

This chapter traces the political, economic, and cultural changes that combined to enflame business's "crisis of confidence" and incite its political mobilization in the late 1960s and early 1970s. In the process, it suggests that this experience marked a departure from the early postwar years often described as one of "liberal consensus." To be sure, many historians now challenge the notion that a general peace pervaded business-government relations in the twenty years following World War II, so the very term requires careful qualification. Traditionally, the "liberal consensus" framework argued that the intense class-oriented battles between labor and business of the Progressive and New Deal periods cooled down markedly after the war, when Cold War imperatives prompted both sides to unite around ideals of liberal democracy and the promise of mass consumption. As a result, each side moderated a little and accepted the other. Scholars who embrace this view point out that although organized labor reached the height of its power in the mid-1950s, when 35 percent of the workforce was unionized, the expulsion of communists from labor ranks and George Meany's conservative leadership of the AFL-CIO represented concessions to business. At the same time, the Republican Party under Dwight Eisenhower resisted more conservative efforts to roll back the New Deal state. Despite Ike's tepid actions on civil rights and blustery threats of "massive retaliation" in foreign policy, he made no effort to undermine the new social compact or Keynesian economics. Indeed, Eisenhower and his corporate allies—both Democrat and Republican— recognized the legitimacy of organized labor and the reality of social welfare, much to the consternation of conservatives like Robert Taft, Barry Goldwater, and, ultimately, Ronald Reagan.[14]

Recent scholarship, however, has convincingly demonstrated that many prominent business leaders never accepted New Deal–style liberalism and in fact campaigned actively and vehemently for its rollback from the 1930s onward. After the downfall of the American Liberty League in the early 1940s, for instance, recalcitrant organizations like the U.S. Chamber of Commerce and the National Association of Manufacturers (NAM) retained their anti-Roosevelt mantle and argued publicly against New Deal programs like Social Security and the 1935 Wagner Act, under which the federal government formally recognized workers' collective bargaining rights. Those groups also played a large, if not decisive, role in the passage—despite Harry Truman's veto—of the Taft-Hartley Act of 1947, which scaled Wagner back and paved the way for "right-to-work" states.[15] Organized labor likewise remained militant, confronting management through strikes and boycotts over issues like high consumer prices, factory relocations, and other intrusions on workers' rights by employers.[16] These conflicts between labor-liberalism and a profoundly conservative anti–New Deal impulse clearly strained at the boundaries of the supposed consensus.

Nevertheless, the persistence of conservative antistatism does not mean that we should reject entirely the claim that a measured truce pervaded business-government relations from the late 1940s through the mid-1960s. Although historians should not overstate the level of harmony among business leaders, labor leaders, and liberal politicians, the *existence* of dissent mattered less than the *influence* of the dissenters. After all, "consensus" need not imply that everyone agreed with each other all of the time but merely that the sharpest conflicts did not dominate the mainstream. The history of organized business groups exemplifies the point. Although the NAM and the Chamber of Commerce remained virulently antilabor and continued to rail against the New Deal, their role on the national political stage shrank remarkably after World War II. Indeed, their unflinching faith in self-correcting markets and staunch opposition to Keynesianism combined to minimize their influence. Rather, in the 1950s and 1960s, the "voice of business" in national politics largely emanated not from those organizations but rather from what political scientists dub "accommodationist" business associations like the Committee for Economic Development (CED) and the Business Advisory Council (BAC). Such organizations provided industrial expertise to government officials on such issues as war-industry management, reconversion, and economic planning, but they neither lobbied nor dictated the policy agenda. Although some historians, adopting a framework of corporate liberalism, have rightly suggested ways that such business groups shaped policy to their advantage behind the scenes, they remained subordinate to government and viewed themselves as such.[17]

To say that many corporate executives "accommodated" liberal Keynesianism and the general contours of the modern regulatory state does not mean that they were always happy about it, of course. Conflicts arose frequently over a variety of policy issues, including corporate taxes, racial integration in the workplace, price controls, and foreign trade. As a general rule, however, the leaders of accommodationist business groups kept their ideological rants to a minimum, and their counterparts at arch-conservative organizations found themselves largely on the outside looking in during the first few decades after World War II.[18] This dynamic began to change, however, during the 1960s, as powerful political and economic forces converged to upset the institutional environment and destabilize that fragile consensus. In its place emerged the "crisis of confidence," which would ultimately invert the power dynamics within the business community and create opportunities for conservative organizations to supplant the accommodationists and organize a broad-based movement in opposition to liberal policies.

BUSINESS AND THE POLITICS OF THE 1960S

Many Americans in the 1970s, no less than today, had a hard time taking seriously the idea that top corporate executives and the directors of national business associations suffered crippling fits of fear and doubt or that they constantly bemoaned their political and cultural impotence. The capitalist class, after all, included the wealthiest people in the country and their daily work affected millions of lives. What factories to open and close, what products to sell and for what price, and how much to pay employees? Such decisions touched workers and consumers, as well as their families, across the country and around the globe, making claims of weakness sound spurious, even silly. What's more, any objective analysis of their political clout would conclude that these were intensely powerful men, able to gain an audience with senators, governors, and the president at their whim. Such access and influence lay simply beyond the imagination of regular people, even those (always an unfortunate minority) who engaged actively in the democratic process. As political scientist David Vogel put it (some years after his sleuthing for the Conference Board): "Through the middle of the 1960s, the political position of business certainly appeared to be a privileged one."[19] And yet by the latter years of that decade, these rich and powerful men collectively began to sweat. By the early 1970s, they had entered into a full-blown panic.

So what changed when the times were a-changin'?

The short answer is that those tumultuous years witnessed a fundamental political and economic restructuring. On the domestic front, the late 1960s saw the triumph of what scholars have called a "rights-conscious revolution" that expanded political battles beyond the traditional frameworks—labor versus business, rich versus poor—to include myriad interest groups organized around race, gender, ethnicity, religion, consumption, and environmental protection. For many business leaders, the most important consequence of this new type of politics was the proliferation of regulations designed to protect specific groups of people from the excesses of corporate capitalism. At the same time, the late 1960s witnessed the end of the extended period of growth and prosperity that the United States—particularly its manufacturing sector—had enjoyed since the end of World War II. Although practically no one openly suggested that the lauded "American Century" would soon come to an end, the stresses of renewed foreign competition from Germany and Japan, the strength of certain labor unions, and the maturation of traditional industries combined to place real pressure on corporate profits.[20]

The longer answer is that the fragile accord that business leaders had struck with the modern American state began to unravel, erratically and sometimes imperceptibly but significantly nonetheless. Despite widespread prosperity during most of the 1960s, many prominent business leaders began to feel increasingly isolated from the political power structure. Any such decline in their status or political importance was, of course, relative; wealthy industrialists remained very influential men. But compared with the halcyon days of Republican president Dwight Eisenhower and the 1950s, a growing number of executives *felt* more like outsiders to policy than they had before.

Politically, the sense of isolation that ultimately led to business's crisis of confidence began with the election of Democrat John F. Kennedy in 1960. Although Kennedy had only superficial policy differences with his Republican opponent, Richard Nixon, the youthful Massachusetts senator struggled to convince business leaders that he shared their goals and vision. Partisan stereotypes played a role. Many business leaders agreed with investment banker Henry Alexander (chairman of Morgan Guaranty Trust Company, later J. P. Morgan & Co.), who described the Eisenhower administration as "a turn away from the direction of constantly more government intervention," which had been the rule since 1933.[21] What, he asked, would a Democratic restoration under Kennedy look like? For his part, Vice President Nixon fueled those fires during the 1960 campaign, warning business leaders that a Kennedy White House would find itself at the mercy of radical labor leaders, to whom it would owe its political fortunes. Moreover, many businesspeople interpreted Kennedy's campaign promise to "get this country moving again" as a call for an inflationary economic policy that would hurt their bottom lines.[22]

On a personal level, Kennedy's biography didn't help matters. Many business leaders grumbled about this scion of privilege whose only postnavy career had been politics and who had never had to meet a payroll. According to journalist Hobart Rowan: "The average big businessman had a proper respect for Kennedy's wealth, but regarded him as a rich man's son who had no real understanding of the role of profit or other business problems."[23] Of course, Nixon had also practiced politics as a profession and had never made a payroll, and there was certainly no love lost between the East Coast business establishment and the child of middle-class Quakers from suburban California.[24] But Nixon at least belonged to the GOP, party not only of Eisenhower but also of Nelson Rockefeller and, at least by common stereotype, the business community since the 1850s. While the national Democratic Party certainly catered to business interests—and historically depended on support from businesspeople—its longstanding links to populist politics, farmers, immigrants, and organized labor weakened any claim it could make to be the "business party." Indeed, according to eminent business historian Herman Krooss, only three of the thirty-one businesspeople who donated more than $1,000 during the 1960 election gave to the Democratic Party.[25]

Kennedy wrestled with the charge that he was "antibusiness" throughout his brief presidency, despite his decision to appoint business-friendly conservatives to important cabinet positions and to marginalize liberal firebrands like Arthur Schlesinger Jr. and John Kenneth Galbraith when it came to economic policy.[26] A minor but telling brouhaha involving Commerce Secretary Luther Hodges highlighted the fraught relations between top business leaders and the Democratic administration. A self-made textile factory owner from North Carolina, where he had also been governor, Hodges did not typify a "Kennedy liberal" and perhaps might have appeared as an earnest business ally. An early architect of the "New South," he supported government-funded research and development and played an instrumental role in the construction of the Research Triangle Park in his home state. Like other sunbelt political entrepreneurs, Hodges worked to bring new business to the region, inaugurating a pattern of capital flight from North to South in the early postwar years that would bear tremendous fruit, in large part by recasting labor politics, by the 1970s and 1980s.[27] Although Hodges believed strongly in investment and capitalistic growth, his regional and class allegiances as a populist southern Democrat complicated his interactions with businesspeople, especially northern industrialists. On a cultural level, he remained deeply hostile to what he perceived to be the privileged status of old-money, eastern establishment business elites. When Hodges assumed the reins at the Commerce Department in January 1961, that animosity quickly turned into a high-profile flare-up with the kings of large industrial firms and their major representative organization, the Business Advisory Council (BAC).

The BAC dated back to 1933, when Franklin Roosevelt formed it by executive order at the behest of his first commerce secretary, Daniel Roper. Formally lodged in the Commerce Department, the BAC consisted of approximately fifty chief executive officers from major industrial and financial corporations who provided free, unfettered economic advice for the secretary and, by extension, the president. According to the organization's most prominent historian, Kim McQuaid, this "business cabinet" constituted "a quasi-public advisory agency that was *in* the government, but not *of* it." That is, the member CEOs enjoyed direct access to the White House, but they also retained a large degree of institutional autonomy—they financed their own meetings and kept the minutes private. This is not to say that the BAC dictated policy: as an advisory body, the group could not lobby. In some cases, it proved instrumental, helping create and operate the National Recovery Administration of 1933–35, for instance. In others, the White House overruled its opinion, as with the Wagner and Social Security acts of 1935. From the high points of the New Deal through the 1950s, however, the BAC retained its privileged position within the Commerce Department as, in McQuaid's phrase, "the most important forum for . . . compromise-minded managers" from the country's big businesses, including titans like U.S. Steel and General Electric.[28]

Luther Hodges was not a big businessman and made clear up front that he wanted immediate changes at the BAC, including a more diversified membership that included small and midsized companies, greater regional variety, and a more explicit role for the commerce secretary in the group's structure and operations. In addition, he wanted to reform the BAC's traditions of autonomy and secrecy, citing the imperatives of transparency and democracy in a body officially lodged in the government. In short, Hodges envisioned an end to the BAC's exalted, privileged status. In July 1961, after months of tense and often viciously personal wrangling between Hodges and the top brass at the BAC, the chief executives rejected the secretary's proposals and instead voted to formally disaffiliate themselves from the Commerce Department. Dropping the term "Advisory" from their title, they became simply the Business Council, a private consortium of CEOs from large corporations dedicated to articulating their collective policy preferences to the government and the public. Kennedy worked feverishly to mend fences with the individual CEOs at the Business Council, distancing himself politically from Hodges in the process. Nonetheless, the face-off contributed to the president's reputation as less than fully supportive of business.[29]

Less than a year after the Business Council bolted from the federal government, an even higher-profile showdown developed between Kennedy and major industrial leaders: the famous "steel crisis" of 1962. The steel industry had been central to the history of industrial political economy in the United States since Andrew Carnegie broke the Homestead strike in 1892. In the postwar period, the politics of prices for steel and wages for steelworkers led to a pitched confrontation in 1952 when the threat of a strike in the midst of the Korean War prompted Harry Truman to nationalize the steel industry, only to be overruled by the Supreme Court.[30] Yet the federal government's heavy involvement in labor-management relations in steel persisted. In 1959, during another fiery round of contract negotiations between steel companies and the United Steelworkers union, members of the Eisenhower administration (particularly Vice President Nixon) convinced the steel companies to accede to higher wages in the interest of labor peace and yet to keep the sale price of steel constant—absorbing the loss. Three years later, during yet another round of contract negotiations, the steel industry confronted a new president who had made price inflation enemy number one. According to wage-price guidelines issued by the Kennedy administration, unions had to demonstrate an increase in worker productivity to justify a pay raise, thus preventing companies from passing through higher labor costs into the price of an essential commodity. Using his leverage with the unions, Kennedy ensured minimal wage increases, and he fully expected the steel companies to fulfill their end of the bargain and keep prices down.

For Roger Blough, chairman of the United States Steel Corporation and chairman of the now independent Business Council, Kennedy's imposition of wage-price guidelines and apparent coziness with the steel unions represented an intolerable intrusion on the industry's ability to set its prices and remain profitable. In a face-to-face meeting in the Oval Office in April 1962, Blough handed Kennedy a memo—which he had already distributed to the press—announcing that U.S. Steel would raise its prices by 3.5 percent, effective immediately, despite the guidelines. Within hours, U.S. Steel's major competitors, including Bethlehem, Republic, and Jones & Laughlin, announced similar price hikes. Faced with such intransigence, not to mention the real possibility of unpopular inflation stemming from the higher price of steel, John F. Kennedy briefly declared war on Roger Blough. Famously telling his staff that "steel men were sons of bitches," the president launched a rhetorical and legal assault on "Big Steel" and, by implication, overprivileged corporations in general. Taking to the airwaves, Kennedy lambasted steel executives "whose pursuit of power and profit exceeds their sense of public responsibility" and who displayed "such utter contempt for the interests of 185 million Americans."[31] He didn't mention Blough by name, but he didn't have to: no one could doubt the object of Kennedy's ire. At the same time, the U.S. Department of Justice, conveniently headed by Kennedy's brother Robert, began to investigate whether Bethlehem Steel had colluded with U.S. Steel to raise its prices in violation of antitrust law. In the end, the public shaming and not-so-subtle threat of legal action worked. Blough rescinded U.S. Steel's price increases, and Kennedy notched a public victory, but at a price. Distrust and discord between the Democratic president and important elements of the business community persisted, foreshadowing later clashes between liberals and business leaders over the politics of inflation in the 1970s.[32]

When Lyndon Johnson assumed the presidency upon Kennedy's death in November 1963, business relations with the White House improved slightly but not enough to overcome the emerging partisan schism between the Democrats and many corporate leaders. As a skilled legislator with a long history of forging agreements among opposing groups, Johnson struck many businesspeople as more approachable than Kennedy had been. Unlike in 1960, when business support overwhelming went to Nixon, business partisanship was subdued in the 1964 election and corporate executives by and large backed Johnson against Barry Goldwater. (To be sure, the real "business candidate" in 1964 was New York governor Nelson Rockefeller, whom Goldwater defeated in the primaries on a wave of anti-establishment populist conservatism.)[33] As president, Johnson worked hard to foster mutual understanding and common goals with business leaders. In January 1964, he invited members of the Business Council for dinner at the State Dining Room to hear a preview of the State of the Union Address. One executive gushed: "It's the first time in our history that we've been invited to dine in the White House—it didn't even happen under Ike!"[34]

Business's honeymoon with Johnson was short-lived, however. The new president's eager commitment to Great Society spending programs and reluctant escalation of the war in Vietnam strained the federal budget, yet he balked at pushing for higher taxes. Fiscally hawkish business leaders objected to the growing deficits and fretted over the possibility of inflation. In addition, many corporate leaders detected in Johnson the same partisan traits they had viewed suspiciously under Kennedy, including his sustained commitment to wage and price guidelines. As one administration staffer explained, many business leaders complained that the president was "always bashing big business but never bashing big labor."[35]

The Stirrings of Mobilization: PACs and Lobbying

During the Kennedy-Johnson years, increasing numbers of business leaders thus came to believe that the ship of state was sailing away without them. Asserting their collective influence over policy would require greater political infrastructure than the business community had traditionally employed. Although the highest-profile debates over business involved major industries like steel and macroeconomic questions of wages and prices, the institutions of collective action that ultimately permitted broad-scale business mobilization in fact emerged from specific debates in a different field: the medical profession. During the early 1960s, debates over the pharmaceutical and health insurance systems galvanized the medical community and prompted new forms of political organizing, campaign funding, and lobbying—tools that the broader business community would later appropriate.

As they would in the 1990s and 2000s, liberal proposals to regulate and reform the health care industry prompted a major conservative backlash in the 1960s. The reform movement involved two complementary planks: imposing stricter regulations on pharmaceutical products and providing government-run health insurance for elderly and poor Americans. In 1959, Senator Estes Kefauver (D-TN) launched a highly publicized investigation into the pharmaceutical industry in the wake of mounting concerns about high drug prices and investigations of price-fixing among drug manufacturers. Kefauver's hearings led to a legislative push, propelled by widespread outcry over birth defects linked to the sedative thalidomide, that resulted in the 1962 Kefauver-Harris Amendment to the 1938 Federal Food, Drug, and Cosmetic Act, which increased regulations and disclosure requirements on drug manufacturers. A few years later, congressional liberals successfully passed the Social Security Amendments of 1965, creating Medicare and Medicaid. Both reforms prompted vociferous objections by conservatives; indeed, lobbying from the pharmaceutical industry rendered Kefauver's law significantly weaker than its backers had hoped. Critics of Medicare and Medicaid charged health insurance for the old and poor represented a treacherous slide toward the type of nationalized health care practiced in Western Europe, and those fiery protests united political conservatives in a vague battle cry against "socialized medicine."[36]

The fiery political debates over national health insurance and pharmaceutical regulation prompted the American Medical Association (AMA) to form the first conservative—indeed, the first nonlabor—PAC in 1961 to raise money for candidates who opposed increased governmental regulation of and involvement in the medical profession. The creation of the AMA's PAC marked a signal change in the national political landscape because the legal status of PACs remained ambiguous in the early 1960s. The 1907 Tillman Act, which barred corporate campaign contributions, and the 1943 Smith-Connally Act, which extended that prohibition to labor unions, still governed, but those laws did not specify whether those institutions could collect and redistribute funds that were freely given by individual employees or members (that is, money that did not come directly from their coffers). Beginning with the CIO's PAC in 1943 (the first political action committee in the United States), trade unions relied on their political clout to evade legal issues. Corporate managers, on the other hand, adhered more strictly to the letter of the law but developed other strategies to funnel money to politicians. For example, many companies allowed employees to charge campaign activities to their corporate expense accounts; retained managers and staff on the payroll while they worked for campaigns; and offered pay raises to employees with the explicit understanding that they would donate the extra money to specific political candidates. Both companies and unions also evaded campaign finance laws by employing the same lawyers and public relations firms as candidates and then overpaying those vendors for legitimate services, effectively funneling money to campaigns. Such measures, while technically illegal, grew increasingly common as the costs of running campaigns increased with the spread of television in the 1950s and 1960s.[37]

Such evasive techniques remained far less efficient than aboveboard political action committees, so the AMA's decision to form a PAC opened an important door to more coordinated corporate fund-raising, and it came at an opportune time. In the second half of the 1960s, many public affairs executives and professional Washington Representatives noted a clear shift in the congressional terrain in which they had previously operated quite comfortably. The increasingly liberal stance of non-southern Democrats on issues like civil rights and social welfare, as well as the consolidation of the Goldwater wing of the Republican Party at the expense of Northeast liberal Republicans, changed the constitution of each party's caucus and led to a sea change in legislative strategy. Prior to this change, according to one insider, Washington Representatives had worked on specific issues with members of Congress they knew personally, and the most entrepreneurial used their contacts with committee chairmen or, in many cases, Senate Majority Leader Lyndon Johnson, to great effect. Johnson's departure for the vice presidency (and ultimately the White House) blocked off many of those inroads, and the increased push to weaken the power of committee chairs further destabilized the status quo. Corporate lobbyists in particular felt outgunned under the new dispensation. Many noted with dismay that their opponents in organized labor, because its campaign finance strategy matched its lobbying prowess, successfully targeted not only policymakers but also the composition of Congress.[38]

Following the AMA's example, a handful of directors from the National Association of Manufacturers (NAM) established the country's first corporate PAC, the Business-Industry Political Action Committee (BIPAC) in August 1963. The group's first president, Texan Robert Humphrey, left his position as the NAM's public affairs director to dedicate himself full-time to running a freestanding organization that he felt would be better suited to influence campaigns without becoming bogged down in legislative minutiae. Despite BIPAC's official independence, its original board members retained their affiliation with the NAM, and the group in its early years relied on significant seed money from existing business groups. Highly conscious of the potential legal snarls related to coordinating corporate campaign donations, the new organization retained well-heeled D.C. tax lawyers from the firm of Miller and Chevalier, who advised BIPAC to create a bifurcated organizational structure. On one side stood the educational arm, which could promote a "business" perspective in political debates through the media and in the workplace. The financing arm, on the other hand, would collect voluntary contributions from individual people, usually from within specific corporations, and redirect those funds to politicians.[39]

In the group's early years, BIPAC leaders worked hard to establish credibility by stressing their reputations as chief executives from well-respected manufacturing firms, many of whom had been active in the NAM. Its board of directors grew quickly and, quite by design, included well-known heads of oil companies, utilities, and financial services firms. Moreover, BIPAC's educational arm funded "political education" efforts, publishing a newsletter to explain the political process, the dynamics of specific local and national races, and the importance of voting, especially on "business" issues and for "business" candidates. According to Robert Humphrey, BIPAC aimed not to fund winners, necessarily, but to provide financial assistance to candidates with principled pro-business positions who found themselves in tight, competitive races. As a result, success came slowly; in 1964, for example, most of its candidates lost, including two Republican Senate candidates—Texas oil executive George H. W. Bush and Tennessee lawyer Howard Baker (running to replace the recently deceased Estes Kefauver). In the midterm elections of 1966, however, the group fared much better, and its support contributed to major conservative victories. Moreover, although BIPAC involved itself primarily with federal elections, its leaders encouraged business activism at the state level as well. Although "political power ha[d] shifted from the states and localities to Washington" since the 1930s, a BIPAC report argued, "electing a fiscally-minded state legislature [remained] vital to the economy of the state and the nation."[40]

Although BIPAC's message resonated with many conservative businesspeople, the organization struggled during the 1960s because of persistent uncertainty about the legality of political action committees. That ambiguity was only resolved in 1975 when the Federal Election Commission (FEC)—created by Congress to enforce new campaign finance laws passed in 1971 and 1974—issued its Sun Oil decision, officially sanctioning corporate PACs, whose numbers skyrocketed in the next few years. That growth was particularly stark in comparison with the number of labor PACs. Between 1974 and 1978, the number of business PACs shot up from 89 to 784, while labor PACs increased by only 16, from 201 to 217. The total number of corporate PACs peaked at approximately 1,800 in the late 1980s and settled around 1,600 from the mid-1990s to 2012. Prior to the reforms of the mid-1970s, however, BIPAC largely remained a lone voice in the wilderness.[41]

Even as Kennedy-Johnson policies propelled the drive for more formalized corporate campaign financing, the changing mechanics of business-government relations in the 1960s likewise bolstered business leaders' clamor for greater institutional power and collective action. Although Johnson tried to appear friendly to business concerns—touting fiscal discipline, noninflationary growth, and concern for the international balance of payments—his particular style ultimately confirmed corporate leaders' sense of isolation from the inner circles of power. On legislation ranging from free trade to public housing to taxes, Johnson distinguished himself by making strategic use of ad hoc committees of business leaders to promote his policies. In 1967, leading industrialists formed the Emergency Committee for American Trade, an ostensibly independent group that promoted Johnson's position against trade quotas. The president also pushed the Business Council to create an offshoot organization called the Business-Government Relations Council to facilitate information sharing among lobbyists for large firms. That new group, according to the administration, existed "solely for liaison with the federal government and [would] not take policy stands on political issues." Although such institutions brought business leaders more directly into the political process, they also highlighted their inherent weakness: business provided advice *when called upon*, but the politicians set the agenda.[42]

Business's continued reliance on firm-specific Washington Representatives ironically exacerbated this growing sense of isolation. Wealthy corporations had long relied on professional public affairs firms such as the prestigious Hill and Knowlton, founded as a "corporate publicity" office in 1927, as for-hire mouthpieces both to the consuming public and, especially since World War II, to government officials and policymakers. But in addition to those hired guns, large companies also retained in-house experts, many of whom registered as lobbyists under the 1946 Federal Regulation of Lobbying Act, which required anyone who was paid primarily to influence legislation to register with Congress and report all lobbying income. Although the total number of Washington Representatives increased steadily during the 1960s, before exploding in the 1970s and 1980s, the vast majority of companies could not afford such tailor-made representation and instead relied on trade associations to defend their interests. Yet even firms that employed in-house lobbyists engaged in precious little collaboration or collective work. Some Washington Representatives skillfully forged contacts with legislators and won specific favors for their firms—a subsidy here, a government contract there—while others proved notably ineffective. But successful or not, company-specific lobbyists focused narrowly on their employers' needs, not the concerns of the broader business community.[43]

Amid the contentious politics of the 1960s, however, business leaders sought opportunities to bring their lobbyists together. For example, in late 1964, Henry Ford II (CEO of the eponymous car maker) learned that the Johnson administration intended to release a report that criticized the private retirement system and made far-reaching recommendations for pension reform. Ford instructed his Washington Representative to form a committee of lobbyists from fifty companies to generate broad-based industry opposition. To chair that committee, Ford appointed Sidney Weinberg, a senior partner at Goldman Sachs and member of many corporate boards, including that of the Ford Motor Company (his nickname was "Mr. Wall Street"). Under Weinberg's leadership, the Washington Pension Report Group grew to include 125 companies whose lobbyists paid numerous visits to government officials and members of Congress, presenting a unified front against the pension reform recommendations. This brief episode provided a glimpse of the possibility that broad-based collaboration among lobbyists might bring, but it also highlighted the challenges involved. According to Ford's Washington Representative, Weinberg's leadership proved essential to holding the committee together. When Weinberg died in the summer of 1969, the committee faltered, and liberal politicians led by Jacob Javits ultimately pushed through the public pension reforms known as the Employment Retirement Income Security Act, or ERISA, in 1974.[44]

Many top executives interpreted the dissolution of the Pension Report Group as a clear signal that their status in Washington politics remained perilously fragile. Although that group, along with the Johnson administration's ad hoc business committees and the Business Council, would later provide vital institutional grounding for the Business Roundtable, its fate reinforced a declension narrative during the late 1960s. Washington Representatives and trade associations, business leaders remarked, had simply stopped getting the job done. Firm- and industry-specific strategies could successfully win particular favors, but they had little effect against broader policy initiatives—whether on pension reform, taxes and budgets, wage-price guidelines, or national health care. Given the shifting political sands in Congress and public support for policy proposals that seemed to cut against core business interests, disorganized and haphazard lobbying looked increasingly powerless. By the end of the 1960s, creeping inflation and weak productivity growth combined with a hostile political culture to undermine business leaders' confidence. But those economic and political factors provided only part of the context. Adding essential fuel to the fire, business leaders noted with chagrin their painful inability to halt what they saw as an avalanche of debilitating new government rules restricting business affairs—known collectively as "social regulations."

STRUCTURAL CHANGES, STRUCTURAL CONSEQUENCES

While partisan tensions and conflicts over labor and health care policy certainly captured business leaders' attention in the first half of the 1960s, a combination of policy developments and destabilizing macroeconomic changes came to dominate their concerns by the 1970s and underscore the growth of business's crisis of confidence. On a policy level, the American regulatory state underwent a historic reconfiguration that enflamed political passions among many businesspeople. At the same time, the deteriorating national economy and the decline of America's manufacturing dominance contributed to the growing sense of crisis within the business community. For many corporate leaders, these two phenomena fit hand in glove, and a growing number argued with mounting fervor that liberal economic policies were wreaking havoc on the national economy and business's future.

Between roughly 1965 and 1975, a new regulatory regime succeeded— although it did not always supplant—the systems put in place first during the Progressive Era and then by the New Deal. Both earlier reform moments had created powerful federal institutions to fetter the operations of private market actors, but each emerged in response to the specific problems of its time. Between the turn of the twentieth century and World War I, Progressive reformers reacted to the economic instabilities generated by rapid industrialization and the rise of large corporations with regulations designed to manage competition and hold large institutions accountable to the principles of democracy. A generation later, during the Great Depression, the Hoover and Roosevelt administrations incorporated various regulatory impulses into a regime aimed fundamentally at navigating the wild vicissitudes of a failing economy. Government bodies like the Civil Aeronautics Board and the Interstate Commerce Commission (established in 1887 but expanded in the 1930s to regulate trucking and busing as well as railroads) created stable markets by restricting access and entry, setting prices and routes, and otherwise curtailing free competition. At the same time, the Securities and Exchange Commission provided stability for investors by promoting transparency in the financial community.[45]

In the postwar years, however, the turmoil of the early industrial period had long since settled and memories of the Depression began to fade.

A new age, marked by industrial maturity and economic prosperity, bred a new critique of the existing regulatory structures, particularly among political activists who claimed to speak for "the public interest." Intellectually linked to the New Left, this growing movement argued that the Progressive and New Deal regulatory regimes served business interests at the expense of "the public." The federal government, public interest activists claimed, had become little more than a tool of privileged interests for preserving their own profits and protecting their industries from competition. Such critiques, while certainly not new, galvanized a broad coalition of neoprogressive reformers to lobby for new laws to protect people *from* business. By the mid-1960s, public interest activism generated new legislation ranging from equal employment (an outgrowth of the civil rights laws of 1964 and 1965) to consumer and environmental protection, from the Kefauver-Harris Amendment that strengthened the Food and Drug Administration in 1962 to the National Highway Safety Act of 1966 and the Air Quality Act of 1967. During the Nixon administration, the public interest movement reached the height of its influence, shepherding the creation of omnibus new federal bodies like the Environmental Protection Agency (EPA) and the Occupational Safety and Health Administration (OSHA), which generated myriad new rules on everything from chemical emissions to workplace safety requirements.[46]

Thus by the late 1960s, the dominant thrust of regulatory politics in the United States had shifted from protecting a range of interests from business abuses, especially other businesses, to protecting *people* from business. Although most New Deal and Progressive Era policies had constituted "economic regulation," the public interest movement concentrated far more on "social regulations." These two forms were vitally different. *Economic* regulations governed economic behavior—the things companies did to make money—by restricting entry, prices, and so on. *Social* regulations, on the other hand, targeted what economists call the "externalities" of doing business—negative spillovers of economic activity whose costs are borne by society at large, such as pollution, labor injustice, and racism. By design, the industry-specific regulations of the earlier periods provided advantages for certain companies and industries over others; the new social regulations, by contrast, generally increased compliance burdens across all firms and industries.

The explosion of new social regulations in the late 1960s aroused business's ire in large part because they thwarted the traditional power dynamics of regulatory governance. Both the environmental and consumer movements cut their teeth at the state level, championing legislation to establish independent regulatory commissions. However, by the early 1970s, their efforts turned squarely to the federal government and to specific laws that adopted a far stricter model of regulation. Environmental activists, for example, bemoaned the fact that state regulatory commissions not only suffered severe staff shortages but also frequently saw their memberships overrun by representatives of the very industries the agencies set out to regulate. The practice of "regulatory capture," observed as far back as the 1880s, seemed to confirm the institutional power of entrenched minority interests over the public good. To confront this dynamic, reformers increasingly pushed reforms that centralized regulatory authority in specific administrators who answered directly to the president, who faced public accountability through the electoral process. The 1970 amendments to the 1963 Clean Air Act, for example, aggressively shifted the onus of environmental regulation from the states to the federal government, empowered a single administrator to enforce its provisions, and codified specific regulatory requirements in law. Critics branded such provisions "command-and-control" regulation, but proponents argued that only this type of regulation could permit the public interest to overcome the influence of powerful businesses and industries. According to political scientists Richard Harris and Sidney Milkis, the command-and-control regime aimed "specifically to avoid bureaucratic discretion and undue industry influence in the administrative process." The centralization of environmental and consumer protection thus marked a deliberate attempt to reduce the sway of the regulated over the regulators.[47]

New social regulations represented an affront to business not only through their procedural mechanism, which certainly increased their effectiveness, but also through their spirit, which many corporate leaders interpreted as an affront to their integrity. In October 1972, the chairman of the Council of Better Business Bureaus (BBB), Elisha Gray, clearly expressed the business community's widespread umbrage during a Business Council meeting. The council members, all chief executives at the country's largest industrial, commercial, and financial firms, had assembled for their twice-yearly retreat weekend in Hot Springs, Virginia, where Gray took the opportunity to depict the rapid uptick in laws purported to protect consumers since the late 1950s. "Whereas none of us would quarrel with some of the earlier business standards . . . such as the Child Labor Law," he explained, "we have every reason to be alarmed at . . . some of the more recent laws [that] begin to cut to the very essence of the free enterprise system . . . by the removal of incentives[,] . . . restriction of design and product possibilities . . . [and] the usurping by government agencies of the function of our customer relations." As the head of a private organization explicitly dedicated to monitoring corporate behavior and preserving the good name (and profitability) of socially responsible firms, the BBB chairman argued that social regulations intruded directly on that prerogative and portended something far more sinister. At the rate they were going, Gray warned, the political forces behind the new laws threatened to "dismantle the free enterprise system in the next ten years."[48]

In the early 1970s, Elisha Gray's dire prediction was as commonplace as it was hyperbolic. Although jeremiads about the coming demise of "free enterprise" had echoed across corporate conference centers for years, the new social regulatory regime appeared to provide specific evidence of a fundamental realignment that both reinforced business leaders' sense of their waning political influence and created significant cost pressures at a time companies could least afford them. After twenty-five years of nearly unquestioned manufacturing dominance, American firms saw their grip on global trade slip in the late 1960s amid the revival of foreign competition, especially from Japan and Germany. Moreover, the after-tax profit rate (for nonfinancial firms) hit a peak in 1965 that it would never see again.[49] By the 1970s, this crisis of profitability morphed into a more general economic contraction, made worse by rising inflation. Productivity growth rates fell by half, even as real wages stagnated and real GDP per capita, which had increased by 35 percent under Kennedy and Johnson, rose by a paltry 12 percent under Nixon and Ford. In 1971, the United States clocked a trade deficit in merchandise—Americans bought more from than they sold to the world—for the first time since the 1890s. The following year saw the collapse of the Bretton Woods system of international monetary policy, which regulated worldwide capital flows and relied on the dominance of the dollar, dealing a major blow to American economic prestige. Dependable growth gave way to a series of recessions—in 1969–70, 1973–75, 1980, and 1981–82—each more severe than the last and typically dubbed "the worst since the Great Depression." At the same time, price inflation accelerated after 1965 through a combination of deficit spending and monetary mismanagement, punctuated cruelly by severe supply shocks, particularly in energy.[50]

The deteriorating economy weighed heavily on the minds of business executives. Although many recognized the growing threat from foreign competitors, most prominent corporate leaders argued that American business could easily remain dominant in global manufacturing so long as domestic policies favored continued productivity growth. According to a NAM brochure, the "U.S. standard of living depends directly on a high level of productivity . . . [in order] to pay wages far above those of other countries [and] stay competitive in world markets." Through the mid-1970s, therefore, politically active business leaders trained their sights on the threats to profits and productivity that emerged from trade barriers, as well as labor and regulatory policies, and far less on the changing international context as such.[51]

To make the case against liberal economic policies clear, the U.S. Chamber of Commerce sent its in-house economist Carl Madden to Congress to provide the "business" perspective on the 1970 "Economic Report of the President" prepared by Richard Nixon's Council of Economic Advisors. Madden, a tall, portly man who had formerly worked as the dean of business at Lehigh University, grumbled to the assembled members of the Joint Economic Committee that, contrary to the popular view, the late 1960s had represented anything but a period of peace, love, and prosperity. Rather, he explained, the Johnson administration's rampant federal spending had left "an unhappy legacy . . . of unrealized full-employment budget surpluses, escalating government deficits, and accelerating inflation." Despite the "loose rhetoric . . . of affluence and abundance" that liberal policymakers boasted of, America at the dawn of the 1970s was "not nearly so affluent as some have appeared to believe," Madden warned.[52]

Industrial leaders like Chicagoan Pete Venema, chairman of the NAM in 1972, also read the macroeconomic tea leaves as an indictment of existing domestic policy. Venema, like many executives of his generation, had risen from a middle-class background to excel in college; in 1932 he earned a chemical engineering degree at Armour, which later became Illinois Institute of Technology. Shortly thereafter he began a lifelong career at Universal Oil Products Company of Illinois, where he worked his way up from the pilot plant division through the patent department and then to executive status, leaving only temporarily to earn a law degree from Georgetown in 1942. In 1955 he became Universal's chairman of the board and chief executive officer, and in later years he distinguished himself as president of his alma mater and a powerful spokesman for the NAM. Addressing fellow executives at an industrial relations conference, Venema bemoaned the dire state of American manufacturing, which faced "[h]igh costs for labor and material, backbreaking tax loads . . . an aging industrial plant . . . [and] trade barriers which inhibit our competitiveness in foreign markets." The inevitable result, Venema predicted all too correctly, was that American industry would soon find itself "being outproduced and outcompeted by almost every industrial nation in the free world."[53]

Corporate leaders like Venema and business-minded economists like Madden argued that faced with such economic instability, American corporations could ill afford the mounting regulatory compliance costs that new social regulations—from the EPA and OSHA to consumer product safety and measures to protect striking workers—would create. Although

Figure 1.1. This sign, reprinted in the Chamber of Commerce's newsletter in May 1972, captured the persistent anxiety among many businesspeople that excessive federal regulation—especially government agencies like OSHA and the EPA—would drive small companies out of business. Courtesy of Hagley Museum and Library.

business handwringing about liberal policies toward labor and regulation had formed a mainstay of political discourse for generations, these men's vitriolic attacks gained rhetorical potency as the economic vitality of the postwar period slipped away.

At the same time, few if any business executives in the early 1970s accurately predicted America's economic future—including the globalization of production and distribution, not least through advances in communication technology, and the rapid rise of the financial services industry. Although some theorists have claimed that business leaders responded to an acute crisis of capitalism in the late 1970s by mobilizing politically to enact a neoliberal takeover of the state, such arguments miss the chronology: business's mobilization started well before the contours of the crisis in capitalism became apparent and in fact aimed to *prevent* the evisceration of domestic manufacturing. Economic insecurity and specific policy shifts thus laid a vital foundation for the business community's political mobilization, but by themselves proved insufficient. A different set of factors—less quantifiable but equally vital—manifested on a psychological and cultural level within the business community and played an essential role in pushing business's crisis of confidence to its breaking point.[54]

THE CULTURAL ASSAULT

Businessmen are people, too. While they might often wish to present themselves as unemotional, hyper-rational, nearly robotic decision makers—and indeed certain economic models suggest as much—in reality, major corporations as well as mom and pop stores are all run by human beings, with the virtues and failings that we all possess. Despite the wealth, success, and generally quite well-developed egos of the men who ran America's largest firms and top business associations in the 1960s, they still had very human desires to be validated and appreciated. So while partisan politics, structural policy change, and real economic uncertainty underlay corporate leaders' political mobilization, the stark rise in public antagonism to business as a social institution provided the final straw.

For many businesspeople, the increase in social regulations provided clear evidence of a cultural turn. In the mid-1960s, pollsters calculated that more than half of Americans expressed "a great deal of confidence" in the leaders of major companies, a record high for the modern polling era. But by the early 1970s, only 28 percent indicated such support, and after Watergate and the 1975 recession, the Harris polling company put the figure at 15 percent.[55] Reflecting back in 1976, pollster Daniel Yankelovich, whose firm monitored public attitudes, concluded that social regulations since the mid-1960s had arisen directly as a consequence of that drop in public confidence. "Without the mistrust," according to Yankelovich, "we would have had regulations, but [they] would have been ones in which both the business sector . . . and the political sector entered into a civil dialogue, both sides contributing, and reaching the kind of creative compromise for which our polity is famous."[56]

Yankelovich was only partly correct, since the boom in social regulations had actually begun with consumer protection and equal employment laws in the early to mid-1960s when business—even big business—boasted historically high public approval rates. In reality, the push for environmental, consumer, and workplace regulations grew from a confluence of historical factors, including the increasingly partisan composition of Congress, the proliferation of new types of knowledge about risk and prevention, and rising expectations born of the general prosperity. Nonetheless, Yankelovich's analysis reaffirmed a central narrative that business leaders seized on, linking the new regulatory order to business's collective inability to prove its mettle to the public. At the 1975 annual meeting of the Business Roundtable, Alcoa chairman John Harper explained the link clearly. "On the question of whether or not the typical big company is above the law, or whether inflation is caused by business making too much profits, or whether companies tell the truth in advertising, [public opinion] was fairly heavily against business," the chief of the aluminum powerhouse declared. In a democracy, Harper continued, "what the public thinks . . . has a decided effect on the kind of legislation that comes out of Congress."[57]

But as Harper well knew, public opinion by itself did not beget policy; organized interest groups played a vital role in shepherding legislation through Congress. The most important factor in the rise of new social regulations had been the newfound strength of the organized public interest movement, the myriad associations of lawyers, activists, students, and politicians who came to epitomize the sum of all of business's fears. Indeed, many business executives believed that a fundamental moral critique lay embedded in the public interest movement's activism. Through their mere choice of words, self-described defenders of the "public" interest implicitly condemned the "private" sector for its inability to protect consumers, citizens, and the environment. And no one person typified that animus more than a young lawyer named Ralph Nader.

Nader first rose to national attention in 1965 when he published *Unsafe at Any Speed*, a stinging condemnation of "designed-in" flaws in automobiles that gravely endangered drivers and passengers. The American business community famously got off on the wrong foot with Nader when General Motors hired a private investigator to dig up dirt on the consumer advocate's personal life in the hope of smearing his image. The ham-handed plan backfired spectacularly when the public learned about it. GM ate crow, and the resulting legal settlement helped Nader establish a vast institutional infrastructure to expand his activism and public influence. In short order, Nader rode his newfound celebrity as the little guy who challenged the corporate giants to a string of legislative victories, including, quite prominently, the National Traffic and Motor Vehicle Safety Act of 1966.[58]

Nader's star continued to rise throughout the late 1960s and early 1970s. In 1972, a Louis Harris poll found that 64 percent of Americans agreed with the statement: "Nader's efforts go a long way toward improving the quality and standards of the products and services the American people receive." At the same time, only 5 percent agreed that

"Nader is a troublemaker who is against the free enterprise system." Within that 5 percent, however, lay a disproportionate number of corporate leaders and their ideological allies in conservative organizations. The American Conservative Union accused Nader of running a "hate-business campaign" that represented "in essence . . . a movement for far stricter, often absolute regulation of business and market activity." John Post, a conservative lawyer from Texas and the first paid staffer for the Business Roundtable when it was founded in 1972, years later described Nader as "riding tall, wide, and handsome" in the 1970s. According to Post, a gaggle of journalists and cameramen would crowd Nader's press conferences, but when Post emerged afterward to provide the Business Roundtable's opposing view, "nobody filmed it." Against Nader's celebrity, business felt it couldn't get a word in edgewise. Such political and cultural exclusion convinced many corporate leaders that a new political order was afoot.[59]

If the strength of the public interest movement convinced business leaders that the public was turning against them, numerous opinion polls bore out that conclusion. By mid-1975, according to Gallup, Americans had less confidence in "big business" than in any other major national institution. At the same time, however, the public mood in the mid-1970s had also soured on everything, from government to organized religion to the military. Nevertheless, Republican pollster Robert Teeter, who worked for President Gerald Ford (and later Reagan and both Bushes), concluded that the decline in public support for business was steadier and deeper than for other groups. While 34 percent of the public trusted big business, 38 percent of Americans had confidence in organized labor, 40 percent in Congress, 58 percent in the military, and 68 percent in organized religion.[60]

Scholars have long noted the widespread public pessimism that marked American culture in the 1970s, but it remains an underanalyzed phenomenon. In the space of a few short years, the ebullient spirit embodied by civil rights protestors, antiwar demonstrators, and other liberal groups gave way nearly entirely to what author Tom Wolfe called the "Me Decade"—a period of self-loathing narcissism. For filmgoers, one of the period's most iconic moments came in 1976's *Network*, in which newsman Howard Beale suffers a nervous breakdown at the hands of the soulless corporate television machine and gets the whole country screaming: "I'm as mad as hell, and I'm not going to take this anymore!"[61]

What underlay such angst? Historian Christopher Lasch's *The Culture of Narcissism*, published in 1979, argued that the roots of America's despair lay in structural factors related to capitalist individualism and the spread of consumer culture since World War II. In the late 1960s, for example, New Left activists expressly condemned corporate greed and the alleged power of the military-industrial complex, lending a profoundly anticorporate and often anticapitalist strain to antiwar protests, such as the firebombing of Bank of America branches in 1970. Moreover, widespread disgust over the role of corporate political slush funds, exposed through the Watergate scandal, as well as real product safety controversies likewise fueled the flames. Finally, some scholars have submitted that rising income inequality, which began with the economic crisis of the early 1970s and intensified through policy decisions in the Carter and Reagan administrations, has accounted for the long-term decline in Americans' confidence in nearly all major institutions. In all its manifestations, the malaise that beset American culture no doubt contributed to the public's declining trust in business leaders.[62]

Although Americans in general became more pessimistic in the mid-1970s, corporate leaders almost certainly overreacted to a handful of choice opinion polls in their diagnosis of a widespread assault. Yet even if their evidence did not represent society as a whole, it provided powerful ammunition for concerted action, and business leaders took those declining poll numbers seriously. In corporate boardrooms and conference centers across the country, their public speeches and private correspondence overflowed with a run of depressing statistics. Many complained—as they had in the 1880s, 1910s, 1930s, and whenever reformers had challenged the status quo—that the public was terribly ignorant and misinformed. "People don't have much sympathy or understanding for corporations' needs for profits," Alcoa's John Harper explained, "when prices are mounting and they are feeling the pinch." Even as corporate profits declined in the 1970s, executives knew that they often looked like profiteers. Speaking to the American Gas Association in October 1973, the NAM's chairman, Burt Raynes of Rohr Industries, explained that the "average American, not just students, thinks that business makes 28 percent profit on every dollar of sales. And all of us in this room, I think, are quite aware that the actual percentage on sales is closer to 4-1/2 percent." Such misinformation manifested in popular sloganeering, such as the sweatshirt in figure 1.2. Little wonder business seemed under attack.[63]

Moreover, many executives concluded that the public's negativity extended beyond profits and literally threatened the existence of their firms. One of the most outspoken CEOs on this matter was AT&T chief John deButts, the man at the heart of one of the largest antitrust lawsuits in American history. Born in Greensboro, North Carolina, deButts earned an electrical engineering degree at Virginia Military Institute before starting a long career with AT&T, where he rose triumphantly through the ranks. As executive vice president and vice chairman of the board in the 1960s, he had a front-row seat to the intense wrangling between the telecommunications giant and the antitrust division of the U.S. Department

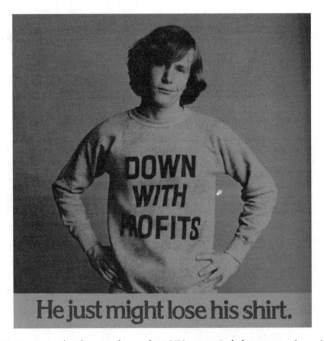

Figure 1.2. Business leaders in the early 1970s worried that many Americans lacked faith in the free enterprise system and its basic tenets, such as the profit motive. In this July 1973 ad from the Chamber of Commerce's newspaper, the business association chastised the young man pictured for failing to see that "profit is an incentive to beat the competition with new and better products," including the very sweatshirt he was wearing. Courtesy of Hagley Museum and Library.

of Justice. Antitrust investigations ultimately led to a formal suit in 1974, by which time deButts had become CEO, and ultimately to the breakup of the "Ma Bell" system in 1984. Years of management experience convinced deButts that poor public relations had been at the heart of the accusations of monopoly that AT&T faced. The company's problems, he insisted, stemmed from a Congress and a Department of Justice who "do not 'hear' what you have to tell them because they are committed to the idea that the company is too big, is beyond regulation, and should—for some philosophical or ideological reason—be cut down to size." Appealing for help to a public relations expert in 1967, he bemoaned, "How do I get those government people to *hear* me—not just listen to me?"[64]

In 1975, still fighting the Justice Department's suit, deButts commissioned a massive study of large firms' public image, which concluded that antibusiness bias ran rampant in the media, not just among journalists but in popular entertainment as well. As deButts summarized: "By television's account, the executive suite is, for the most part, populated by stuffed shirts and scheming scoundrels, both types insensitive to the higher things in life and driven by nothing so much as a barely disguised greed." An anonymous executive echoed the sentiment to David Vogel and Leonard Silk at the Conference Board meetings in 1975: "One little smirk or crack on the *Tonight Show* biases the opinions of millions of Americans." Such treatment, deButts concluded, explained why "poll after poll confirms a steady growth in public skepticism with respect to the earnestness with which business pursues its professed aim of service to the public."[65]

This antibusiness bias from the media and Hollywood, not new but perhaps more visible in the early 1970s, puzzled many business leaders. Why, they asked, were agents of the news and entertainment industries so hostile to business and profit when they themselves worked for large private corporations? Drawing on the work of social and political theorists, some business leaders came to believe that the answer lay in a profound and growing disconnect between the values of free enterprise and the country's dominant mind-set. Scorn for business certainly shaped the work of journalists and entertainers, business leaders believed, but its roots lay far deeper in national culture.

In an influential article in the *Wall Street Journal* in May 1975, the writer and "godfather of neoconservatism" Irving Kristol explained the prevalence of antibusiness bias by invoking a phenomenon sociologists called the "New Class." This group, Kristol argued, included "college-educated people whose skills and vocations proliferate in a 'post-industrial society' (to use Daniel Bell's convenient term)." Specifically, they were the professionals and experts "who make their careers in the expanding public sector . . . [and] the upper levels of the government bureaucracies." Because members of the New Class flourished in the public sector, Kristol claimed, they actively worked to siphon power away from private enterprise and toward themselves. Moreover, as cultural elitists, the New Class disdained any society shaped "by the preferences and appetites of ordinary men and women" through their consumption choices and market transactions.[66] That elitism and their own drive for power in turn explained their adversarial stance toward free-market capitalism, he concluded.

Kristol's explication of the New Class theory, like most rhetorical invocations of the period, did not emerge ex nihilo. Indeed, business leaders had lodged similar complaints about Franklin Roosevelt's "Brains Trust" of New Dealers from Harvard Law School during the 1930s.[67] But in the 1970s, the notion took on a particular salience among many businesspeople because it reinforced their practical objections to new social regulations and other liberal economic policies. One Connecticut businessman responded to Kristol's editorial by claiming that the New Class had taken over not only academia and the media but also Congress and government bureaucracies. Elitist experts at the EPA, for example, with "vestigial business knowledge" imposed "severe restrictions on industry without any scientific in-depth studies and facts."[68] Clinton Morrison, an executive with the First National Bank of Minneapolis, invoked Kristol's theory in a stump speech during his one-year tenure as chairman of the U.S. Chamber of Commerce in 1975. Free-market critics in the New Class looked down their noses at business, Morrison declared, "precisely because the market is so vulgarly democratic." Anything less than a purely market-driven economy, Morrison argued, was inherently elitist and reflected "a belief that it is better for some central authority to plan for us than for us to plan for ourselves."[69] In sum, the New Class theory helped business leaders make sense of the rising power of the public interest movement and the intentional bureaucratization of regulation, as well as the persistent antibusiness spirit they sniffed out of the news media and entertainment industry.

The "us versus them" vision implicit in the New Class theory also resonated with many business leaders because it appealed to their self-image as guardians of a virtuous and traditional middle-class ethic. The most politically active businesspeople during the 1970s were not, by and large, the products of the nation's elite. To be sure, they were college educated, male, and white—historically the best indicators of upward mobility in the United States.[70] Yet most had attended small colleges or public universities, not exclusive Ivy League schools. Despite their wealth, prestige, and close contacts with presidents and senators, these men saw themselves as products of the American middle class where success flowed from hard work and integrity. Business was the domain, as one executive remarked, of "the guy who scrambles to the top of the heap." The New Class professionals, so overrepresented within the government bureaucracy, typified a sense of entitlement and superiority that exacerbated status anxieties among many business leaders. Indeed, as one executive remarked to Silk and Vogel, "[t]he government is full of bright, long-haired, arrogant young lawyers right out of Harvard Law School whose main goal in life is to harass us."[71]

New Class theory thus redrew traditional notions of class struggle away from "manager versus worker" and toward "elite versus everyman," appealing directly to business leaders' self-image. By pitting hard-working businesspeople against elitist (but ultimately ill-informed) academics and professionals, the theory helped connect top business leaders (by all accounts "elite" in their own right) with other conservative political organizations. Even at the highest levels, many corporate leaders saw themselves as part of Richard Nixon's "Silent Majority," who took offense at 1960s social upheavals led by overprivileged college students who rejected their flag and their heritage.[72] To many corporate leaders, public antagonism toward business simply marked the continuation of the culture wars of the 1960s, most pronounced among young people. In 1977, NAM chairman Heath Larry, a retired U.S. Steel executive, reflected that former student radicals had brought their perverse values into the world of work in the 1970s. Those notions emerged, he claimed, "in preference for the environment over improved technology, in aversion to bigness, in revolt against the 'rat race,' in decline for respect for authority and disinterest in material possessions." Now that "many of the young people who marched against conventional values . . . hold positions of power in Washington," Larry suggested, their tendency to blame "the system" turned into support for collectivist, socialist policies.[73]

If the counterculture and the general tenor of what historian Allen Matusow called "the unraveling of America" in the late 1960s contributed to business leaders' sense of isolation and aggrievement, cultural changes and unrest in organized labor only further drove the point home.[74] The contested relationship between employers and workers has long formed the foundation of industrial political economy, but even these age-old tensions felt increasingly unfamiliar in the 1970s. Labor's institutional culture shifted perceptibly in the aftermath of the late 1960s in the face of critiques by a younger generation, in the words of labor historian Nelson Lichtenstein, about "corporate power, routine work, union bureaucracy, and the racism and sexism endemic to working-class culture."[75] As United Auto Workers president Walter Reuther declared in 1970, America now boasted "a new breed of workers [sic] in the plant who is less willing to accept corporate decisions that pre-empt his own decisions."[76] That rebellious spirit animated a major strike wave that rocked industrial relations in the early 1970s. Unrest in those years included wildcat strikes by federal postal workers, widespread sanitation walkouts, and recurring protests at GM's Lordstown, Ohio, plant between 1972 and 1974.[77] In the end, the anti-authoritarianism that underlay that tremendous uptick in strike activity helped weaken labor politically by decreasing their leaders' clout. With a note of irony, one executive remarked to Silk and Vogel: "[AFL-CIO president George] Meany is the best ally we have. Unions have knowledge of costs, margins, profits. We need an alliance between the capital sector and organized labor to protect the free enterprise system against anybody else."[78] For men like that executive, "anybody else" increasingly meant the new generation—those antibusiness radicals who firebombed the banks, picketed the defense companies, and selfishly launched wildcat strikes despite their leaders' wishes.

A vicious storm thus raged across the American political landscape, and the business community found itself right in the middle of it. The social, cultural, and economic dislocations that intellectual historian Daniel Rodgers has recently categorized as the opening salvo in an "Age of Fracture" fundamentally altered longstanding patterns of accommodation between corporate leaders and the political sphere and begat a new era in the politics of business. Drawing on his interviews at the Conference Board meetings as well as his longtime observations of American business and economics, *New York Times* columnist Leonard Silk concluded that the spirit and culture of American executives themselves had profoundly changed. The chorus of complaints about the federal government, the regulatory state, and the New Deal social welfare system, while present for decades, acquired a new tenor and a fiercer urgency in the early 1970s. "Just as much of the public sees powerful business corporations dominating the rest of society and the governmental process," Silk told an audience of Conference Board members at the Waldorf-Astoria Hotel in September 1976, "businessmen see just the reverse. They believe they themselves are dominated by other forces in the society; by populist politicians and their supporters, by government bureaucrats, by labor unions, by farm groups, citizen groups, consumer groups, the press and the electronic media." For growing numbers of business leaders, the pressures had become all-consuming—from social regulation legislation to weak profits to a cultural abyss of antibusiness venom—and allies seemed few and far between. The consensus of the early postwar years had fractured irrevocably by the early 1970s, replaced by a deep and foreboding sense of crisis. No longer able to tap their old political allies or rely on their outdated methods of political entrepreneurship, corporate leaders increasingly talked themselves into an inescapable truth. They would have to do it themselves.[79]

CHAPTER 2

A New Life for Old Lobbies

> According to the Soviet social science textbook *Obshchestvo Ve-deniye*, the U.S. Chamber of Commerce determines "the political course of the United States."
> —Richard L. Lesher, president, Chamber of Commerce of the United States, April 1976

IN SEPTEMBER 1976, during the brief window between the hoopla surrounding the bicentennial of the Declaration of Independence and the hotly contested presidential election in which Jimmy Carter ran Gerald Ford out of office, the 108-member board of directors of the National Association of Manufacturers (NAM) held a meeting in Colorado Springs to debate nothing less than the future of their eighty-year-old organization. Three months earlier, the NAM's president, Doug Kenna, had triumphantly announced an agreement to merge with the U.S. Chamber of Commerce and create the "National Association for Commerce and Industry." The combined strength of this proposed super-lobby would eliminate organizational "redundancy" and streamline the NAM's and the Chamber's central mission: to shape business-related legislation and to provide a mouthpiece for the united voice of the entire business community. Despite the merriment surrounding America's 200th birthday, the country's economic future looked especially bleak in 1976. Productivity, profit, and employment rates had all declined in recent years, and inflation and the public's animus toward business were up. Combining the forces of the two stalwarts of American industry would at long last, according to Chamber of Commerce president Richard Lesher, put the business community in a position to combat the "growing bias in this country against the private sector."[1]

The proposed merger of the NAM and the Chamber emerged from the widespread clamor for businesspeople to take collective action in response to the political perils they believed they faced. Businesspeople, according to an oft-cited refrain, had to learn the political lessons that labor had used to such success in the decades since the New Deal and engage in national legislative debates and policymaking more directly and concretely. By the early 1970s, corporate leaders broadly agreed that on issues from economic planning to social regulation, business simply found itself outfoxed at every turn. Just as labor's successful use of political action committees had helped inspire the creation of the Business-Industry Political Action Committee (BIPAC) in the early 1960s, so too did the merger of the American Federation of Labor (AFL) and the Congress of Industrial Organizations (CIO) in 1955 provide a model for joining the country's largest employers' associations together in one institution. Political power, business leaders and their political allies believed, had to be cultivated, and unity begat strength. As one Republican congressman sympathetic to the NAM-Chamber merger wrote: "Without political clout, no legislative agenda can be possible."[2] Committed to institutional change, business activists tapped into a long history of strategic borrowing from their political opponents; the immediate pressure of their "crisis of confidence" helped them overcome institutional inertia and adopt a reformist agenda.

As vehicles for a united, pan-business political offensive, the leaders of the NAM and the Chamber believed that their size, experience, and diversity of membership gave them a unique advantage that a merger would only strengthen. Each association had a long history that dated to the Progressive Era (the NAM was founded in 1895; the Chamber in 1912), and each boasted small companies as well as Fortune 500 corporations on its roster. Of the two, the NAM was considerably smaller and somewhat more focused, comprising 13,000 member firms predominantly from the manufacturing, construction, and extractive industries, as well as a number of financial institutions. The 100,000-member Chamber of Commerce, the self-described voice of "Main Street" commercial interests, comprised service and manufacturing companies—including nearly all NAM members—as well as professional organizations, local and state chambers of commerce, and trade associations. Although leaders of both groups stressed that approximately 80 percent of their members were small companies, both also represented the nation's largest industrial and financial services corporations, which tended to pay higher dues and exerted disproportionate influence on policy.[3]

Yet despite overlapping memberships, shared political goals, and the high hopes of their leaders, the proposed merger fell apart when the NAM's board of directors voted it down. Although NAM president Kenna had promised that manufacturers would make up 80 percent of the combined organization's board of directors and that "no effort would be made to force together state manufacturing associations with state chambers of commerce in individual states," board members worried that integration with the Chamber would inevitably shift focus away from manufacturing interests. As the president of a small electric company opined, "NAM is a manufacturing oriented organization today; however, what will it be after the merger?" Yet even in failure, the effort to create a union between these two powerhouses testified to the powerful drive for a renewed political offensive as business's crisis of confidence reached its peak in the mid-1970s. Although the NAM board ultimately placed industrial solidarity over pan-business unity, the merger had only been conceivable in the first place because both organizations had recently undergone a profound convergence of organizational structure and political strategy. Indeed, in the years leading up to the failed merger, these one-time dinosaurs of organized business had reinvented themselves by deliberately expanding beyond their historic functions to become dominant forces in national politics.[4]

The institutional developments at the NAM and the Chamber—the new life breathed into these old lobbies—grew directly from the political and economic upheaval of the late 1960s and early 1970s and paved the way for effective pan-business lobbying in the years ahead. The tumultuous 1960s had altered the landscape of Congress and party politics, particularly through the rise of public interest liberalism and its demands for greater federal intervention with regard to employment equality, consumer and worker protection, and environmental stewardship. The civil rights movement ended one-party rule in the South, creating a growing number of contested congressional races, and the Republican Party shifted further to the right on economic and social welfare issues. Congressional reforms, particularly the Legislative Reorganization Act of 1970, reduced the power of committee chairs and opened Washington to a barrage of interest group activists, lobbyists, and campaign funders. And finally, federal election reforms and the legalization of political action committees fundamentally changed the financing structure of congressional campaigns and the possibilities for various interests to shape policy.[5]

In this new political context, business leaders at the NAM and the Chamber refashioned their public image, refined their approaches to lobbying, and broadened their policy prescriptions. Maintaining their traditional focus on labor power and government "interference" in the market, they organized around issues like wage-price controls, the Davis-Bacon Act, and the minimum wage. At the same time, they expanded their horizons to reflect the new policy debates, inveighing against the proliferation of environmental protections and consumer product safety laws, and in particular against the expansion of federal regulatory authority through agencies like OSHA. Although scholars do not typically employ the framework of "social movements" to describe the activism of economic elites—and the men who ran the NAM and the Chamber certainly qualified as elite—business leaders' strategies frequently mirrored those of their antagonists in the environmental and consumer movements. In addition to developing powerful lobbying infrastructures aimed at the levers of power in Congress and, to a far lesser extent, state legislatures, these business associations also engineered a political "ground game" by mobilizing supporters at local levels. Indeed, they distinguished themselves in the 1970s by forging deep networks among business owners, politicians, policy entrepreneurs, and intellectuals. In revitalizing their position in American politics, they helped create a sense of common purpose among businesspeople and like-minded political allies, a vital characteristic of any social movement. Even when they failed to achieve their stated objectives, such as uniting into one organization or, as we will see, "educating" the public about the virtues of free enterprise, they created a lasting political coalition with profound ramifications in the future.

RISE OF THE OLD GUARD

As the old lions of the American business community, the NAM and the U.S. Chamber of Commerce had seen their influence on policy ebb and flow with the currents of American politics from the Progressive Era through the 1960s. The NAM, the smaller of the two, had the distinction of being older. During the Depression that followed the Panic of 1893, financiers like J. P. Morgan engineered the country's first corporate merger movement, not only spawning mass concentrations of capital in highly integrated firms but also making industrial policy a paramount concern for businesspeople at all levels. In 1895, more than three hundred industrialists convened in Cincinnati to promote industrial development and the freer trade of American manufactured goods both within the United States and abroad. They aimed to strengthen reciprocal protectionist tariffs and thus limit imports from Europe, which threatened to outcompete American manufacturers under the "tariff for revenue only" policies of the Wilson-Gorman Tariff Act of 1894. One of that original meeting's primary conveners, Ohio governor William McKinley—whose eponymous tariff act of 1890 had been replaced by Wilson-Gorman—saw in the nation's manufacturing community a chance to shore up his bid for the Republican Party's presidential nomination. Together with his campaign manager, Marcus Hanna, McKinley believed that an organization of manufacturers would help him woo economic elites in the South who had voted nearly lockstep with the Democratic Party since the Civil War. McKinley and Hanna hoped to shift focus to national economic issues, including trade policy, rather than regional politics. (And indeed, they were modestly successful: McKinley performed far better in the South than any other Republican candidate in the post–Civil War era, nearly carrying Atlanta on his way to national victory in 1896, although the Democrats largely retained their grip on the Solid South, as they would until the 1960s.) The NAM's devotion to national economic growth and foreign trade helped blur regional lines, and the group became an important political vehicle for the McKinley campaign.[6]

Given the NAM's subsequent reputation as an antistatist hard-liner organization, the fact that it emerged from a spirit of cooperation between manufacturers and the federal government appears ironic. Yet in its early years, the association actively supported a vigorous federal government—after all, only Washington could establish and enforce protectionist tariffs. After McKinley's victory, however, many of the NAM's high-tariff legislative demands came up short, including the tortuously slow creation of the Department of Commerce (finally established in 1903). Employers began to doubt the benefits of the association, and membership declined. In response, the NAM's leaders shifted their focus from foreign trade to a more energizing issue: fighting the rising power of labor unions. The "labor question" entailed policies that stretched from laws governing work stoppages to the eight-hour day, thus presenting more concrete issues for manufacturers. Buoyed by its newfound antilaborism, the NAM's rolls swelled, nearly tripling (to 2,742) between 1902 and 1907, and the group cemented what would become its long-lasting reputation as a hardnosed antagonist to unions. But that strategic switch came at a cost: as the NAM focused increasingly on shop-floor issues, the inroads its founders had crafted with politicians and policymakers atrophied. Within a decade, business-oriented Republicans in Washington complained loudly that while the NAM clearly articulated the antiunion position, no organization projected the overall "voice of business" to policymakers.[7]

Into that void stepped the U.S. Chamber of Commerce, truly a product of its time. The rapid and unprecedented growth of industrial production at the end of the nineteenth century fundamentally reshaped America, yielding not only massive and vertically integrated corporations but also the fiery politics of trust-busting, populism, and unionism. At the same time, the rise of modern management at those large industrial corporations generated a deluge of economic data and rich policy debates. In 1903, Congress responded to this new chapter in the history of capitalism by creating the Department of Commerce, formalizing the federal government's interest in the mechanics of industrial society. No sooner had the ink dried than government officials and policymakers began to call for direct input from business owners to help them create policies to nurture and regulate industry. Some sought to work through city and state-run chambers of commerce, which had promoted trade on the local level since the early nineteenth century but had no national organization. By 1910, members of the Taft administration proposed a *national* Chamber of Commerce that would comprise businesspeople from across industries and regions and operate as a clearinghouse of statistics, perspectives, and analysis that legislators could use to formulate policy.[8] Heading into his reelection campaign, which he would lose in a three-way race with Theodore Roosevelt and the ultimate victor, Woodrow Wilson, William Taft believed such an organization could have a political as well as policymaking function. Like his Republican predecessor McKinley, Taft believed that nationalizing business issues would help bring southern businessmen to his side in the campaign. (His strategy failed, and the president lost the South badly on the way to a nationwide electoral wipeout.) In April 1912, hundreds of delegates from state and local business associations accepted Taft's invitation to convene in Washington, where they officially inaugurated the United States Chamber of Commerce.[9]

As the administrative operations of the American state and the industrial business community expanded dramatically during the 1910s and 1920, the NAM and the U.S. Chamber of Commerce cemented their positions as ardent defenders of private enterprise. As the self-proclaimed voice of *all* business, the Chamber acquired a greater national profile than did the NAM, which remained relatively small and narrowly focused. In the 1920s, the NAM's membership peaked at more than 5,000 owner-operators of mostly small and midsized manufacturing firms (those that did less than $10 million in sales per year—approximately $1.7 billion in current dollars—or employed fewer than 2,000 employees), concentrated in the Northeast and Midwest.[10] The Chamber, on the other hand, cast a longer shadow and played an important role in major Progressive Era policy debates, including the creation of the Federal Trade Commission. In historian Robert Wiebe's words, it quickly became "the most successful national association of the progressive era."[11] By 1929, the Chamber boasted nearly 14,000 individual people and companies on its membership rolls, as well as more than 1,500 state and local organizations from across the country. For the group's leaders, the involvement of such a diverse constituency clearly demonstrated that "business" had a harmonious set of interests regardless of region or industrial sector. In the 1920s, President Calvin Coolidge, perhaps with some exaggeration, proclaimed that the Chamber "very accurately reflect[ed] . . . public opinion in general."[12]

Despite its sunnier public presence, the Chamber joined the NAM in ardent opposition to government policies that infringed on business prerogatives. Antagonism between business leaders and progressive politicians only escalated during the Great Depression, which discredited the business class in general and fueled public distrust of large corporate interests in particular. The NAM did little to bolster its stock with many Americans when, in the first year of the Depression, its president heartlessly prescribed the harsh medicine of laissez-faire capitalism. If poor Americans "do not . . . practice the habits of thrift and conservatism, or if they gamble away their savings in the stock market or elsewhere," he asked, "is our economic system, our government, or industry to blame?"[13] Prominent leaders at the Chamber of Commerce, at first, were less strident. Under President Hoover and during the early years of Franklin Roosevelt's term, liberal businessmen like Gerard Swope of General Electric and retailer Edward Filene (founder of the liberal research group the Twentieth Century Club) preached a brand of corporate liberalism that championed collaboration between business and the state, particularly through the economic planning boards created under the National Recovery Act. That honeymoon proved short-lived, however, and the Chamber broke publicly with Roosevelt in 1934 before joining the NAM in full-throated condemnation of Social Security and the National Labor Relations Act the next year.[14] Those hallmarks of the Second New Deal, the two business associations charged, violated the "American way" and reeked of socialism.[15] In the years to come, the NAM in particular became a haven for virulently anti–New Deal executives, many of whom also supported the rabidly anti-Roosevelt American Liberty League. At the same time, the group's membership increasingly skewed toward larger firms, and its obstructionism became legendary, cementing a reputation that would last for generations. Indeed, its leaders openly proclaimed at their national convention that the NAM was "out to end the New Deal," and its activism—however ineffectual—backed up such intransigence: of the thirty-eight major federal proposals on which the group took a position and which subsequently became law between 1933 and 1941, the NAM opposed thirty-one.[16]

Of course, neither the NAM nor the Chamber made good on its hopes "to end the New Deal," whose central elements survived World War II to become embedded in the fabric of American political economy. After the war, both organizations retreated somewhat from their screeching anti-Roosevelt vitriol, but they retained staunchly conservative positions on fiscal policy, welfare, and organized labor. As historian Robert Collins has argued, the business community in general softened its once-rigid take on Keynesian economics, accepting a certain level of deficit spending to boost consumption and business growth.[17]

While they brokered a modest rapprochement with the New Deal state over Keynesianism and, to a very slight extent, Social Security, the NAM and the Chamber nonetheless proved unwilling to bend on labor issues. The National Labor Relations Act of 1935—the Wagner Act—had changed the world of labor-management relations into which the business associations had been born by empowering the National Labor Relations Board to regulate collective bargaining and ban certain antilabor practices. The New Deal's support for unionization had also spurred the creation of the CIO, which emerged from and then split with the AFL.

Unlike its older counterpart, the CIO appealed primarily to industrial unions and lesser-skilled, often more radical workers, much to the chagrin of business leaders already predisposed to distrust labor. Indeed, the much-publicized presence of communists within the CIO, coupled with popular outrage over the strike wave that industrial unions launched shortly after the end of World War II, galvanized a conservative antilabor pushback that the NAM and the Chamber fully endorsed. As the Cold War rapidly redefined American politics after World War II, red-baiting politicians and their business allies accused the CIO of subversion. They threw fuel on the fire by blaming the 1946 strike wave for the onset of postwar inflation and the dramatic rise in consumer prices. (Both charges were exaggerated: while the CIO certainly counted communists and "sympathizers" among its members, its leadership also included adamant anticommunists like ex-socialist Walter Reuther of the United Auto Workers; moreover, rising prices mostly reflected the "catch-up" effect after the government ended wartime price controls, which in fact precipitated the strikes.)[18]

In 1947, the fiercely antilabor factions within the business community—most vividly on display at the NAM—finally achieved an important policy victory after fifteen years of frustration. During the election of 1946, the Republican Party rode a wave of New Deal fatigue and distaste for labor unrest to win majorities in both houses of Congress. The following June, an antilabor, antiliberal, and anticommunist coalition secured passage of the landmark Taft-Hartley Act, which amended the National Labor Relations Act and became law when Congress overrode President Harry Truman's veto. Although the new legislative strength of the Republican Party proved critical to the successful veto override, the coalition drew considerable support from conservative Democrats as well. In the House, 106 out of 177 Democrats voted to override Truman, as did 20 out of 42 Democratic senators; the Republicans voted more in lockstep. A bipartisan victory against organized labor, Taft-Hartley barred communists from leadership roles in unions by mandating "loyalty oaths," prohibited shop-floor supervisors and foremen from joining unions, and banned certain types of labor resistance (such as sympathy strikes and secondary boycotts). Most important for the future of business and labor politics, Taft-Hartley also included a "right-to-work" clause, which amended the Wagner Act to permit state legislatures to ban "union shops"—labor contracts that required workers to join a union before being hired (although they could leave the union thereafter). The right-to-work section of Taft-Hartley ultimately led to a bifurcated labor structure in the United States, in which some (mostly northern and midwestern) states permitted union shops and others granted employers far more power to resist unionization.[19]

The fruit of a ten-year struggle to roll back labor's New Deal gains, the debate over Taft-Hartley provoked an energetic lobbying campaign that exposed the important institutional divisions within the postwar business community. Business leaders who identified with the "accommodationist" groups, such as the Committee for Economic Development, which advised policymakers on budgetary issues, largely stayed on the sidelines. The chief executives at the Business Advisory Council mostly supported the bill, but they were hamstrung by their institutional structure and could do no lobbying. The NAM and the U.S. Chamber, on the other hand, threw themselves into the thick of things, pushing their anti-union message not only in the halls of Congress but also on the shop floor itself. The NAM in particular invested heavily in workplace propaganda, producing and distributing flyers and "educational" material designed to persuade workers to oppose dictatorial "union bosses." Such overt lobbying by business caught labor's supporters by surprise and provoked fierce concern. CIO president Philip Murray, for example, railed against what he called the NAM's "national propaganda campaign" as labor leaders of all stripes recognized anew the serious challenge that ultraconservative business activists presented. Indeed, labor's bruising defeat pushed CIO and AFL officials to mend their fences and paved the way for their formal reaffiliation in 1955.[20]

Taft-Hartley provided a brief moment of rejuvenation for the old-time business lobbies, but it was far from the complete repudiation of New Deal labor policy that its most ardent proponents at the NAM and the Chamber sought. As labor historians have argued, the law strained but did not break the labor movement, and it actually reinforced the government's commitment to collective bargaining as the centerpiece of labor-management relations. Just as important, the rabid anti-unionism that the NAM and the Chamber displayed during the lobbying effort severely tapped their political capital, cementing their reputations for right-wing rigidity. By the 1950s, each group saw its status and political clout decline notably, particularly after the conservative wave that produced Republican congressional majorities crested and the Democrats regained control of both houses in 1954 (a hold not relinquished in the Senate until 1980 and in the House until 1994).[21]

Although both groups saw a drop in their relative power in Washington politics, the NAM took the worst of it. In 1951, publisher and business-oriented conservative Malcolm Forbes editorialized that the NAM took such extreme policy positions against labor that its support of any legislation amounted to a "kiss of death." Such hostility to all aspects of the liberal state both reflected and shaped the NAM's membership. By the early 1960s, the group attracted primarily midsized family-run companies—80 percent employed fewer than five hundred people—

and its executive leaders hailed from all regions of the country. The group also acquired a reputation for reactionary politics, made worse by the exploits of its board member Robert Welch, a California candy manufacturer who founded the rabidly right-wing, conspiratorial, and isolationist John Birch Society in 1958. Nattering negativism and paranoid racism do not a winning political lobby make. For many Americans, as one trade magazine summarized in the early 1970s, the NAM stood out as "the bad guys."[22]

The Chamber of Commerce suffered the taint of right-wing radicalism less than the NAM did, but it nonetheless saw its immediate influence on policy decline. After brief flirtations with corporate liberalism during World War II, the organization settled into a traditionally conservative orientation. It advocated fiscal conservatism (balanced budgets with low taxes) but also reluctantly embraced Keynesianism, especially federal stimulus spending in times of recession. Unlike the firebrands at the NAM, its leaders cultivated a staid and mostly nonconfrontational posture, reflecting in large part their diverse constituency. The organization played only a minor role in the Eisenhower and Kennedy administrations and occupied what historian Robert Collins has called "the middle of the new spectrum" of business-oriented politics. In his 1969 dissection of power brokers in Washington, political scientist Lewis Dexter dismissed both the Chamber and the NAM as mostly irrelevant. "It is interesting to note," he wrote, "how, in almost every conversation I have ever had in which these are referred to, someone will point out how ineffective [they] are."[23]

The NAM Goes to Washington

In the late 1960s and early 1970s, as I argued in the previous chapter, corporate executives and business owners from across the industrial spectrum and in all regions of the United States became increasingly insecure and anxious. The crisis of confidence hit home especially hard at the NAM and the U.S. Chamber of Commerce, where leaders who had for decades hailed themselves as defenders of a united business community now confronted a growing sense of voicelessness and cultural isolation. Bemoaning private enterprise's apparent political impotence, the NAM and the Chamber both worked hard to reinvent themselves by reorganizing their political strategies, expanding their memberships and operations, and forging crucial inroads with other conservative and business-oriented organizations.

The NAM began its turnaround first, largely because its leaders realized earlier how far the group had to go to regain mainstream credibility and cultivate allies within government rather than simply screaming from outside the gates of power. In 1962 the NAM's first full-time president, Werner P. Gullander, came onboard with a clear mandate to improve the organization's public image and political effectiveness. Like many mid-century business leaders, Gullander was a product of middle America. The son of a Swedish missionary and pastor, he graduated from the University of Minnesota in 1930 and began a career in accounting at General Electric. He ultimately became executive vice president for finance at General Dynamics, a defense conglomerate and government contractor, before taking the reins at the NAM. During the 1960s, Gullander purged the NAM of its radical, Bircher members and created a leaner but more moderate organization. He also prevailed on those NAM members that retained Washington Representatives to take a more conciliatory approach to lobbying government officials—to helpfully explain business's positions rather than rant and rave about affronts to free markets. "[W]e must look to other means of influencing legislation," he told NAM staffers, "by shedding light, not just heat, on the subject."[24]

Gullander's reforms laid the groundwork for a sea change at the NAM after the pragmatic Minnesotan retired in 1972. To replace him, the association hired forty-nine-year-old Edgar Douglas Kenna, who had gained some measure of national fame as a college football star during World War II. Leaving his native Mississippi in 1942 after spending his freshman year at Ole Miss, Doug Kenna transferred to West Point and led Army to an undefeated 1944 season, going All-American in the process. A hard-charging quarterback and halfback (who also captained Army's tennis team and was named All-American in basketball), the 5'11", 180-pound standout was West Point's valedictorian in 1945, served a postwar tour of duty in Germany, and returned to coach at Army before entering the private sector in 1949. There he parlayed his athletic prowess, competitive nature, and leadership skills into business success, rising to management positions in firms across a number of diverse industries. By the time he became NAM's second full-time president (before Gullander, leaders had served one-year chairmanships while continuing to run their own companies), Kenna had garnered experience in electronics, aerospace, farm equipment, and financial services.[25]

Gullander had set the wheel of change rolling by trimming the NAM's membership and adopting a less strident tone; Kenna cast himself as an innovator with structural reform on his mind. The organization he inherited, stripped down to 12,000 member companies, retained its focus on small and midsized firms (83 percent of members employed 500 or fewer workers). Even as the NAM shrank, however, the political world it operated in grew increasingly complex. For Kenna, the rapidly changing dynamics of business-government relations required the old organization to expand its legislative focus beyond its traditional bugaboo—organized labor—and develop sophisticated policy recommendations and legislative action plans on a variety of business issues. The proliferation of liberal reform legislation, most especially OSHA in 1970, raised the political stakes for small manufacturers in particular. In response to the concerns about regulatory capture voiced by public interest activists like Ralph Nader and a growing cohort of like-minded legislators in Congress, many new social regulations tightly proscribed the administrative functions of regulatory agencies, intentionally leaving little discretion to regulators themselves. Even more than in the past, Kenna believed, business's "affairs ha[d] become interwoven with Government," and the NAM needed "to be in a position where we can work more closely with Congress, the Executive branch and the Regulatory agencies."[26]

Committed to engaging in national policymaking more directly, the NAM moved its headquarters from New York City to Washington, D.C., in 1973. It also created a Government Affairs Division that aimed, Kenna said, to keep NAM staffers "in touch with the rapidly changing scene on the Hill." That division reported directly to the NAM's leaders "about the bills which are bottled up, those which are likely to move and unfolding situations which could have special urgency for business." Kenna's Washington-based strategy also allowed the organization to coordinate testimony before congressional committees and other government agencies by "executives who have a story to tell about what effect a given proposal would have on their company or industry." Such a focus reflected the group's newfound commitment to direct lobbying of both lawmakers and officials at regulatory agencies whose daily decisions affected the NAM's member companies.[27]

Within a few years, the NAM's shift in focus to Washington politics led to structural and organizational changes that heralded the arrival, as the group's president proclaimed in 1978, of a "New NAM"—a more effective and less abrasive vehicle for "supporting the business viewpoint in the governmental process." Working from the nation's capital, NAM staff members found it easier to track bills moving through Congress and to monitor, as one leader explained, "what the priorities are in the Committees on the Hill." A "situation room" at the Washington headquarters helped NAM staffers determine the status of key legislation—on labor law, consumer protection, price and wage controls, international trade, and a bevy of other issues—and use that information to identify which legislators they should target.[28]

Although the NAM remained, as it had always been, a national organization principally concerned with federal policy, its leaders recognized that business's political success depended to a large degree on mobilizing sympathetic politicians, activists, and organizations at the local and state levels as well. "Business," after all, represented far more than a national interest group. The "New NAM" thus created a Public Affairs Committee to centrally coordinate seven field branches, which in turn organized telephone and mail campaigns to municipal and state elected officials. Mirroring the direct-mail techniques pioneered by conservative Republican activist Richard Viguerie in the 1960s, the NAM created what one leader called "a 'rifle-shot' approach to alerting the business community to opportunities for taking effective action on important issues." In addition to keeping business owners around the country informed about specific happenings in legislative circles, this strategy also served a vital movement-building function: it strengthened network ties between the NAM's national leaders and its members across the country, the heart of a "grassroots" community.[29]

The Chamber Gets the Memo

While the NAM's structural reinvigorations stemmed from a strong but ill-defined sense that its persistent negativity hampered its cause, reform at the Chamber of Commerce boasted more concrete origins. During the 1970s, the Chamber increased its membership approximately fourfold, dramatically scaled up its direct and indirect lobbying activities, forged lasting ties to other conservative political organizations, and strengthened its networks with local affiliates, trade associations, and individual business owners around the country. Those foundational changes arose in direct response to a somewhat infamous 1971 strategy memorandum written by corporate lawyer Lewis Powell. The son of Virginia farmers, Powell earned a law degree from Washington and Lee University and a master's degree under the tutelage of Felix Frankfurter at Harvard Law School in 1932. From there, he entered the world of corporate law in Richmond, launching a career that included a stint as the president of the American Bar Association, positions on several corporate boards of directors, and ultimately a seat on the U.S. Supreme Court. In the summer of 1971, Powell received a request from his neighbor and friend Eugene Sydnor, president of a chain of department stores and fellow member of the Richmond social elite. Chairman of the Chamber of Commerce's Education Committee, Sydnor lamented his organization's somewhat sleepy political posture, particularly given rising anxiety among conservative business leaders. Knowing that he and Powell saw eye to eye on the real problems that stemmed from the lack of collective political activity by business, Sydnor asked his neighbor to lend his gravitas and pen a strategic analysis—it was a mission statement—of ways the Chamber could respond to the challenges business faced.[30]

The resulting memorandum, ominously titled "Attack on American Free Enterprise System," quickly made its way to the Chamber's top leadership in August 1971. (Powell accepted Richard Nixon's second offer to join the Supreme Court—the first one had come in 1969—in October of that year; he took his seat on the bench in January 1972.) Powell's memo summarized the widespread belief that a cultural assault on the values of capitalism lay at the heart of business's political impotence and the spread of stifling regulatory laws, inflationary spending, productivity-squashing labor laws, and high taxes. Moreover, Powell contended, public distrust of businesspeople translated into a more general skepticism of the capitalist system itself. Only by directly confronting that cultural challenge and actively asserting the benefits of the "free enterprise system," he argued, could business leaders hope to release their shackles and make a better tomorrow. And although many business groups would have to participate, "no other organizations appear to be as well situated as the Chamber" to lead the charge. As the country's largest employers' association, Powell wrote, the Chamber boasted "a strategic position, with a fine reputation and a broad base of support." Its role, he insisted, was "vital."[31]

Although Powell's memo was an "eyes only" document intended for Sydnor and the higher-ups at the Chamber, *Washington Post* political reporter Jack Anderson caught wind of it and broke the story a year later, once Powell was firmly ensconced on the Supreme Court. The whiff of corporate cronyism proved too powerful for Anderson, a liberal—and avowedly anti-Nixon—columnist who wrote frequently about corruption in government and business.[32] Anderson described the Powell Memorandum in sinister terms, the nefarious attempt by powerful corporate interests to subvert the democratic process, and the document has remained a potent symbol among critics of corporate power on the political left ever since. Indeed, some commentators go so far as to suggest that the memorandum itself prompted a "corporate takeover" of American politics.[33]

The reality of the Powell Memorandum is much more complicated, however. Conceptually the document broke little new ground; business leaders had been voicing many of the same concerns for years, if not as eloquently or persuasively. Thus rather than a clarion call for a counter-mobilization by conservative businesspeople, the Powell Memorandum is better understood as a tool for institution building. As legal scholar Steven Teles has argued, the memorandum called specific attention to the hegemony of legal liberalism in the judicial system, to which conservative lawyers and politicians later provided intellectual counterpoint by modifying law school curricula and creating national organizations like the Federalist Society. Quickly spreading beyond the Chamber of Commerce, the memorandum achieved a wide readership within conservative political circles and its main arguments—often quoted verbatim—became important talking points in the halls of think tanks, policy meetings, fundraisers, and conferences.[34]

More important, the memorandum left a profound legacy at its specific institutional target. Eugene Sydnor, one director among many at the Chamber of Commerce, circulated the document widely, making sure it hit the desk of the group's chief decision makers. Perhaps nothing reflected so clearly the bureaucratic culture that dominated the creaky Chamber of Commerce than its leaders' initial response to Powell's rousing call for action: they formed a committee. Early in 1972, the Chamber's Committee to Interpret Business met for the first time and committed itself to "interpreting"—that is, translating—the benefits of free enterprise for non-businesspeople. For the Committee to Interpret Business, "selling the American way to the American people" had to become "the No. 1 priority for the nation and the business community," and the Chamber thus created a special task force on the Powell Memo to deliver specific recommendations.[35]

While it awaited the task force's results, the Chamber's board of directors responded to Powell's suggestion that the Chamber become the national leader of a broad-based business movement by retooling the group's leadership structure. Since 1912, the Chamber's chief officer had been its president, a business owner or chief executive, often with a national reputation, who served as the group's spokesman for a year but didn't quit his day job. To create greater strategic and organizational coherence at the highest level, the Chamber created a permanent presidency in 1974 and renamed the yearly position as chairman of the board of directors. Mirroring the process at the NAM through which Werner Gullander became the full-time leader, the Chamber elevated longtime executive vice president Arch Booth to be its first president.[36]

The task force on the Powell Memo reported back in 1973 with a set of specific policy recommendations. The first was to resume contributions to the Business-Industry Political Action Committee (BIPAC), which had lapsed since the 1960s. The Chamber's board voted to donate $25,000 to BIPAC's Political Education Division, which promoted issue items and provided information about the political process—such as how to lobby, vote, or raise funds for candidates—but did not directly contribute to political campaigns. By limiting its contributions to BIPAC's "educational" function, the Chamber hoped to remain above the fray of electoral politics and thus retain its influence with as wide a range of policymakers as possible.[37]

The Chamber also dramatically expanded its organizational structure by creating several affiliated groups. These included a think tank called the National Chamber Foundation, whose purpose vice president Thomas Donohue explained as "conducting and publishing research on public policy issues of critical importance to the stability of the enterprise system." Another new organization, Citizen's Choice, worked to generate political enthusiasm among a network of tens of thousands of "rank and file workers, professionals and retirees" by sending them "a monthly newsletter, special action alerts on important legislation, [and] access to a toll-free telephone hotline number providing weekly updates on pending legislation." Calling itself a "grassroots" organization, Citizen's Choice played a vital role in the Chamber's indirect lobbying: as national leaders pinpointed specific legislators whom they wished to persuade on any given vote, they could tap into a vast network of "regular people" to bombard their representatives with constituent mail. Finally, perhaps the most influential new affiliated organization, the National Chamber Litigation Center (NCLC), emerged in direct response to Powell's concerns about the judicial system's hostility to business. While Citizen's Choice promoted indirect lobbying through grassroots mobilization, the NCLC represented a different approach—direct legal challenges to regulatory enforcement. Beginning in 1977, the group pooled corporate resources to defend individual companies that faced legal actions regarding workplace safety, equal opportunity, or antitrust laws.[38]

The flurry of activity that overtook the formerly lackluster Chamber of Commerce in the aftermath of the Powell Memorandum climaxed with the arrival of an entrepreneurial new leader, Dr. Richard Lesher, in 1975. A former business school professor with a Ph.D. in business administration, Lesher had previously worked as an administrator for NASA and had forged his bona fides within the manufacturing community as president of the National Center for Resource Recovery. As head of that industry-funded research organization dedicated to extracting usable materials (copper, iron, even natural gas) from industrial waste, Lesher had worked to improve recycling technology and promoted its virtues to businesses by stressing the cost savings it entailed. When sixty-eight-year-old Arch Booth announced his retirement from the Chamber in 1975, the board of directors looked to Richard Lesher to assume the helm.[39]

Booth was a Kansas native who began his career on the staff of the U.S. Chamber in 1943 after running the Wichita chamber of commerce and became executive vice president in 1950 at the age of forty-three. Although he held the title of "president" only for the last year of his tenure, he had been the group's highest-ranking permanent leader for most of those twenty-five years and thus left an indelible stamp on the organization's culture. According to Chamber senior vice president Carl Grant, Booth was a "tight-fisted" manager who maintained strict personal control over day-to-day operations, perpetuating a traditional and

Figure 2.1. In this undated photo, a staff member at the U.S. Chamber of Commerce prepares a mass mailing for Citizen's Choice, a "grassroots organization" the Chamber created to lay the groundwork for indirect lobbying through a massive network of informed and energized local business owners and professionals. Courtesy of Hagley Museum and Library.

conservative aura throughout the association. He penned a weekly syndicated business column called "The Voice of Business," which appeared in local and national newspapers across the country, oversaw the publication of the Chamber's monthly in-house journal, *Nation's Business*, and appeared as a guest speaker on a low-profile radio program that the Chamber ran.[40]

For Richard Lesher, only forty-one years old when he replaced Booth, such public outreach represented an important but incomplete part of the Chamber's grand strategy. A careful student of the Powell Memorandum, Lesher believed that the Chamber could only achieve the public visibility it needed by creating a technologically sophisticated media operation through which it would serve the business community as both a communications hub and a policy house. In the late 1970s, Lesher thus oversaw the creation of a satellite television network that linked local and state chambers of commerce and offered specialized programming and videoconferencing. The main component of that American Business Network was a weekly half-hour debate program called *It's Your Business*, which Lesher moderated. After 1982, the Chamber broadcast the show directly from a state-of-the-art studio in its headquarters in Washington, D.C. (across Lafayette Square from the White House). As cable television spread across the country in the 1980s, the Chamber went with it. Its two-hour morning business news program, *Nation's Business Today*, began airing on ESPN in 1985. Although Lesher's gung-ho approach to new media raised the Chamber's public visibility, some conservative holdouts at the staid institution bristled at his public presence, claiming in particular that the debate show *It's Your Business* amounted to self-promotion. Nonetheless, the results proved undeniable: under Lesher's leadership, the U.S. Chamber rose from the ashes in a few short years to become a major voice in the politics of business.[41]

Richard Lesher's public communications revival at the Chamber helped fuel tremendous growth. In addition to taking on new permanent staff members and vice presidents hired to run the multimedia communications network, Lesher also expanded the group's sales force and aggressively courted new member companies, local chambers, and trade associations. As a result, the Chamber's membership rose from 50,000 in 1970 to more than 200,000 by the early 1980s. Indeed, the membership boom and the communications blitz reinforced each other. The benefits of membership, sales representatives told potential recruits, included a subscription to *Nation's Business*; that growth in readership increased the magazine's advertising base, generating new revenue that it used to augment the quality and relevance of its reporting.[42]

Lesher's organizational and spiritual revivalism at the Chamber of Commerce in many ways reflected the broader trajectory of conservative activism in the United States in the 1970s. Like many other conservative organizations, the Chamber deployed modern and sophisticated methods, such as television, radio, and computer-generated direct mail solicitations, in the service of increasingly traditionalist, strident, and confrontational politics. Young leaders like Lesher vocally rejected the alleged postwar "consensus" by which prominent business leaders made peace with New Deal liberalism, from Keynesianism to public interest regulations. Instead he helped bring the conservative critique more fully into the mainstream of national politics during the 1970s, joining in a larger project that built on longstanding antistatist ideas and unapologetically advocated for unfettered enterprise. Responding to the rise of new social regulations that limited regulators' discretion and encouraged inflexible "command-and-control" rule making, the new Chamber president delivered a vitriolic stump speech around the country in 1975 and 1976 provocatively asking: "Can Capitalism Survive?" "Did you know," Lesher railed, "that Agents of the Occupational Safety and Health Administration can raid a place of business any time they want . . . [and that] the Environmental Protection Agency has the power to destroy a city?"[43]

Lesher's ideological fervor bolstered the Chamber's image as a conservative crusader for business interests but contrasted sharply with the generally more conciliatory approach that dominated large national business associations like the Business Council and the Committee for Economic Development, which were run by executives and business owners themselves, rather than political activists. Nowhere did this tension appear clearer than in the series of debates over "corporate social responsibility" that unfolded within business circles in the 1970s. Amid plummeting public approval ratings, only exacerbated when the Watergate scandal revealed deep patterns of corporate corruption, business leaders turned introspective, asking what they had to do to convince Americans that they performed a positive social function. John Harper, CEO of aluminum giant Alcoa, had laid out the major features of the social responsibility debate as early as 1967 in an article for the *Public Relations Journal*. Bristling against stricter environmental and consumer safety regulations, many corporate leaders called for massive resistance to the government's assault on their autonomy. Blazing a middle ground, Harper contended that the American people had a legitimate right to worry about things like pollution, product safety, and workplace health, but business leaders could respect those complaints without surrendering operational control to heavy-handed regulatory authorities. Indeed, business leaders could "prevent further regulation best by anticipating needs and meeting them voluntarily." In essence, Harper's article repeated a longstanding argument, articulated as early as the Progressive Era, that far-sighted actions by business leaders could provide a hedge against governmental overreach. Even as an increasingly distrustful public called ever louder for legislative remedies, most business leaders clung to Harper's optimistic prescription.[44]

For Richard Lesher, on the other hand, Harper and businessmen like him preached nothing short of appeasement. In a fiery editorial in the summer of 1976, Lesher loudly denounced the persistence of public debates over the "long list of things business is or ought to be involved with," including "health care, the environment, product safety, [and] equal employment opportunity." Such wrangling, Lesher declared, missed the broader point. Americans should not debate business's social responsibility, he claimed, when "the one MAJOR social good that business performs isn't even on the list: IT CREATES JOBS." In a country facing a severe recession (official unemployment was 8 percent in 1976 and GDP growth had flatlined since 1973), Lesher insisted that business's social function *was* its economic function. "Next time you're discussing the 'social good' business does, point out that it does PLENTY. . . . But the number ONE good is: IT CREATES JOBS."[45]

By dismissing the very notion of corporate social responsibility, Lesher clearly articulated the key strategic differences between the Chamber of Commerce and big-business organizations. In fact, Lesher's argument mirrored very closely the claims long espoused by Milton Friedman, the University of Chicago economist and chief proponent of the monetarist critique of Keynesianism. For years, Friedman had worked to rehabilitate neoclassical economic thinking in intellectual circles, arguing that the government obstructed the liberating operations of the market by distorting incentives and that, in a philosophical sense, the greater good would arise through the free exercise of enlightened self-interest. In the late 1960s and early 1970s, Friedman's star rose dramatically, aided by a faltering economy, growing distrust in the prescriptions of Keynesian demand management, and, in no small part, the network of conservative activism to which Richard Lesher hitched his wagon at the Chamber.[46]

In a famous article in the *New York Times* in 1970, Friedman inveighed against the very notion of "corporate social responsibility." From an economic perspective, he claimed, corporations were artificial entities that only existed to pursue profit. Since "[o]nly people can have responsibilities," the whole premise of the debate was flawed. (According to this argument, a corporation that failed to make a profit would soon cease to exist, all other things being equal, so its only true function must be profits.) Friedman thus distinguished between corporations (a legal creation) and the human beings who ran them (who could logically be said to have social responsibilities). Lesher, on the other hand, invoked far less nuance and took a more overtly political stance, arguing that neither businesses nor businesspeople owed anything to society except economic growth, and any efforts to control corporate autonomy necessarily compromised prosperity. As the Chamber of Commerce expanded its structure, media presence, and lobbying under Richard Lesher's leadership, its commitment to its founding principles and its antagonistic posture toward the liberal state crystallized.[47]

SELLING THE MARKET

The drive for renewal, revival, and restructuring that swept the old-time Chamber of Commerce and the NAM in the early 1970s emerged from the palpable panic among corporate leaders. In all corners of the business community, executives and small business owners, as well as their paid representatives at trade and employers' associations, decried their cultural isolation and voicelessness in the wake of rising foreign competition, declining profit margins, and heightened regulatory responsibilities. Public hostility to business appeared to be growing, especially among what Lewis Powell called "perfectly respectable elements of society"—schoolteachers, ministers, college professors, and journalists.[48] "Americans do not understand their own economic and business systems," declared the Chamber of Commerce's newsletter. As a result, according to another executive: "Every day in a piecemeal way, the public unwittingly destroys the free market." Business, it appeared, simply could not get its message across.[49]

Corporate leaders' fixation on that problem prompted an explosion of efforts to recast Americans' understanding of business and economics and to rehabilitate the public image of corporations as well as the men (and sometimes, rarely, women) who ran them. Collectively called "economic education," such programs targeted primary and secondary schools, universities, the media, and the public at large. "Economic education," the NAM's Public Affairs Committee proclaimed, was dedicated to the proposition "that society's ills can be overcome through the workings of the free enterprise system." For leaders at major employers' associations, this project became an all-consuming passion in the mid-1970s.[50]

Of course, the idea of "educating" the public about the virtues of business and capitalism far predated the 1970s. From their inception, the NAM and the Chamber had dedicated great resources to "teaching" the public about the glories of the free enterprise system and the perils of socialism (a term wantonly waved around, whether it fit the situation or not). In the 1920s and 1930s, the NAM helped member firms organize "company unions" and then bombarded factory workers with "informative" brochures and fliers to build support for those in-house boards that undermined independent unionization efforts. During the legislative fight over the Taft-Hartley Act in 1946 and 1947, the NAM developed a shop-floor strategy, providing workers—a captive audience—with information about the threats posed by communists in the labor movement and the virtues of the "right to work." Moreover, in 1945, a former Chamber of Commerce director named Leonard Read created the Foundation for Economic Education, the country's first libertarian think tank, which published uncountable brochures and pamphlets, even record albums, preaching the laissez-faire gospel. While the Chamber itself focused more on concrete policy than abstract philosophy, it, too, published and distributed educational material, producing booklets with titles like "The American Competitive Enterprise Economy," "Understanding Economics," and "Freedom v. Communism." Indeed, throughout the postwar period, business leaders beat the drum of public education unceasingly.[51]

But the drive for economic education in the 1970s unfolded amid a different public climate. In many circles, economic libertarianism was on the march through think tanks like the Heritage Foundation and the Cato Institute, the beneficiaries of massive grants of private capital, which produced thoughtful and politically viable policy recommendations to actively roll back New Deal–era labor laws and new social regulations. By the end of the decade, Milton Friedman would produce a popular television documentary, *Free to Choose*, expounding on the benefits of capitalism and free markets. New organizations also flourished on college campuses, including Students in Free Enterprise, which by the late 1980s sent people wearing giant pencil costumes to junior high classrooms to carry the pro-capitalist message to preteens. (Friedman, in *Free to Choose*, had riffed on Adam Smith's famous description of pin production by explaining that no individual person could actually make a graphite pencil; only the profit motive could bring it into existence.) In the long run, the stakes of this intellectual movement were enormous. Free-market fundamentalism argued that "the state" and "the market" existed in separate and antagonistic spheres and that the market became increasingly "free" as state power declined. Such a vision explicitly denied the notion that states, through their legal and administrative functions, in fact *constituted* markets. Thus, rather than mediate the claims of competing interests on the market, economic libertarians claimed that policymakers should unilaterally eliminate state activity and allow market forces to govern society. To be sure, such extreme neoliberalism rarely manifested in a pure form in any serious policy debates, but by the 1980s and 1990s it would significantly permeate national discourse and place major limitations on policy options.[52]

The debates over economic philosophy that entrepreneurial activists like Richard Lesher engaged in during the 1970s thus fit snugly into a longer intellectual project. Moreover, during the early 1970s, economic education projects also provided a tremendous opportunity for the crusty old business lobbies to expand their influence. Renewed attention to such programs permitted the NAM and the Chamber to develop new physical infrastructure and vital networks, both within the business community and between corporate leaders and other conservative activists. The NAM's Public Affairs Committee, created in 1975 as part of the group's organizational revival, ran workshops that provided businesspeople with stock speeches and audiovisual aids, encouraging them "to seek out speaking engagements on college campuses and before educator audiences and student groups at all levels." The NAM also created an Organization Services Department in 1975 to establish relationships with local business groups and community organizations such as the American Legion, to which it mailed "packaged programs" on various business issues.[53]

Public outreach efforts targeted both specific legislation and general business topics, especially the question of profits. In the aftermath of the oil embargo by the Organization of Petroleum Exporting Countries (OPEC) in late 1973, inflation quickly became the nation's number one economic problem, and many consumers blamed corporate fat cats for price gouging. Prominent liberals in Washington—and many campaigning for Congress, including a young Arkansan lawyer named William Clinton—demanded a "windfall profits tax," similar to provisions imposed during the two world wars to prevent profiteering. In 1973, the Chamber of Commerce produced and sold a "Profits Kit" that included charts, articles, and "suggestions on how to use the materials to get the story out—to employees in your plant or office, to customers, to your community through newspaper ads, radio spots, posters, stickers, buttons, and reprints." Written by the group's in-house economist, Carl Madden, the kit proudly declared that "Profit is *not* a 4-Letter word!"[54]

In their campaigns for economic "literacy," business leaders targeted the medium as well as the message. As I argued in chapter 1, complaints that the national media suffered a "liberal bias," while certainly nothing new, grew louder and more pitched in the early 1970s. From Walter Cronkite's famous denunciation of the Vietnam War effort to Woodward and Bernstein's exposé of Watergate (and to a far lesser extent, their colleague Jack Anderson's "outing" of the Powell Memorandum), journalists achieved infamy in conservative circles. "It makes me sick to watch the evening news night after night and see my husband and the efforts of his industry maligned," the wife of one executive complained in 1975.[55]

For the NAM and the Chamber, media relations constituted a vital part of their "education" strategies. The NAM's first reformist president, Werner Gullander, instituted what he called a "press-panel 'sales' approach" with journalists, inviting them to sit onstage with him during his public appearances and creating an informal media roundtable. In 1975, the NAM's Public Relations Committee launched a series of public seminars to forge contacts between business leaders and writers and editors, particularly from business and financial news outlets. As president, Doug Kenna used his personal connections with television network executives to improve communication and understanding between executives and journalists—businesspeople would acknowledge the importance of helping journalists meet deadlines and agree to provide truthful, verifiable statistics for business articles; in return, journalists would try to address businesspeople's complaints about biased coverage.[56]

While businesspeople loved to whine about the media, many also believed that Americans' ignorance of business developed long before they became consumers of the news. Changing hearts and minds thus required catching them while they were young and impressionable, in the nation's schools. But schoolteachers, a Chamber researcher reported, "seem[ed] to be ignorant of the business world and economics." Indeed, according to one poll, "the majority of high school teachers and students thought a high standard of living comes by limiting profits." In the mid-1970s, the Chamber of Commerce used its publishing infrastructure and distribution networks to produce and sell an elaborate educational program for high school students called "Freedom 2000." The materials included a teacher's manual, comprehension and discussion questions, and an animated motion picture. In the movie, aliens visited Earth to learn why some societies were wealthier than others. Spoiler alert: the reason was "an economic system in which the rights and choices of the individual are of paramount importance." That message directly reinforced many business leaders' central argument against aggressive consumer and environmental protection legislation by subtly suggesting that caveat emptor and self-monitoring by business were preferable to command-and-control regulations.[57]

Although businesspeople often bemoaned the poor *content* of high school economics education (which they claimed ignored such concepts as the profit motive, the intersection of supply and demand, and the division of labor), programs like "Freedom 2000" and a similar one from the NAM called "Remember the Future" generally avoided specific issues and aimed instead for a more visceral reaction, hoping to boost students' appreciation of the free enterprise system and of corporations. Other outreach programs likewise worked to build personal connections across political and generational lines, including the Chamber's College-Business Symposia. Launched in the late 1960s amid antiwar and antiestablishment campus activism, these events were coordinated by the national office but sponsored by local chambers of commerce and trade organizations, bringing what one participant called "the gray-flannel

Figure 2.2. This animated public service announcement, produced for the Chamber of Commerce by Hanna-Barbera studios in 1973, explained the Chamber's position on striking a "balance" between fighting pollution and promoting economic growth. Courtesy of Hagley Museum and Library.

group" into contact with the "bushy hair and sideburns" crowd. Business groups also sponsored seminars and summer camps for high school and college students that included business simulation activities that allowed participants to make decisions about marketing, financing, and even labor relations.[58]

A final forum for economic education that saw a burst of activity in the early 1970s concerned print, television, and radio advertising. Although the NAM, the Chamber of Commerce, policy institutes, and corporations had "advertised the American Dream" since the rise of mass consumer advertising in the early twentieth century, the rapid spread of television and the urgency of the moment led pro-business activists to invest substantial sums of money in increasingly elaborate campaigns. In 1972, the Chamber of Commerce's Education Committee (chaired by Eugene Sydnor, procurer of the Powell Memorandum) hired Hanna-Barbera Studios, famous for their prime-time family shows *The Flintstones* and *The Jetsons*, to create a series of animated public service announcements (PSAs). The disarmingly playful thirty- to sixty-second cartoons broached complex economic problems, including foreign trade, pollution, and product safety, in simplified tones. They then cut to the live-action grandfatherly visage of Arch Booth, who explained how "free markets" offered the cure to any problem. In the case of pollution, as figure 2.2 shows, Booth calmly explained the necessity of trade-offs: "Clean air, land and water are vital to all of us," he said. "But so are jobs, food, clothing and housing. We have to weigh the total impact on the environment along with the economic and social costs in order to clean up." Like the packaged programs for high school and college students, such advertisements trafficked in platitudes and generalities, framing business debates in terms of personal freedom, economic opportunity, and the perils of socialism. Although spurred by complaints that the public suffered from an unsophisticated understanding of economics and business, most economic education programs in fact provided little more than philosophical propaganda.[59]

The Limitations of Economic Education

During the go-go period of institution building and ideological fervor in the early to mid-1970s, economic education programs were all the rage among business elites. Longstanding associations like the NAM and the Chamber, as well as the Foundation for Economic Education, expanded their earlier initiatives, and new organizations joined the fray. But did their efforts pay off? Although the quantity and breadth of economic education material clearly rose, one might well question its effectiveness. It simply strains credulity to suggest that any individual person saw a billboard, ate pancakes over a placemat touting free enterprise, or read a magazine advertisement and then fundamentally revised her political beliefs. Yet by bombarding the public with fervent praise of private enterprise and unflinching condemnation of organized labor and government bureaucracy, the campaigns may well have shaped the zeitgeist, however difficult it might be to measure their precise effect.

By the standards that business leaders set for themselves, however, the public education push did not meet its primary goal of raising Americans' opinion of business. Millions of dollars and years of speeches, packaged programs, textbooks, brochures, and ad buys did not move the needle on public confidence in business at all. The number of Americans who claimed to have "a great deal" of confidence in the leaders of major corporations (the closest proxy in the surveys to "business" as a social institution) declined from 50 percent in the 1960s to 20 percent by the mid-1970s and never rebounded. Even during the "Reagan recovery" of the mid-1980s and the roaring 1990s, rarely did more than 30 percent of Americans proclaim "a great deal" or "quite a lot" of confidence in corporate leaders. (The most common amount of confidence was "some" and that figure hardly changed from the 1970s to the present.)[60]

In time, association leaders, corporate executives, and even think-tank activists and journalists acknowledged this failure and began a strategic retreat from their best-laid plans. In 1977, NAM president (and former U.S. Steel executive) Heath Larry opined that "so many countless efforts to overcome 'economic illiteracy' have been funded by industry that it's almost scandalous." Thus while employers' associations never fully abandoned public outreach as a strategy, they increasingly dedicated themselves to hot-button legislative issues, mobilizing grassroots lobbying campaigns and directly pressuring policymakers. Even the Chamber's vaunted television programming, which continued until Lesher stepped down as president in 1997, typically dealt with specific policy matters rather than a broad-based campaign to revive faith in business or capitalism itself.[61]

The campaigns for economic education failed—at least on their own terms—because corporate leaders and the heads of business associations fundamentally misinterpreted the public's mind-set and critique. In truth, there never was a broad-based "attack on the free enterprise system." Faith in free-market capitalism ran deep in the nation's political tradition, and historically, socialistic alternatives to a free enterprise economy garnered very little support. The dominant question in the history of American political economy has never been "capitalism or socialism?" but "what type of capitalism?" According to a survey taken in the summer of 1971, exactly as Lewis Powell penned his memorandum, 66 percent of Americans agreed that the "free enterprise system" provided the best path to a higher standard of living, while only 20 percent thought "government help" was the best route. In 1978, a poll conducted for the business-friendly U.S. News and World Report concluded that the "public's concern is with business per se, not with the system within which it operates," a view supported by many other national surveys.[62]

Moreover, no evidence suggests that Americans' aggregate understanding of economics was any lower in the mid-1970s than it had been in the mid-1960s, when business enjoyed very high approval ratings. At least one member of the NAM's Education Committee had cautioned as much in 1973, telling fellow members that "[e]conomic literacy and the anti-business bias prevalent today are not the same problem."[63] More likely, to the extent that public outreach efforts changed the nation's political conversation, they did so by "educating" Americans about the (allegedly pernicious) effects of regulations and unions on economic prosperity, not by rehabilitating the image of business itself. For example, between the mid-1960s and the early 1980s, the percentage of Americans who believed that government went "too far" in regulating business increased from 40 percent to 65 percent, and those numbers have remained as high ever since, even during the Great Recession that began in 2007. The degree to which such a shift in public sentiment reflected propaganda campaigns by business, as opposed to general antigovernment sentiment and the absolute growth of the regulatory state, is impossible to measure, but that shift certainly did not bring with it greater public confidence in business leaders.[64]

Public confidence in business leaders simply moved on a different scale than either faith in free enterprise or formal understanding of business and economics, but many business leaders were slow to come to grips with that fact. Their reluctance is perhaps understandable if we consider their mind-set—if you believed in and understood the system, they felt, it only followed that you would have faith in the men who ran it to the best of their ability. But the American public did not think that way, especially in the 1970s. Public cynicism toward business emerged as part of a broader set of cultural trends, born of dislocation and malaise and fueled by economic doldrums, foreign policy failings, and political scandals. Americans' faith in *all* social institutions—the military, the government, labor, even religion—declined during this period, and in most cases public confidence never recovered the high levels of the 1950s and 1960s.[65]

And yet in an important sense, the economic education programs did not fail but in fact formed an integral part of a major political mobilization. On the most straightforward level, these programs reaffirmed and solidified fundamental philosophical commitments to the primacy of markets and demonstrated to conservative politicians that corporate leaders could be staunch allies in what activists framed as a culture war against the excesses of New Deal liberalism. Just as important, the economic education programs helped reenergize the sleepy old business lobbies. Initiatives like the Hanna-Barbera PSAs and the media blitzes by the NAM's Public Affairs Committee convinced members that these groups stood ready to take the fight directly to antibusiness elements in government, academia, and the press. Indeed, the very process of funding, creating, and distributing economic education packages, programs, television and radio spots, and print ads required leaders of the national organizations to strengthen ties with their tens of thousands of members. Public relations campaigns naturally have multiple audiences, and in this case, unifying the internal audience yielded a more important legacy than persuading the external audience. Strengthened networks *within* business associations proved invaluable to later lobbying, as these public relations campaigns generated a common identity that helped business groups overcome collective action problems and speak increasingly with a single voice.

OLD LOBBIES IN A NEW AGE

The U.S. Chamber of Commerce and the National Association of Manufacturers reinvented themselves in the late 1960s and early 1970s in direct response to the acute challenges business leaders believed they confronted. As powerful mouthpieces for a business-oriented approach to solving economic policy problems, these two organizations formed part of a far larger movement of libertarian and economically conservative political actors that revolutionized both lobbying and politics. Indeed, the aggressive and often hyperbolic fear-mongering of men like Richard Lesher helped strengthen strategic and ideological ties between business associations and a burgeoning conservative intellectual movement. Born of the same antiregulatory, antilabor spirit that animated the NAM and the Chamber, conservative and libertarian think tanks invoked fevered Cold War rhetoric to condemn liberalism, warning that America could easily follow England and France down the slippery path first to socialism and then to Soviet-style communism. Conservative pundits, politicians, and intellectuals read and quoted extensively from the Powell Memorandum and helped popularize the notion that public interest regulations, labor unions, and even affirmative action and civil rights represented a blatant attack on "free enterprise" and a deep threat to America's economic health.[66]

Think-tank directors and the academic scribblers they employed believed strongly that businesspeople themselves, organized through associations like the NAM and the Chamber, would ultimately prove essential to any successful challenge to the reigning liberal orthodoxy. In 1975, the president of the American Enterprise Institute, William Baroody Sr., told a conference of NAM public affairs executives that think tanks like his simply could not do the job alone. To save free enterprise and free society, Baroody warned, "nothing less than the total involvement at the very top echelons of the corporate ladder is required."[67] Yet despite support from conservative intellectuals, the quest to form a united business front against liberal political culture faced significant challenges. The age-old tensions between confrontation and accommodation persisted, as the conflicting interpretations over corporate social responsibility demonstrated. Success, leaders at the NAM and the Chamber came to realize, would come not only by injecting themselves into the political process but by crafting a coherent and uncompromising conservative critique that they could nonetheless persuade the general public to support. As a result, the nation's oldest business associations both reinvigorated their institutional operations and recaptured the fire of their youth by casting themselves as ideological partners with the think-tank community. Their media outreach and local grassroots organizing likewise testified to this revived spirit: the days of consensus-building appeasement among the business class had to yield to a new policy of direct confrontation. In turn, this ideological coherence gave business activism the aura of a real social movement that legitimated individual sacrifices in the name of a greater goal.

This rejuvenation of business lobbying achieved success not by preaching a vague and generalized faith in free markets but by targeting specific issues and shaping public debate about those policies. As the later chapters in this book explore, organized business leaders ultimately developed a sophisticated strategy: whether lobbying Congress or the public at large, they framed policy debates in terms of material self-interest and positioned the "business view" as the least objectionable. Working with intellectual leaders and political partners, they successfully vilified the other side—organized labor, government bureaucracies, and public interest activists—and strengthened their institutional unity and capacity for collective action in the process. Finally, by skillfully managing their growing networks of local and state-level organizations, the NAM and the Chamber bolstered their lobbying effectiveness by engaging business owners and like-minded economic conservatives in a common project.

Not all business leaders felt satisfied with these old lobbies, however, despite the new life breathed into them in the early 1970s. As the contours of global capitalism shifted, particularly through the crisis of inflation and the rapid rise in foreign competition from Japan and Germany, many leaders of the industrial manufacturing community in particular felt an acute level of anxiety over their international and domestic economic standing. For many big-business executives, who were historically less politically confrontational than the NAM and the Chamber, the broad-based and ideologically oriented strategies those old groups developed with such gusto appeared insufficient to address the enormity of the challenges. In the following chapter, we turn to those manufacturing giants who came together, amid overlapping crises of productivity, profitability, and industrial decline, to form a new business lobbying organization that would revolutionize the practice of corporate influence by the middle of the 1970s: the Business Roundtable.

CHAPTER 3

The Birth of the Business Roundtable

> People of the same trade seldom meet together, even for merriment
> and diversion, but the conversation ends in a conspiracy against the
> public, or in some contrivance to raise prices.
> —Adam Smith, *An Inquiry into the Nature and Causes of the
> Wealth of Nations* (1776)

THE LINKS CLUB IS ONE OF NEW YORK CITY'S most exclusive and elite social organizations. Although officially a golf club and a part of the United
States Golf Association, it has no course of its own but occupies a stately
four-story brick townhouse between Park and Madison, two blocks east
of Central Park. The building, located at 36 East 62nd Street, was built
in 1890, and the Links Club took up residence upon its founding in 1916
by Charles Blair Macdonald, a golf booster and course architect. The
club's first members were Macdonald's close friends, members of the Progressive Era New York bourgeoisie who counted in their number several
bank presidents, prominent attorneys, and "men of leisure." Like all of
the city's esteemed "gentleman's clubs" (not to be confused with the other
kind of "gentleman's club"), the Links Club remained in the decades after
its creation a beacon for economic elites.

From its earliest years, the Links Club catered to the city's business
leaders. Slipping through an unmarked door below street level, corporate executives would enter the main foyer to find a welcoming fireplace
and, to the rear of the first floor, a private dining space called the Oak
Room. Before them lay an ornate staircase that spiraled counterclock-
wise to the top floor of the townhouse. The pale green walls (in homage
to golf links) gave off a warm glow, and herringbone patterns marked
the hardwood floors of the long halls. The club's second floor held the
library, which featured wood panels brought from a room in England
designed by Sir Christopher Wren, cornice molding, leather chairs, and a
Rembrandt Peale portrait of George Washington. The dining room, one
floor up, housed a painting of former member Dwight D. Eisenhower.[1]

By the 1960s, the Links Club had become a preferred social gathering
spot for America's most powerful chief executives. Many corporations,
such as General Electric, AT&T, and major airlines, had their headquarters in New York, as did the commercial banks and investment houses on
whose financing those giants depended. Moreover, other big companies

operated within striking distance of the big city, from DuPont in Delaware to Xerox in Connecticut. And although the heart and soul of American industrial manufacturing lay in the heartland, industrial leaders knew that their corporate interests lay as much in East Coast power centers as in their traditional home bases. General Motors CEO Richard Gerstenberg, for example, received mail both in Detroit and at the GM Building on Fifth Avenue. In the age of the corporate jet, steel executives from Pittsburgh, automakers from Detroit, and rubber and tire chiefs from Ohio frequently and easily made their way to the Big Apple—and to the Links Club. Retreating to this oasis, away from the bustle of the city crowds and the demands of their corporations, executives could relax at the bar and enjoy each other's company.

The simple brick façade of the modest-looking townhouse thus disguised the monumental power brokering that occurred behind its hardwood doors. Most of the time, business leaders came to socialize—to complain about the government and make plans to play golf. Indeed, house rules barred members and their guests from conducting business in the dining rooms and other "public" spaces within the club. On the upper floors, however, private meeting rooms provided the perfect location for privileged, off-the-record conversations.

One such room hosted a gathering on the night of March 27, 1973, that included the incoming and outgoing chief executive officers of General Electric, the heads of AT&T and aluminum giant Alcoa, and the retired CEO of U.S. Steel, Roger Blough, by then a partner at the Manhattan corporate law firm White & Case. All five men served on the governing Executive Committee of the "March Group," a loose affiliation of big-business CEOs that had officially formed at the Links Club just one year earlier. They also all sat on the leadership board of an even newer organization called the Business Roundtable, created just six months earlier by the merger of two slightly older groups that handled labor relations and inflation issues, particularly in the construction industry. Given the pronounced overlap in leadership between the March Group and the nascent Business Roundtable, Blough and the other four executives concluded that the two organizations should formally join forces. A month later, again in an oak-paneled conference room of the stately brick townhouse on 62nd Street, a larger group of businessmen voted their agreement, and the leaders of American industry put the Business Roundtable into its final form. In the months and years ahead, the chief executives of the March Group quietly but unmistakably took over the Roundtable from the inside, completing a half-decade's work of uniting the CEOs of the country's largest corporations into a singular political powerhouse that would make an indelible imprint on the history of business and politics in the United States.[2]

The Business Roundtable, a consortium of chief executive officers from approximately 150 of America's largest publicly and privately held corporations, holds a unique place in the history of business lobbying. It emerged in direct response to business's crisis of confidence and quickly became a powerful symbol of business leaders' desire to shape politics as well as an expression of their collective power. Unlike older business associations, the Roundtable faced no institutional obstacles from an entrenched culture or obstructionist reputation. In addition, the Roundtable took center stage in the world of business lobbying during a key moment of economic realignment that both bolstered its ambitions and ultimately limited its range of influence. During the late 1960s and early 1970s, global capitalism underwent profound and irrevocable changes, and American industrial manufacturing began to lose its global dominance. The first decade of the Roundtable's activism coincided with the dramatic shift of production away from the United States, the permanent decline of both productivity growth and unionization, and the supplanting of manufacturing by financial services as the nation's most important industry. The specific policy threats that drove the leaders of American big business to create the Business Roundtable reflected these shifting dynamics, even if few executives accurately understood the degree of change they faced. Indeed, while the first generation of Roundtable leaders exuded optimism that they could confront the challenges industrial manufacturing faced through better domestic policymaking, their organization in many respects represented a last-ditch gambit by the long-established multidivisional industrial firms that had formed the heart of industrial capitalism since the late nineteenth century. Its birth reflected their collective insecurities and anxieties, and its political strategies shaped how American industrialists would confront the new world order.

Founding Brothers

Although the Roundtable would eventually become one of the most powerful members of a broad-based corporate mobilization that lobbied for a wide range of "pro-business" policies, its origins lay in a subset of American industry that faced very specific economic concerns by the late 1960s. The original Business Roundtable—before it absorbed the March Group in the spring of 1973—formed in October 1972 through the merger of the Labor Law Study Committee (LLSC) and the Construction Users' Anti-Inflation Roundtable (CUAIR). The former brought together lawyers and public affairs professionals dedicated to employment and union issues, while the latter united companies who shared a common interest in reducing the costs of construction and the strength of the building trades unions. Both constituent groups, therefore, reflected the political struggles of America's oldest, largest, and, by the 1970s, increasingly imperiled industries.

The Labor Law Study Committee had its roots in the politics of labor, particularly the aftermath of President Lyndon Johnson's 1964 landslide victory over Republican Barry Goldwater that brought the Democratic Party overwhelming majorities in both houses of Congress (68 members in the Senate; 295, or 57 percent, in the House). Taking office in January 1965, the 89th Congress launched a juggernaut of liberal reforms, including the most important elements of Johnson's Great Society program—Medicare, Medicaid, the Voting Rights Act, the Immigration and Nationality Act, and various War on Poverty and housing measures. Yet even though the AFL-CIO pronounced that term "the most productive congressional session ever held," organized labor failed to achieve one of its most critical goals: the repeal of section 14(b) of the Taft-Hartley Act of 1947. This provision, for two decades the greatest thorn in labor-liberalism's side, permitted state legislatures to ban certain types of employer-union agreements, including the union shop. A total of nineteen states, mostly in the South and West, had enacted such bans and effectively ground unionization efforts there to a halt. Despite months of intense lobbying by national and local labor organizations as well as liberal allies in and out of Congress, proponents ultimately failed to overcome a Senate filibuster and the repeal died in the fall of 1965. In the end, the measure was doomed by President Johnson's decision to place a higher priority on Medicare and other Great Society programs, as well as by the intransigence of southern and western Democratic senators who feared a business backlash in their right-to-work states.[3]

As those senators predicted, labor's push to repeal 14(b) sparked a massive organizational response by employers. The National Right to Work Committee, formed in 1955 to combat unionization, certainly received an organizational boost from the struggle, but so did smaller organizations, including the newly formed LLSC. This group of public affairs and labor relations executives took shape in 1965 when three corporate vice presidents—Fred Atkinson of Macy's, Doug Soutar of American Smelting and Refining, and Virgil Day of General Electric (GE)—met informally for lunch in New York City. Commiserating over labor's political offensive, the men agreed that managers from across the industrial spectrum needed a formal outlet to collectively voice their opposition to the repeal of 14(b). Once that legislative threat subsided, according to Virgil Day, the executives kept alive the concept of a labor-oriented managers' group. Most important, they sought a means to take the political offensive and "reverse the process of always waiting until [they] had to meet some union pressure." Day, who had long represented GE in labor negotiations and hearings before the National Labor Relations Board (NLRB), hired the top three management-oriented labor attorneys in the country to conduct an intense study of the National Labor Relations Act and report back with what Day called "an analysis of the labor problem from the standpoint of potential legislative remedies."[4] Some months later, those lawyers offered a series of specific amendments to the law that would benefit management, suggestions that Day immediately presented to the now officially constituted LLSC that he headed.

In the years after the 14(b) repeal battle, the LLSC expanded both its operations and its membership. It quickly grew to include approximately sixty member companies, typically represented by public affairs and labor relations executives, usually at the rank of vice president (like the group's founders). Following the recommendations of Day's lawyers, the group called for specific changes to labor law, including an expansion of right-to-work laws, tighter rules for secret ballots in union elections, and requirements that employees vote before launching a strike. In addition to working with sympathetic politicians to craft legislative proposals, the LLSC also conducted legal research and raised money for employers embroiled in cases before the NLRB. By the early 1970s, the organization counted among its members a wide range of industrial powerhouses, from steel and aluminum producers to utilities and airlines to automobile and chemical manufacturers. Despite their disparate markets and operations, these companies found common cause both in their large size and in their intimate dealings with organized labor.[5] Far removed from its origins as an informal lunch group, the LLSC formalized its research and advocacy operations and opened a Washington headquarters. In 1972, it hired a full-time executive director, William Beverly Murphy, a sixty-five-year-old Wisconsin native and former chairman of the Business Council (1965–66) who had recently retired as CEO of Campbell's Soup.[6]

Between 1965 and 1972, the LLSC expanded its focus beyond labor law to the larger question of union power and its effects on the national economy, particularly through the increasingly visible problem of inflation. The Consumer Price Index, which tracked the cost of a standard basket of goods, increased at an annual rate of 1.3 percent in 1964 but more than 6 percent in 1970.[7] During the LLSC's early years, the relationship between rising prices and the power of organized labor came to dominate the group's mission.

During the 1960s, public debates about the causes of inflation largely revolved around two distinct, though not mutually exclusive, explanations known as "demand-pull" and "cost-push." According to the demand-pull model, inflation resulted when aggregate demand increased faster than the overall economy's capacity to produce goods and services, most often because of deficit spending by the federal government. Cost-push explanations, on the other hand, attributed higher costs of finished goods to increases in the costs of factors of production (such as labor and raw materials). Today nearly all economists agree that while supply shocks can drive up prices in the short run, long-term inflation is fundamentally a monetary issue: excessively rapid growth of the money supply leads to higher prices. (The classic, if oversimplified, formulation is "too much money chasing too few goods.") Indeed, in the 1950s and 1960s, many economists took an essentially monetarist view—only when the money supply expanded, they argued, could increases in factor costs or aggregate demand lead to higher prices.[8] Nonetheless, such theories remained largely confined to economists and specialized policymakers until the mid-1970s, when entrepreneurial public intellectuals—chief among them Milton Friedman—succeeded in popularizing monetarist arguments. The public affairs executives at the LLSC, like most Americans in the late 1960s, still viewed inflation primarily in terms of demand-pull and cost-push models.

Arguments about demand-pull inflation reflected the widespread acceptance of the central tenet of Keynesian economics. In 1936, British economist John Maynard Keynes published his *General Theory of Employment, Interest, and Money*, beginning a decade-long process of convincing the non-communist world that in times of recession or depression, the government's proper role was to stimulate economic activity by spending more money. So well entrenched was Keynes's theory by the late 1960s that most observers blamed inflation on the Johnson administration's "guns and butter" policy—increased spending on the war in Vietnam after 1965 combined with greater outlays for Great Society initiatives at home. Such spending, without any offsetting increases in taxes (until the 1968 tax surcharge, which proved too little, too late), led to significant growth in the federal budget deficit: the shortfall between the government's revenue and its expenses rose from $3.7 billion (or .5 percent of GDP) in FY 1966 to $25.2 billion (or 3 percent of a larger GDP) in FY 1968. Adjusting those figures as a share of the total economy, those deficits totaled approximately $70.9 billion and $418 billion, respectively, in 2011 dollars. (In 2011, for comparison's sake, the U.S. federal budget deficit was approximately $1.5 trillion and 11 percent of GDP.)[9]

Most business leaders considered themselves fiscal conservatives; they relished the idea of pinning inflation on an expansive federal bureaucracy and saw the link between deficit spending and inflation as only natural. Even so, many executives entrenched in labor negotiations saw the demand-pull explanation as incomplete. As prices continued to rise in the late 1960s, many in the business world cried out against what they viewed as an equally important factor: *cost-push* inflation, which arose when the costs of production increased. For most industrialists, the chief villain was the price of labor. When powerful unions won new contracts that raised workers' pay faster than productivity increased (i.e., when firms paid workers more for the same output), industrial executives claimed that they had no choice but to pass along the higher costs by raising the end prices of their products. They described this phenomenon as "wage-push" inflation, a specific flavor of cost-push. Most industrial affairs executives openly rejected the possibility that companies could actually absorb higher labor costs *without* raising their prices by cutting other types of expenses. In his memoir, corporate attorney Haliburton Fales recounted a conversation with his boss, U.S. Steel CEO Roger Blough, in which Fales was "sufficiently naïve to suggest to Roger that CEOs . . . voluntarily limit[] their own compensation." In response, Blough explained that "boards of directors had to have the flexibility to attract the best possible executives and that limiting their options would be disastrous for U.S. business."[10] For members of the LLSC as much as for Roger Blough, such reasoning reigned unquestioned. The "excessive power of unions," committee members declared, was "a potent-factor in the wage-price spiral" that wracked the economy by 1971 and "helped bring on recession and rising unemployment."[11]

Convinced of the clear link between labor power and inflation, members of the LLSC decided by the early 1970s that real success required a concerted effort to target public opinion. Like most other politically engaged businesspeople, the LLSC leaders believed that the public tended to lionize labor and demonize management and that such poor public relations played a significant role in labor's superior political organization and legislative successes. Yet macroeconomic events appeared to create a new opening when, in the summer of 1971, an international monetary crisis combined with rising inflation compelled President Nixon to impose a mandatory freeze on wages and prices, followed by a system of strict price controls. (See chapter 4 for a detailed account of the price control program.) According to a consultants' report to the LLSC, three-quarters of Americans—including nearly two-thirds of union households—supported the administration's wage and price controls in the name of fighting inflation, despite the fact that the program severely limited the possibility of pay raises for workers. Such apparent willingness to share the sacrifice created what the LLSC's consultants called "the most favorable climate in years for the mobilization of public opinion towards fair and constructive action for labor law reform." The LLSC thus placed a particularly high priority on "expos[ing] the <u>fact</u> of labor power and its <u>impact on the average citizen</u>" to garner support for the National Labor Relations Act amendments it proposed, reaffirming its commitment to using public opinion as a political strategy.[12]

ROGER'S ROUNDTABLE

The belief that cost-push inflation stemmed from "excessive union power" extended far beyond the LLSC. Indeed, it had been an article of faith within antilabor rhetoric from the nineteenth century through the New Deal. During most of the postwar period, inflation remained mild by historical standards, although it certainly aroused passions in the aftermath of World War II and the Korean War.[13] Nonetheless, although inflation would not become the nation's dominant political issue until the mid-1970s, the notable rise in the cost of labor and materials starting in 1965 proved essential for the mobilization of the businesspeople who were most directly affected by that inflation. And no industry protested rising costs as vehemently as the construction industry. In the late 1960s, pitched debates raged over the power of building trades unions in the construction industry, spawning the second organization that would ultimately form the Business Roundtable: the Construction Users' Anti-Inflation Roundtable.

Construction workers—carpenters, welders, electricians, pipefitters, and so on—possessed higher skills than average manual laborers and their wages traditionally outpaced those in manufacturing as a whole. By the late 1960s, as the business magazine *Fortune* argued some years later, "construction wages began to get out of line" with the rest of the economy.[14] Beginning with the recovery after the 1960–61 recession, the construction industry boomed; profit rates nearly doubled between 1960 and 1966, and wages rose accordingly. Yet when the economy slowed again later in the decade, construction wages continued to rise significantly faster than manufacturing wages. Labor-oriented economists and policymakers suggested that the discrepancy arose from a disproportionate boom in private, commercial, and highway building in the late 1960s, as well as the fact that high unemployment rates in construction mitigated the long-term costs of higher hourly wages.[15] For industrial executives and managers, however, the only explanation for high construction wages lay in the overwhelming and outsized strength of the construction unions, which the Chamber of Commerce's economist called "the most powerful oligarchy in the country."[16]

In November 1968, just two weeks after Richard Nixon won the presidency, the Chamber of Commerce convened a two-day National Conference on Construction Problems to which it invited construction firms and other large industrial companies, including representatives of the Ford Motor Company, U.S. Steel, and First National City Bank.[17] The Chamber's president for 1968, Winton M. "Red" Blount, declared that labor relations in construction were "chaotic," if not "despotic," and hoped that a national conference would galvanize a response. Founder and president of Alabama-based Blount Brothers Construction, Red Blount knew from his long experience in the booming Sunbelt South the challenges of negotiating with building trades unions. The threat of strikes had led to "unbelievably high" wage settlements even as "productivity [was] declining at an alarming rate," he told the assembled conference-goers. Most important, he explained, individual construction firms could not deal with the industry's "major and chronic problems that could spell its very extinction as we know it." Acting alone, Blount claimed, contractors too often felt such intense pressure simply to finish a given project that they bowed to union demands, acquiescing to higher wages that drove up prices down the line. Rectifying this dynamic required what Blount called a "joint cooperative effort" among all interested parties, including "contractors, builders, owners, trade association representatives, economists, [and] government experts."[18]

Blount's conference piqued the interest of industry professionals, and the Chamber of Commerce immediately appointed a special task force to formulate specific recommendations. That task force included many of the labor relations executives already active on the LLSC, such as Virgil Day, and worked with a similar group established by the NAM, ultimately recommending a new organization to strengthen business's bargaining power. The secret to reducing union clout, the task force reasoned, lay in uniting construction companies and another vital constituency: construction *users*. "Users" was the term business leaders employed to denote construction firms' biggest clients: large corporations that commissioned major building projects—including factories and retail space—and thus paid the higher prices that resulted (so the thinking went) from excessive construction union power. Uniting the buying power of industrial titans like General Motors, Alcoa, and U.S. Steel, the task force concluded, would strengthen construction firms' resolve and help them resist wage demands from their unions.[19]

The Construction Users' Anti-Inflation Roundtable (CUAIR) thus emerged from the suggestion of the Chamber's task force in the summer of 1969. At its head stood Roger Blough, former steel chief and a man whose very name had a visceral effect on supporters of labor. According to some sources, Blough initially rebuffed the call to head a new business group until several chief executives prevailed upon him to take charge. His own attorney contradicted that assessment, however, and claimed that Blough had been angling to head up exactly such a construction users' group since retiring as CEO of U.S. Steel earlier that year.[20] In either event, Blough represented the perfect pick for the job in many ways. A former chairman of the Business Council, he was one of the best-known corporate executives in the country, in both business and political circles. Tall and lean, vibrant at age sixty-five, he exuded a strength and confidence that came not only from his experience as a top executive but also from his poor upbringing in rural Pennsylvania, where he worked his way from a one-room schoolhouse to Yale Law School.[21] In another sense, however, Blough made for a somewhat ironic inflation fighter. The 1962 steel showdown with President Kennedy, after all, had begun when Blough insisted on raising U.S. Steel's prices, despite the administration's warning that such a move would spark cost-push inflation. Ironic or not, however, Blough demonstrated an ironclad commitment to curbing construction industry wage demands, and he brought that steadfast zeal to the newly formed CUAIR.

Headquartered in New York City, the CUAIR comprised representatives from more than one hundred major corporations from the mining and extractive (Bethlehem Steel, Alcoa), chemical (Dow, DuPont), automotive (GM, Ford), food (Heinz, Nabisco), and retail (Macy's, J. C. Penney) industries, among others. (See appendix 3.1.) Affectionately known as "Roger's Roundtable" in a nod to Blough, the group became an important nexus for information sharing and political organizing for a network of "local user groups" in cities across the country. As contractors' associations and construction companies confronted strikes, work stoppages, and contract negotiations, they benefited from logistical support from CUAIR member firms. From New York, where its leaders could enjoy dinner meetings at the Links Club, Blough's CUAIR coordinated negotiating strategies for these local user groups and facilitated dialogue among member firms.[22]

Roger Blough's commitment to working with the large companies that made up the bulk of the organization's national membership led him to effectively cut smaller contractors—companies like Winton Blount's—out of the planning process. According to General Electric CEO Fred Borch, Blough's strategy reflected his assessment that contractors were simply "pawns of the unions" and that user companies could do better on their own.[23] Blough's preference for nonconstruction companies became especially apparent as he expanded the CUAIR's strategies and began to advocate on national policy issues in addition to supporting local user groups in their struggles with construction unions. No stranger to high politics, he drew on his experiences advising Kennedy on tax policy as a member of the Business Council's Treasury Consultant group and working with Johnson on housing and urban employment.[24] Early in 1971, Blough appeared before Congress to present the CUAIR companies' case against the Davis-Bacon Act, the Depression-era law that required construction workers on government projects to receive the prevailing local wage. By preventing contractors from importing cheaper labor and guaranteeing federal support for local economies, Blough declared, Davis-Bacon served as "an engine of inflation" that "spread high city rates to rural communities." When Richard Nixon temporarily suspended Davis-Bacon in an effort to stem rising inflation shortly thereafter, Blough quickly took credit (although his testimony was by no account the deciding factor) and told a local user group: "We've made progress, but too little."[25]

Determined to do more, Blough turned his attention to the CUAIR's organizational strategy via a bit of old-fashioned horizontal integration. Given the group's focus on national legislation and the important role large corporations played in its activism, Blough concluded that his goals and methods overlapped considerably with those of the LLSC. Since each organization worked to embolden management in labor negotiations, they naturally appealed to the same constituencies, a conclusion supported by their overlapping memberships. Thirty-seven of the 58 LLSC companies had also joined the CUAIR, which included 113 member firms. Moreover, firms that participated in both groups held a disproportionate number of leadership positions. Beverly Murphy, who became the LLSC's first full-time director in 1972, had served on the CUAIR before he retired from Campbell's Soup; and the CUAIR's chairman was none other than GE vice president and LLSC founder Virgil Day. Indeed, once the two groups combined, six of the ten men on the Executive Committee represented firms that had belonged to both groups. (See appendix 3.1.)[26]

In August 1972, Blough began advocating loudly for a merger. Given their common goal, as Blough put it, to "creat[e] a better industrial relations climate and . . . more constructive national policies," joining forces seemed eminently sensible.[27] But bringing together the unified voice of major corporations promised more than efficiency gains in organizational politics. The merger carried symbolic importance as well, representing a long-awaited step toward putting business on par with organized labor. Like the failed merger between the NAM and the Chamber of Commerce a few years later, the union of the LLSC and the CUAIR called to mind the 1955 merger of the AFL and CIO, a move that—for many top executives and conservative politicians—had marked the arrival of "Big Labor" in American politics. Hailing the combination of the two groups as "a step in the right direction," a Republican congressman from Illinois declared that labor had long coordinated its political activities through the AFL-CIO, and now business had finally put itself in a position to "make its point more effectively by doing likewise."[28]

The merger of the LLSC and the CUAIR resembled the creation of the AFL-CIO in other ways as well. The union of the two labor giants, which had been rivals since 1935, ultimately shifted power to the larger and less radical AFL, largely by installing its head, George Meany, as the president of the combined federation. Meany's ascent had confirmed CIO members' fears that their specific agenda and more aggressive strategies would take a backseat in the new organization.[29] In much the same way, some labor law experts at the LLSC warned that despite the leadership overlap, the two groups in fact employed very distinct agendas. DuPont's public relations chief, for example, wrote to his CEO that "the 'anti-inflation' thrust of the Roundtable [CUAIR] contrasted to the 'union-management power balance' objective of the LLSC." That is, the LLSC prided itself on working within the legal system to restrain union *abuses*, but the CUAIR's jawboning and Roger Blough's vehement rhetoric could come off as an affront to unions *in general*. Like a good PR man, the DuPont executive fretted about the optics and warned that being associated with the hard-headed CUAIR could compromise his lobbying efforts with Congress and the LLSC's campaign for specific labor law reform.[30]

Blough and his LLSC counterpart Murphy papered over such reticence by creating a power-sharing agreement between the two organizations. Each group appointed a full-time executive director, one to head the "construction committee" and the other to lead the "labor-management committee." Having ironed out those technical details, Blough made good on his longstanding desire to create a singular lobbying voice for large industrial corporations and to take the fight over inflation directly to the unions. On the evening of October 16, 1972, several dozen well-heeled corporate executives met privately deep in the Links Club and voted to combine the two organizations into "The Business Roundtable—For Responsible Labor-Management Relations." (The clunky subtitle disappeared within a year.) Perhaps to mollify LLSC members who still worried they would lose clout, Beverly Murphy became the group's first chairman, while Blough and Fred Borch, the soon-to-retire CEO of General Electric, took the title "co-chairmen"—one notch down. The rest of the Executive Committee included: John deButts (CEO: AT&T), Richard Gerstenberg (CEO: General Motors), John Harper (CEO: Alcoa), Shearon Harris (CEO: Carolina Power and Light); J. K. Jamieson (CEO: Exxon); Charles B. McCoy (CEO: DuPont), and David Packard (CEO and founder: Hewlett-Packard). These CEOs not only represented the inner circle of American industry. Nearly to a man, they also all headed yet another consortium of executives—known as the March Group—whose ultimate incorporation into the Business Roundtable would define the organization's unique strategy and policy agenda well into the future.

THE MARCH GROUP

On March 22, 1972, a handful of men led by Alcoa CEO John Harper and GE chief Fred Borch met privately at the Links Club to make official what had until then been a haphazard tradition of get-togethers by chief executives. In a gesture toward their nonchalance, they named the group after the month in which they met. Far less structured and hierarchical than the LLSC or the CUAIR, the March Group met at the Links Club irregularly, when members could get together, about once every six to eight weeks. While Harper and Borch provided the organizational impetus for the initial meeting, Borch later recalled that the group "was very informal. . . . Titles meant nothing." Roger Blough was nominally the secretary; he took minutes and collected dues from the individual participants who financed the meetings themselves. As a group, they issued no publications and hired no permanent staff. In some respects, the March Group was little more than a small cohort of friends who socialized and talked business. But these were more than just beer buddies. They happened to run forty-six of the country's largest corporations, and the agenda-setting Executive Committee included a dozen of the most economically influential industrial leaders in the world.[31]

The March Group lasted only a year as an independent entity before it merged with the Business Roundtable in the summer of 1973. But its fleeting official existence belied the long tradition of overt political strategizing by industrial CEOs at a certain social club on 62nd Street in Manhattan. Indeed, the origins of the March Group, and thus also the Roundtable, extended back many years to a regular set of meetings convened by Ralph Cordiner, General Electric's chairman and chief executive officer in the 1950s.

Although General Electric had enjoyed a reputation for liberal, even progressive, leadership since the early twentieth century—counting among its chiefs pro-Roosevelt Democrats like Gerard Swope and Owen Young in the 1930s—Ralph Cordiner did not fit that mold. Born on a wheat farm in Walla Walla, Washington, Cordiner worked his way toward an economics degree at local Whitman College by selling washing machines before graduating in 1922 and beginning a career with General Electric. After stints at Schick, Inc., and the War Production Board in the early 1940s, he returned to GE, where he became president in 1950 and chairman of the board in 1958.[32] His years among the electronics giant's leadership made him a fierce partisan for business, opposed to labor and any governmental restrictions on corporate prerogatives. In 1959, GE joined twenty-eight smaller electrical manufacturing companies in pleading guilty to price-fixing and bid-rigging. Although Cordiner himself narrowly escaped prosecution, seven executives received one-month jail sentences and the company paid nearly half a million dollars in fines. The episode cemented Cordiner's ardent opposition to conciliation between business and liberal government; he became so antagonistic, in fact, that the Business Council removed him as its head in 1961.[33]

In addition to the bid-rigging charges, Cordiner faced major labor relations problems as well, particularly during the strike wave that followed World War II. As newly empowered labor unions fought for wage increases to compensate for the end of wartime price controls, GE's executives hired an aggressive labor relations specialist named Lemuel Ricketts Boulware. Under the so-called Boulware regime, GE established a reputation for taking a hard line in labor negotiations and successfully restrained many union demands.[34] Cordiner, however, worried that other industries would not prove as skillful in their labor negotiations and that the downstream consequences for his company could be severe. If car manufacturers, for example, acceded to union wage demands and raised their prices, Cordiner believed, the resulting inflation would drive up GE's supply costs. Although car companies themselves might weather the storm, consumer electronics manufacturers, which faced greater foreign and domestic competition and higher price sensitivity among their customers, could suffer a major loss of sales. As Cordiner's successor as CEO, Fred Borch, put it, "Auto labor rates could have killed us."[35]

Since excessive labor power in any industry threatened all industries, Cordiner reasoned, the solution lay in pan-industrial collective action, which led him to New York and the Links Club. During his tenure atop GE, Cordiner began calling regular meetings of fellow chief executives who also faced tense negotiations with CIO-backed unions. (Even after the AFL-CIO merger in 1955, business leaders maintained their stigma against "CIO unions"—those heavy industry and manufacturing unions that assumed greater strength during the Depression and developed a reputation for radicalism and intransigence.) The "Links Group," as Cordiner described his circle of associates, included chief executives from automotive and machinery manufacturers, communications, and rubber, steel, and aluminum companies. Believing that they could not trust newspaper coverage of ongoing negotiations in other firms, the executives met in the privacy of the club to share, according to Borch, "the honest story on what labor offers really were and what the real settlements were."[36]

Much of the impetus for the informal Links Group arose from industrial leaders' growing frustration with the Business Council, an association to which they all belonged and that supposedly represented large corporate interests in Washington. Although the Business Council had formally declared its independence from the Commerce Department in 1961, largely to gain a freer advocacy hand, many CEOs still complained that it remained merely an advisory body. By tradition, the council did not take political positions, endorse candidates, conduct research, issue policy statements, or participate in lobbying (although its member companies could and certainly did do all those things individually).

Although the Business Council's political role may have been too limited for some members, it nonetheless constituted an important forum for
bringing high-powered executives together, typically in lavish surround-
ings. For example, a group of executives prevailed upon Roger Blough
to head up the CUAIR at one of the group's "work-and-play" weekends
at the posh Homestead Resort in Hot Springs, Virginia. At the same
time, the council also performed a socializing function for executives as
they made their way up the corporate ladder, a dynamic illustrated by
Charles B. McCoy's reception after his promotion to CEO and chairman
of the board of directors of the E. I. Du Pont de Nemours Company late
in 1968. At the council's next retreat weekend at the Homestead, the
group's chairman (who happened that year to be Fred Borch of General
Electric) reserved a special place in the receiving line, "[i]n order that you
[McCoy] and Mrs. McCoy may meet the members and their wives." In
that way, during the Chairman's Reception in the resort's Empire Room,
McCoy officially joined the club.[37]

In the late 1960s, the Business Council boasted approximately 150
members, all chief executive officers, most of whom regularly attended
the group's meetings—both in Washington and, twice a year, at the
Homestead Resort. Although not all the council executives shared the
same degree of enthusiasm about political activism as the members of
the Links Group, nearly all major industrial CEOs who were interested
in politics actively participated in the Business Council. Between 1969
and 1972, two sets of factors converged to push to the breaking point
the frustrations of exactly those men, who had been meeting for years at
the Links Club, grousing at the Homestead, or, in some cases, working
on Roger Blough's CUAIR. The first was the downturn in the national
economy—shrinking profits, recession, declining productivity growth,
and, of course, inflation. The second was Republican president Richard
Nixon's apparent inability to do anything to halt the economic and regulatory policies of his liberal Democratic forebears. While Johnson had
been president, corporate leaders had been able to blame the budget deficits and new regulations on party politics. Nixon—nominally the head of
the "pro-business" party—offered no such cover. Convinced that sounder
fiscal and monetary policy, as well as less costly regulations, could reverse
the decline, many executives began to demand direct action. "I think we
all recognize," wrote Alcoa CEO John Harper to his fellow industrialists,
"that the time has come when we must stop talking about it, and get busy
and do something about it."[38]

In the early 1970s, Harper and Borch emerged as galvanizing leaders
of a growing coalition of like-minded executives. In the twilight of their
respective careers, the two men shared similar life stories that shaped
their politics. Borch, the son of an electrical engineer and born in Brook-

lyn, grew up in Ohio and studied economics at Western Reserve University (later known as Case Western) in Cleveland; he joined General Electric at age twenty-one with his newly minted degree in hand.[39] Harper grew up in Louisville, Kentucky, where he started to work for an Alcoa facility at the age of fifteen. (He earned $12 a week for a summer job in 1925, or somewhere in the neighborhood of $600 a week in 2013 dollars.) Still working for the company to which he would dedicate his life, he put himself through college at the University of Tennessee, graduated with a degree in electrical engineering, and joined Alcoa full time in 1933.[40] Harper and Borch typified a generation of men who spent their entire careers with one employer, rising through the ranks to top management as their corporations grew ever larger in the mid-twentieth century. Their professional lives also coincided fully with the New Deal order, and by the time they approached retirement, their frustrations with business-government relations had boiled over.

Harper and Borch fully endorsed the complaints that echoed among members of the Links Group, the LLSC, the CUAIR, the Business Council, and myriad trade associations by the late 1960s. Harper in particular seized on the old saw that business failed at "telling its story," particularly when compared to organized labor. Unions, these men believed, simply played all aspects of the political game better. Labor PACs dominated the campaign finance world, while BIPAC, the only major corporate PAC before 1970, struggled to make a difference. Labor likewise dominated the lobbying front. Policy battles were won and lost in the cloakrooms of Congress, but despite greater reliance on Washington Representatives, large corporations felt organizationally outmatched, as their lobbyists frequently reminded them.

Yet the problem, Harper and Borch argued, was not a shortage of business associations. To the contrary, they believed that Washington had too many business lobbyists and that the cacophony of voices drowned out the central message. Moreover, the plethora of business groups, trade associations, and ad hoc committees, not to mention the proliferation of firm-specific Washington Representatives, created real risks of wasted effort. "We must," John Harper argued, "use more effectively the vast time, talent, and resources of the business community."[41] The Committee for Economic Development, a nonprofit research organization in the "corporate liberal" model that included both business leaders and economists, was, for Borch, "largely academic" and lacked "the clout we wanted on fast moving issues." For their part, the NAM and the Chamber of Commerce tended to draw leaders from their small and midsized constituents, leaving the Links Club firms without the influence they wanted and, because of graduated membership dues structures, felt they paid for. Finally, the Business Council, however helpful in greasing social wheels, could not lobby directly and retained a focus on the White House that, particularly by 1970, appeared increasingly misguided. Although Arthur Schlesinger Jr. coined the term "imperial presidency" to describe the modern executive branch, Congress in fact exerted a far greater degree of influence over domestic economic and regulatory policy in the mid-twentieth century. (Schlesinger's critique largely concerned foreign policy.) Since the 1930s, however, Business Council members had prided themselves on working with the president, chief executive to chief executive. To truly take action in politics would require breaking away from a president-focused strategy and working actively with Congress to propose, shape, and frequently curtail legislation.[42]

This panoply of failed models left Harper and Borch deeply frustrated. Despite widespread agreement about the need for collective business action, the exact method for creating a united business movement looked anything but obvious. In 1971, the two men found themselves spending significant time in Washington on a variety of projects and began meeting regularly with other interested parties to discuss ways to increase big-business executives' direct clout with Congress. Harper organized planning sessions with several of the most prominent and well-placed Washington Representatives, many of whom had begun forming ad hoc coalitions to combine their resources, staff, and strategies on specific legislative issues. "The principal ingredient missing in these ad hoc groupings," the Washington Representatives insisted, "is the direct involvement and guidance of the chief executive officers."[43] Members of Congress and other Washington fixtures concurred. Secretary of the Treasury John Connally and Federal Reserve chairman Arthur Burns, for example, each conveyed to Harper and Borch early in 1972 their belief that the voices of business leaders themselves had insufficient weight in policy debates. (Early reports on the creation of the Business Roundtable suggested that Burns and Connally in fact instructed the CEOs to create the group. In reality, the plans were already in the works when the officials met. As Borch put it, somewhat evasively, Burns and Connally "appreciated our effort.")[44]

Most of the executives at Harper and Borch's meeting at the Links Club on March 22, 1972, had attended such meetings since the Cordiner/Boulware days, but at long last they had created something official. The March Group aimed to fundamentally revolutionize the practice of corporate lobbying by involving CEOs in political strategy and coordinating the operations of Washington Representatives. Indeed, only corporations that retained permanent paid lobbyists could join, a policy that excluded the small and midsized companies that relied on trade associations or hired-gun lobbyists. Believing so strongly that disorganization among large corporations led to legislative weakness relative to labor and other interest groups, the March Group leaders worked to streamline communication and strategy between lobbyists and chief executives. Although they recognized the importance of traditional methods of influencing politics, particularly funneling donations to political campaigns, the March Group members' real innovation was their commitment to using chief executives as lobbyists themselves. Only through direct involvement and clear top-down coordination could they change the dynamics within the nation's capital.[45]

To that end, the March Group CEOs divided themselves into four task force committees, each devoted to a specific legislative area: taxation, international trade, consumerism, and environment. At the head of each task force sat a particularly motivated chief executive who not only coordinated activities among Washington Representatives but also worked to "rally support within the business community" for the issues under his purview. Task force chairmen contacted fellow CEOs, arranged group meetings with lawmakers, and wrote policy white papers that helped executives explain their policy preferences to their employees and local communities. This structure established the groundwork for both direct and indirect lobbying: by reaching out to employees and local media in their corporate hometowns, March Group members could generate grassroots-level enthusiasm for their policy preferences; chief executives could then provide evidence of that local support directly to lawmakers whom they met in person.[46]

The March Group also provided an institutional forum for executives to finally take action on their long-held complaints about the climate of public debate. "The business community," John Harper said, "just has not been communicating effectively, and this has led to a poor understanding of our economic system; and this had led to unwise laws and regulations." Men like Harper and DuPont's Charles McCoy echoed the NAM and the Chamber's desire to create economic education projects that would "tell business's story" and bolster executives' public standing. McCoy, for example, called for using the combined financial and logistical resources of the March Group companies to promote better training in business and economics in the nation's secondary schools.[47]

Many Washington Representatives agreed in principle with the importance of improving business's public image, but they worried that the collaboration represented by the March Group would itself add fuel to the fire and lead to severe "public relations hazards." "We believe that business has very serious problems with the intellectual community, the media and youth," a group of professional lobbyists told their March Group bosses, "[and] that the continuing hostility of these groups menaces all business." Especially given the "supercharged political climate" leading up to the 1972 election, the PR-savvy Washington Representatives urged the CEOs to keep their efforts "informal and as private as possible." As a result, the organization issued no press releases to herald its arrival, and the executives conducted their meetings quietly.[48]

Finally, the March Group explicitly avoided partisan politics, not least because its leaders included proud Democrats like Harper as well as steadfast Republicans like Roger Blough. More important, however, the executives believed that their ability to influence sitting members of Congress depended on building relationships of mutual trust and respect; embroiling themselves in the thick of election battles would certainly strain those ties. Following the same logic, the March Group did not coordinate campaign giving to groups like BIPAC or individual candidates, setting a precedent that the Business Roundtable perpetuated. Indeed, although the Roundtable's member corporations used PACs and other vehicles to influence campaigns, the organization itself has never formed or directly contributed to a political action committee. Ironically, the men whose explicit goal was to increase big business's "voice" took great steps to appear silent. A combination of insecurity and keen strategizing led to the first rule of the March Group: you don't talk about the March Group.

Uniting the Voice of Big Business

In April 1973, just one year after it formed, the March Group integrated its task forces into the structure of the Business Roundtable. The redundancy in leadership and resources convinced the March Group CEOs that a merger made good sense. "No one wanted to create just another organization," John Harper explained. At the same time, Borch and other executives worried that merging with the Roundtable could potentially hamper its "longer-range public-economic-education effort" if the combined group acquired the "antilabor image" associated with the CUAIR and LLSC.[49] As the combined voice of America's largest industrial corporations, the executives knew, the Business Roundtable ran the very real risk of embodying the public's fears of corporate malfeasance and collusion. In the end, however, Roger Blough managed to convince his fellow industrial executives that the logic of integration outweighed the potentially negative optics of affiliation. By the summer of 1973, Harper replaced Beverly Murphy as the organization's chairman and the March Group dissolved into the ether from which it had come.

As its leaders worked to codify the Roundtable's organizational structure, institutional identity, and political strategies in the months after the merger, the exact nature of the organization remained in flux. Structurally, it contained a hodgepodge of committees and task forces, including the original labor law and construction committees, as well as the Public

Information Committee (PIC). The first two adopted distinct tactical approaches although they shared an overriding concern with labor power and inflation, while the latter, a holdover from the LLSC, focused on business's public image and thus adopted a distinct strategic objective. The inclusion of the March Group's four task forces only muddied the waters further, since they focused specifically on pending legislation within tightly drawn categories (consumerism, taxes, environment, and trade). Further complicating matters, the combined Business Roundtable's leadership core included a mix of chief executive officers, public affairs executives, and labor lawyers. The group also retained the CUAIR's "local user groups," the state-level consortiums of manufacturing companies that organized collectively to confront construction unions but generally refrained from direct lobbying on either the state or federal level. The Business Roundtable remained, as Blough described it in the spring of 1973, "an amalgam of loosely knit but highly professional committees."[50]

When John Harper took the reins that summer, everyone seemed to agree on the basic problems the new organization needed to confront, but members differed—sometimes heatedly—over how to structure the group and where to set their priorities. The CEOs still worried that the industrial relations people would tar the whole group with an "antilabor" brush, and the public affairs specialists complained that the CEOs focused too narrowly on policy to the exclusion of public outreach (pockets of enthusiasm for economic education notwithstanding). Consultants commissioned by the PIC reported that the CEOs showed "little articulation of [the] basic problem" of business's image, validating the complaints from the public affairs executives. The consultants' report, however, was "not well-received" by the labor-management committee, according to its D.C.-based director, who felt slighted that the group had hired a permanent president to run the organization from New York. That turf battle only compounded tensions over strategies and priorities.[51]

Within a few years, however, Roundtable leaders replaced the complex system of committees with a more streamlined structure. The division between "labor law" and "construction" that had marked the original merger eventually dissolved, and the March Group's model of issue-specific task forces predominated. That consolidation represented the ultimate triumph of the chief executive officers over the industrial relations executives and labor lawyers. By the late 1970s, the group's structure and mission largely fell into sync and the Roundtable operated as the March Group had: a CEO chaired each task force and marshaled his own company's personnel and resources to produce position papers and coordinate legislative action. The Roundtable itself maintained a very small administrative staff, did not register as a lobbyist in its own name, and did not actively coordinate fund-raising for political campaigns. The group dedicated most of its attention to issue-specific lobbying in national politics and, although it retained a New York office into the 1990s, it devoted the bulk of its efforts to Congress.

The one holdout to this organizational redesign was the PIC, which, under the leadership of AT&T Vice President for Public Relations Paul Lund, came to embody the conflict between idealistic proponents of public outreach and the executives who remained steadfastly concerned with direct lobbying. Based in New York, the PIC in 1974 and 1975 proposed a massive public relations blitzkrieg to target everything from children's television to high school textbooks to radio talk shows. Tapping into the same spirit that animated "economic education" programs at other employers' associations and think tanks, the PIC hoped to reshape the public's negative opinions about big business in particular. Its most elaborate and expensive project was a collaboration with *Reader's Digest* in 1975 for which the Roundtable paid approximately $1.2 million (or about 90 percent of its annual dues revenue; around $4 million in 2013 dollars) to run three-page advertisements each month. The advertisements, dotting the pages of an already fairly conservative magazine, extolled the virtues of big business, the importance of profitability, and the pitfalls of inflation and regulation.[52]

Initially, the chief executive officers who increasingly held sway over the Business Roundtable felt optimistic about the *Reader's Digest* project. Both John Harper and DuPont's Charles McCoy, the Executive Committee's liaison with the PIC, actively supported the plan, expensive though it was. But when public opinion polls showed no change in the public's views of business after the program had run for several months, they balked and pulled the plug one year into a proposed three-year plan. Such a quick retreat from "pro-business" advertising suggests that the Roundtable's leaders quickly realized their naiveté. Long-term changes in public perceptions of business and economics, no matter how essential to their political success, would not come quickly or easily. As more Roundtable leaders adopted this more realistic assessment, the PIC found itself increasingly marginalized within the organization. When its strong-willed chairman Paul Lund died at age fifty in 1975, its role faded rapidly; by the mid-1980s it had disappeared entirely from the group's organizational structure.[53]

Despite that retreat from an overt economic-education agenda, positive public relations remained a critical part of the Roundtable's operations, albeit without the Pollyannaish expectation of instant gratification. Throughout the 1970s, Roundtable CEOs took deliberate steps to increase their media presence, offer reasonable and sympathetic explanations for their policy preferences, and reinforce their belief that society as a whole benefited when large corporations did well. Thus in 1975, six CEOs appeared on NBC's *Meet the Press* in a panel conversation about the place of business in American society and politics. Representing a cross section of industries, from automobiles to banking to retail, the men bragged to moderator Lawrence Spivak that they were working hard to overcome their natural disinclination toward the media. "Most of us are relatively inarticulate," quipped Reginald Jones, Fred Borch's successor at GE, "as I think your viewing audience is probably already realizing." Throughout the show, the executives made a real effort to portray themselves as civic-minded, honest, and patriotic, but their appearance was also somewhat disingenuous. Although all six executives held prominent positions at the Business Roundtable, that common allegiance remained unstated during the hour-long interview. Their failure to mention the work of their young lobbying organization reflected their continued concern that the American public would look askance at overt political collaboration by the country's top industrial leaders. The impulse for silence, honed in the days of the Links Club and the March Group, still reigned. Even as they struggled to improve big business's image and "tell their story," Roundtable executives felt pressure to maintain a low profile.[54]

The Businessman's Lobby on the Cusp of a New Order

The Business Roundtable formed in the early 1970s in response to the widespread conviction that the industrial manufacturing community faced deep, existential threats. On one level, such pervasive anxiety among top executives may appear surprising. After all, the men who led corporations like DuPont, U.S. Steel, and General Electric universally enjoyed great wealth, considerable power, and extraordinary social and political connections. Many, as we have seen, had not been born to such privilege and had put themselves through school before ascending the corporate ranks. Along the way up, they became socialized into an elite universe of golf and tennis retreats and Manhattan social club dinners. Despite those privileged positions, however, their apparent decline in direct legislative influence signaled a broader pattern of political and economic vulnerability, pushing these men to new levels of collaboration. Powerful executives like John Harper, Fred Borch, Charles McCoy, and Roger Blough felt such concern for the future that they jettisoned their parochial corporate allegiances and worked hard—after hours and without direct compensation—to create a new vehicle for political influence.

At the same time, those trepidations should not surprise us, since they emerged from the same environment that prompted a broader political mobilization among businesspeople, particularly the rejuvenation of the U.S. Chamber of Commerce and the National Association of Manufacturers, as well as the blossoming of economically conservative think tanks and aggressive business-oriented PACs. To review the story so far: Beginning in the mid-1960s, big-business executives eyed the newly robust regime of environmental and consumer protection regulation with increasing alarm. The new political strength of liberal reformers, both in Congress and within the community of organized interest groups, compounded their conviction that the political terrain many had navigated for a generation had shifted beneath their feet. Through its regulatory, appropriations, and taxing operations, the U.S. Congress came to exert a far greater influence over the national economy by the late 1960s, and corporate executives who had grown accustomed to dealing with the president through the Business Council increasingly recognized the need to work with the national legislature. Moreover, Congress in the 1960s became more partisan and its membership less secure. Conservatives wielded far less influence within the Democratic Party in the wake of the civil rights movement and many Republican legislators embraced more confrontational postures toward New Deal and Great Society fiscal policies and government programs. In that new political environment, a growing and self-identified "conservative movement" united grassroots groups, think tanks, and corporate benefactors on a platform of social traditionalism, economic libertarianism, and militant foreign policy, providing clear allies for organized business leaders. Finally, changes to campaign finance laws in 1971 and 1974 further destabilized the political order by encouraging the proliferation of political action committees that traded campaign cash for issue loyalty, encouraging congressional candidates to adopt less compromising positions on everything from environmental regulation to abortion and tax policy. The political mobilization of business, including the creation of the Business Roundtable, both emerged from and helped drive this vital moment of political flux.

This new dedication to Washington politics fundamentally changed business leaders' approach to their longstanding struggle with organized labor. As this chapter has shown, the companies that constituted the Labor Law Study Group and the Construction Users' Anti-Inflation Roundtable had deep roots in the politics of labor, especially in the construction industry. Rising inflation and the creeping productivity crisis of the late 1960s convinced increasing numbers of public relations and labor law specialists within the industrial manufacturing community that a company-by-company strategy would ultimately prove insufficient to tackle the threats posed by rising costs and strong unions. To be sure, corporate managers retained the traditional leverage that came from their place in the industrial political economy: the power to relocate plants both within and increasingly beyond national borders in response to divergent state and local conditions. Indeed, as labor historian Jefferson Cowie has shown, capital moves more easily than labor, and in the 1960s and 1970s increasing numbers of American manufacturers sought cheaper labor and weaker regulations by shipping their productive facilities away from the Northeast and Midwest.[55] Yet while industrial leaders continued to "vote with their feet," the men who formed the Roundtable also worked deliberately and collectively to further nationalize their conflict with organized labor. As the following chapter shows, inflation and labor power continued to provide powerful organizational fuel for organized business interests. Indeed, by the late 1970s, Roundtable strategists largely abandoned efforts to mobilize "local user groups" to fight state and municipal battles with unions, choosing instead to lobby directly against labor-liberal legislation in Congress, where they achieved notable victories during the Ford and Carter administrations.

The Business Roundtable concentrated, in its early years, on labor power and inflation, particularly within the construction industry, because of the fragile position its member companies maintained within American capitalism. As the lobbying arm of large, vertically integrated industrial corporations, the Roundtable brought together a particularly vital group of corporations at a unique historical juncture. In the early 1970s, "big business" meant vertically integrated, highly capitalized firms that operated with remarkable stability in highly regulated markets and faced few threats from new technologies or upstart domestic competitors. Newfangled and often short-lived conglomerates, which burst onto the scene of American business in the late 1950s and early 1960s, were conspicuous by their absence in the ranks of the Roundtable. Moreover, although New York banks provided vital financing and strategic advice for Roundtable firms, including seats on their boards of directors, financial services companies did not form a major part of the Roundtable's constituency. Rather the corporations that formed the heart first of the March Group and then of the combined Business Roundtable represented the lions of traditional American industrial capitalism, including aluminum and steel, automobile manufacturing, and chemical production.

The composition of the Roundtable is telling because, as the following chapters illustrate in greater detail, this industrial manufacturing community would not survive the economic crisis of the 1970s with nearly the level of economic dominance that it once boasted. Between 1965 and 1973, precisely the years in which the Roundtable's constituent parts took shape and merged, the manufacturing sector's share of total U.S. profits fell by 2.7 percent per year, and the return on capital investments in manufacturing likewise declined. The resulting crisis of profitability contributed to the long-term stagnation of industrial manufacturing in the United States and the rise of a service- and finance-oriented economy.[56] By the 1980s, as the final chapter of this book argues, the composition of the leadership structure of the Business Roundtable would shift to reflect the new prominence of financial services, pharmaceuticals, and telecommunications.

The industrial executives that put the Business Roundtable together readily professed the belief that their political clout had slipped since the early 1960s, yet they remained silent on—perhaps ignorant of—the international structural forces that underlay their weakening economic position. Top corporate leaders watched their year-to-year profitability decrease and clearly understood that rising foreign competition, particularly from Japan and Germany, applied new pressure to their bottom lines. But in the early 1970s, few businesspeople had a clear sense of the magnitude of this phenomenon, much less a name for it: deindustrialization. Indeed, the vagueness of the foreign threat both compounded executives' anxieties and compelled them to focus their energies on domestic factors that, ostensibly at least, lay more firmly in their sphere of influence. Thus did most Roundtable executives earnestly believe that the root of their problems lay with federal policy and could thus be solved by greater political coordination at home. For these dinosaurs of the Fordist economy, the paramount concerns remained inflationary fiscal and monetary policy, labor power, taxes, and social regulations. With those problems addressed, they reasoned, manufacturing's profitability and the strength of American industrial exports would take care of themselves. History would prove them wrong.

From the dark recesses of the Links Club to the halls of Congress, the executives who formed the Business Roundtable took pride in their young organization but insisted that the uphill struggle had just begun. "Overall, it becomes clear to me that business must take an active, aggressive role in developing understanding of and support for the free-market system by reestablishing the public's confidence in business," John Harper said in 1975. "Without question," he added, "we have our work cut out for us." Myriad policy battles loomed on the horizon, Continental Can CEO Robert Hatfield explained, as liberal politicians in Congress declared "a virtual open hunting season" on private enterprise. Powerful constituencies mobilized around labor law, environmental and consumer safety regulation, antitrust policy, and national economic planning. In the first years of its life, the young lobbying organization would confront some of the most intractable economic and political challenges of the twentieth century, including, as we will now explore, the most vexing economic beast to emerge in the 1970s: inflation.[57]

APPENDIX 3.1: Original Member Corporations of the "The Business Roundtable—For Responsible Labor-Management Relations" upon the Merger of the Labor Law Study Committee and the Construction Users' Anti-Inflation Roundtable, October 13, 1972

Source: Archives of the Business Roundtable.

CR = Member of Construction Users' Anti-Inflation Roundtable
LL = Member of the Labor Law Study Committee

CR	LL	Allied Chemical Corporations
CR	LL	Aluminum Company of America
CR	LL	American Can Company
CR		American Cyanamid Company
CR		American Electric Power Company
	LL	American Metal Climax
CR	LL	American Smelting and Refining Company
CR	LL	American Telephone and Telegraph Co.
CR	LL	The Anaconda Company
CR		Arizona Public Service Company
CR	LL	Armco Steel Company
	LL	Armstrong Cork Company
CR		Ashland Oil and Refining Company
CR		Atlantic Richfield Company
CR	LL	Bethlehem Steel Corporation
CR		Boise Cascade Corporation
	LL	Broadway-Hale Stores, Inc.
	LL	Brown & Root, Inc.
CR		Burlington Industries, Inc.
CR		CPC International, Inc.
CR	LL	Campbell Soup Company
CR		Carolina Power and Light Company
	LL	Chase Manhattan Bank
CR	LL	Chrysler Corporation
CR		Cincinnati Gas and Electric Company
CR		Cities Service Company
CR		Cleveland-Cliffs Iron Company
CR		The Cleveland Electric Illuminating Company
CR		The Coca-Cola Company
	LL	The Columbia Gas System, Inc.
CR		Consolidated Edison Company of New York
CR		Consumers Power Company
CR	LL	Continental Can Company, Inc.
CR		Continental Oil Company

CR		Corning Glass Works
CR		Crane Company
	LL	Crown Zellerbach Corporation
CR		Cyclops Corporation
CR		Dallas Power and Light Company
CR		Dayton Power and Light Company
CR		Detroit Edison Company
CR	LL	Dow Chemical Company
CR		Duke Power Company
CR	LL	E. I. du Pont de Nemours & Co.
CR		Eastern Air Lines Co.
CR		Eastman Kodak Company
CR		Eaton Corporation
CR		Federated Department Stores, Inc.
CR	LL	Firestone Tire & Rubber Company
	LL	First National City Bank
CR	LL	Ford Motor Company
	LL	General Cable Corporation
CR	LL	General Dynamics Corporation
CR	LL	General Electric Company
CR		General Foods Corporation
CR		General Mills, Inc.
CR	LL	General Motors Corporation
CR		General Tire & Rubber Company
CR		Georgia-Pacific Corporation
CR	LL	The B. F. Goodrich Company
CR	LL	Goodyear Tire & Rubber Company
CR		Gulf Oil Corporation
CR		H. J. Heinz Company
CR		Hercules Incorporated
CR		Ideal Basic Industries, Inc.
CR		Ingersoll-Rand Company
CR	LL	Inland Steel Company
	LL	International Harvester Company
CR	LL	International Nickel Company
CR		International Paper Company
CR		Iowa-Illinois Gas & Electric Company
	LL	Irving Trust Company
	LL	Johns-Manville Corporation
CR	LL	Jones & Laughlin Steel Corporation
CR	LL	Kaiser Industries Corporation
CR	LL	Kennecott Copper Corporation
CR		Koppers Company, Inc.

CR	LL	R. H. Macy & Company
CR		Marcor, Inc.
	LL	McGraw-Edison Company
CR		The Mead Corporation
	LL	Minnesota Mining & Manufacturing Company
CR		Mississippi Power & Light Company
CR		Mobil Oil Corporation
CR		Monsanto Company
CR		NL Industries, Inc.
CR		Nabisco, Inc.
CR		The National Cash Register Company
CR	LL	National Steel Corporation
CR	LL	Olin Corporation
CR	LL	Owens-Corning Fiberglass Corporation
CR		Pacific Gas & Electric Company
CR		J. C. Penney Company, Inc.
	LL	Pennzoil United, Inc.
CR	LL	Phelps Dodge Corporation
CR		Philadelphia Electric Company
CR		Phillips Petroleum Company
CR		The Proctor & Gamble Company
CR		Public Service Company of Colorado
CR		Public Service Company of Oklahoma
CR		Public Service Electric & Gas Company
CR	LL	Republic Steel Corporation
	LL	Revere Copper & Brass, Inc.
	LL	Roadway Express, Inc.
CR		Scott Paper Company
CR	LL	Sears, Roebuck and Company
CR	LL	Shell Oil Company
CR		Southern California Edison Company
CR		Southern Company
CR		Sperry Rand Corporation
CR	LL	Standard Oil Company (Indiana)
CR		Standard Oil Company (New Jersey)
CR		The Standard Oil Company (Ohio)
CR		Stauffer Chemical Company
	LL	Sun Oil Company
CR		TRW, Inc.
CR		Tenneco, Inc.
CR		Texaco, Inc.
CR		Texas Electric Service
CR		Texas Gulf Sulphur Company

CR		Texas Instruments Incorporated
CR		Texas Power & Light Company
CR		Union Camp Corporation
CR	LL	Union Carbide Corporation
CR		Union Electric Company
CR		Union Oil Company of California
CR	LL	Uniroyal, Inc.
CR	LL	United Aircraft Corporation
CR		United States Steel Corporation
	LL	Utah International, Inc.
CR	LL	Westinghouse Electric Corporation
CR	LL	Wheeling-Pittsburgh Steel Corporation
	LL	Whirlpool Corporation
CR		Xerox Corporation
	LL	Youngstown Sheet & Tube Company

APPENDIX 3.2: Leadership of the Business Roundtable upon Incorporation of the March Group, Spring/Summer 1973

Source: Archives of the Business Roundtable.

Executive Committee

W. B. Murphy, Chairman	Campbell's Soup	
Roger Blough, Co-Chairman	White and Case	(March Group)
Fred Borch, Co-Chairman	General Electric	(March Group)
John deButts	AT&T	(March Group)
Burt Cross	Minn. Mining and Manufacturing	(March Group)
Richard Gerstenberg	General Motors	(March Group)
John Harper	Alcoa	(March Group)
Shearon Harris	Carolina Power and Light	
J. K. Jamieson	Exxon	
Charles B. McCoy	DuPont	(March Group)
David Packard	Hewlett-Packard	
Stanford Smith	International Paper	(March Group)

Other Members of the Policy Committee

Karl Bendetsen	Champion International Group
Benjamin Biaggini	Southern Pacific
Willis Boyer	Republic Steel
Donald Burnham	Westinghouse

Stewart Cort	Bethlehem Steel	
Russell DeYoung	Goodyear	
Henry Ford II	Ford Motor Company	(March Group)
Robert Hatfield	Continental Can Company	
Reginald Jones	General Electric	
Brooks McCormick	International Harvester	
John McLean	Continental Oil	
Louis Menk	Burlington Northern	
Frank Milliken	Kennecott Copper	
Shermer Sibley	Pacific Gas & Electric	
Donald Smiley	Macy's, Inc.	
Edgar Speer	U.S. Steel	
J. E. Swearingen	Standard Oil Company (Indiana)	
Pendleton Thomas	B. F. Goodrich	
C. C. Tillinghast Jr.	Trans World Airlines	
Lynn Townsend	Chrysler Corporation	
Maurice Warnock	Armstrong Cork	
Perry Wilson	Union Carbide	
Robert Wilson	Boeing	
T. A. Wilson	Roadway Express	
Arthur Wood	Sears, Roebuck	

CHAPTER 4

Business, Labor, and the Politics of Inflation

> I don't go along with the idea that sees us as heroes on inflation
> and villains on unemployment. That will take us to a point where
> no conservative will ever be elected again.
>   —Richard Nixon, February 1969

> Present high inflation threatens the economic security of our
> Nation. . . . Inflation is a symptom of economic distress. . . .
> Our whole society, the entire American family, must try harder
> than ever to live within its means.
>   —Jimmy Carter, March 14, 1980

SINCE THE 1920S, the United States Chamber of Commerce has occupied
a grand three-story limestone building straight across Lafayette Square
from the White House, in the heart of Washington, D.C.[1] On January 20,
1972, this stately headquarters on H Street, half a city block on all sides
and encircled by Corinthian columns, hosted the Chamber's annual Association National Affairs Conference, an opportunity for Chamber members to discuss national political issues and their role in policymaking. In
the realm of national politics, the 1,200 corporate executives and trade
association representatives who convened in Washington that winter day
certainly had plenty to fret over, not least the fortunes of the Republican
Party. Just fourteen months earlier, the GOP and many business-backed
candidates had suffered a severe bruising in the 1970 midterm elections,
and President Richard Nixon's prospects for reelection looked doubtful
given the weak economy, the resurgence of antiwar activism, and the
continued power of organized labor within the Democratic Party. Despite
that outlook, an even more pressing problem dominated the conference:
the previous summer, the Nixon administration, through its Economic
Stabilization Program, had established the country's first-ever peacetime
experiment in mandatory wage and price controls, and the now half-
year-old system proved endlessly vexing to the Chamber's members. (The
tens of thousands of military personnel fighting and dying in Vietnam,
Laos, and Cambodia at the time likely quibbled with the term "peacetime," but the phrase nonetheless dominated the discourse.) How, the
Chamber conference's attendees wondered, had inflation grown so out
of hand that the federal government—run by Nixon, a supposedly pro-

business Republican—had begun *controlling* prices? How did the program affect their firms and industries? And more important, what could the business community do about the ever more ominous problem of inflation?[2]

Richard Nixon's wage and price controls program, a little-remembered episode that nonetheless dominated the administration's domestic economic policy for nearly three years, began with a nationwide price freeze in August 1971. By executive order, no producer could raise the price of any good or service higher than it had been the previous month, no landlord could a hike a rent, and no worker could receive a higher wage. Although Nixon had vowed to oppose such heavy-handed government action earlier in his term, political and economic circumstances conspired to force his hand. After nearly a decade of expansion, the American economy entered a recession in 1970. Then, in the summer of 1971, an international monetary crisis erupted. Under the Bretton Woods agreement of 1944, the U.S. dollar effectively served as the world's reserve currency, and the United States promised to redeem dollars for gold at a fixed rate of $35 per ounce. By 1971, foreign central banks had assembled enormous stockpiles of greenbacks and threatened to redeem them immediately, but the United States did not have sufficient gold stocks to back up the dollars in global circulation. To prevent a devastating run on American reserves, Nixon suspended gold convertibility and asked Congress to pass several measures to stimulate the flagging economy. But both the devalued dollar and Nixon's stimulus programs threatened to put upward pressure on inflation, which had been edging higher since 1965 and reached a 5 percent annual rate in the summer of 1971; hence the wage and price freeze. That fall, the administration replaced the out-and-out freeze with "Phase II" of the controls program, a convoluted system of councils, boards, and commissions designed to gradually liberalize prices and wages while still keeping inflation within a low target range of 2 to 3 percent. By January, when the Chamber held its meeting, business leaders joined the rest of the country in a struggle to understand the complex bureaucracies involved in the new regime.[3]

Phase II wage and price controls required certain firms—depending on their industry and number of employees—to petition the government for permission to raise their prices or else face tax penalties for noncompliance. But which firms, which prices, under which circumstances, and at what penalties? The details were murky, highly politicized, and deeply frustrating. Confused and anxious, the Chamber's directors saw the Association National Affairs Conference as an opportunity for their members to learn more about the intricacies of the program as well as to voice their collective concerns about inflation, government-led economic planning, and their sense of relative powerlessness in the political process. For many, the biggest highlight came when John Connally, Nixon's treasury secretary, rose to address the assembly.[4]

Under the Economic Stabilization Program, Secretary Connally chaired an agency called the Cost of Living Council, which coordinated the entire operation and thus served as the public face of the anti-inflation campaign. A conservative Democrat and former Texas governor who was wounded during the Kennedy assassination in 1963, Connally appealed to many businesspeople as a self-made man who had worked his way through law school before parlaying his legal practice into a lucrative career in the oil industry. The tall, charismatic politician comported himself with what Henry Kissinger described as "swaggering self-assurance," and he practiced fierce political loyalty. In the 1960s, he had worked hard for his fellow Texan Lyndon Johnson; by the 1970s, he transferred that devotion to Nixon, who tapped him to head Treasury largely to appeal to conservative southern Democrats.[5] Taking the podium to address the Chamber of Commerce's convention, the fifty-four-year-old Connally displayed the southern bravado for which he was famous, and he minced no words defending his boss and challenging his fellow businessmen. According to the Chamber's newsletter, the secretary "launched a particularly hard-hitting off-the-cuff talk that chastised the business community for dragging its feet in supporting the Administration's efforts to revitalize the economy."

"This Administration," Connally thundered, "has defended the American business enterprise of this nation far more than you've defended yourselves." At business's behest, he continued, Nixon had pushed through Congress a massive stimulus package, including investment tax credits, other tax cuts, and reforms to foreign exchange rates that made American manufacturers more competitive abroad. "You asked for it. You got it. But what have you done with it? Nothing!" Connally roared. Meanwhile, he added, "The rest of the world is at work while we're worrying. . . . They're out-working us; they're out-thinking us; they're out-planning us day after day." Business leaders' handwringing and incessant complaining in lieu of action, Connally maintained, had in fact created the need for the very wage-price controls system that now bedeviled them. Nixon had been forced to implement the controls, the secretary claimed, because employers made irresponsible and selfish decisions to raise prices and accede to wage demands, despite their effect on the national economy. Until business asserted itself against labor unions, he threatened, the controls would continue. "When you make up your minds that you can no longer . . . expect anybody to support unconscionable and unreasonable wage demands, and when you realize you can't continue to raise your prices in an unconscionable fashion, we will end controls. . . . It could be next summer or next fall or maybe it will be four years from now—I don't know. It depends on you."[6] Accusing his fellow business leaders of whining about government even as they kowtowed to labor, Connally put a fine point on many Nixon administration officials' frustration with the leadership of the business community. If the Chamber conference participants had sought sympathy from one of their own, they found none in John Connally.

The leadership of the Chamber of Commerce did not take kindly to such a dressing-down. For years, as the previous chapters argued, business leaders had bemoaned their political impotence in the face of liberal regulatory policies and labor activism. Despite Nixon's conservative reputation and his "New Federalism" initiatives that devolved social welfare spending to the states, his embrace of not only price controls but also more muscular social regulation—including especially the EPA and OSHA, both created in 1970—reinforced many business leaders' conviction that he was at best a fair-weather friend. To hear a prominent member of his administration publicly mock business for what corporate leaders perceived to be their greatest weakness stung deeply and ruffled more than a few feathers.

Several days after the speech, Chamber executive vice president Arch Booth wrote Secretary Connally a letter, which the organization subsequently published for its members, that aimed both to stick up for the business community and to refocus the debate on the causes of and solutions for inflation. After perfunctorily thanking the secretary for his time, Booth launched a pointed defense against the charge that business could do nothing but whine and drag its feet. Although Connally's "tough-love" approach challenged business leaders to be strong and forthright, Booth hastened to point out how weak and ineffective firms really were—essentially validating Connally's premise. "It's easy to suggest that business must be tougher in resisting unreasonable wage demands," Booth protested. "But when a strike results, who suffers? Not the strikers, who receive welfare checks, food stamps, and other government aid." Citing the classic business-conservative view of collective bargaining, Booth implicitly argued that in any contract negotiation, management and labor naturally exercised equal economic power, and the government thus should leave them to negotiate freely on their own. Ideally, Booth believed, the state should act as a neutral arbiter to ensure a level playing field for the two competing sides, yet labor partisans in Congress routinely stacked the deck against employers. The minimum wage, welfare, and government construction contracts all bolstered labor's collective power unfairly, Booth claimed, to business's detriment. If the Nixon administration really wanted to empower employees, he told Connally, the place to start was redressing this imbalance of power, not with maligning business leaders for their justifiable complaints.[7]

As Booth and Connally's testy exchange demonstrated, the business community's vague political anxieties crystallized around specific policy battles in the early 1970s. Indeed, fiery debates over price controls presaged a decade-long battle over the politics of inflation—whom to blame for it and how to fix it—that loomed large over American politics and profoundly shaped the development of organized business lobbying. The controls program itself brought business leaders' frustrations, both with their political opponents and with themselves, into sharp relief. On one hand, corporate leaders argued that mandatory price restrictions flew flagrantly in the face of free-market economics and would surely lead to disaster—business failures, supply shortages, layoffs. Moreover, many believed, the very fact that the economy had devolved to a point that controls appeared necessary reaffirmed how politically weak business had become in national policymaking. At the same time, many businesspeople reluctantly accepted the controls, at least for a time, because of their intense fear of inflation. This inability to decide which was worse—the disease or the treatment—spawned a sense of political paralysis that only exacerbated business leaders' collective sense of impotence.

This chapter traces the complex politics of inflation from the onset of wage-price controls in 1971 through the peak of America's inflationary experience during the Carter administration. During those years, the country's major business associations successfully mobilized a powerful lobbying operation by negotiating the new political terrain that inflation created. From the frustrating nadir, typified by the public spat between Connolly and Booth, organized business leaders rebounded mightily, successfully engaging in both ideological debates and interest group politics to bolster their institutional unity and achieve clear policy victories.

The source of business groups' revival in the 1970s lay in their successful navigation of the politics of inflation. Historically, battles over price instability emerged along the class lines created by an industrial political economy—they pitted the interests of workers against those of employers, or labor against capital. According to a simplified model, modest increases in nominal prices tended to redistribute wealth downward by shrinking the value of accumulated wealth while reducing the real value of debt. Traditionally, this tendency meant that financiers championed stable-money policies while debtors (particularly farmers) pushed for inflationary policies. In the aftermath of World War II, the class-based divisions over inflationary policies continued, albeit in a revised form. As Keynesian economic thinking came to dominate American policymaking, most economists accepted the Phillips Curve, which predicted that inflation and unemployment moved in opposite directions. The stewards of national economic policy thus faced a clear trade-off: pursue price sta-

YOUR DOLLAR IS GETTING SMALLER

Figure 4.1. Images like this, published by the U.S. Chamber of Commerce to promote a television special in 1971, expressed the common argument that inflation functioned as a type of tax on all Americans. In it, the greedy caterpillar of price instability eats away at the purchasing power of the American dollar. Courtesy of Hagley Museum and Library.

bility (to the primary benefit of capitalists and employers) or risk some inflation in the interest of expanding economic growth and job creation.[8]

As the quotes that begin this chapter indicate, those classical conceptions dissolved during the 1970s. Speaking at the beginning of his term, Richard Nixon recapitulated—and then rejected—the traditional view that Republicans, because they favored business, put inflation fighting ahead of economic growth, while Democrats, the party of the working class, worried instead about unemployment. For Nixon, that traditional political model promised nothing but ruin. Yet by 1980, Democratic president Jimmy Carter precisely reversed Nixon's calculus, calling for national sacrifice among consumers in defense of price stability and accumulated capital. The worm had turned, and business-oriented inflation fighting became Carter's top priority, negative consequences for workers be damned.

This transition occurred because, during the 1970s, the politics of inflation increasingly revolved around middle-class consumers, a category that muddied the easy distinction between "labor" and "capital." As wages failed to keep pace with rising prices, consumers felt the pinch. Purchasing power declined, and the higher cost of everyday goods outweighed the advantages of a smaller debt load. But who should pay the price of reducing inflation—corporations through their profit margins, or workers through their paychecks? As an interest group, consumers held no inherent loyalty to either business or labor, so union and corporate leaders competed fiercely for their support. Couching their policy preferences in terms of pocketbook politics, political agents from each side blamed the other for the high cost of living, and each insisted that

Figure 4.2. Business leaders saw themselves in direct conflict with labor for the support of middle-class consumers. Here, members of the U.S. Chamber of Commerce perform that conflict by imitating striking workers to "protest" the advantages they believed labor wielded over business, particularly among policymakers (such as those who favored "food stamps for strikers") and in collective bargaining agreements that rewarded "strike violence" with "wage increases in excess of productivity gains." This event occurred at the Union Power Luncheon during the Chamber's 1971 annual meeting. Courtesy of Hagley Museum and Library.

the other shoulder the painful burden of resolving it. On one hand, labor and other left-leaning political activists castigated excess profits, executive compensation, and corporate greed. On the other, business leaders and their surrogates denounced the inflationary effects of wage demands that outpaced productivity as well as wasteful government spending.[9]

The contentious debates over inflation in the 1970s sharpened the battle lines between labor and business, fueling the right-wing critique of liberalism as well as corporate leaders' political mobilization.[10] Wading into the thick brambles of wage-price controls, labor law, and economic planning, organized business groups took up those political challenges and emerged triumphant. Yet as this chapter demonstrates, their success did not come easily. Although the collective mouthpieces of the business community yearned mightily to engage in national politics, they faced substantial obstacles. Their ambivalence over wage-price controls and the penchant for worrisome handwringing for which Connally chastised the Chamber of Commerce reflected a much larger trend. Maintaining a united front on such contested policy issues and making a confident political case against organized labor required a good deal of energy and coordination, not to mention deep pockets and tremendous will. By successfully running the gauntlet of inflation, organized business groups achieved important victories. By demonizing liberal notions of economic planning and dampening public support for labor, they established themselves as a powerful force in national politics.

THE POLITICS OF WAGE-PRICE CONTROLS

Long before Richard Nixon announced his Economic Stabilization Program, the major mouthpieces for American business had staked a clear position against using mandatory price controls to curb inflation. Prior to 1971, the country's only experiences with compulsory price-fixing by the federal government had unfolded amid the exigencies of war; in the aftermath of each world war and the Korean War, business leaders placed themselves at the forefront of the political push to abandon controls and allow market mechanisms once again to determine the going rate for goods, services, and labor. In the 1960s, both before and after the escalation of hostilities in Vietnam, Presidents Kennedy and Johnson each administered price "guideline" programs, although the annual inflation rate hovered around 3 percent for most of the decade. Under those voluntary programs, government experts determined acceptable percent increases for wages and prices industry by industry. In lieu of formal legal power, the government relied on moral and political suasion, the process called jawboning, to compel unions and firms to comply. Among employers' associations and the heads of major industrial corporations, however, even voluntary guidelines provoked howls of protest. According to a NAM subcommittee: "Attempts to reduce inflationary pressures through 'guideposts' for wage-price behavior or selective controls are both self-defeating and destructive to the economy."[11]

The end of the Kennedy-Johnson period and the advent of the Nixon administration provided some relief for business leaders who continued to fret about price controls. Ironically, Richard Nixon had cut his teeth in government as a bureaucrat with the Office of Price Administration, which implemented national price controls during World War II, but the Republican president made his philosophical opposition to mandatory controls clear early in his term. Nonetheless, in the summer of 1970, opinion polls showed that the public increasingly supported the use of price controls to rein in inflation. In a cynical move, congressional Democrats passed the Economic Stabilization Act that August, giving the president the authority to impose price controls and hoping that Nixon would bear the political costs for *not* doing so.[12] For their part, corporate leaders insisted that the government keep this newfound power in the drawer. "[T]he only occasion when wage, price and rent controls might be used," a Chamber of Commerce executive warned Congress, "would be during extreme emergency conditions involving an imminent external threat to the national security."[13]

But the case for price controls persisted. Many policymakers and economists argued that the "psychological expectation" of inflation could only be reversed by strict government action. According to this argument, people who anticipated inflation tended to behave in ways that actually *caused* inflation. For example, workers would demand larger pay raises to offset future increases in the price of consumer goods, and companies would increase their prices preemptively because they expected higher labor and supply costs to cut into future profits.[14]

Moreover, the demands of electoral politics also pushed Nixon to reassess his stance. Chastened in the 1970 midterm and struggling in the polls, the president worried that appearing to side with business interests could damage his already weakened prospects for reelection. Moreover, Nixon simply did not feel as beholden to business as many corporate leaders had hoped a Republican president would be. In part, this was personal: Nixon viewed the "East Coast establishment"—including top industrialists and financiers—with loathing and jealousy, a bias some scholars have suggested had roots in his sense of social inadequacy as a teenager.[15] Just as important, Nixon calculated that he had little to lose politically by distancing himself from big business but much to gain. While business-oriented conservatives would never back his opponent, Nixon could structure his domestic policies to woo traditionally Democratic voters, including white ethnics, poor southerners, and members of the working class.[16]

Ultimately, a perfect political and economic storm forced the president's move. Amid mounting public clamor for direct action against inflation, a lackluster economy, an international monetary crisis, and, eventually, the encouragement of all his economic advisors, Nixon came around. On August 15, 1971, he announced a "New Economic Policy," including a complete freeze of wages, prices, and rents. With that announcement, the Republican president business conservatives had hoped would undo Great Society liberalism and liberate free enterprise from excessive regulation instead inaugurated what *Time* magazine called "one of the most complex of bureaucratic exercises" known to the modern presidency.[17]

But a funny thing happened on the way to national economic planning. Despite their outspoken prior hostility to price controls, most prominent business leaders greeted Nixon's freeze with cautious enthusiasm. The chairmen of General Motors and Chrysler declared themselves "pleased" and "delighted" with Nixon's dedication to solving the inflation mess, and the president of Republic Steel called the New Economic Policy "a bold, progressive, forward-looking program." The head of Pan American Airlines told Nixon that the wage-price freeze could "spark a revival for the lagging air travel industry." Financial institutions were particularly supportive, and many lenders promised not to raise interest rates (which were technically not frozen), easing the flow of credit to firms that might need cash but could not raise prices.[18] As the chairman of Metropolitan Life Insurance assured the president, "the general feeling [among top executives] was one of pleasure and relief that a firm and broad policy of action was taken."[19] Even the NAM and the Chamber of Commerce accepted the move as a fait accompli and offered clear, if not ebullient, votes of confidence. Chamber president Archie K. Davis, head of Wachovia Bank, praised Nixon's "bold and decisive leadership in moving against our domestic and international economic problems." And looking forward, NAM president Werner Gullander pledged "the wholehearted cooperation of the industrial community to supporting President Nixon's efforts to control inflation."[20]

If chief executives and association leaders appeared to turn on a dime and accept mandatory price controls, their gestures of support in fact masked severe apprehensions, which many, quite diplomatically, reserved for private venues. In the fall of 1971, for instance, the Chamber of Commerce produced a twenty-minute slide show for local business leaders that described August 15, 1971, as "doomsday for free enterprise in America." According to the Chamber's public relations department, the freeze had been a necessary evil, brought on by "an intolerable economic crisis"— spiraling inflation, declining productivity gains, increased competition from foreign manufacturers, and shrinking exports. Despite its official support, however, the organization implored its members to remain vigilant and help keep the administration focused on the "root causes" of inflation: "union power and excessive government spending."[21] Perhaps, the Chamber suggested, this "doomsday" scenario had a silver lining from a public relations perspective: an opportunity to raise "public awareness of our economic problems" and provide the American voter "a compelling reason for listening to—and understanding—rational solutions to our economic ills." Using the freeze as a teachable moment, Chamber directors launched a major public information campaign that included full-page ads in Washington-based newspapers in the fall of 1971 that declared "Let's Freeze Government Too!"[22]

Offering a tepid yet favorable response to the freeze, despite the cognitive dissonance involved, business leaders played the politics of inflation shrewdly by aligning themselves with public opinion and against the major mouthpieces of organized labor, which largely criticized Nixon's decision. Although labor and its legislative allies had long supported the concept of price controls—or "incomes policy"—in general, the AFL-CIO leadership, as well as a vocal minority of the rank and file, complained that such a program, administered by ostensibly business-oriented Republicans, would focus too much on wages, hurting workers. The wage-price freeze threatened to nullify pay increases that had been negotiated but not yet implemented, giving "the working man," in the words of a Louisiana-based member of the United Papermakers and Paperworkers union, "the short end of the deal."[23] But Americans in general—and even a majority of union households—looked quite favorably on the plan. In the summer of 1971, the Gallup organization reported that 70 percent of the public supported the measure, a figure that only grew as inflation dropped from 4.6 percent to 3.8 percent that fall. Critics argued that inflation had in fact started to decline before August 15 (a claim economists later validated), but the program's apparent success surely bolstered its popularity.[24] That combination of public support and labor opposition created a golden opportunity for business leaders and economic conservatives. *Business Week* magazine, for example, argued for the freeze precisely because labor opposed it. Although a few outspoken conservatives—most prominently William F. Buckley Jr. of the *National Review* and economist Milton Friedman—criticized the plan as essentially statism, most conservatives joined business leaders in shelving their philosophical disappointment and forging a consensus view that economic reality demanded harsh medicine.[25]

In the fall of 1971, as the administration rolled out "Phase II" of the controls program, members of the business community continued to profess qualified enthusiasm. Many, like PepsiCo CEO Donald Kendall, couched their support in terms of political and economic necessity. Kendall, a prominent Republican who had accompanied then vice president Nixon to Moscow in 1959 and witnessed the Kitchen Debate with Nikita Khrushchev, told Nixon that while he "normally believe[d] in the free market place," it had been "necessary to put on controls." More ominously, Kendall also warned that Nixon had no choice but to maintain the program until inflation declined; abandoning the fight against inflation now would give "the opposition . . . a specific campaign issue for 1972."[26]

While corporate leaders like Kendall focused on the political stakes, others confessed that the program's actual mechanisms made the medicine easier to swallow, whatever their ideological misgivings. As John Connally took pains to explain at the Chamber's association meeting in January 1972, the administration had largely developed the architecture of the controls program with business interests in mind, and each of Phase II's most important components relied heavily on business input. The Pay Board, modeled after World War II's War Labor Board, comprised fifteen members, five each from organized labor, business, and the "public"—that is, people who did not represent any union or company—who determined when workers could receive higher wages and how much. The Price Commission, which regulated the end prices that companies could charge, consisted of seven members from the public led by a business school dean.[27]

Indeed, the vicious politics of inflation flared most vividly at the Pay Board, whose tripartite nature pitted labor representatives like AFL-CIO president George Meany against the "business" and "public" members. After a series of bitter 10 to 5 votes in which the public and business representatives voted for far more restrictive wage increases against the labor contingent, four of the labor members quit the board. In Meany's words, they refused "to be a part of the window dressing for this system of unfair and inequitable Government control of wages for the benefit of business profits." Only Frank Fitzsimmons of the Teamsters remained, and Nixon rearranged the board to include only one representative from labor and one from business. The spat convinced many corporate leaders that Connally was right to present the controls as "business-friendly"— anything that made Meany so furious couldn't be all bad.[28]

Business leaders also appreciated that the White House so openly defended the importance of corporate profits. For example, the Pay Board declared early on that it would rule on petitions for wage increases based solely on improvements in worker productivity, exactly as management wished.[29] And although the Price Commission had an explicit mandate to trim corporate profits (on the theory that net revenues exceeded costs only because prices were too high), it issued major exemptions when profits came from gains in productivity or sales. Such a focus on productivity and capital reinvestment took much of the ideological sting out of price controls, even as it fueled labor's accusations that Phase II offered too much to business. Indeed, shortly before he quit the Pay Board, George Meany ranted that the Price Commission was "more concerned with profit margin maintenance and total profit expansion" than with actually keeping prices down for consumers. Widespread consensus about the need to combat inflation, as well as Phase II's institutional favoritism toward business, softened the hard edges of government-mandated price controls.[30]

BUSINESS TURNS AGAINST CONTROLS

Despite those soft edges, many business leaders remained ambivalent about the wage-price controls program, as the Chamber members' testy exchange with John Connally brought into focus. Many believed that business's tacit acceptance of the controls exposed a crucial ideological inconsistency that would ultimately weaken their defense of free enterprise in the long term. By June 1972, a Chamber committee recommended that the organization formally renounce the controls program and begin to work against it. The board of directors, however, voted against the proposal, persuaded that the controls had in fact reduced inflation somewhat and that ending them abruptly, in the words of their in-house economist, "would restore market discipline but would threaten stability from a possible price surge." The risks of inflation, the board concluded, simply outweighed the benefits of returning to a market-based system.[31]

Leaders at the NAM likewise disputed what public position to take on the controls. Congress would have to reapprove Nixon's authority to mandate price controls in the spring of 1973, and the NAM's leaders believed their organization should play a major role in that debate, one way or another. When twelve men and one woman on the NAM's Ad Hoc Committee on Phase II failed to reach consensus on the program in November 1972, the group's chairman polled more than one hundred executives on the board of directors, hoping to locate "the views of industry." Instead he found only more ambivalence.[32] Ultimately, despite its clear philosophical predisposition to "free enterprise," the NAM's Executive Committee granted Nixon a guarded vote of confidence to continue the controls.[33]

Although the NAM and the Chamber struggled to achieve consensus among their vast memberships, the newly formed Business Roundtable found greater success articulating a clear defense of free markets and opposition to the price controls regime. Born right in the thick of Phase II—the LLSC and the CUAIR merged in October 1972—the Roundtable represented the sum of management's fears about inflation. Moreover, its streamlined and hierarchical structure facilitated consensus building among its members.

Just one month after the merger that brought it into existence, the Business Roundtable launched its first official foray into the world of direct lobbying in response to growing frustrations with Phase II. In November 1972, Roger Blough led a Washington-bound contingent that included John Harper of Alcoa, Richard Gerstenberg of General Motors, John deButts of AT&T, and Beverly Murphy, the retired CEO of Campbell's

Soup and the Roundtable's chairman. The five men arranged a private meeting at the White House with budget director Caspar Weinberger, Council of Economic Advisors (CEA) chairman Herbert Stein, and Federal Reserve chairman Arthur Burns, where they forcefully argued for an immediate end to the controls program. Such a display of unanimity among the leaders of major corporations no doubt impressed administration officials, who did not hear as much consensus from other corners of the business community. Yet the officials doubted, in Murphy's words, "that controls in one form or another could be lifted without serious economic effects"; rather, they persuaded the Roundtable CEOs that they were actively working on "alternate plans to replace the present control program." This seminal meeting thus marked a vital coming-of-age for the big-business CEOs who formed a united front against economic planning, even as it reaffirmed the uphill struggle for influence they faced. For their part, the Roundtable CEOs focused on the silver lining. Despite failing to stop the controls immediately, the nascent business group lauded itself (privately) for opening a direct pathway to policymakers.[34]

Tensions between business and the administration dissipated slightly in January 1973 when Nixon, claiming imminent victory over inflation, announced Phase III of the Economic Stabilization Program, which made price controls even more palatable to business by jettisoning the Pay Board and Price Commission and implementing broad standards rather than rigid regulations.[35] But that brief moment of optimism proved to be short-lived. The administration's hopes that inflation would continue to decline in 1973 were summarily dashed when, freed of Phase II strictures, many firms quickly raised prices to catch up on lost revenues. Moreover, a global economic expansion led to greater consumption and production, and an unexpected shortfall in wheat, grain, and rice harvests around the world caused unregulated agricultural prices to spike. Wholesale inflation hit an astounding 21 percent annual rate in the first three months of 1973, and consumer staples like food and petroleum grew especially dear.[36] Nixon faced widespread criticism that his "voluntary" program was merely a sop to business and his administration scrambled desperately to recover.[37] To curry favor with consumers, the president flexed Phase III's muscle in late March by freezing wholesale and retail prices for beef, pork, and lamb.[38] To allay public fears that his administration looked out only for big business, he required all firms with more than $250 million in annual sales to submit prior notice of any price changes, even though inflation was by then rooted in food and commodities.[39] And in June the president threw a Hail Mary pass: Freeze II, a two-month moratorium on price, but not wage, increases, followed by Phase IV controls. This new plan, in Nixon's words, entailed "tighter standards and more mandatory compliance procedures" for corporations but did not change the standards for wages, which, the president claimed, had "not been a significant cause of the increase in prices."[40]

In the short term, the policy shift fanned the flames on all sides. By mid-July, 75 percent of Americans claimed to support Nixon's economic policy. The freeze on food and petroleum, where heightened demand and near-capacity production systems caused gasoline prices to creep ever higher, garnered particularly high praise.[41] Organized labor also began to reconsider its longstanding skepticism in light of Phase IV's fixation on prices rather than wages. Frank Fitzsimmons of the Teamsters applauded Nixon for "look[ing] a serious national problem right in the eye and . . . tak[ing] bold action."[42]

To be sure, the Manichean politics of inflation meant that policies that pleased labor drove business to distraction, and Freeze II brought none of the accolades and solidarity that business leaders had offered Nixon when the whole program began in August 1971. Walter Wriston, CEO of First National City Bank and a member of the Business Roundtable's Policy Committee, offered Nixon a (deeply flawed) history lesson, claiming that wage-price controls would lay waste to freedom and prosperity: "There is no instance in recorded history, since the Roman Emperor Diocletian first put controls on 900 items in the third century, when such action has halted inflation," he said. Contradicting himself, Wriston said that even though the first freeze "did a great deal to break up the psychology of inflationary expectations," resurrecting such a policy only proved that "Government intervention in free markets becomes addictive."[43] By siding with the consuming public and labor, Richard Nixon had squandered whatever goodwill he had with conservative business leaders.

Meanwhile, Phase IV prompted an immediate about-face among the boards of directors of the NAM and the Chamber, who had struggled so mightily to achieve a consensus in defense of free markets. Inflation raged as fiercely as ever, but without preferential treatment from the government, ideology prevailed and business leaders declared war on the Economic Stabilization Program. In September 1973, the NAM's board of directors voted overwhelmingly to steadfastly oppose the continuation of wage and price controls and immediately began publicizing its new creed. A fiery brochure called "Why NAM Is against Wage and Price Controls" provided a coherent set of talking points for the NAM's network of member companies, arguing that Phase IV typified "a tendency that is politically inevitable in any system of controls—a marked bias against profits."[44] The Business Roundtable's leaders likewise declared that continuing controls could "only aggravate dislocations which inevitably follow an extended period of interference with the operation of free markets."[45]

Events on the ground gave credence to business leaders' new mantra as the economy deteriorated rapidly in the summer of 1973. Bare shelves at grocery stores, layoffs, shuttered factories, and the grotesque slaughter of unmarketable farm animals by the thousands all testified to the market dislocations generated by Freeze II.[46] When Nixon ended food price controls in August, grocery bills skyrocketed. Then just as the food price shock normalized, OPEC cut off oil exports in retaliation for American support for Israel in the Yom Kippur War of October 1973. The embargo brought the already strained petroleum industry to near collapse and pushed overall inflation rates even higher. As energy eclipsed food prices as the country's primary economic woe, the White House transferred gasoline price controls to the new Federal Energy Office.[47] Organized business groups, finally able to articulate their long-held case against government interference in the operations of the free market, at last found a more attentive public. Support for Phase IV decreased rapidly, as confidence in the government's ability to restrain inflation through controls waned.[48]

Organized labor likewise solidified its opposition to price controls in the fall of 1973, despite some union leaders' support for the second, labor-friendly freeze during the summer. Framing the context in strict class terms, AFL-CIO president George Meany argued that an acceptable controls program remained theoretically possible, even desirable, but only if it placed the cost burden on well-paid businesspeople by limiting profits and dividends; hardworking union members should not suffer through restricted wages. Since Meany could not imagine that the Republican president would ever institute such a program, a better approach would be no controls at all.[49]

The issue ultimately came to a head in Congress in the winter and spring of 1974 in debates over whether to reauthorize Nixon's price controls program. The original Economic Stabilization Act of 1970 provided only temporary authority, so the reauthorization debate presented organized business groups a tremendous opportunity to exercise their new commitment to pan-industrial mobilization and lobbying. In the final months of his doomed presidency, Nixon himself remained detached from domestic policymaking, utterly consumed by the Watergate scandal. In his absence, White House economic advisors meekly advocated a temporary reauthorization of the controls to allow them to wind the program down on their own timetable. Thus, after years of hedging their bets over inflation, organized business leaders at last prepared to use their institutional force to lobby Congress in the name of free enterprise.

In February, NAM president Douglas Kenna and Chamber of Commerce treasurer Charles Smith testified before the Senate, projecting interorganizational unity as well as statistical evidence of widespread opposition to the controls within the business community. The headache of compliance, submitting formal price-increase notifications, reassessing tax obligations, and submitting labor agreements for federal oversight—not to mention the ideological stigma of government-mandated prices—convinced approximately 95 percent of NAM member firms to favor "a prompt termination of controls." The deep networks that these national institutions had forged between political elites and rank-and-file business owners provided the substantive grist for Smith and Kenna's testimony, in which they unflinchingly dismantled the logic of price controls. Regaling the senators with stories about production delays, shortages, abrogation of contracts, and other inefficiencies, the two representatives of organized business deployed explicit examples from legislators' own constituents to make the case for immediate termination.[50]

The Business Roundtable likewise threw itself into the fray during the final battle against Nixon's wage-price controls. For the young organization, the legislative battle marked a vital shift in focus away from big-business leaders' historically close work with the executive branch. Sensing a real opportunity to shape the debate in Congress, the Roundtable sent a contingent of CEOs to Capitol Hill, including the chiefs of such powerhouses as Westinghouse Electric, B. F. Goodrich, and Continental Can. These executives testified not only on behalf of their own companies but also as members of the Roundtable, the united—and now very public—voice of large industrial corporations. While the NAM and the Chamber, whose members ranged from single-proprietorships to multi-nationals, argued that controls hurt companies of all sizes, the Roundtable executives explained that price controls hurt big businesses in particular by restricting capital accumulation. Firms of all sizes hoped to reinvest their profits, they claimed, but such investment constituted the lifeblood of large multi-unit firms.[51] Like Smith and Kenna, Roundtable CEOs cultivated broader networks to influence legislators. Leading up to the lobbying campaign, the group's chairman, John Harper, exhorted his fellow CEOs "to express their views to Congress and the general public" because the appearance of "grassroots" support among large companies would prove far more influential than the testimony of a handful of powerful executives. "This needs to be done *now* and repeated frequently," Harper insisted.[52]

Organized business leaders worked hard to generate support for their lobbying efforts at all levels, but their efforts likely would have succeeded in any case. With only a tepid defense from the White House and firm opposition from organized labor, the best-funded and most powerful interest group in Washington, the wage-price program was doomed. Nonetheless, a slim majority of Americans still favored mandatory controls, and many liberals in Congress supported the program as a proxy for national economic planning. Other legislators simply wished, as one said, to "cast a vote against inflation" before running for reelection.[53] In the end, however, those gestures proved too little to save the program, and Congress allowed the Economic Stabilization Act to expire. Thus while the campaign against controls certainly did not pose the toughest challenge that employers' associations and their lobbyists would face in the 1970s, it provided an essential training ground for later successes. As April turned to May in Richard Nixon's final year as president, his authority to impose wage and price controls quietly evaporated, and business leaders claimed an important organizational victory.[54]

THE UNFINISHED CAMPAIGN AGAINST INFLATION

Corporate leaders wasted no time congratulating themselves for the demise of the Economic Stabilization Program. Indeed, Wallace Bates, president of the Business Roundtable, declared that the young organization had been a "material factor" in educating Congress and the public about the economic distortions that controls had caused.[55] At the same time, no one assumed that the political battle was over, especially as a "catch-up" bout of inflation rocked the economy after the controls expired. Chamber of Commerce economist Carl Madden, for one, believed that direct price controls would surely "come back from time to time if we have these spurts of inflation."[56] According to Roundtable co-chairman Roger Blough, even if the controls remained dead, inflation would remain, and high prices would continue to stoke public animus toward the business community. "Living in a control-less environment may sound inviting," he said, "but . . . every corporation's action will be subject to the severest sort of critical assessment from here on out."[57]

As the winter of OPEC's discontent made way for the inglorious summer of Nixon's resignation, 1974 turned out to be the worst year for price stability since World War II; the 11 percent annual rate would only be surpassed during the second energy crisis of 1979 and 1980. In the months after the Economic Stabilization Program lapsed, printing presses at the NAM and the Chamber hummed furiously with new brochures, mailings, and reports as business leaders redoubled their public lobbying about the causes of inflation and the perils of controls. Publications like "Wage and Price Controls: A Failure in History, Theory, and Practice" and "Inflation Losers: You, Your Family, Your Country" spread business's message broadly by highlighting two essential points. First, inflation resulted *exclusively* from excessive government spending and labor power; and second, mandatory controls only made it worse. Through tremendous public outreach, organized business groups sought actively to

capitalize on their organizational strength and maintain a coherent public front.[58]

Corporate lobbying groups also fought the specter of a return to price
controls by remaining vigilant with government officials, a task facilitated somewhat by Nixon's resignation and Gerald Ford's ascension to
the White House on August 9, 1974. In one of his first acts in office, the
new president convened a conference of economists to propose solutions
to the perplexing inflation problem. While some of the economists at
the conference urged monetarist solutions, following Milton Friedman's
suggestion to rigidly target the money supply, and others invoked the
"old time religion" of reducing government spending and budget deficits,
nearly all the participants rejected the possibility of a return to controls.
Although business leaders could take comfort that the first part of their
message remained dominant, many voiced continued frustration that policy debates did not adequately appreciate the role of labor power. Shortly
after the conference, Roundtable chairman John Harper complained to
Alan Greenspan, chairman of Ford's CEA: "We think it a disservice for
anyone to infer that the new labor increases this year have been reasonable." Highlighting fiscal and monetary policy was fine and good, but if
the economists with Ford's ear failed to implicate labor, Harper claimed,
they implicitly left too much blame on business, and the country risked
a repeat of 1971.[59]

Compared with Nixon, however, Ford's dedication to the entrenched
problems of inflation struck many business leaders as a breath of fresh air.
Even before the Watergate scandal swamped Nixon's presidency, many
corporate executives had grown weary of his ambivalent attitude toward big business and his willingness to accept liberal economic policies
in hopes of rallying political support. Gerald Ford, on the other hand,
shared none of Nixon's personal insecurities about elite eastern corporate
leaders and actively reached out to the increasingly organized representatives of the business community in Washington. Indeed, Ford's embrace
of business prompted heated criticism, typified by a Herblock cartoon in
the *Washington Post* that showed corporate fat cats hoisting "Good Old
Jerry"—the college football star who had nearly turned pro—onto their
shoulders while the man on the street opined: "He seems like such a nice
guy, I wish he was on our side." (See figure 4.3.) Even Ford's "Whip Inflation Now" campaign, mocked bitterly for its big red WIN buttons and
meaningless gestures of solidarity, reflected a spirit of voluntarism—not
mandatory price restrictions—that sat well with many business leaders.

Ford inherited a presidency weakened by both Watergate and the
steady increase in congressional influence over domestic policy. Any honeymoon the new president may have enjoyed when he famously promised
an end to America's "long national nightmare" evaporated when he is-

Figure 4.3. In 1975, *Washington Post* cartoonist Herblock joined many liberals in denouncing Republican president Gerald Ford's close ties to corporate interests and business lobbyists. A 1975 Herblock Cartoon, © The Herb Block Foundation.

sued a blanket pardon of Richard Nixon one month after taking office.[60] With the Republican Party in disrepute, many business leaders looked at the upcoming 1974 midterm elections with dread, fearing that the coming liberal onslaught would reinvigorate organized labor, bolster the drive for increased regulations and social spending, and otherwise enflame inflationary pressures in the economy. Playing defense, the Chamber of Commerce launched a substantial campaign for an "inflation-proof Congress" by promoting business-friendly candidates in federal, state, and local elections. Although the Chamber did not directly contribute money to campaigns, donating only $25,000 to the educational (i.e., noncampaigning) arm of the Business-Industry Political Action Committee (BIPAC), the group counted on its national networks of associations and firms to support candidates who were committed to spending cuts and a hard line toward labor. Already in the midst of a major revitalization effort, the Chamber used the inflation issue to mobilize support at its grassroots through a three-part kit with segments called "Test Your IQ (Inflation Quotient)," "Test Your Candidate's IQ," and "To Fight (or Not to Fight) Inflation: How Did Your Congressman Vote?"[61]

Such meager electioneering, however, proved utterly ineffective, and the Democratic Party surfed the mighty anti-incumbent wave to major victories. Although the Democrats had suffered a bruising humiliation with Nixon's defeat of George McGovern in 1972 and had barely held onto their majority in the House of Representatives, the electoral success of "Watergate babies" in 1974 bolstered their ranks by 50 members in the House and brought their Senate majority to 60. Many of these freshmen representatives had campaigned as anti-Nixon liberal reformers and replaced moderate Republicans from the North, dramatically shifting the composition of the Democratic caucus away from its more conservative southern members.[62] For many corporate leaders, the new shape of Congress reinforced the need to work with and influence incumbent legislators rather than hold out hope for a new crop of business-oriented "inflation-proof" politicians. The fact that many of the new Democrats represented suburban constituencies for whom consumer issues, especially prices, trumped traditional labor-liberal allegiances provided an important opening for business.

BETTER LIVING THROUGH INDIRECT LOBBYING: COMMON SITUS AND LABOR LAW REFORM

The political and economic climate of the mid-1970s thus encouraged the dramatic rise of indirect, or grassroots, lobbying by employers' associations. Although the NAM, the Chamber, and the Roundtable, as well as their well-heeled member corporations, retained Washington Representatives from trade associations and individual firms, they also found great success mobilizing "ordinary" constituents to influence fence-sitting legislators. By energizing local businesspeople about specific issues and providing them with prepackaged information, form letters, and talking points, Washington-based groups combined their longstanding desire to "tell business's story" with the pressing need to shape votes in Congress.

The politics of inflation and business's ongoing campaign to keep the focus on organized labor created a vital laboratory for indirect lobbying. Among its earliest successes was the campaign against a labor practice known as common situs picketing, which arose on construction sites where subcontractors employed workers from multiple unions simultaneously. Although current law permitted workers to strike only over a grievance with their actual employer, pro-labor legislators pushed a reform to allow solidarity strikes, increasing pressure on management to respond to strikers' demands. The ensuing legislative battle not only accomplished an important goal for business leaders but also renewed enthusiasm and cohesion among a wide range of firms, trade associations, and employers' groups.

Common situs picketing exemplified the type of policy that enraged business-oriented conservatives and corporate leaders, who believed it would tip the scales of collective bargaining decisively against business and toward labor. "In our opinion," Roundtable chairman John Harper wrote, "the adverse impact of common situs picketing on the construction industry, as well as on industrial companies which use contractors in their plants, would seriously affect the cost, quality, and completion of industrial facilities."[63] Such arguments fell on deaf ears in the Democratic majority in Congress, which passed a bill permitting the practice in the fall of 1975. At first, President Ford looked for some excuse to support the measure, recognizing his party's persistent weakness with working-class voters. According to Under Secretary of Commerce James A. Baker, conservatives in his administration ultimately convinced him that the legislation would "strike hardest at small business and nonunion craftsmen and contractors, particularly minorities." More important, Ford knew he faced a powerful political threat from former California governor Ronald Reagan, then preparing a primary election battle for the Republican nomination. Since Reagan, an avowed conservative, looked likely to tap into antilabor and pro-business sentiment, Baker warned Ford that "failure to veto will be political suicide as far as the nomination is concerned." In January 1976, Gerald Ford issued the first veto of his brief administration, killing the common situs bill.[64]

Early the next year, however, after Democrat Jimmy Carter ousted Ford from the White House, pro-labor legislators again began to push a common situs bill through Congress. Knowing that they could not rely on a presidential veto, a cohort of employers' groups led by the Roundtable, the NAM, and the Chamber organized a substantial indirect lobbying campaign to stop the measure in the House instead. Coordinating with several contractors' associations, they mobilized support from construction company owners and local civic groups, all of whom peppered their representatives with a coordinated message denouncing the bill.[65]

Through its Construction Committee, a holdover from Roger Blough's CUAIR, the Business Roundtable mobilized its "local user groups" around the claim that the law "would increase work stoppages in an already strike-prone industry, and would significantly increase construction costs."[66] The bill's sponsor, Representative Frank Thomas (D-NJ), expected the bill to pass the House by seven or eight votes but expressed surprise at the "massive" lobbying against it. In late March, 88 Democrats, largely from the South, joined 129 Republicans to defeat the measure (14 Republicans and 119 Democrats voted for it).[67] By coincidence, the news of the bill's failure broke just as the NAM opened its annual meeting at the Hilton hotel in Washington, prompting loud cheers from the attendees. Seizing an opportunity to play the politics of inflation, the NAM's president, former U.S. Steel executive Heath Larry, told a journalist that the bill's demise "ought to be a great deal of satisfaction to the public at large" because it would have dramatically increased inflation. The public should not support measures that would encourage strikes, Larry added, because "[p]icket lines are threats, not freedom of speech, and they've always been."[68]

As it turned out, the common situs fight merely provided a prelude to a much more substantial battle between organized business and organized labor. Late in 1977, the AFL-CIO judged that, with Democrats in control of Congress and the presidency, the time was propitious to push comprehensive labor law reform. The bill labor wanted would restore some of the losses it had sustained in the Taft-Hartley Act of 1947 by increasing penalties on employers who committed unfair labor practices, granting unions greater access to employment sites for organizing, and enlarging the NLRB.[69] Speaking for the business community, the Chamber of Commerce argued that the bill was "designed to make it easier for unions to organize non-union workers." Labor's demands, the Chamber continued, were "inflationary" and "would have a substantial impact on small business, would expand the federal bureaucracy, and would tilt the basic labor law in favor of organized labor."[70]

As they had against the common situs bill, Washington-based employers' groups and trade associations coordinated a massive lobbying blitz against the labor law reform bill, both in Congress and among the grassroots. According to *Business Week*, the CEO of Sears, Roebuck sent a personal appeal to retired Sears employees, explaining his belief that the labor bill "could push our country down the road to a labor- and government-controlled economy." Reports by the Chamber of Commerce promised that, if passed, the bill would bolster union membership by millions.[71] In the halls of Congress, business lobbyists skillfully tracked down potential allies to support a Senate filibuster. As an aide to one such target, Florida Democratic senator Lawton Chiles, recalled: "I don't think they missed a single possible opponent of that bill in our state."[72] Yet message counted as much as medium. The legislation, business lobbyists insisted, threatened not just large employers but small business owners and, most important, consumers, who would bear the higher prices caused by excessive labor power.

The political fight over labor law reform after years of high inflation and economic instability was a high-water mark for organized business as well as a turning point in industrial labor relations. Indeed, as many scholars have noted, the acrimony and ill will that the fight generated between union and business leaders—many of whom had worked constructively, if combatively, for years—never dissipated. The executive council of the AFL-CIO called the business offensive "a conspiracy of convenience between corporations, trade associations, and extreme right wing groups." Indeed, many industrial leaders recognized that the cost of deteriorating labor-management relations could potentially outpace the gains of defeating the bill. The Roundtable's Policy Committee voted to join other business groups in opposing the law, but only by a vote of 19 to 11; many of the largest and most heavily unionized members, like GE and U.S. Steel, worried that their opposition would simply antagonize their own workforce. But other corporations, particularly retailers and those in low-skill industries like textiles, led the charge to prevent labor law reform, and the Roundtable's leadership gave the group's combined clout to the lobbying effort.[73]

In the spring of 1978, conservatives led by firebrand senators Orrin Hatch (R-UT) and Jesse Helms (R-NC) led a filibuster against labor law reform, boasting significant support from the organized business community. After nineteen days and six failed efforts to invoke cloture, the bill's proponents finally gave in. *Business Week* hailed business's "new lobbying weapon [that] combines the power of new coalitions in Washington with grassroots organizations that reach into virtually every congressman's home district." Labor's supporters also expressed shock, calling the "unprecedentedly broad coalition of business groups" that brought down the bill a "catastrophe for American labor." The next month, UAW president Douglas Fraser publicly resigned from a high-profile labor-management committee, chaired by former labor secretary John Dunlop, which sought to foster dialogue between union leaders and major industrial CEOs, including Roundtable members Reginald Jones (General Electric) and Irving Shapiro (DuPont). "The leaders of industry, commerce and finance in the United States have broken and discarded the fragile, unwritten compact previously existing during a past period of growth and progress," Fraser bitterly explained. For their part, however, corporate leaders could only see the defeat of labor law reform as a victory. By expanding the political debate on labor beyond simple negotiations between workers and managers to include broader economic implications, business groups had aroused enthusiasm among their members and greater public support for their position. By arming their professional lobbyists with that constituent voice, they achieved results in Congress, reaffirming the potential of the pro-business grassroots, or what Chamber president Richard Lesher called "the only lobbying that counts."[74]

LOBBYING CONGRESS: THE END OF ECONOMIC PLANNING

Business's newfound institutional cohesion, catalyzed by the contentious politics of inflation, paved the way not only for increasingly effective forms of indirect lobbying but also for greater influence with policymakers. Indeed, the shifting balance of political power after the Democratic Party's gains in 1974 and 1976 forced executives and employers' associations to craft coalitions directly with policymakers whose first instincts did not always match business's priorities. With a Democrat again in the White House and more liberals in Congress, many conservative corporate leaders feared a return to liberals' traditional focus on unemployment and economic growth rather than a robust campaign against inflation. The continued tension between those apparently antithetical policy goals manifested in the prolonged struggle over a piece of labor-liberal legislation designed to guarantee employment for all Americans: the Humphrey-Hawkins Act.

In 1974, as the economy spiraled deeper into recession, liberal senator Hubert Humphrey (D-MN) and Congressman Augustus Hawkins (D-CA) proposed the "Equal Opportunity and Full Employment Act," which, in form and spirit, mirrored a 1946 plan to craft a national economic planning system. The legislation called for the government to achieve "full employment" (usually calculated at 3 percent unemployment) through fiscal and monetary policies, including the direct creation of government jobs. The 1946 Employment Act had in fact become law, but only after a coalition of business leaders and antilabor conservatives from both parties watered down its language and enforcement provisions.[75] Thirty years later, Humphrey and Hawkins hoped that the Democratic Party, finally shed of its conservative southern constituency, could use its post-Watergate strength to pass a more robust labor-oriented full employment bill. The original versions of their legislation instructed the government to provide "equal opportunities for useful and rewarding employment" to all Americans and proposed a "Job Guarantee Office," responsible to the president, to set "such policies and programs as may be needed to attain and maintain genuine full employment."[76]

Humphrey-Hawkins won strong support from the AFL-CIO, other labor groups, and liberal activists. Business leaders, however, decried the plan as "a political gimmick." In a series of articles commissioned by the Business Roundtable, business economist Ross Wilhelm of the University of Michigan articulated business's central argument against the full employment bill: artificially reducing unemployment, either through expansive fiscal and monetary policy or, as a last resort, through "phony, dead-end jobs" that paid "prevailing union wage rates," would necessarily increase inflation. "The inflationary wage requirements built into the Humphrey-Hawkins Bill would compound the inflation problem and would bring back double-digit inflation," Wilhelm argued.[77]

Between 1974 and 1978, business organizations lobbied hard against the bill, sending executives to pay personal calls to senators, promoting packaged editorials like Wilhelm's, and mobilizing letter-writing campaigns. Despite years of indirect lobbying, however, the measure remained quite popular in the Democratic-controlled Congress. In May 1978, Bethlehem Steel CEO Lewis Foy, who chaired the Roundtable's National Planning and Employment task force, exhorted his fellow CEOs to direct their attention to the Senate Banking Committee. Although business groups had long made the defeat of Humphrey-Hawkins a top priority, Foy claimed, most committee members had heard very little opposition to the bill, receiving few letters and practically no personal visits.[78] Although the Roundtable, the NAM, the Chamber, and other business organizations clearly and vociferously opposed the bill, their message had not sunk in with policymakers—a sign that their newfound lobbying prowess was far from omnipotent.

Many corporate leaders remained hopeful that they could defeat Humphrey-Hawkins, as they had with common situs picketing and the labor law reform bill. Others, however, recognized that the labor-liberal alliance's political strength and the general popularity of raising employment during an economic downturn gave the legislation an air of inevitability. Nonetheless, in the summer of 1978, corporate lobbyists successfully marshaled a skilled political coalition in Congress to thoroughly defang the legislation from within. Taking advantage of labor's institutional weakness after its high-profile loss on labor law reform, corporate lobbyists and congressional conservatives, especially Orrin Hatch, managed to remove nearly all enforcement power from the bill. In an eerie echo of 1946, the final version of the law, which Carter signed with some fanfare in the fall of 1978, bore little resemblance to the original. In tellingly vague language, the act asserted "the responsibility of the Federal Government to use all practicable programs and policies to promote full employment, production and real income, balanced growth, adequate productivity growth, proper attention to national priorities, and reasonable price stability." Although liberal legislators could boast that they had voted for full employment, the bill that had originally promised to inaugurate a full-scale system of national economic planning changed practically nothing. (Its one major effect was to prohibit sex, racial, and religious discrimination in government programs—a notable milestone but unrelated to combating unemployment.) In fact, the bill's language actually reinforced the conservative business position on the importance of fighting inflation, a policy goal that appeared to contravene robust job creation and economic stimulus.[79] In the end, business lobbyists succeeded by playing the politics of inflation in the debate over unemployment and compelling key congressional allies to view policy choices in terms of that classic trade-off.

Lobbying Carter: The Final Death of Price Controls

Building on their success against labor and Humphrey-Hawkins, organized business lobbyists continued their string of policy victories by derailing any liberal hopes of reinstituting wage and price controls to combat inflation. After peaking in double digits in 1974—as a result of the OPEC embargo, food shortages, and the end of Nixon's controls— the national inflation rate declined during the recession of 1974–75 and remained around 6 percent for the next two years. Although prices rose more slowly, the ever-higher cost of living and 7 percent unemployment during the Ford years created severe economic strain, and signs of decreasing productivity made future inflation appear likely.[80] By January 1978, the inflation rate stood at 6 percent per year—high by the standards of the early 1960s but quite low compared to several years earlier. In his State of the Union Address that month, Jimmy Carter made clear his deep concern about inflation and, to the delight of conservatives, his conviction that the blame fell squarely on government deficit spending. Yet while he pledged fiscal restraint and a balanced budget, he also called for widespread collaboration in the fight against inflation, asking "government, business, labor, and other groups" to voluntarily hold down their wages and prices.[81]

Prominent corporate leaders approved.[82] DuPont CEO Irving Shapiro, who had succeeded Charles McCoy in 1974 and taken over as Business Roundtable chairman from John Harper in 1976, declared himself "impressed with [the president's] recognition that many of our problems must be solved by the private sector; that government cannot solve them." Carter's openness to business's perspective on inflation no doubt pleased Shapiro, a proud Democrat who supported Carter in 1976 and sought to build bridges between Democratic politicians and elite corporate leaders. Although he worried that the president's "plan to establish a voluntary anti-inflation effort raises the spectre of wage-price guidelines," Shapiro remained "reassured by the President's stated dislike of controls."[83]

While Carter claimed to put inflation front and center in 1978, he struggled to avoid a hard choice between two traditional inflation-fighting strategies. The first, favored by many business leaders and other economic conservatives, was to "engineer a recession" to bring prices down. The second was mandatory wage and price controls, still a popular fallback option among many liberals. Rather than choose the rock or the hard place, Carter charted a politically safer (but economically dubious) middle by invoking the creed of "voluntarism" and shared sacrifice—not only by firms but also by workers and consumers. He repeated his calls for firms to hold down prices but also asked all Americans to tighten their belts and restrain their spending habits. To the chagrin of traditional Democratic constituencies, Carter promised "specific governmental actions . . . to tighten budgets, rationalize government regulations, reorganize the bureaucracy and increase productive investment."[84]

But neither Carter's jawboning nor his pledge to trim the governmental fat did much to curb inflation. Resolving to put some teeth into his request for voluntary price and wage vigilance but rejecting mandatory controls, Carter instead announced a formal system of voluntary wage and price standards, or guidelines, on October 24, 1978. To head the new program, the president tapped liberal Keynesian economist Alfred Kahn, best known to the public for overseeing airline deregulation as chairman of the Civil Aeronautics Board.[85] Kahn became Carter's new "inflation czar" and led the Council on Wage and Price Stability (COWPS), a holdover from the Ford administration that set voluntary standards, adjudicated petitions for exemptions, and pursued various strategies to encourage compliance.

COWPS called on labor organizations to demand pay raises of no more than 7 percent per year, allowing them to keep up with inflation but not put upward pressure on it. Moreover, as Kahn explained to the Chamber of Commerce, President Carter asked "every business to hold down any price increase to one-half percent below the rate of increase during the 24 months from the beginning of 1976 to the end of 1977." A firm that had increased its prices by an average of 6 percent during those two years, for example, would be limited to a 5.5 percent increase in 1979. As a loophole, the program allowed another route to compliance for firms that experienced huge cost increases. According to Kahn, "if your costs are going up rapidly, you may pass them on through price increases even if that puts you over your price increase limit. But if you pass on costs, you are not supposed to increase the amount of your profit by more than 0.5 percent, except as the volume of your sales goes up."[86]

While these standards were officially "voluntary," COWPS had considerable leverage to urge business and labor to respect them. For workers, the administration used a carrot: if inflation rose above 7 percent, workers whose unions had respected the ceiling would receive an offsetting tax credit. For business, a stick: in order to sign federal contracts worth more than $5 million, companies would have to prove that they were complying with the price standards.[87] Such a system meant that for firms that did significant business with the government, very little about the plan was truly "voluntary."

Although price controls, even "voluntary" ones, violated sacred tenets of free-market economics, Carter's willingness to blame government for inflation won his plan support from some prominent business leaders. After delivering a keynote address to the Business Council in December 1978, for example, the president received a vote of confidence from an unlikely source: the group's chairman, North Carolinian John deButts, CEO of AT&T and a founding member of both the March Group and the Business Roundtable. Departing from the council's tradition of policy neutrality, deButts interrupted the president's question-and-answer session to offer his two cents. "I happen to believe that the President is sincere and will succeed in his efforts" to reduce government spending and regulation, deButts told his fellow executives on the council. "I believe that it is incumbent upon us in the business community . . . to find a way to comply with the standards established by our President."[88]

Similarly, if not so emphatically, the chairman of the NAM also urged his far larger membership to comply with the voluntary price standards. Herbert Markley, the president of ball-bearing manufacturer Timken Company from Canton, Ohio, further urged NAM members to write the president personally ("if you can conscientiously do so") to state their intentions to comply.[89] Embracing the spirit of the "New NAM," Markley rejected the organization's historic role as obstructionist and antistatist and argued that business stood to gain politically by working constructively with the government. Such a shift in tone prompted a fierce backlash from many NAM members, however. One manufacturer accused Markley of trying to "appease" the president by conceding ground on the inflation debate. "I know and certainly you must know that inflation will be stopped only when the government spends no more money than it takes in," the member angrily wrote. Despite such blowback, the NAM's leaders worked hard to build bridges with the administration in the late 1970s, even inviting Alfred Kahn to deliver a luncheon address at the group's spring conference in Washington in March 1979.[90]

Carter's modest success generating support from business leaders owed largely to his personal appeals. A month after announcing the price standards, he wrote directly to business leaders and pledged to do everything in his power to fight inflation by reducing government spending in return for their promise to comply with the price guidelines.[91] The president also pitched his program by using social and political networks in Washington to target important corporate leaders even more directly. In late 1978, White House staffers convened the first of several meetings with what they called the "Group of Nine"—the country's most powerful business and trade associations. Meeting first in Vice President Walter Mondale's office (where Carter dropped by) and later in the Business Roundtable's Washington headquarters, the group included the heaviest hitters of organized business in the late 1970s: GM's Thomas Murphy and GE's Reginald Jones from the Business Roundtable, Donald Seibert from J. C. Penney (who headed the National Retail Merchants Association as well as the Roundtable's inflation task force), AT&T's John deButts from the Business Council (as well as the Roundtable), NAM chairman Herbert Markley, and Richard Lesher from the Chamber, as well as representatives of the National Federation of Independent Business, the New York Stock Exchange, the American Bankers Association, and the American Retail Federation.[92]

The Group of Nine meetings revealed a broad spectrum of opinions and reactions to Carter's plan. As he had during the Business Council meeting, deButts strongly urged firms to comply but reiterated that the council did not take formal policy positions. Markley also reaffirmed his support and said he soon expected an "avalanche" of supportive letters. The Roundtable leaders demurred somewhat; Jones claimed many businesspeople did not believe the program was "voluntary" because of the sanctions the administration threatened against noncompliant firms. Similarly, Seibert argued that retail stores worried that consumers would unfairly blame a store for any price increase, even one that was in line with the guidelines.[93]

Although the leaders of the NAM and the Roundtable generally treated the voluntary standards as regrettable but unavoidable, the Chamber of Commerce offered no such conciliatory tone. Represented at the meetings by its full-time president, Richard Lesher, as well as its short-term chairman, Shearon Harris, president of the Carolina Power and Light utility company, the Chamber "more or less stalled on the issue," according to a White House staffer. Accosting Carter's standards as vague and fearfully predicting that compliant firms could be sued for price-fixing under antitrust laws, Harris and Lesher refused to follow their counterparts at the NAM and encourage their members to comply. Instead, Harris took a more aggressive approach, proposing a litany of twenty-eight actions for the federal government to undertake to fight inflation all by itself, including reducing the regulatory burden, encouraging exports, lowering taxes on firms, and decreasing labor's bargaining power.[94] For his part, Lesher berated Alfred Kahn for proposing that the federal government publicize the names of noncompliant companies and encourage consumers to boycott them, accusing the inflation czar of antibusiness bias. Although Kahn promptly clarified that the government would simply urge Americans to be "prudent buyers," the Chamber remained steadfastly opposed.[95]

Such diverse responses, from deButts's enthusiasm to Lesher's defiance, typified the persistent challenges business leaders faced as they worked to unify around any proposed remedy for inflation. Echoing the contentious experiences of Phase II controls in 1972, the heads of mobilized business groups wrestled with competing imperatives: their fear of inflation and their hostility to heavy-handed government interference in markets. The White House staff members who had so hopefully convened the Group of Nine soon understood that the business leaders all expressed severe reluctance to embrace the president's anti-inflation program. In short order, the Carter administration realized that it would be unable to tap these business groups' indirect lobbying prowess to shore up national support for voluntary guidelines.[96]

Indeed, business's collective patience with Carter and the price standards ran thin very quickly. In 1979, another oil shock rocked global economies as the Iranian Revolution unsettled the political order in that country and disrupted petroleum supplies. Inflation rose rapidly even as the COWPS price- and wage-setting standards grew more complicated and, in the minds of many business leaders, onerous. That fall, the president of the National Association of Realtors told Kahn that the program had failed to "remain 'simple, voluntary and largely self-enforcing.' The standards have become increasingly detailed and complex, considerable effort has been made to induce compliance, and a cumbersome reporting and exception approval system has been created."[97] Many of the business leaders who had defended the voluntary guidelines program a year earlier now called for its complete abolition. For example, the NAM's full-time president, Heath Larry, whom Commerce Secretary Juanita Kreps had singled out for his cooperation in late 1978, had grown far less positive about price standards by the fall of 1979.[98] Roundtable chairman Thomas Murphy of General Motors warned that despite the administration's professed opposition to mandatory controls, he worried about "the establishment of pay and price advisory committees which might be interpreted as a step in that direction."[99] Finally, in the summer of 1980, as Jimmy Carter's political fortunes waned, the Roundtable came out against wage and price guidelines entirely, telling Carter that they "distorted public understanding of the causes of inflation" and that gaining public support for hard but necessary policy choices would only be hampered "if the misconception is allowed to persist that voluntary wage and price restraint can substitute for them."[100]

As business leaders finally stopped hedging their bets and came out in force against Carter's middle path on inflation, a growing segment of the broader public joined them. By the end of the 1970s, the nation's decade-long battle with price instability had taken its toll on the political class; while opinion polls suggested that a razor-thin majority of Americans might still be open to wage and price standards, no political will existed to pursue them.[101] Although the voluntary guidelines program limped on until the end of Carter's term and Kahn maintained his post at COWPS until 1980, the administration's anti-inflation emphasis shifted dramatically at the end of 1979 when the new Federal Reserve chairman, Paul Volcker, launched a radical monetarist policy. Between 1979 and 1982, the Fed's aggressive program of targeting the money supply successfully wrung inflation out of the economy by sparking a massive economic recession, exactly the scenario Johnson, Nixon, Ford, and Carter had struggled to avoid.[102]

If Richard Nixon's experiment in wage and price controls was tragedy, Jimmy Carter's was farce. Both presidents tried to construct policies to appease their traditional political opponents while frustrating their allies: Nixon by appealing to middle-class consumers and unions despite business's objections to controls; Carter by watering down his policy options in an effort to stay in business's good graces. Neither succeeded, but Nixon managed to avoid paying the political price, mostly because he succumbed instead to the self-inflicted wound of Watergate. Carter, on the other hand, lost his presidency largely on the weakness of his economic stewardship. Yet the two anti-inflation policy episodes that bookended the 1970s proved pivotal for organized business groups. In both 1971 and 1978, corporate leaders had to face down the inherent contradictions between their fear of inflation and their opposition to government involvement in the economy. In both cases, business leaders initially gave the president the benefit of the doubt but ultimately turned on him as the effort to exert government control over prices limped into meaninglessness.

THE TRIUMPH OF THE POLITICS OF INFLATION

The experience of stagflation in the 1970s fundamentally reshaped American politics at a critical moment in recent history. Aggregate price levels first approached worrisome levels in the late 1960s, the result of Johnson's guns-and-butter policies and monetary mismanagement by the Federal Reserve, but inflation exploded to crisis level in the wake of the 1973 OPEC oil embargo. The second oil shock, in 1979, revived the crisis, which only abated after the severe recession of the early Reagan administration wrung inflationary impulses out of the economy and international oil prices fell. During the roughly fifteen years in which inflation topped the list of America's economic woes, however, an essential realignment unfolded in national politics. Organized business groups, which began that period full of sound and fury but not signifying much, established themselves as formidable lobbyists on a host of economic issues and deftly navigated the treacherous politics of inflation. That experience galvanized business leaders to engage more actively and assertively in national politics, take their long-simmering antagonism to organized labor to the frontlines of debate, and formulate an increasingly effective counterattack against traditional liberal governance.

Of course, the crisis of inflation did not plague the United States alone but afflicted industrial economies the world over. From Europe to Asia to Latin America, the oil shocks and turmoil in international exchange markets spawned vicious cycles of higher prices and lower productivity, as well as political turmoil and regime changes.[103] But different political systems respond to common pressures in idiosyncratic ways, and the American business community's response to the challenges of inflation unfolded in the unique context of the American political system. The contrast with West Germany, fast becoming a primary industrial rival for manufacturers in the United States, offers a compelling lesson. Postwar German economic policymaking reflected the country's long corporatist tradition, which extended back to Bismarck in the 1870s and urged constant and institutionalized cooperation among business and labor organizations. Indeed, the West German constitution of 1949 formally enshrined corporatist principles by guaranteeing legal protection for both employers' associations and labor unions; in practice, wage contracts negotiated by leading associations, such as the employers' group Gesamtmetall and the union IG Metall, provided models for other industries to follow. Although the oil shocks of the mid-1970s presented West German policymakers with the same hard choices that their American counterparts faced, the crisis manifested in different ways politically. Institutionalized corporatism tended to promote industrial cooperation rather than confrontation; indeed, in 1978, precisely as American industrial relations dissolved in the heated lobbying over labor law reform, Social Democrat Helmut Schmidt achieved a measure of common ground (and a multibillion Deutschmark economic stimulus program) between business and labor groups.[104]

But in the United States, efforts at industrial cooperation fared poorly. The Nixon administration's mandatory wage-price controls bureaucracy certainly represented an attempt to centralize fundamental aspects of industrial production, including wage rates and production schedules. For a time, the controls even managed to stem the scourge of price inflation, but business leaders supported the program only as long as their priorities remained administrators' top priority. Once Nixon, bowing to public pressure and his own disinclination toward the business establishment, placed a higher premium on wages and consumers than on profits, the increasingly unified business community turned against the controls and invoked classically conservative notions of free markets to condemn top-down economic controls as a matter of principle. In so doing, business leaders helped cement their standing with more ideologically libertarian members of the burgeoning conservative political establishment, many of whom came to view corporate leaders not as self-interested hacks but as intellectual and political partners in their campaign against liberal economic policies.

Moreover, as inflation continued to wreak havoc in the aftermath of the controls experiment, business lobbyists successfully exploited the political cleavages the crisis exposed. In their campaigns against labor law reform and full employment, organized business groups deliberately framed their policy preferences to capitalize on the growing animus toward the federal government. The politics of inflation permitted corporate lobbyists to link bureaucracy, labor power, and deficit spending to the growing sense of cultural detachment and malaise, for which President Jimmy Carter served as a potent symbol.

The contentious politics of inflation thus catalyzed business's political mobilization and the organization of a coherent pan-business lobby. Successes against common situs picketing and labor law reform drew directly from business leaders' renewed focus in the aftermath of the Nixon controls; their rejection of Carter's weak tea compromise solidified their role as dominant players in national politics. Ultimately this process drove a major wedge between representatives of industry and representatives of labor, doing irreparable damage to any hope for renewed goodwill or mutual collaboration. Corporate lobbyists learned to frame old arguments in new and modern ways by forging common cause with both lawmakers and, as the next chapter explores, an increasingly anxious, cynical, and politicized national constituency: the American consumer.

CHAPTER 5

The Producer versus the Consumer

> Just a few years ago, consumerism for most corporations was a
> cloud no bigger than a man's fist, a fitful disturbance that would
> surely pass as quickly as it materialized. Today, consumerism is
> swirling around U.S. business like a tornado, shattering old
> assumptions, shaking the foundations of major industries.
> —*Sales Management Magazine*, c. 1970

AMERICAN TELEVISION VIEWERS tuned to NBC around midnight on Saturday, December 11, 1976, would have encountered what appeared to be the holiday edition of a low-budget talk show called "Consumer Probe." That night's guest, Irwin Mainway of Mainway Toys, cut the perfect swath as a stereotypical greasy and unscrupulous businessman, complete with a dark three-piece suit, aviator sunglasses, a thin mustache, and a thick Chicago accent. The show's host, a somewhat indignant and self-righteous consumer advocate, took Mainway to task for what she called the "unsafe toys for children" that his company manufactured and marketed. The litany of questionable products included the "Pretty Peggy Ear-Piercing Set," "Mr. Skin Grafter," and "Johnny Switchblade: Adventure Punk," a rubber doll from whose arms sprouted two sharp knives when you pressed his head. Accused of peddling what was "by no means a very safe toy," Mainway took umbrage. To the contrary, he insisted, nothing was wrong with Johnny Switchblade. "[L]ittle girls buy 'em, you know, they play games, they make up stories, nobody gets hurt. I mean, so Barbie takes a knife once in a while, or Ken gets cut. There's no harm in that." The host then produced another product, "Bag O' Glass"—a clear plastic sack filled with what she called "jagged, dangerous glass bits." Again Mainway defended the product's logic and his company's integrity. "The average kid," he said, "picks up, you know, broken glass anywhere. . . . We're just packaging what the kids want."

"So, you don't feel that this product is dangerous," the host pressed.

"No," Mainway declared. In fact, his company was a model corporate citizen. "Look, we put a label on every bag that says: 'Kid! Be Careful! Broken Glass!'"

Of course, NBC viewers late on a Saturday evening in 1976 were actually watching *Saturday Night Live,* the irreverent sketch comedy program then in its second season. The unctuous Irwin Mainway was played by Dan Aykroyd, while guest host Candace Bergen portrayed the humorless consumer advocate. Giving voice to the opprobrium of consumer rights activists across the country, Bergen's character concluded that Mainway's entire product line was "really unsafe and should rightfully be banned from the market." Insulted yet again, Mainway pointed out that *no* toy could be 100 percent safe, so the accusation was unfair. (His exact words were: "Hold on a minute, sister. . . .") To drive his point home, he graphically demonstrated how easily he could get a painful splinter from a wooden block, strangle himself with the cord of a toy telephone, or choke on a large foam ball. Crestfallen, the host ended the interview. "Well, this is certainly a very sad situation," she berated Mainway. "One of the precious joys of Christmas warped by a ruthless profiteer like yourself."[1] Mainway, foam ball blocking his airway, flailed his arms wildly as the show faded to black.

Playing to *Saturday Night Live*'s generally young, urban, and liberal audience who would welcome consumer hero Ralph Nader as host just one month later, the show's writers unsurprisingly cast Aykroyd's character as outlandish and hyperbolic. At the same time, Candace Bergen also invoked unsympathetic derision as the scolding, self-righteous consumerist. By mocking both sides—the criminally negligent "ruthless profiteer" and the schoolmarmish social do-gooder—the satire, perhaps unwittingly, encapsulated the hotly contested politics of American consumer product regulation in the mid-1970s.

On one side of this struggle stood business leaders, who produced and sold products to an ever more selective, vigilant, and risk-averse consuming public. On the other stood the consumer rights movement, a subset of the larger liberal reform movement that also championed stricter workplace safety and environmental protection laws and achieved significant success lobbying the federal government in defense of what its supporters called the "public interest." *Saturday Night Live*'s short romp through consumer politics revealed the major contours of that debate. Candace Bergen's declaration that "Teddy Chain Saw Bear" and "General Tron's Secret Police Confession Kit" should be "rightfully banned from the market" by federal decree surely seemed reasonable, but viewers were left to wonder about the role of caveat emptor as an alternative to the strong arm of the regulatory state. Moreover, Dan Aykroyd's claim that *no* product (not even a foam ball) came with absolutely no risks echoed the business community's longstanding complaint: social regulations were inherently arbitrary, discriminatory, and insufficiently attentive to the costs of compliance or the real likelihood of harm. Such unrealistic demands for perfect products, many businesspeople claimed, led inexorably to business failures and higher prices. At a time of persistent inflation, how could such debilitating consumer product regulations *really* serve the consumer's best interest?

For the writers and actors at *Saturday Night Live*, both sides of this debate lay open to ridicule, suggesting the evolving nature of consumer politics in the mid-1970s. And indeed, as this chapter shows, the national debate over consumer protection underwent a remarkable transformation during the mid-1970s largely in response to the successes of an increasingly mobilized and organized corporate lobbying community. Once a relatively uncontested social goal, consumerism emerged from the contested politics of a stagflationary decade as a fraught clash of interests. The country's most famous consumer champion, Ralph Nader, had shot to popularity in the late 1960s, but his glow wore off during the malaise of the Carter years. Public opinion polls recorded that trajectory: in 1974, 73 percent of Americans professed some or a great deal of respect for Nader, and in 1975, 76 percent agreed that it was "good to have critics like Nader to keep industry on its toes."[2] Between 1976 and 1979, however, national confidence in Nader fell from 64 to 52 percent (and those with "a great deal of confidence" dropped from 28 to 16 percent). More telling, the percent of respondents with hardly any or no confidence in him rose from 18 to 34 percent.[3] Indeed, in 1971, only 5 percent of survey respondents agreed with the claim frequently made by business activists that "Nader is a trouble maker who is against the free enterprise system." But by 1980, a full quarter of respondents to a General Electric poll claimed that "more activity by people like Ralph Nader" would hurt the economy.[4] While GE's poll likely reflected a skewed base, it highlighted a general trend confirmed by the political battles discussed in this chapter.

The decline of Nader's symbolic potency mirrored a real drop in support for regulatory legislation, which helped nurture a deregulatory impulse and the increased salience of business- and market-oriented political discourse. Several vital factors underlay this shift in American politics, including an increasingly organized and well-funded intellectual challenge to liberal policies, devastating inflation and economic stagnation, and political and cultural anxieties that generated distrust in government in the wake of Vietnam and Watergate. This antistatist mood, ironically abetted by the likes of Nader and his public interest reform movement, which criticized the government for colluding with powerful interests, created essential space for yet another vital development: the sophisticated lobbying campaigns engineered by organized business associations and prominent corporate leaders. Although their success was far from complete—the success of antismoking and auto-safety campaigns as well as antifraud protections for senior citizens stand out as notable pro-consumer achievements—the business movement largely halted the tide of liberal reform legislation, especially concerning consumer product regulation, by the end of the decade.

To analyze the mechanisms of business lobbying as well as its effect on the shifting politics of consumer product regulation, this chapter traces the origins, rise, and slow death of Ralph Nader's biggest legislative priority for the consumer movement in the 1970s, a consumer protection agency in the federal government. Designed to institutionalize consumerism by inserting what Nader called a "consumer perspective" into the national regulatory apparatus, the Consumer Protection Agency (CPA) was a constant fixture on the congressional docket from 1969 to 1978. Despite widespread and well-placed support, however, it failed to become law, ultimately defeated by the overwhelming lobbying of united and effective corporate interests. The agency's final loss in 1978 marked a turning point in regulatory and consumer politics. Not until lawmakers created the Consumer Financial Protection Bureau (CFPB) as part of the Dodd-Frank Act of 2010 did a comprehensive government agency designed to protect consumers regain legislative legs; even then, the CFPB faced administrative and conceptual limitations, with purview only over financial matters.[5]

The story of the proposed Consumer Protection Agency exposes the shifting political terrain on which organized business leaders operated during the 1970s. Just as the politics of inflation discussed in the previous chapter broke down along classical fault lines, pitting business against labor, so too did the politics of regulation highlight a dichotomy between the interests of "producers" and "consumers." For activists like Ralph Nader, consumer advocacy meant putting the needs of consumers ahead of profits and rewards to producers. Bemoaning the final defeat of the CPA in 1978, one of Nader's top deputies, attorney Mark Green, predicted that "the influence of producers' interests on regulation will continue."[6] Although business leaders protested that such a distinction between consumers and producers rang false because *everyone* was a consumer, the old-fashioned categories remained mainstays of the debate. President Gerald Ford, for example, articulated precisely that division in an address to the Chamber of Commerce in 1975 by declaring his solidarity with business leaders in their campaign to reduce the costs of social regulations. "Ultimately," Ford told the businessmen in the crowd, "all such costs are paid by you, the producers, and your wives, the consumers."[7]

Ford's comment, intended to blur the distinction between producers and consumers, in fact highlighted it by articulating the highly gendered nature of the politics of consumer protection. While businessmen and their wives clearly shared a desire for affordable and safe products, they naturally, in Ford's telling, approached the issue with different priorities and perspectives. Political debates over consumer protection in general, and the Consumer Protection Agency in particular, frequently stereotyped consumer advocacy as feminine, weak, and dependent, from Candace Bergen's portrayal of the prim and judgmental "Consumer Probe" host on *Saturday Night Live* to widespread decrees that a hyper-regulatory "nanny state" threatened to emasculate the nation. Finally, insinuations by Nader's political opponents that the unmarried consumer advocate was gay testified to the prominent place of gender and sexuality in consumer-related public policy debates.

For business leaders, the discursive dichotomy between producing and consuming—including its class and gender overtones—provided a framework for challenging the notion that one side represented the "public interest" while the other stood only for private gain. As this chapter argues, business lobbyists' ultimate deflection of legislation to create a Consumer Protection Agency hinged on their ability to reframe debate over the bill and cast its proponents as elite special interests rather than champions of the general welfare. Uniting their networks of energized businesspeople and tremendous resources, business associations launched a major offensive against the CPA. Deploying a strategy also used successfully by other conservative political activists, anti-CPA lobbyists parlayed economic anxiety and the public's inherent distrust of bureaucracy to break the back of the consumer movement by the end of the 1970s. At the same time, they successfully advanced the argument that corporate interests in fact aligned with consumers' welfare. Although they failed to dethrone "consumerism" completely, they applied just enough pressure on the legislative system to deplete its political momentum. As with their work against the labor law bill and Humphrey-Hawkins, business groups' indirect lobbying against the CPA halted the tide of the liberal reform agenda and permanently altered the landscape of American politics.

PRODUCERS AND CONSUMERS

The modern consumer rights movement emerged in the 1960s, but its origins lay in the reformist politics of the late nineteenth and early twentieth centuries, a response to the rapid changes wrought by urbanization and industrialization. During the Progressive Era, muckraking writers like Ida Tarbell and Upton Sinclair helped raise public awareness of the dark underside of industrial capitalism, exposing the exploitative working conditions, crushing poverty, and dangerous products that accompanied mass production, mass distribution, and mass consumption. Citizens' groups like the National Consumers League emerged, first on local stages and soon as national organizations, bringing attention to the ravages of industrial society, lobbying for local health ordinances and safer working conditions, and organizing boycotts to protest issues from corruption to racial discrimination. In the process, Progressive reformers cultivated a political identity for consumers as conscientious citizens who could, when organized, use their collective purchasing power to fight for social change.[8]

At the level of policy, industrialization inspired fundamental changes in the regulatory role of government at both the state and federal levels. Stifled by a political tradition of minimal state interference in the conduct of business, policymakers slowly responded to the changing economic landscape. In the last half of the nineteenth century, for instance, organized farmers convinced several state governments to empower departments of agriculture to set quality controls on meat. By 1906, Congress officially nationalized the process of regulating food and pharmaceutical products with the Pure Food and Drug Act, whose passage owed largely to organized consumer groups. That legislation laid the groundwork for national product safety standards and affirmed consumers' importance as a political force.[9]

Consumers' growing political identity received a boost from the rapid advance of industrial capitalism, as diversified and integrated national firms increasingly provided the goods Americans used in their daily lives, from mouthwash and shaving cream to radios and automobiles. By the 1920s, professionalized advertising agencies urged Americans to see themselves as discriminating consumers by marketing products in deeply personalized terms. In the 1930s, the economic deprivations of the Great Depression gave rise to yet another manifestation of consumer identity. While Herbert Hoover tried to revive the economy on the supply side through such programs as the Reconstruction Finance Corporation, which supplied federal loans to businesses, Franklin Roosevelt predicted in 1932 that "in the future we are going to think less about the producer and more about the consumer." The National Recovery Administration, the public face of the first New Deal between 1933 and 1935, included consumer councils among its myriad code-writing bodies, and the Federal Food, Drug, and Cosmetic Act of 1938 granted the Food and Drug Administration (FDA) stronger regulatory authority. Moreover, the mandate of the Federal Trade Commission (FTC) also underwent a major transition during the 1920s and 1930s; originally designed to protect individual firms from the uncertainties of the marketplace, the FTC under the New Deal increasingly worked to protect consumers from abuses by business. The Roosevelt administration's job creation, personal home loan, Social Security, labor relations, and direct aid programs, while experimental and haphazard at first, ultimately congealed into an ideologically coherent policy regime focused on defending citizens' purchasing power. As the Keynesian faith in the government's power to promote growth and employment through demand-side stimulus came to dominate policy debates, the New Deal made the federal government the guardian of the consumer's material interest.[10]

In the aftermath of World War II, economic policymakers continued to place a premium on what historian Meg Jacobs has called "pocketbook politics," but the experience of the Great Depression fundamentally altered popular ideas about what constituted the "consumer's interest." Earlier consumer crusades had targeted poverty and economic dislocation in addition to quality of life issues—such as those arising from diseased meat or unsafe drugs—but consumer politics in the postwar years came to revolve nearly exclusively around economic questions: who could purchase what, and for how much? Many consumer activists, for example, used their purchasing power to challenge racial discrimination, protesting stores or restaurants that hired African American workers but refused to cater to African American clients. Others mobilized over the cost of everyday consumer goods, most notably during strikes over the price of meat when war-time price controls ended in the mid-1940s. In an increasingly modern and technologically oriented society, consumers demanded greater information about products, and consumer organizations played a vital role securing access to such data. Moreover, consumer activism was not limited to the United States. In war-torn Europe and parts of the developing world, citizens also organized themselves as consumers to navigate the uneasy transition to growing affluence.[11]

Yet while consumerism as a political identity flourished, explicit focus on consumer *protection* declined significantly between the 1930s and the early 1960s. Although precise measurements of public concern with any particular issue are impossible to attain, the incidence of the term "consumer protection" in five national newspapers tells a striking story. Used 50 times in 1940, the term appeared only 5 to 10 times per year through the 1950s; in 1960, it was used 23 times but skyrocketed from there, doubling to 50 in 1965 and hitting 750 in 1971. (Usage declined slightly at the end of the 1970s, reached 550 in 1985, and settled into the 200 range from 1990 to 2008.) Similarly, popular magazines devoted increasing attention to consumer protection in the 1960s: the *Readers Guide to Periodical Literature* listed 4, 9, and 6 articles under that heading in 1963, 1964, and 1965 but 32 and 48 in 1969 and 1970, respectively.[12] Although such figures are not an exact proxy for public interest, they certainly show an increase in media attention to the politics of consumer protection and thus corroborate the notion that after decades on the back burner, product safety reemerged as a vital political topic in the 1960s.

That reemergence corresponded with the protracted economic boom of the 1960s that decisively recast Americans' expectations of material goods and produced what historian Lizabeth Cohen has called "the third wave consumer movement." While the first wave of consumer activism emerged in the Progressive period to confront the perils of industrial society and the second wave took shape during pits of despair during the Depression, this third wave grew from the warm glow of affluence.[13] As living standards rose, Americans increasingly rejected caveat emptor as a sufficient standard and demanded greater protections against unscrupulous vendors and hazardous products. As with environmental laws, the push for consumer protection began, unevenly, at the state level. In 1957, New York and Rhode Island became the first states to enforce deceptive trade practice laws through bipartisan state commissions. In the 1960s, growing numbers of states passed laws regulating such practices as the sale of consumer debt from stores to financial institutions, the advertisement of prescription drugs, and the return policy for items purchased from door-to-door salespeople. State-level consumer protection varied significantly by region, however. The ethos of consumerism found greater support among wealthier and better-educated citizens, who formed the bulk of the third-wave consumer ethos. State regulation flourished, therefore, in richer states whose populations included higher percentages of middle- and upper-class liberals. The South, where conflicts over racial desegregation seeped into all political issues that involved strengthening the hand of government, enacted fewer and weaker consumer protection laws than other regions.[14]

On both the state and federal levels, the politics of consumer protection thrived when liberals—Republicans as well as Democrats—did well electorally, such as in the midterm election of 1958 and Lyndon Johnson's landslide reelection in 1964. Tapping into the ethos of third-wave consumerism on the campaign trail in 1960, John F. Kennedy helped nurture the revival of a consumer identity rooted in protection by promising to be "a high-powered lobbyist" for the consumer. Two years later, he reinforced that message by proclaiming a "Consumer Bill of Rights," including the right to safe products, to information about them, to choice among goods, and to a voice in politics. Kennedy's proclamations both confirmed consumerism's newfound importance as a political force and, perhaps more important, signaled the shift in the locus of consumer protection politics toward the federal government. Discrepancies in state regulation, both in focus and enforcement, convinced consumer activists to turn their focus to the federal government. By the 1970s, the FTC beefed up its prosecution of deceptive trade practices, frequently using the experience of state commissions as a model. It also increasingly collaborated with state governments to launch antitrust and consumer protection lawsuits.[15]

In addition to benefiting from top-down support, consumerism gained strength from national outrage over stories of death and injuries that resulted from faulty, unsafe, or polluting products. In 1962, for example, Americans recoiled in horror at stories of "thalidomide babies" born with serious birth defects linked to an antinausea medication their mothers had taken while pregnant. Although many states passed their own consumer product safety legislation, issues such as thalidomide stretched so far beyond state borders that local action seemed insufficient, especially since the types of industries involved operated on a national—even international—level. Liberal policymakers in the federal government channeled the public's shock into tremendous support for the Kefauver-Harris Amendment to the Federal Food, Drug, and Cosmetic Act in 1962, which required pharmaceutical manufacturers to provide proof of their products' safety. In the years that followed, Congress passed dozens of other laws designed to protect consumers from inferior or untested products, compel truth-in-advertising, limit environmental pollution, and regulate marketplace transactions.[16]

Organizationally, third-wave consumer politics shifted into high gear in the mid- to late 1960s, propelled by a sophisticated infrastructure of local, state, and national organizations and prominent leaders. Long-standing groups like the National Consumers League and the Consumers Union, founded in the 1920s and 1930s, respectively, found themselves joined by newcomers like the Consumer Federation of America, founded in 1967, and myriad state-level organizations. With the publication in 1965 of his seminal exposé of the car industry, *Unsafe at Any Speed*, a young lawyer from Connecticut named Ralph Nader emerged as one of the consumer movement's most influential leaders. Boasting degrees from Princeton and Harvard Law School, Nader recalled the classical muckraking tradition of the Progressive Era by denouncing corporate greed and accusing automobile executives of willfully peddling lethal products. His advocacy for automobile safety directly propelled the National Highway Safety Act of 1966 and, soon thereafter, the requirement that all cars come equipped with seatbelts. By the end of the decade, Nader established national networks of public interest law firms, research groups, and grassroots organizations, including Public Citizen and Congress Watch, cementing third-wave consumerism's growing influence.[17]

By the time Richard Nixon assumed the presidency in 1969, eight years of consumer-oriented Democratic presidents had firmly cemented the goals of consumer protection in national politics. On the campaign trail, Nixon had hinted that he might abolish the position of White House Special Assistant for Consumer Affairs, established under Johnson, but public outcry quickly convinced him that he could ill afford to appear "anticonsumer."[18] Instead, in April 1969, Nixon appointed Pennsylvania Republican Virginia Knauer to that post; in 1971, he expanded her powers by executive order and created the Office of Consumer Affairs in the Executive Office of the President.[19] In that role, Knauer became the most vocal consumer activist within the White House, where she lobbied successfully for a plank in the Republican Party Platform to support an independent consumer agency.[20] That platform also endorsed the Consumer Product Safety Commission (CPSC), a regulatory agency charged with writing and enforcing safety standards. Although Nixon worried about expanding the federal bureaucracy, Knauer convinced him to sign the CPSC into law, which he did "with reservations" in October 1972, days before cruising to reelection.[21]

For many business leaders, the CPSC joined the ranks of the EPA and OSHA on the greatest-hits list of antibusiness social regulation, which they viewed as the ill-conceived product of American culture's deep bias against free enterprise. Indeed, as the consumer movement gained strength, conservative business leaders grew increasingly vocal about the inherent anticorporate prejudice that it embodied. At New York's Waldorf-Astoria hotel in April 1970, the NAM's Marketing Committee organized a conference on industry's "crisis in credibility." Donald Gaudion, the chairman of that committee and CEO of New Jersey–based chemical company Sybron, Inc., reminded attendees about the dramatic decline in "[f]aith in the honesty and responsibility of American business" since the mid-1960s, worsened by consumerism's inherent critique of business's integrity. "Demands by consumer advocates for more and more protective legislation," Gaudion argued, "raised doubts in the public mind. . . . Once doubt about industry's good faith is implanted in the public mind, all industry is suspect, and each company suffers a loss of respect from its employees and its community."[22]

Such consternation echoed throughout the business community. Also in 1970, the Chamber of Commerce's Consumer Issues Committee produced and distributed a filmstrip called "The Consumer Revolution" that opened with ominous images that invoked terrifying "signs of revolution" in America: "Restless youth demanding sweeping changes. . . . Militant minorities battling for social and economic change. . . . Rioting in our cities. . . . Bombing office buildings. . . . Marches on Washington." Last on that list: "Angry consumers protesting rising prices and other problems of the marketplace." All of these were part, the narrator explained, of a frontal assault on basic American institutions. "Business is one of the battlegrounds," the filmstrip proclaimed, "[and the] battle has a name: Consumerism." In that context, many business leaders saw nothing forced about linking Ralph Nader with the Black Panthers and the

Weather Underground—all were subversive, un-American, and deeply threatening.[23]

However, like Richard Nixon, business leaders were only too aware of consumerism's massive public appeal, and their instinct for self-preservation meant that they reserved their most vitriolic denunciations for private conversations. The Chamber of Commerce's incendiary film-strip, for example, explicitly addressed trade association audiences, not the general public. More publicly, corporate leaders and business asso-ciations took pains to acknowledge legitimate consumer concerns and to promote business's social responsibilities. The Chamber, for example, adopted and publicized a "Business-Consumer Relations Code," which de-clared business's civic obligation to health and safety, high quality at low prices, clear warranties, and the elimination of fraud. The code formed the centerpiece of a major public relations campaign designed "to en-courage businessmen in general and trade and professional associations in particular to take a more positive role in the consumerism front."[24]

To be sure, many corporate leaders genuinely believed that consumers had legitimate grievances and that business bore clear social responsibil-ities—to safe products as well as to the environment, workplace condi-tions, and social justice. Even so, they also realized the political and stra-tegic advantages that came from taking such an accommodating posture toward consumerism. Embracing the spirit of welfare capitalists of ear-lier generations, some prominent chief executives believed that making public peace with consumer activists could in fact help preserve business prerogatives. In 1975, the CEO of SC Johnson explained to his fellow Business Council executives during a retreat weekend in Hot Springs, Vir-ginia, that his company had removed fluorocarbon propellants from its aerosol products because Americans wanted "business to make voluntary decisions on our own terms and not dictated by government regulation, but reflecting the <u>consumer's</u> self-interest."[25] The Chamber of Commerce promoted its Business-Consumer Relations Code in the same spirit. Ac-cording to Chamber president Ritter Shumway, ignoring consumer issues would only add "*new* layers of bitterness to consumers' attitudes toward business," but an effective response by business would "counter the flood of legislative 'remedies.' "[26] This strategy of accommodation reflected the American business community's long history of deflecting new regula-tory requirements by shrewdly, if cynically, responding to the public's concerns.[27]

Other business leaders, however, firmly rejected such calls to em-brace the spirit—if not the methods—of consumerism. Many concurred with conservative economist Milton Friedman, who famously argued in 1970 that business's only "social" responsibility was to generate prof-its.[28] Friedman, of course, had the luxury of not selling anything to the consuming public; most businesspeople did not feel free to be quite so strident. Nonetheless, major employers' associations like the NAM and the Chamber of Commerce frequently tried to split the difference and articulate their anticonsumerist message with a softer touch. For example, the Chamber's effort to promote business values through televised public service announcements in 1972, discussed in chapter 2, included a spot on the role of consumers in society. Over a busy street scene, Chamber executive vice president Arch Booth explained that all those people—"businessmen, housewives, doctors, lawyers, laborers, teachers, students"—were also "bosses . . . the public, the consumers . . . in our economy." Consumers were "bosses" because they, not the government, "determine what shall be produced by what they buy." The cartoon simultaneously validated consumers' social and economic importance and blurred the distinction between "producer" and "consumer," so vital to the consumer movement's political project. Yet the colorful ad could not hide the creeping nervousness just below the surface. Despite Booth's affectionate, grandfatherly comforts, the rapid rise of consumer protection politics clearly struck a note of fear into an already jittery business community. In both its prejudices and practices, business leaders believed, organized consumerism posed a significant threat to profits and, more important, corporate autonomy.[29]

INSTITUTIONALIZING THE MOVEMENT: THE CONSUMER PROTECTION AGENCY

Among the many ironies of the presidency of Richard Milhous Nixon is this: on the subject of consumer protection legislation, both the liberal reform movement and the business community believed fervently that the president was in the other's pocket. After Nixon put his signature on legislation creating OSHA and the CPSC and, by executive order, created the EPA, lawyers at the Chamber of Commerce warned the group's members starkly about "the tremendous clout which the government now has to regulate manufacturers, distributors, retailers, private labelers and importers of hundreds of different consumer products—in the name of safety."[30] The president of the Grocery Manufacturers of America, an attorney from Cincinnati and former lobbyist for Sears, Roebuck named George W. Koch, complained to a White House aide that Nixon's apparent embrace of consumerism had left many of his business supporters in a "frustrating lurch."[31]

Yet at the same time, consumer advocates viewed Nixon with deep suspicion, responding to the Republican's inauguration in 1969 by jump-starting a particular consumer protection initiative that had been incubating for a decade. Beginning in 1959, liberal members of Congress led by Estes Kefauver had proposed legislation to establish a cabinet-level "Department of Consumer Affairs." By the mid-1960s, Kefauver had died and the mantle fell to a cohort of younger legislators from both parties, many of whom had been elected in the liberal wave of 1958. Just two months after Nixon's inauguration, one of the Senate's most liberal and consumer-oriented Democrats, Abraham Ribicoff of Connecticut, invited Ralph Nader to help his Senate subcommittee draft a bill that would protect consumers against the potential setbacks the incoming administration might launch. To the surprise of many congressional liberals, the consumer hero strongly argued against Kefauver's idea of a "Consumer Department" in the president's cabinet. Rather than add another layer of regulatory bureaucracy or create another cabinet position accountable to the president, Nader proposed to institutionalize the consumer movement by inserting the "consumer voice" into the proceedings of regulatory agencies through a new type of government body: the Consumer Protection Agency.[32]

During its legislative career from 1969 to 1978, the specific title of the government body Nader had in mind changed several times for both political and practical reasons. It was alternately known as the Agency for Consumer Protection (ACP), the Agency for Consumer Advocacy (ACA), and the Office of Consumer Representation (OCP), but those names usually described much the same structure and purview. Despite the minor protests of certified public accountants, the final bill that Congress voted on (and rejected) in 1978 called for a Consumer Protection Agency (CPA), and that is the term most historians have used to refer to the bill throughout its lifetime.

No matter its technical name, the agency Nader proposed would possess a unique structure that reflected his critique of both corporate power and the regulatory state. Nader embraced a strand of populist liberalism that deeply distrusted all instances of concentrated power, very much in the Jeffersonian tradition. That Jeffersonianism extended to Nader's conception of the business corporation, which he also viewed through the antiquated prism of the nineteenth century. Prior to the rise of general incorporation laws shortly before the Civil War, all corporate charters in the United States came directly from state legislatures, and in rare cases Congress—that is, corporations existed only by the grace of the government and only when elected officials believed the corporation served the public good. Even the arch-Federalist Supreme Court Chief Justice John Marshall, decreeing that private contracts superseded state prerogatives in *Trustees of Dartmouth College v. Woodward* (1819), nonetheless captured the early republic's attitude toward corporations: "The objects for which a corporation is created are universally such as the government wishes to promote," he wrote. "They are deemed beneficial to the country."[33] Ralph Nader similarly understood corporations as *public* institutions that carried *social* responsibilities, a vision that underlay his long and unsuccessful campaign to require federal charters for large corporations and put "public" representatives on corporate boards of directors.[34]

If Nader's conception of the corporation differed from the more individualistic vision that most businesspeople espoused, his notion of the state itself also departed from that of most mid-century liberals. His Jeffersonian populism reflected a deep distrust of centralized state power as well as corporate power, and he worried acutely about the expansion of government bureaucracies and the administrative apparatus of the state. He thus parted ways with labor-oriented Democrats and union leaders who saw a robust federal government as the key to preserving the public good. Nader refused to support a "Department of Consumer Affairs" because he believed that adding more governmental structures only compounded the real threats to civic participation in government and the promises of democracy. Instead he argued that the principle aim of policy should be to decentralize power through procedural reforms that subverted both the state and corporations to the common goals of all citizens—the "public interest."[35]

Nader's politics deeply informed his fixation on the problem of *regulatory capture*, which to him was the primary reason that consumers were not adequately represented in government. The theory of regulatory capture, promulgated widely by political scientists in the mid-twentieth century, argued that the immutable logic of large organizations inevitably caused regulated firms and industries to manipulate and control the decisions of the very agencies charged with regulating their conduct. Individual government regulators, according to this view, shared so many repeated transactions with representatives of the firms they regulated that they developed intellectual and personal empathy for them, and so made rules in their interests. In a more sinister sense, many critics opined the famous "revolving door" through which former government insiders found lucrative positions working for regulated firms as lobbyists, parlaying their contacts and deep knowledge into special favors for their employers. Nader believed that additional layers of regulation, including a cabinet post, would not address the structural problem at hand but simply create another regulator who could be captured by industry. Rather, to truly institutionalize the "consumer's voice" in government would require the fundamental reform of regulatory *procedures* themselves.[36]

Nader thus proposed a Consumer Protection Agency that would oversee and influence the process of administrative rule making by regulatory agencies, not promulgate regulations itself. Instead of crafting rules, the CPA would have statutory authority to oversee regulations and policies written by all government agencies to ensure that they reflected the best interest of consumers and that industry insiders did not wield undue influence on administrative decision making. The CPA would have the authority to audit a wide range of agencies, from the Office of Economic Opportunity, which handled employment fairness, to the Securities and Exchange Commission, which set transparency requirements. Moreover, it would act as a clearinghouse for public grievances, from high costs to faulty products to product recalls. Finally, the CPA would conduct research into consumer issues, facilitating the work of consumer protection agencies within the federal government and state-level commissions. And to avoid conflicts of interest and allow the agency a broad range of oversight, Nader insisted that the agency possess administrative independence; it should be positioned outside of any department (such as the Treasury or the Federal Reserve) and report directly to the Executive Office of the President.[37]

Most important, the CPA would fundamentally alter the process of regulatory decision making in Washington because it would have legal standing to intervene before federal regulatory agencies, boards, and courts. Making the case for the CPA to supporters, Joan Claybrook of the group Public Citizen argued that regulatory agencies, including the EPA and OSHA, operated "in a quasi-judicial capacity, holding hearings, listening to arguments, and making decisions." Corporations used their tremendous financial resources to hire expert witnesses and provide complex data to support favorable regulations. Since "consumers" were disparate, unorganized, and not centrally funded, regulators frequently did not hear opposition to the industry view, so the Consumer Protection Agency would fill that void. Agency lawyers would fact-check corporate claims, compel regulatory agencies to use their subpoena power to obtain data directly from regulated companies, and appeal any decisions that went against consumer interests. Thus, from its inception, the CPA embodied deep skepticism about state power, bureaucracy, and the potentially corrupting influence of corporate power. If Ralph Nader was Jeffersonian in his political vision, he was Brandeisian in his policy prescriptions.[38]

Almost nothing about the proposed CPA sat well with the vast majority of business leaders, especially those who were active in Washington-based employers' associations. Nader's theory of the corporation as a public institution struck many as anachronistic at best, destructively socialist at worst. More than a century of law, not to mention hundreds of years of liberal property-rights philosophy, affirmed that the corporation was a collection of private contracts and a sacrosanct and autonomous part of the body politic, capable of paying taxes, suing in court, and owning property. To deny that corporations enjoyed private status was to discredit the entire concept of free enterprise; if corporations were public, what stood in the way of the nationalization of industry? Moreover, many conservatives believed that Nader's fixation on regulatory capture reinforced the consumer movement's affront to corporate integrity: the theory effectively indicted all business leaders as nefarious fat cats who undermined democracy for their own ends rather than the virtuous producers of prosperity, as they far preferred to see themselves.

As proposed in 1969, the Consumer Protection Agency thus combined consumerism's instinctive distrust of business with social regulation's costs of compliance—the worst of both worlds. Politically active business leaders loudly condemned the plan. The proposed agency, according to the NAM's director of government affairs, threatened to install "a tax-supported consumer activist group within the government." Such an agency would boast "unprecedented investigatory powers over the private sector and the rest of government." Killing the bill in Congress became one of the business community's top priorities.[39]

ORGANIZED BUSINESS ON THE MARCH

The corporate offensive against the Consumer Protection Agency began quickly. In the late spring of 1969, just weeks after Nader and Ribicoff announced their proposed agency, several dozen Washington lobbyists organized regular meetings to coordinate an industry response. Major employers' groups and trade associations, particularly the NAM, the Chamber, the National Federation of Independent Business (NFIB), and the Grocery Manufacturers of America (GMA), took the lead mobilizing the Washington Representatives from their most prominent member firms. From the beginning, these organized corporate representatives acknowledged the daunting challenge they faced in opposing the CPA. In fact, George Koch of the GMA (no relation to the Koch Industries family), bestowed the code name "RW80D" on the group at its earliest meetings. The appellation referred to Jules Verne's *Around the World in 80 Days*, whose lesson, Koch told his fellow lobbyists, was "nothing is impossible." Despite consumerism's tremendous popularity and conservatives' relatively weak position in Congress, the lobbyists knew that many avenues lay before them. James Madison's ingenious, not to say infuriating, system of safeguards against the "mischiefs of faction" meant that stopping a bill was much easier than passing one. In the United States, reactive lobbying had an inherent tactical advantage over proactive lobbying.

Organized business's counteroffensive against the Consumer Protection Agency centered institutionally around that ad hoc committee, which rebranded itself the Consumer Issues Working Group (CIWG) by

1973. At its helm stood Washington veteran Emmett Hines, the director of government relations—that is, chief paid lobbyist—for construction materials manufacturer Armstrong Cork, who structured the CIWG as a coordinating body through which CPA opponents exchanged information, crafted lobbying strategies, and divided up public relations tasks. Lacking a formal structure or legal existence, the group relied on its members for financial and logistical support, including staff and office space. While early meetings attracted representatives of several dozen firms, by 1977 the CIWG counted more than four hundred members, including industrial giants like Bethlehem Steel, Maytag, Ford, United Airlines, and most major oil companies. But throughout its battle against the CPA, the CIWG's most significant institutional support came from employers' associations—the NAM, the Chamber, and, upon its creation in 1972, the Business Roundtable—which tapped widespread and growing lobbying infrastructure to work vigorously against the bill.[40]

The corporate lobbyists and association representatives in the CIWG understood well that the idea of the CPA—like the consumer movement in general—enjoyed great popularity among the public and tremendous support from lawmakers in both parties. Indeed, even most moderates endorsed the concept; Republican representative Gerald Ford of Michigan pronounced it "a sound, workable bill" in 1971.[41] Deeply anxious about the business community's negative public image, many corporate leaders worried that the very impression of a coalition of industrial interests working against the bill would push fence-sitting legislators over to the consumer movement's side, if only so they would not have to face constituents' accusations that they caved to pressure from "big-business lobbyists." Recognizing this dynamic, the NAM's marketing director specifically encouraged members to stress their position as independent, nonaffiliated small business owners when they wrote anti-CPA letters or telegrams to their elected officials. "Your letters will be more effective," he explained, "if you omit any reference to NAM or its materials."[42]

Fighting an uphill battle, CIWG lobbyists focused on specific strategic objectives, looking for congressional allies who could help them thwart the majority's will and stall the bill. In 1970, the bill raced through subcommittees in the House and Senate with near unanimity. In December, the CPA passed the full Senate 74 to 4, and observers predicted a similarly lopsided victory in the House.[43] Knowing the bill would surely pass a floor vote and that even if opponents could convince Nixon to veto it Congress would override that veto, the CIWG turned its fire on the last procedural gauntlet the legislation had to run. Before any bill could come to the floor for a vote, it first had to pass muster with the House Rules Committee, a bipartisan fifteen-person body that decided what legislation went to the floor, when, and under what conditions for debate. In the two days after the Senate vote, the CIWG lobbyists worked feverishly to persuade conservative members of the Rules Committee to block the bill from moving forward. In a telling example of strategic arm-twisting, one lobbyist from the NFIB leaned on Texas Democrat John Young by reminding him about the small business owners in Young's district. Although the idea of a CPA might be good in theory, the lobbyist told the congressman, it contained a few provisions that had to be "smoothed out and structured" or it else would be too burdensome for small companies. Some 286,000 NFIB members had come out against the CPA, the lobbyist continued, and 21,000 of them lived in Texas.[44] Under such pressure, Representative Young joined six others in voting against sending the bill to the full House. With one member absent, the Rules Committee deadlocked 7 to 7, and the bill died.[45]

After such a close vote and with continued momentum in Congress, consumer advocates blazed ahead with another version of the CPA bill once the new Congress, elected during the midterm election of 1970 that saw significant liberal and Democratic Party gains, took office. In October 1971, the House passed a new CPA bill 344 to 44. To Nader's chagrin, this new legislation slightly restrained the proposed agency's investigative powers, despite efforts by Nader allies in the House to pass strengthening amendments. Nonetheless, the somewhat weaker bill still called for an independent agency with jurisdiction to participate in formal regulatory and other rule-making procedures. With such overwhelming support, proponents hopefully set their eyes on the upper chamber, where only four senators had voted against the CPA the year before.[46]

Few consumer advocates predicted, however, that two of those lonely votes from 1970—archconservative Democrats Sam Ervin of North Carolina and James Allen of Alabama—would ultimately succeed in leading filibusters in two successive Congresses, stalling the advance of the CPA through shrewd parliamentary procedure backed by the growing lobbying weight of the CIWG. Ervin, the seventy-six-year-old veteran of World War I who had achieved national prominence as a vocal opponent of civil rights legislation, took credit for leading the 1970 floor fight against the CPA when he tried, largely without success, to insert industry-specific loopholes and exemptions into the legislation.[47] Philosophically, Ervin opposed the expansion of federal regulatory power over states, which he believed the bill embodied. More specifically, he agreed with the Chamber of Commerce's argument that more robust consumer regulations would likely compel business to disclose corporate secrets, such as recipes or chemical formulas.[48] Not coincidentally, the North Carolinian's business constituents included major tobacco companies, who worried, as an attorney for R. J. Reynolds wrote to Ervin, that an activist CPA might place "the power to destroy the tobacco industry . . . squarely in the hands of the Federal Trade Commission."[49] Allen, also a segregationist southern Democrat, expressed concern that the CPA would be inherently hostile to other government agencies and thus urged compromise legislation that denied the CPA subpoena power and specifically protected private corporate information.[50]

Ervin and Allen became natural allies with the CIWG lobbyists, and as the campaign for the CPA reemerged in 1972, the Washington lobbyists worked furiously to assist their filibuster. According to Senate Rule XXII as it then stood, two-thirds of all members present and voting had to vote for cloture in order to end debate and bring a measure to a vote; Ervin and Allen therefore had to convince 32 fellow senators to reject cloture to maintain a successful filibuster. Throughout the summer of 1972, the senators worked closely with CIWG representatives to identify allies and secure their support. With particularly enthusiastic assistance from George Koch and the GMA, CIWG lobbyists supplied the senators with information, data, talking points, and even prepackaged speeches to prolong debate and counter arguments by CPA proponents. Ervin put forward a compromise that he called an "Amicus Amendment," which would have reduced the CPA's authority over federal agencies to the same level of influence that an amicus curiae brief has in a lawsuit. The ploy failed to sway any CPA supporters, but it provided Ervin and his growing list of conservative allies some political cover from charges that they were openly hostile to consumers.[51]

Through their logistical support for Ervin and Allen's filibuster, organized business groups demonstrated their growing skill at managing indirect lobbying campaigns. All summer long, lobbyists targeted specific senators and mobilized businesspeople in their constituencies to bombard them with telephone calls, letters, telegrams, and often personal visits. Such a barrage aimed not only to shape the senators' own thinking but also to assure them that important voters would defend their decision and that they could take a stand against bureaucracy without drawing the wrath of consumers. The quality, not just the quantity, of constituent mail thus figured prominently into this strategy, suggesting a unified "letterhead theory of indirect lobbying." All else being equal, letters from the owners of small companies or middle managers at large firms that arrived on embossed company stationery appeared to carry more weight than hastily scrawled personal notes. Such business correspondence overwhelmingly urged senators to join the filibuster and reject the CPA or else water it down with Ervin's Amicus Amendment. By providing their members with specific language and point-by-point arguments, the CIWG groups helped ensure that anti-CPA mail also appeared more authoritative than the simple slogans ("Consumers need a voice") that senators tended to hear from CPA proponents.

In September 1972, the CPA bill made its way through committee and headed toward the Senate floor. Sam Ervin, who had unsuccessfully argued against the bill in committee, loudly promoted his Amicus Amendment, and quietly shored up support for a filibuster, received the following letter from a constituent: "Having read newspaper accounts of your opposition to SB3970, which would set up an independent Consumer Protection Agency, I am writing to commend you for your stand and to express the hope that you will continue to oppose this unwise legislation when it is deliberated upon the floor of the Senate."

The letter came on formal personal letterhead, clearly typed and personally signed from a businessman in Charlotte. In a remarkable testament to the coordination of the anti-CPA movement, Ervin also received the same letter, in exactly the same wording, from a businessman in Raleigh. And several more from men in Charlotte, at least two of whom used the same corporate suite address (but did not identify their company). Such a coordinated campaign reflected the supreme skill the bill's opponents displayed in rallying businesspeople at local levels and giving the impression of broad-based support. (Evidence of coordination also belied the claim that the letter writer got his information from newspapers—clearly he got it from the person who gave him the form letter.)[52] Moreover, the coherence and sophistication of the anti-CPA grassroots effort clashed starkly with the more traditional methods of lobbying employed by Naderite organizations like Public Citizen, which worked their standard coalitions in Congress and believed that they still could achieve a strong showing.

On October 5, 1972, as the 92nd Congress approached a preelection recess, Ervin and Allen's filibuster faced its final test and passed. The bill's proponents mustered only 52 votes for cloture, far below the two-thirds majority needed, and the bill died for that session of Congress. (Sixteen senators missed the vote, but their presence would not have altered the outcome.) The 30 senators who voted against cloture included 18 out of 45 Republicans, mostly from the Midwest and West, and 12 Democrats, all but one of whom hailed from the former Confederacy. The liberal reform movement badly misjudged its support in Congress, and the anti-CPA forces deftly tapped into the traditional home of anti–New Deal conservative politics and the power of the filibuster to kill the measure.[53]

Two years later, in August 1974, the House again passed the CPA, this time by a smaller but still substantial margin of 293 to 94. Once again, conservative senators Allen and Ervin led a filibuster, prolonging debate both in committee and on the Senate floor, and relying on logistical support from the CIWG lobbyists to keep their members in line. During the long summer that culminated in Nixon's resignation in August, Ervin—who had bolstered his credibility with many liberals through his dogged chairmanship of the Senate Watergate Committee during the previous eighteen months—successfully pushed through an amendment exempting small businesses from the CPA's oversight powers. Although such a concession may have paved the way for greater support from the small business community, the various organizations working through the CIWG remained united in opposition. Explaining that logic, the NFIB's lobbyist wrote to Ervin that although he was grateful for the exemption, he worried that it would not survive a conference with the House. Arguing that "[w]ithout it, the Consumer Protection Agency is totally unacceptable to the small business community," the NFIB lobbyist reaffirmed his stark opposition.[54]

Once again, liberal senators and their allies in the consumer movement worked hard to convince just enough filibustering senators to change their mind and vote for cloture. Lobbyists for the pro-CPA Consumer Federation of America published a target list of "swing senators" whom they hoped to bring to their side. Of their top fifteen, eleven were Republicans, illustrating the strong link between southern Democrat antistatist conservatism and opposition to the Consumer Protection Agency.[55] The final cloture vote on September 19, 1974, echoed the same partisan and regional dynamic. CPA supporters managed to muster 64 votes, three shy of the two-thirds majority they needed to invoke cloture. (Edward Kennedy [D-MA] and William Fulbright [D-AR] were absent, but their votes would not have changed the results.) The 34 senators who voted against cloture included 21 of the 42 Republicans in the chamber, plus Conservative James Buckley of New York, and 12 Democrats, all but one of whom came from the South. Indeed, seven of the Republicans hailed from the South, meaning that more than half the filibuster strength came from the former Confederacy.[56]

The CIWG's successful use of parliamentary procedures to defeat the CPA in 1970, 1972, and 1974 emboldened the business community and enraged liberal consumer activists. *Washington Post* journalist Jack Anderson, who had leaked the Powell Memorandum in 1972 and devoted much of his writing to exposing corporate malfeasance, described the CIWG as "an awesome array of industry nabobs," and Nader railed against corporate "special interests" that had waged a "massive campaign to defeat the bill."[57] Yet the hair's-breadth margins of the cloture votes diminished any sense of victory for business lobbyists. According to Nixon aides, CIWG leader Emmett Hines called the White House to express "concern, verging on alarm, of significant portions of the business community" that the Nixon administration might consider a compromise measure, warning starkly against emboldening bipartisan consumer advocates and alienating the business community.[58] Even after the successful filibusters, Hines knew the battle was far from over.

A New Front: The Battle for Public Opinion

In truth, business lobbyists had done little more than buy themselves more time. Public opinion polls confirmed that Americans still liked the idea of a CPA, so its passage appeared to be a question of when, not if. Depending on how pollsters asked the question, 50 to 65 percent of Americans supported the CPA between 1974 and 1976, while only around one-third opposed it (the remainder did not understand it enough to have an opinion).[59] The Watergate scandal and Nixon's resignation in 1974 stiffened public sensitivity to underhanded business dealings (such as those that funded Nixon's secret slush funds), bolstering support for the measure in principle. Moreover, the 92 "Watergate babies" elected in the fall of 1974 altered Congress's ideological makeup, and 7 of the 35 senators who had filibustered the CPA left office by January—including Sam Ervin, who retired.[60] Anti-CPA lobbyists understood well that their strategy had to extend beyond legislative parlor tricks and actually reshape public debate about the bill they hoped to defeat permanently.

Anti-CPA lobbyists knew that convincing legislators to oppose the bill would require vigilance and unity, but maintaining a united and committed front frequently proved challenging. CPA supporters—including Nader groups and Republican Virginia Knauer, who stayed on in the Ford administration as director of the Office of Consumer Affairs—published the names of several companies that actually supported the bill, hoping to win over undecided members of Congress. CIWG lobbyists retorted quickly that such firms represented a distinct minority and continued to argue, quite accurately, that the majority of major firms and business associations steadfastly opposed the CPA.[61]

But business opposition frequently appeared broader than it was deep—CIWG lobbyists worried that the bill did not arouse a sufficient sense of urgency among many businesspeople. After all, a decade of strong consumer protection laws, both state and federal, had not yielded apocalyptic results. Perhaps key legislators and their business allies would lose interest in fighting the CPA or even come around to accepting some version of it. Combatting such potential lethargy required convincing businesspeople that the proposed bill represented a far more dire and devastating federal intrusion on business than anything that had come before. Making that case, the Chamber of Commerce published a short opinion piece called "Consumer Protection Agency: You Think You Don't Have a Stake in It? Well, Read On." The article stressed the proposed agency's subpoena and interrogatory power and conjured horror stories of over-regulated small business owners brought to ruin by a dictatorial "Administrator of the CPA," who would monitor their every move. Invoking the same vague yet ominous specter of intrusive "big government" that had animated conservatives' ideological opposition to the New Deal state for decades, the Chamber of Commerce claimed that the CPA would create a bureaucratic nightmare for small business owners.[62]

Because their grip on the levers of power in Congress remained so tenuous, anti-CPA lobbyists focused on the public square as much as the cloakrooms of the Capitol. And by 1974, as consumer advocates prepared to ride the liberal tailwinds toward another pass at the bill, no business group was better suited to take on that dual challenge than the Business Roundtable. The wealth and resources of its member corporations created a vital infrastructure for organized informational campaigns. In late 1974, the Roundtable inaugurated its public relations campaign against the CPA by paying $25,000 to the highly reputable Opinion Research Corporation (ORC) of Princeton, New Jersey, to survey Americans about consumerism and consumer legislation.[63] According to the ORC's poll, 75 percent of respondents opposed "setting up a Federal Consumer Protection Agency over all existing consumer-related agencies." Instead they favored "making existing agencies work better and more effectively." Thirteen percent of those surveyed said they did favor the CPA, but half of those respondents changed their minds when the pollsters told them the cost would be "at least $60 million for the first three years." Moreover, most poll respondents claimed that the best recourse for faulty products lay with retailers, manufacturers, or better business bureaus, not with the federal or state government.[64]

The ORC poll thrilled the Roundtable's executives, who heard exactly what they had wanted to and quickly disseminated the results to their allies in the CIWG for widespread distribution. Firms and associations wrote editorials, cartoons, position papers, and talking-point memos for newspapers across the country during the winter and spring of 1975, creating a blitz of apparently scientific anti-CPA publicity. Most anti-CPA propaganda reaffirmed business's longstanding arguments about the link between regulations and inflation, business failure, and job losses but now included the exciting news that the American public finally shared those sentiments. Over the next three months, the White House collected 245 editorials that invoked the "75 percent" figure as proof that members of Congress who backed the CPA in fact ignored the will of the people.[65]

Perhaps the best-known pundit who used the ORC data to attack the CPA in the spring of 1975 was a certain B-movie star and avowedly conservative former California governor. The Roundtable's survey, Ronald

Reagan wrote, confirmed that most people opposed creating "another big bureaucracy which is bound to mushroom (don't they all?)." Moreover, Reagan insisted, the consumer movement's complaints about business were largely unfounded, since "[o]nly 13 percent said they had been treated 'unfairly' as consumers." Linking antiregulatory politics to populist complaints about liberal elitism, Reagan claimed that the CPA bill would merely create a forum for "professional consumerists" and "bureaucrats" to make policy by "equat[ing] their own opinions with those of all consumers."[66] Tapping into the same antistatist and antibureaucratic rhetoric that had shot him to national political prominence during the Goldwater campaign in 1964, the future president relied on his celebrity among conservatives to spread the message further than business associations could by themselves. The day Reagan's editorial appeared, GMA president George Koch slyly forwarded it to a staffer in the Ford White House, noting, "The pressure continues to mount for a veto." Given rumblings that Reagan would challenge Ford for the Republican nomination the next year, Koch's message resounded clearly.[67]

The ORC poll provided excellent ammunition for anti-CPA conservatives and business groups, but, as consumer advocates pointed out, it reflected a profound polling bias. An investigation by the Congressional Research Service of the Library of Congress lambasted the polling company for asking a loaded question that posited a false choice between creating "an additional Consumer Protection Agency" and making simple improvements to existing agencies. "By repeating the point that the agency would be 'additional' four times in the course of the question," the report concluded, "this item may well have focused the concerns of the respondents on *the size of government bureaucracy*. It is consequently very difficult to know if respondents were reacting to the Consumer Advocacy Agency or if they were expressing their dismay with the complexity and size of government [italics added]." Indeed, differently phrased Gallup and Harris polls showed that the CPA remained popular.[68] Senator Charles Percy of Illinois, a liberal Republican and fervent CPA supporter, claimed that his "own mail and conversations with consumers around the country" convinced him that the bill was both good policy and a political winner.[69] But for business lobbyists, the ORC poll provided a valuable lesson: framing mattered, and public antipathy toward government bureaucracy provided a politically useful countermeasure against antibusiness bias.

The ORC survey constituted only part of a multipronged public relations blitz against the CPA bill. Advertising in *Reader's Digest*, for example, the Business Roundtable mocked the consumerist notion that companies should make perfect products. "Have you ever stopped to think what it would cost to build a television that would 'never' fail or wear out? Many thousands of dollars."[70] The anti-CPA movement also led to political cartoons, such as one that depicted the agency as an obese, over-bearing mother figure, locking the consumer in a bear hug and declaring: "I'd just love ya to death!" The cartoonist commented: "Just what we need. . . . Smother Love" (see figure 5.1).[71]

This cartoon and dozens more portrayed the CPA as an emasculating threat to individual choice, while others adopted a more menacing tone and cast the proposed agency as an all-seeing "Big Brother." In the years to come, such invocations of the "national nanny" formed an increasingly prominent part of conservative critiques of regulation, including, quite prominently, efforts by the FTC to regulate advertisements during children's television programming in the late 1970s. As FTC chairman Michael Pertschuk observed, that meme spread deeply throughout political culture, manifesting in such stalwart organs of the "liberal establishment" as the *Washington Post*. Longstanding conservative attacks on heavy-handed consumer regulation thus gained increased prominence through the CPA battle, and the basic message was simple: bureaucratic meddling would wreak havoc on producers and, by extension, consumers.[72]

Even as business activists deployed advertisements, editorials, and cartoons to weaken public support for the CPA in general, they also honed their arguments about the bill's details in an effort to win points with specific legislators. The proposed legislation's treatment of labor unions, which business lobbyists believed was hypocritical and unfair, provided perhaps the most fruitful line of attack. In the original version, the CPA administrator's jurisdiction would have extended to the NLRB on issues "directly concerning a labor dispute involving wages or workplace conditions affecting health and safety." That is, the CPA could theoretically have ruled *against* workers' interests if it judged that they conflicted with consumers' interests (by driving prices up, for example). In need of support from organized labor after the failed efforts in 1970 and 1972, the CPA's supporters in Congress removed that language from the 1974 and 1975 versions, leaving the NLRB beyond the CPA's purview. According to Senator Sam Ervin, this "labor exemption" would apply "whether or not the CPA administrator might determine that these [activities] could result in a substantial effect on the interests of consumers."[73] For business lobbyists as well as conservative politicians like Ervin, this change smacked of unscrupulous deal making and liberal favoritism to labor. Michigan Republican Robert Griffin, long a critic of union privilege but otherwise disposed to support consumer issues, voted against the bill because he believed that exempting the NLRB meant the CPA catered to "special interests."[74] This fixation on the "labor exemption" thus represented a shrewd tactic by corporate lobbyists, at least on the margins.

Figure 5.1. In May 1975, as conservative pressure grew for President Ford to veto the Consumer Protection Agency, *Richmond Times-Dispatch* editorial cartoonist Carl E. "Chick" Larsen lampooned Ralph Nader's plan as an overbearing mother. Courtesy *Richmond Times-Dispatch* and the Special Collections and Archives at Virginia Commonwealth University.

Although consumer issues attracted tremendous support, labor remained as divisive as ever.

Yet despite the CIWG's massive public relations blitz and intense lobbying, the proposed Consumer Protection Agency remained popular with the public and retained significant support in Congress as the bill ran the legislative gauntlet once again in 1975. Without Ervin to lead another filibuster, CIWG lobbyists failed to prevent cloture when the Senate considered the bill in the spring of 1975. Indeed, one executive at the NAM complained that "Consumer militants have been busy telling Senators and the Administration that 'business has given up the fight.'"[75] Heading into the summer, the House appeared poised to approve the measure as well, and all eyes turned to the only remaining obstacle in its path: the newly installed holder of the presidential veto, President Gerald R. Ford.

The Slow Death of the CPA

Ascending to the presidency under unprecedented circumstances in the summer of 1974, Gerald Ford encountered a deeply divided, angry, and distrustful country. The national nightmare of Watergate, combined with military failure in Vietnam, the energy crisis, and inflation, had bred widespread discontent, which Jimmy Carter would later term "a crisis of confidence." The voting public, as White House pollster Robert Teeter commented to Chief of Staff Dick Cheney, was "more alienated and more cynical than at any point in modern times." Widespread public animus, Teeter claimed, extended to "the government, businesses, unions, school systems, media, churches, and even stores where people shop." But this variety of targets shared a vital common feature: they were all *big*.[76] At the heart of America's malaise in the mid-1970s was a classical critique of concentrated power and inaccessible, unaccountable, undemocratic elites. Fear of "bigness" cut both ways in debates between business leaders and consumer advocates, as each camp tagged the other as "Big"— "Big Business" on one hand and "Big Government" on the other. In the short term, the public aimed its anger over Watergate squarely at corrupt politicians like Nixon and former vice president Spiro Agnew, as well as their greedy corporate benefactors, rather than the federal government. Over time, however, conservative politicians, intellectuals, and activists successfully used that discontent to build a powerful critique of bureaucracy and, by extension, government itself. The story of the endgame for the Consumer Protection Agency legislation brings into sharp focus the way some conservatives—particularly organized business lobbyists— linked populism with antigovernment sentiment in the interest of weakening the regulatory state.

Like many moderate Republicans, Gerald Ford had supported the CPA earlier in the decade, but in the spring of 1975 the president found himself torn. In April, the new Senate—without Sam Ervin in it—broke an anti-CPA filibuster and passed the bill, sending it to the House of Representatives. With liberal ranks swelling with Watergate babies, House approval seemed certain and business lobbyists pressured Ford for a veto. On one hand, Ford deeply respected the opinions of business leaders, and knew he could ill afford to alienate conservative and business-oriented voters. On the other, as the head of the Republican Party, Ford bore the brunt of public criticism over the cronyism and corruption that Watergate had exposed. Senator Robert Dole, Republican from Kansas (and Ford's future running mate), urged the president to take a centrist path by proposing a politically acceptable alternative policy.[77] White House advisor Bill Baroody Jr. agreed, warning that an outright veto would paint Ford as "reactive, negative, anticonsumer and a 'tool of big business.' "[78] Splitting the baby, however, just might work.

To reconcile the consumer movement's demand for representation with business's insistence on less bureaucracy, Ford thus proposed a series of "Consumer Representation Plans," which would require the heads of regulatory agencies to analyze their operations and demonstrate that they properly represented the "consumer interest." Although presented as a compromise, Ford's suggestion completely discounted Ralph Nader's fundamental concern about the *process* of regulatory governance, since simply telling agencies to look out for consumer interests did nothing to prevent regulatory capture. Moreover, the proposal in fact reinforced the false choice that the Opinion Research Corporation poll had proposed between creating a new super-agency and "making existing agencies work better."[79] Yet despite protestations from consumer groups, such distinctions proved difficult to explain to many voters, and Ford's alternative to the CPA served its most important political function: it provided cover for legislators, and the president, to oppose the CPA while still insisting with some plausibility that they cared about consumer protection.

In September 1975, Ford announced that he would veto the CPA if it passed the House. In response, CIWG lobbyists identified 84 persuadable representatives and launched a full-court press. O. Pendleton Thomas, CEO and chairman of B. F. Goodrich and chairman of the Business Roundtable's consumerism task force, beseeched the group's 150 members to use their gravitas to lean heavily on those wavering lawmakers, and their lobbying bore fruit in November. Although the House of Representatives passed the CPA bill, the small margin—208 to 199—meant no chance to override a presidential veto.[80] In a bitter irony, consumer advocates had finally achieved passage in both houses of Congress, but they decided against reconciling the two versions only to see their bill vetoed, and so the CPA once again ended up in the legislative waste bin.[81]

With the 1975 vote, the anti-CPA coalition finally succeeded at more than manipulating parliamentary procedure, even though its ultimate victory had rested on the threat of a veto. At long last, business lobbyists could boast that their message had begun to sink in, as support for the CPA began to soften even among Congress's most liberal members, especially the Watergate babies. Indeed, nearly a third of the new Democratic House members voted against the CPA in the fall of 1975. Typical of this group was freshman representative Christopher Dodd (D-CT), who had run for office on a platform of price controls, environmental protection, and other liberal causes. Unlike his father, Senator Thomas Dodd (D-CT), who had voted for the CPA in 1970 just before retiring, the younger Dodd decided that a new, autonomous agency would only add "a new layer of bureaucracy" to the federal government. While he agreed that corporations often captured regulators, Dodd embraced Ford's Consumer Representation Plan alternative, arguing that Congress should redress the imbalance of power *within the existing structure*.[82] Dodd's language, if not his sympathies, exactly mirrored the coordinated message of business lobbyists. More important, the freshman legislator calculated that business's message would resonate with his upper-middle-class constituents in the Connecticut suburbs.

The defeat of the CPA bill in 1975 thus represented a significant, if incomplete, triumph for organized business groups. The NAM, for example, which had rated the bill one of its "major national legislative issues" and lobbied hard against it, praised the "united business community" for stopping the CPA.[83] "The surprising shift in Congressional sentiment," its leaders boasted, "was the fruit of more than five years of intensive and effective action by the NAM organization in concert with individual members and a host of national, state and local business associations."[84] But business lobbyists knew they had failed to achieve a knockout punch. The CPA retained majority support in Congress and in public opinion polls. When Jimmy Carter narrowly defeated Gerald Ford in 1976, the political calculus changed yet again. No longer able to count on a presidential veto, corporate lobbyists knew they would have to stop the bill directly on Capitol Hill.

The advent of the Carter administration in January 1977 marked a new beginning for the CPA's supporters. For the first time in the bill's long legislative history, the man in the White House had actively campaigned for the measure and positioned himself as a friend of the consumer in the tradition of his Democratic predecessors, Kennedy and Johnson. Indeed, one of Carter's first acts as president was to reappoint Esther Peterson— longtime consumer advocate, advisor to Kennedy and Johnson, and one of the CPA's original architects—as Special Assistant for Consumer Affairs. Peterson's explicit mandate was to shepherd the Consumer Protection Agency through Congress and to Carter's desk.[85] All she needed was a simple majority in the House and a filibuster-proof majority—amended from 67 to 60 in 1975—in the Senate.[86]

The CPA's supporters and opponents all knew the stakes were high. Writing to a state-level consumer leader, Ralph Nader warned: "If big business can defeat this simple yet compelling idea, they will be encouraged to defeat the entire consumer agenda, nationally and locally, with all that implies against the health, safety and economic well-being of all Americans."[87] For their part, business lobbyists realized that they faced an uphill battle, given the new political environment. By 1977, James Ferguson, CEO of General Foods, had taken over the Business Roundtable's consumerism task force. Imploring member CEOs to remain vigilant and active, he claimed that the "effectiveness of our 'grassroots' campaign could make an important difference in what we believe will be an extremely close vote."[88] In terms of resources and energy, however, business opposition to the CPA had reached the height of its power. More than four hundred companies and trade associations, including the Roundtable, had joined the CIWG, allowing the ad hoc group to coordinate public information campaigns and lobbying strategies on an ever larger scale. As before, larger and wealthier corporations and associations took the lead writing editorials, white papers, cartoons, and advertisements, which the CIWG distributed broadly. The Business Roundtable even hired a public relations company, North American Precis Syndicate, to write negative ads and articles about the bill. Business lobbyists in turn used those pieces, clipped out of newspapers and magazines, to demonstrate public opposition to the bill.[89]

Ironically, business lobbyists' arguments against the CPA actually reflected the same antistatist populism preached by the bill's *supporters*. All sides agreed that wasteful and bloated government bureaucracy drove up prices and ultimately hurt consumers. The salient question remained whether the proposed CPA would make that situation better or worse. Critics portrayed it as "yet another" layer of bureaucracy.[90] To the contrary, Nader insisted, the agency would be "a bureaucracy fighter, prodding other agencies to be responsive to consumers." Yet even in making that case, consumer advocates like Nader consistently framed the CPA as a solution to the problem of government regulation, effectively conceding that, as Ronald Reagan would famously state, "government is the problem."[91]

That mixed message presented challenges to the bill's defenders. As Esther Peterson later recounted, CPA backers struggled to explain the bill to voters because it targeted the process of governance rather than immediate consumer problems. "[W]e didn't say that we were going to see that your zipper's repaired, or that your car was going to be repaired," Peterson explained, but that there would be "a structure for taking care of these questions."[92] Jimmy Carter himself perpetuated the confusion.

On the campaign trail in 1976, Carter had railed against the excesses of big government, promising to halt "the proliferation of new agencies, departments, bureaus, boards and commissions because they add more to an already confused federal bureaucratic structure." But as for the Consumer Protection Agency? "This agency, in my opinion," Carter hastened to add, "is different."[93] Articulating exactly *how* it was different became the greatest public relations problem for the bill's supporters.

CPA supporters further compromised their intellectual arguments for the bill by relying on individualistic and materialistic justifications for the legislation. Given the country's precarious fiscal and economic footing in the late 1970s, as well as their inherently populist worldview, they stressed the agency's relatively low cost. Indeed, at $15 million a year, the proposed CPA would cost just a little more than five cents for each of the 220 million people in America. Put another way, they claimed, a year's worth of effective consumer advocacy equaled "about 5 or 6 HOURS of the Department of Defense's annual budget." Perpetuating this pocketbook justification, the consumer organization Public Citizen organized a "Nickel Campaign" through which CPA supporters mailed the five-cent coins to Congress. (The irony that the coins bore the visage of Thomas Jefferson, secular saint of small-government populists, was likely lost on everyone involved.)[94] Of course, the Nickel Campaign's focus on the CPA's administrative costs completely discounted the substantive conservative critique that consumer product regulation generated high compliance costs for firms. Nonetheless, by engaging business lobbyists and other critics on the question of cost, the consumer movement made a strategic decision to embrace the materialistic and individualistic frameworks advocated by their opponents.

After a tough summer of airmail nickels, editorial wars, and intense personal lobbying, the CPA's future remained uncertain. Powerful and vocal opposition by the CIWG convinced the bill's supporters in the House to redraft the measure in October, offering a variety of incentives to undecided legislators. Although Esther Peterson believed she had just enough votes to pass it in the House (and that Senate passage would be easier), House Speaker Tip O'Neill (D-MA)—an ardent supporter—flinched at the last minute and pushed the vote back to the winter.[95]

On February 8, 1978, the House of Representatives voted on the CPA for the fourth time in as many Congresses. This time, without ambiguity, it fell to defeat, 189 to 227. Peterson's optimistic vote count had been scuttled, perhaps by the delay but certainly by the mounting pressure from organized business, whom consumer advocates quickly blamed for the loss. "This Congress is a wholly owned subsidiary" of American business, Ralph Nader railed.[96] "I am frightened for my country after seeing this demonstration of corporate power," declared Peterson. In twenty-five years in Congress, Speaker O'Neill announced, he had "never seen such extensive lobbying." Yet such a fixation on the *quantity* of business lobbying ignored its real *qualitative* achievement. Not only had CIWG lobbyists and major employers' associations mustered tremendous financial, logistical, and human resources, but they had also succeeded in shifting the dominant discourse, both in Congress and in the public square. As Mark Green, director of Public Citizen, conceded, the most common sentiment among legislators was: "I'm with you on the merits . . . but I can't convince my constituents that this bill is not a move toward big government."[97] The Consumer Protection Agency went down, after a decade of struggle, because organized business lobbyists had changed the conversation.

The American Consumer, Politicized

The final defeat of the Consumer Protection Agency at the hands of a well-oiled and sophisticated lobbying campaign by conservative business groups and corporate executives marked a sea change in consumer politics. In the course of less than ten years, the organized business community had taken what appeared to be a legislative slam dunk for public interest liberals and rendered it politically unviable. Along with their landmark victories against labor law reform and meaningful full employment guarantees, the death of the CPA marked the business movement's true coming-of-age in the late 1970s. United through national employers' associations, the business lobby generated common cause among executives from the Fortune 500 as well as small business owners, from moderates as well as antistatist conservatives, from northern and midwestern industrialists as well as segregationist southern Democrats.

The business mobilization against the CPA succeeded because it mixed sophisticated lobbying tactics with the enthusiasm of vast networks of political and intellectual allies, both of which encouraged prominent business leaders to deploy their own resources and political capital. As the battle wore on, corporate lobbyists honed their ability to read the national mood and frame their message around universal concerns, not narrow business issues. But they also realized that winning in Washington required the skillful manipulation of existing political fault lines. Industrial executives at the Business Roundtable, for example, understood that the greatest opposition to consumer and environmental protection regulations had come from the West and the South, where populist fears of an overreaching government largely reflected persistent antagonisms over racial politics. Although many of them personified the "eastern business establishment" to a fault, Roundtable executives worked hand in glove with populist southern conservatives like Sam Ervin and James Allen to mobilize the successful filibusters that twice thwarted the CPA's forward progress. In the first half of the twentieth century, many southern Democrats had joined the ranks of populist Texan Wright Patman to protect "the little guy" from corporate predation, but after the 1960s, business conservatives managed to undercut those alliances. Organizations like the Business Roundtable forged a strong alliance by finding common ground with populists by opposing an expansive federal government. Moreover, corporate lobbyists worked hard to capitalize on the growing schisms between various factions of liberals, targeting suburban professionals who, while supportive of consumerism in general, worried about government bureaucracy and felt less instinctive common ground with organized labor. In this light, particularly given the historic support for social regulations among northern liberals, the business lobby's success in persuading Watergate babies like Connecticut's Chris Dodd stood out as a singularly important achievement.[98]

Despite the demise of Ralph Nader's number one priority, however, consumerism—like environmentalism—remained a popular and potent force in American politics. Rather than inaugurate a return to nineteenth-century notions of laissez-faire capitalism, the conservative critique of the organized consumer movement operated in a much more nuanced manner, taking full advantage of two dueling political traditions: the primacy of the individual and the pursuit of equality and, by extension, opposition to unfair privilege. As cultural historian Lawrence Glickman has argued, conservatives—including organized business leaders—turned the tide against Ralph Nader by co-opting liberal language and aggressively portraying "professional consumerists" as yet another "special interest" out to gain favor from the state. And even as they demonized liberal consumer activists as weak and implicitly feminine, Glickman argues, conservatives also pushed notions of "laissez-faire consumerism" in the 1980s, lauding consumers as intelligent and independent, with no need for a smothering nanny state.[99]

This focus on economic self-interest ultimately formed a critical part of conservative policymaking in the Reagan administration, from regulation, as the next chapter explores, to issues like antitrust. As political scientist Marc Eisner has argued, historical debates about corporate monopolies in the United States focused on the inherent problem of "bigness," but during the 1970s and 1980s, policymakers concentrated more narrowly on the specific economic effects of price discrimination. Collective disadvantages, in other words, motivated conservative economists and policymakers far less than individual harm. The business community's ideological assault on the consumer movement thus resonated broadly. By eliding consumerism with business-oriented conservative values, this co-optation also helped dissolve the longstanding dichotomy between the "consumer" and the "producer" in popular discourse.[100]

But for the leaders of the organized business community, the legislative defeat of the CPA marked an incomplete victory. The drive to institutionalize the public interest movement through procedural reform to the nation's regulatory structure may have died in Congress in 1978, but the cultural and political forces that underlay its power remained. Indeed, while public interest liberals loudly bemoaned business's newfound lobbying prowess, the men at the heart of that movement saw far more work before them. Fresh from their recent string of policy victories, a growing number concluded that the time for playing defense was over. Rather than manipulate the levers of power in Washington to stop or water down legislation they opposed, many business leaders adopted a proactive posture by proposing and lobbying for much-needed change. Flexing their new muscles, organized employers' associations launched a major campaign to comprehensively reform the nation's regulatory structure.

CHAPTER 6

Uncertain Victory

BIG BUSINESS AND THE POLITICS OF REGULATORY REFORM

He has erected a multitude of New Offices, and sent hither swarms
of Officers to harass our people, and eat out their substance.
—Thomas Jefferson, Declaration of Independence (1776)

THE BUSINESS ROUNDTABLE HELPED DEFINE CORPORATE LOBBYING in
Washington, D.C., in the 1970s, but for twenty years the group also
maintained an office in New York City, where it kept its administrative
and strategic planning functions geographically separate from its lobbying. From its prehistory at the Links Club on 62nd Street, the Roundtable
bounced around Manhattan's hot real estate locations, including stints
on Wall Street, Broad Street, and Lexington Avenue. From 1978 until its
final move south in 1993, member CEOs and professional staff members,
particularly those who worked on nonlobbying issues like construction
industry negotiations, occupied a posh suite in the eight-hundred-foot
modernist skyscraper at 200 Park Avenue called the Pan Am Building
(known since 1992 as the MetLife Building).[1] High above midtown Manhattan, the Roundtable's leadership met frequently to establish policy positions, report on the work of a growing list of task forces and committees, and chart the group's future.

At one such meeting, on November 13, 1979, the group's forty-six-
member Policy Committee convened to debate a particularly heated and
divisive question: should the Roundtable support or oppose a bill to
guarantee federal loans to the Chrysler Corporation, a venerable auto-
maker and, until recently, a prominent Roundtable member? Since the
late 1960s, stiff competition from Japanese firms led by Toyota and Dat-
sun (later Nissan) had chipped away at the market share controlled by
Ford, General Motors, and Chrysler, and by the late 1970s, a decade of
economic turmoil had further undermined the U.S. automotive industry.
Amid high unemployment and spiking gasoline prices, Japanese companies offered smaller, cheaper, and increasingly higher-quality alternatives
to Detroit's gas guzzlers, and their competitive advantage received an
added boost from preferential financing and insurance policies from the
export-oriented Japanese government.[2] Chrysler, the smallest and weak-

est of the Big Three, felt the sting worst of all, and by 1979 the company found itself hemorrhaging cash and on the brink of collapse. Its chief executive officer, John Riccardo, announced in July that the company had lost $207 million in the second quarter, held nearly $4 billion in debt, and had more than $700 million worth of unsold cars sitting on its lots. Total losses for 1979 would reach $1.2 billion (approximately $7 billion in 2013 dollars), the largest recorded annual loss in American corporate history up to that point.[3]

Chrysler chief John Riccardo was the son of working-class Italian immigrants in New York. Trained as an accountant, he became president of the auto giant in 1970, where he worked closely with chairman and CEO Lynn Townsend to weather their industry's ever-growing travails. When Townsend retired in 1975, Riccardo replaced his former boss both as CEO and on the Business Roundtable's Policy Committee. Four years later, as his company faced imminent bankruptcy and failed to qualify for private bank loans, Riccardo prevailed on sympathetic lawmakers to draw up legislation for government-backed loans to save the company. Pushed by public bloodlust to "fall on his sword," in the words of many commentators, Riccardo stepped down as chairman in the fall of 1979, resigned his position with the Roundtable, and turned the CEO's office over to his recently hired company president, Lee Iacocca, who did not join the Roundtable.[4] Also the son of Italian immigrants, Iacocca had risen from the steel-working communities of western Pennsylvania to earn engineering degrees at Lehigh and Princeton before embarking on a managerial career at the Ford Motor Company, where in 1970 he became president under CEO Henry Ford II (also a member of the Roundtable's Policy Committee). In the spring of 1978, Ford fired Iacocca and soon thereafter retired (Ford's immediate successor, Philip Caldwell, joined the Roundtable's Policy Committee in 1981). As both president and CEO of Chrysler, Lee Iacocca immediately became the public face of a major lobbying campaign for a government bailout. President Carter and many lawmakers from both parties announced their support for government aid, but Iacocca knew that getting a bill through Congress would require massive public outreach, not least toward the powerful and organized business interests who threatened to stand in the way.[5]

Hat in hand, Iacocca approached his fellow business leaders and asked for their political support for the bailout. Among the nation's top chief executives, association heads, and other business-oriented policy activists, the "Chrysler situation" presented a major quandary. On one hand, many conservative-minded business leaders philosophically rejected the idea that the U.S. government should loan public money to a company that private financial markets had deemed unacceptably risky. Such government interference in the free enterprise system, many told themselves, represented exactly the threat they had spent the last ten years mobilizing against. In November, the chairman of the Roundtable's Policy Committee, Thomas A. Murphy, urged the group to respect the ideology of free markets and lobby against the bailout. Raised in Chicago, Murphy had earned an accounting degree from the University of Illinois in 1938 and immediately launched a lifelong career at the corporation he would ultimately lead as chief executive from 1974 to 1981—the General Motors Corporation, then still the undisputed worldwide leader in automobile production. Although Murphy's professional stake in his competitor's troubles might suggest an ulterior motive behind his purist pro-market stance, the GM chief in fact had long established himself as one of the Roundtable's more outspoken opponents of government involvement in the market. As Murphy put it, government meddling in free enterprise meant that "inevitably someone—maybe all of us—would lose our freedom."[6] But not all business leaders expressed the same zeal as Murphy to invoke moral hazard and throw Chrysler to the wolves. Indeed, some agreed with Michigan's moderate Republican governor William Milliken, who argued for a bailout in the interest of his recession-wracked state. Between the company itself and its suppliers, Milliken worried, hundreds of thousands of Michigan workers stood to lose their jobs. Letting the company go bankrupt, he concluded, "would be many times more costly to the state and federal government than properly drawn aid programs."[7] Even in the heart of automobile country, therefore, opinions varied widely.

As Iacocca toured the nation drumming up support for Chrysler's bailout, he relied on a variant of Milliken's cost-benefit argument with the general public and many lawmakers. To arouse sympathy and support from his fellow business leaders, however, he employed a different rhetorical strategy. Although scholars have attributed the bulk of Chrysler's disastrous record in the 1970s to bad management, Iacocca worked hard to paint his firm as an innocent victim of rampant overregulation by the federal government. Tapping into business leaders' most visceral anxieties, he argued that the crushing spate of social regulations—from the National Traffic and Motor Vehicle Safety Act of 1966 to the Clean Air Act Amendments of 1970 to the Energy Policy Conservation Act of 1975—had ruined his company. Although emissions and safety standards applied to all car makers, foreign and domestic, Iacocca argued that the research and development costs required to comply with them inflicted a particularly high burden on smaller companies like his—smaller, at least, compared to industry leaders Ford and GM. In short, Iacocca passionately insisted that Chrysler deserved a government bailout precisely because the government had caused its problems.[8]

In the end, Iacocca's pitch to business leaders failed. Under Thomas Murphy's leadership, the Business Roundtable's Policy Committee approved a position statement that "the broad social and economic interests of the nation are best served by allowing this [market] system to operate as freely and fully as possible." The NAM, where Chrysler was also a member, objected to the government playing favorites or, in the phrase that would become increasingly popular in the 1980s and 1990s, "picking winners and losers."[9] Yet although Iacocca failed to shore up any appreciable business support, he ultimately sold the plan where it counted most. In January 1980, Congress passed and Jimmy Carter signed the Chrysler Corporation Guarantee Act, which offered $1.5 billion in loans to the beleaguered automaker. Chrysler was far from the first large American corporation that, having run into hard times, found itself the beneficiary of government largesse. In 1970 and 1971, the Nixon administration engineered rescue packages for the Penn Central railroad company and defense supplier Lockheed Corporation, respectively, both of which eventually rebounded. Following their example, Iacocca also parlayed the government's loan guarantees into an effective revival and restored the company's profitability in just one year; indeed, Chrysler paid back its loans fully in 1983, seven years ahead of schedule.[10]

At the time of the bailout, many political activists within the business world and the burgeoning conservative and libertarian think-tank communities immediately cried foul. Conservatives like former treasury secretary William Simon, an ardent free marketeer who founded the Council for a Competitive Economy to lobby for "free competition, not political favors," charged Iacocca with the greatest of treasons against capitalism.[11] GM's Thomas Murphy, for his part, never backed down from his blunt, not to say uncharitable, decree of "No Federal bailouts." His vocal disgust with the plan, even after Chrysler's turnaround, became legendary among future generations of GM management.[12]

Yet despite such noisy complaints about the bailout itself, many corporate leaders remained sympathetic to Iacocca's arguments about the destructiveness of government regulations. In October 1979, NAM chairman John Fisher told the House Banking Committee that although his group opposed the bailout as a matter of principle, the NAM was a "friend of the Chrysler Corporation" and desperately worried about the "hundreds of businesses, many small and some large, which are in similar . . . circumstances." Bad choices by management may have played a part in Chrysler's troubles, Fisher conceded, but "the market-oriented economy has a way of disciplining such decisions." On the other hand, he claimed, excessive regulations had the opposite effect, thwarting the omnipotent hand of free enterprise. The market, according to Fisher, was "not capable of distinguishing between *voluntary* management decisions which prove to be wrong and therefore uneconomic and those decisions which management is *mandated* to make by government and which prove to be uneconomic and wrong [italics added]." In other words, American companies could successfully manage themselves or else they would go out of business. The far greater danger came from the "host of business regulations enacted by the Congress" that constituted a "form of taxation" and "an expenditure by the company as a condition for staying in business."[13]

A Tennessee native with a Harvard MBA, Fisher had spent his entire career at the Ball Corporation, a glass jar manufacturer founded in Muncie, Indiana, in 1880 that expanded into a major provider of aerospace goods and services in the mid-twentieth century.[14] As Ball's CEO, Fisher had witnessed firsthand the explosion of social regulations since the late 1960s, particularly environmental and workplace safety standards, and believed that the pace of such legislation was accelerating. "There have been at least 25 major pieces of regulatory legislation passed in the five years from 1974 to 1978," Fisher told Congress. Facing stiffer competition, depressed sales, and the high costs of regulatory compliance, companies had fewer profits to reinvest in research and development. Articulating the perspectives of the NAM's small and midsized members as well as large corporations like his own, Fisher decried the uneven effect of regulations. Even when "applied uniformly to an industry," he argued, "they tend to alter the competitive structure of the industry because the cost of compliance falls disproportionately on the smaller firms." Chrysler had fallen to the point where it demanded a government bailout precisely because it lacked the large budget to absorb the added cost of regulatory requirements. The vicious cycle of lower profits and higher costs engendered by social regulations, Fisher concluded, thus imperiled all of industrial manufacturing.[15]

The Chrysler bailout brought the business community's deep frustrations to the fore. To be sure, Chrysler's energetic campaign for government aid, like those of Lockheed, Penn Central, and myriad other corporations before it, clashed both ideologically and politically with the mantra of "free enterprise" around which business leaders had long mobilized. Some corporate leaders, like Thomas Murphy, took a hardline stance (albeit a self-interested one, given his position as head of a major competitor). Others, like Fisher, opposed the bailout more reluctantly, moved as they were by deep frustration over the government policies that had brought Chrysler to the brink of ruin. In an apologetic note to Iacocca explaining why he had voted against the bailout, another NAM director hinted that perhaps the entire debacle had a silver lining.

If business leaders could show the public that government regulations had in fact caused Chrysler's pain, they might yet achieve "the relaxation and reversal of the uneconomic, destructive and debilitating trend of overregulation which has so possessed our federal government in recent years."[16]

The debate over the Chrysler bailout within the business community highlighted persistent tensions over what "free market" solutions really should look like, as well as business's ongoing policy struggle with the liberal regulatory state. By the end of the 1970s, industrial lobbyists led by major employers' associations had notched a number of significant political victories and established themselves as powerful players in national policymaking. As the previous two chapters demonstrated, organized business groups, allied with conservative policy institutions and politicians, had successfully redefined public debates over inflation fighting, unemployment, consumer protection, and labor law. In the process, they played key roles in stopping the forward tide of liberal reform legislation and spreading a market-oriented, antiregulatory vision throughout American political culture. For many lobbyists and executives, however, such achievements represented only a starting point toward loftier goals: the severe rollback of environmental, consumer, and workplace regulations and the comprehensive overhaul of the regulatory apparatus. In pursuit of that agenda, business lobbyists waged a wide-ranging campaign against social regulations that extended from the stagflation of the mid-1970s well into the economic recovery during the Reagan administration.

In the end, however, their efforts led to only mixed results. While business leaders and their conservative political allies successfully recast the national conversation about regulations to focus on costs as well as benefits, their ambitious goal to undo the social regulations of the 1960s and 1970s came up short. Moreover, the contradictory debates over "free markets" dramatized through the Chrysler bailout exposed the challenges that conservative business leaders faced. Although a growing number of Americans shared conservatives' antipathy to "big government" by the end of the 1970s, most still favored bailing out Chrysler in order to save autoworkers' jobs. That fact signaled to business leaders that their liberal political antagonists remained strong and resilient. Indeed, the public's support for the bailout galvanized corporate leaders like John Fisher, who used Iacocca's claim that Chrysler had been regulated into bankruptcy to renew the attack on regulatory excess. Yet despite this enthusiasm, corporate lobbyists would discover that proactively reforming the regulatory regime would prove a much harder nut to crack than thwarting liberal legislation like the Consumer Protection Agency or labor law reform. By the Reagan years, the shifting political and economic environment, as well as the complex politics of regulation, conspired to place limits on organized business.

The Politics of Regulation in the Age of Limits

One of the great ironies of industrial leaders' steadfast devotion to reforming the regulatory state was that the campaign distracted their attention from the larger structural factors that were fundamentally reshaping American business, and indeed global capitalism. If Americans in the 1970s needed further convincing that the fount of prosperity they had enjoyed since the 1940s had come to a halt, Jimmy Carter drove the point home in his inaugural address, telling his fellow citizens that "even our great Nation has its recognized limits."[17] Although the American economy still loomed three times larger than its nearest competitor, Japan, the nation's unquestioned international dominance over industries like steel, oil, agriculture, and even automobiles had become a thing of the past. The rapid rise of German and Japanese manufacturers in the late 1960s flooded the global market, leading the United States to run nearly constant balance of trade deficits after 1971—only in 1973 and 1975 did Americans export more manufactured goods than they imported.[18] In response, the profitability of American industrial firms fell 40 percent between 1965 and 1973. The OPEC embargo of 1973–74 spawned the worst recession since the 1930s, pushing U.S. profitability down another 25 percent. Even after an anemic recovery during the Ford administration, profits in manufacturing remained significantly below their pre-recession levels. Unemployment hit nearly 9 percent during the 1975 recession and remained above 7.5 percent during the 1976 campaign, even as inflation hovered around 5 percent.[19]

As economic historians like Robert Brenner have argued, the crisis of profitability in American manufacturing resulted from overproduction by low-profit firms. Policymakers inadvertently abetted this process by stimulating aggregate demand, allowing low-margin manufacturers to remain in business by selling at high volume, as well as through financial deregulation that loosened restrictions on capital flows. Credit-market deregulation, as sociologist Greta Krippner has recently shown, encouraged corporations to borrow more and devote greater resources to investments and speculation in the financial markets at the expense of production.[20] Yet while industrial executives certainly understood these shifts in the international patterns of production and investment, they frequently overlooked their broader implications and maintained a narrow focus on domestic issues, especially regulatory policy. As the fierce debates surrounding the Chrysler bailout in 1979 demonstrated, executives and their conservative political allies strongly believed that their profitability crisis emerged directly from the spate of regulatory requirements that firms had to comply with, not from growing global imbalances. In their minds, the "malaise" of the 1970s vindicated their long-held arguments against government regulation and provided a perfect opportunity to refocus the national debate on its burdens.

Although business-minded conservatives had complained about regulatory excesses for generations, their campaign for comprehensive reform received a major boost amid the inflation crisis during the presidency of Gerald Ford, whose policy preferences aligned more closely with those of top business leaders than had those of his predecessor. As one participant in a White House business-government relations meeting gushed to presidential assistant Bill Baroody Jr.: "[F]or the first time since arriving in Washington, I felt that industry has the opportunity for valid and open discussion with the Administration."[21] Alcoa's John Harper and GE's Reginald Jones, both members of the Business Roundtable's Executive Committee, served on Ford's Labor-Management Committee, as did several other Roundtable members, including GM CEO Richard Gerstenberg and Walter Wriston of First National City Bank, and Heath Larry of U.S. Steel, who in 1977 became one of the NAM's most influential chairmen.[22]

Declaring the persistent rise in prices his top domestic priority, Ford addressed a joint session of Congress six weeks after taking office to roll out his inflation-fighting agenda, including the much-derided "Whip Inflation Now" (WIN) slogan. In addition to targeting specific inflationary pressures in the food and energy sectors, Ford laid out a broader agenda of reform for the nation's regulatory system. At a recent summit, the president explained, business leaders and economic experts had displayed "very broad agreement that the Federal Government imposes too many hidden and too many inflationary costs on our economy." To check those costs, Ford called on Congress to appoint a National Commission on Regulatory Reform "to undertake a long-overdue total reexamination of the independent regulatory agencies." When Congress showed no sign of taking up his charge, Ford proclaimed by executive order the next month that all new regulations must include an "inflation impact statement" and that the director of the Office of Management and Budget (OMB) would evaluate all such statements and determine which rules "may have a significant impact upon inflation."[23]

Ford's Executive Order 11821 created the first mandatory system of cost-benefit analysis for regulations and, at first blush, appeared to reflect many of the aims of the Consumer Protection Agency then making its way through Congress. Like many business leaders, the president frequently invoked the image of the struggling consumer to make the case against excessive and costly regulations. "All too often," Ford told members of the Chamber of Commerce, "the Federal Government promulgates new rules and regulations which raise costs and consumer prices at the same time, to achieve small or somewhat limited social benefits."[24] But such a superficial confluence of goals belied the profound philosophical and political gulf between Ralph Nader's and Gerald Ford's visions of pro-consumer regulation. As the previous chapter argued, Nader believed that regulatory capture and bureaucratic inefficiencies compromised consumers' well-being, either by driving up costs or by leading to unsafe products, but he fundamentally supported the principle of regulation in the public interest—that government policy should place public safety, worker health, and the environment ahead of private profits. Business conservatives, on the other hand, begrudgingly accepted that Americans wanted safe products and a clean environment but urged policymakers, as they had for years, to weigh those social needs clearly against the tremendous costs they entailed. Regulations, they maintained, inevitably drove up costs for producers, contributing not only to inflation but also to unemployment, pressures on profit margins, and the decline of American manufacturing competitiveness. In reality, regulations rarely operated in such a simplified manner; indeed, many of the rules issued by regulatory agencies actually *improved* American firms' competitiveness by requiring their goods to conform to other countries' regulatory requirements, or otherwise making them more efficient and marketable. Nonetheless, most business leaders viewed the issue in far more narrow terms. Enshrining their perspective into law, Gerald Ford jettisoned the public interest movement's goal of improving regulatory effectiveness in favor of reducing the overall burden.[25]

Business leaders greeted Ford's policy with unmasked enthusiasm. Although the idea of a centralized review of regulations focused on cost-benefit analysis had originated with Army Corps of Engineers construction projects during the Johnson administration and expanded informally to include OMB oversight over environmental rules under Nixon, Ford's executive order formalized the concept for the first time and fundamentally reframed policy debates over regulation.[26] Within weeks of the announcement, the Business Roundtable's Policy Committee appointed DuPont CEO Irving Shapiro to chair its new task force on regulation. Shapiro, the son of Lithuanian Jewish immigrants to Minnesota and the first nonmember of the Du Pont family to lead the venerable chemical company, embraced his new role with gusto.[27] Lauding Ford for casting "the spotlight on the mass of government regulations that increase costs for no good reason," Shapiro urged all Roundtable members to send him a "listing of harmful or unnecessary regulatory practices by any arm of

Figure 6.1. In 1976, the National Association of Manufacturers printed this image on the cover of its "Documentary of the Over Regulation of Business." Typifying many business leaders' exaggerated claims about the deleterious effects of regulation, the cartoon depicts American industry as Gulliver, tied down by myriad regulating Lilliputians—from "Labeling Lords" to "Carcinogen Kids"—as legions more flood down from Congress, itself flanked by massive government bureaucracies. Courtesy of Hagley Museum and Library.

government." Armed with a growing list of anecdotes and cost estimates by member CEOs, Shapiro urged both the administration and business-friendly members of Congress to enact specific legislation to place further restraints on government regulators.[28]

The Business Roundtable's enthusiasm for regulatory reform reflected its long-held animus toward social regulations, both because of compliance costs and, more personally, because such rules implied that business could not be trusted to serve the public good on its own. Liberal reformers agreed with the latter assessment. According to consumer advocate Joan Claybrook, who headed the Consumer Federation of America in the 1970s and worked on public interest legislation like the CPA, "Social regulation took decisionmaking out of the hands of corporate managers and socialized it. . . . Public interest groups essentially democratized the decision process and put something other than profit into the equation." Corporate leaders like Shapiro recoiled because such regulations, by their very nature, purported to substitute government expertise for corporate autonomy.[29]

As the Roundtable trained its sights on the costs of social regulations, a parallel yet distinct political critique developed amid the economic strife of the 1970s that, by the end of the decade, would fundamentally reconfigure several major industries. This "deregulation movement" targeted economic regulations in the transportation, telecommunications, energy, and financial services industries. The regulatory structures that governed such industries had largely developed during the Progressive and New Deal periods amid economic uncertainty, price collapses, and business failures, as well as public outcry over natural monopolies and their unchecked power to command high prices. In many cases, policymakers enacted industry-specific regulations at the behest of corporate leaders who sought protection from competition and the perils of market forces and counted on government agencies to impose order and predictability on their operations by establishing barriers to entry, fixing prices, and determining routes and zones of operation. As historians David Moss and Michael Fein have shown, public interest activists helped shape certain aspects of the Progressive Era regulatory regime, particularly regarding broadcast communication, which largely served the public good throughout most of the twentieth century. In other key industries, however, economic regulations largely favored the entrenched private interests who helped construct them. It was precisely that system of private privilege for highly regulated industries that the "deregulation movement" critiqued and sought to unmake in the 1970s.[30]

The drive for economic deregulation came not from business lobbyists but from a political and intellectual movement that united free marketeers and liberal social reformers. The movement's intellectual godfather, conservative University of Chicago economist George Stigler, forcefully articulated an economic theory of regulation in 1971 that upended policy debates. Rather than promote a public purpose by restraining capitalism's disastrous patterns of creative destruction, Stigler argued, regulation served the exclusive interests of private actors by reducing competition and consumer choice, as well as by inflating unjustified profits. Antistatist conservatives picked up Stigler's theory to inveigh against regulation's threats to market freedom and the twisted inefficiencies of cartelization. At the same time, New Left scholars of the "corporate liberalism" school levied compatible complaints, finding that private interests systematically thwarted the public good by capturing the legislative process to their own ends. Liberals like Ralph Nader, Senator Edward Kennedy, and jurist Stephen Breyer extended this reasoning to argue that regulatory capture begat excess profits at the expense of consumers, workers, and smaller firms. Moreover, they claimed, the logic of regulation meant that capture would always result eventually, even if policymakers took special efforts to establish legal and structural barriers between regulated firms and government regulators. Uniting ideologically diverse players, the deregulation movement thus gained strength from the common belief that economic regulations privileged some companies unfairly and at great cost.[31]

During the late 1970s, this coalition engineered a remarkable wave of statutory deregulation. The Airline Deregulation Act of 1978 paved the way for the disintegration of the Civil Aeronautics Board (CAB), which had established route prices and entry barriers for commercial aviation since the 1930s. The Railroad Revitalization and Regulatory Reform Act of 1976 and the Motor Carrier Act of 1980 similarly loosened the Interstate Commerce Commission's control over railroads and long-haul trucking, although the commission itself continued to exist until 1995. The Federal Communications Commission (FCC) likewise amended its rules to permit greater competition in the telecommunications industry, paving the way for the end of the American Telephone and Telegraph Company's monopoly over long-distance telephone service. Finally, the Depository Institutions Deregulation and Monetary Decontrol Act of 1980 removed federal restrictions on savings account interest rates and permitted bank mergers.[32]

Despite the momentous nature of this legislative juggernaut, the very economic theory that underlay the deregulatory movement also predicted—accurately—that business leaders, however committed to the principles of free enterprise, would play only a bit part in the drama. Since economic regulations privileged existing corporations by limiting competition, the fiercest resistance to deregulation often came from regulated companies like Delta and Eastern in the case of airlines and AT&T in the case of telecommunications.[33] Many of the CEOs of those corporate giants, particularly AT&T's John deButts, played influential roles at the Business Roundtable, which not coincidentally refrained from taking a position on any deregulatory bills. Despite their traditional embrace of overt free-market ideology, the NAM and the Chamber likewise remained on the sidelines.[34]

Business leaders' reluctance to lend their lobbying weight to economic deregulation typified the extent to which social and economic regulations operated according to distinct political and economic logics. As political scientists and interest group theorists have long pointed out, economic regulations exposed fault lines within business, since their effects benefited one group, generally well-established firms, while disadvantaging competitors and upstarts. Social regulations, on the other hand, frequently cut across industries, affected firms of all sizes and regions, and produced few notable "winners." Although occasionally firms that boasted technological superiority in complying with regulations—a cleaner production process, for example—could use social regulations to their competitive advantage, more often such regulations provided a clear and compelling rallying point for industrial leaders by defining a common enemy. Thus while economic regulations tended to divide the business community, social regulations provided an important solution to the collective action problems that frequently hampered efforts to organize firms and industries politically.[35]

Although the campaigns to reform economic and social regulations constituted distinct political projects, public and scholarly debates frequently conflated them, creating a discursive complexity that worked to business groups' advantage. Conservative and business-oriented politicians like Gerald Ford blurred the structural distinctions, lumping agencies like the EPA and the CAB together when blaming regulations for the "tremendous efficiency losses, reductions in productivity, and unnecessary costs to the economy," as Ford told members of the Chamber of Commerce.[36] Liberal deregulators like Ralph Nader and Edward Kennedy, although motivated by their concern for consumers, workers, and social justice, often co-opted the rhetoric of market-oriented conservatives by bemoaning the high costs of economic regulations, essentially making business leaders' case for them. Such framing, crafted through political expediency, created an opportunity for business activists to shift the public debate from economic to social regulations by invoking the same language of costs and inefficiencies. In the late 1970s, the campaign for comprehensive regulatory reform legislation, spearheaded by the Business Roundtable, developed from the rhetorical and political openings the deregulatory movement created.

REGULATORY REFORM

During the presidential election of 1976—the first since the oil crisis, the ensuing recession, the Watergate scandal, and the official end of the war in Vietnam—both Gerald Ford and Jimmy Carter tried to capitalize on voter cynicism by casting themselves as foes of "Big Government."[37] Both charged that the federal bureaucracy had grown bloated, cumbersome, and costly, and each promised wholesale change. While their specific positions reflected their party orientations—Ford catered more explicitly to business's argument that regulation abetted inflation while Carter stressed regulation's pernicious effects on consumers and workers—both candidates favored sweeping reform to both economic and social regulations.

Carter, the victor that year by the fourth narrowest popular vote margin in the twentieth century, originally pinned his hopes for minimizing cumbersome bureaucracy associated with regulation on the passage of the Consumer Protection Agency. The CPA, its boosters hoped, would fundamentally restructure the operation of regulatory agencies and thus reduce regulation's cost and complexity while preserving goals like a clean environment, safe and honest products, and fair and healthy employment practices. But the Carter administration and the public interest lobby ultimately failed to overcome business and conservative lobbyists' claims that the CPA represented more "big government" bumbling that hurt producers—especially small businesses. With the CPA dead in the spring of 1978, Carter joined his predecessor Ford in taking unilateral executive action where the legislative process had failed. On March 23, he issued Executive Order 12044, which extended and expanded Ford's Order 11821 by directing all executive agencies to construct "simple and clear" regulations that "did not impose unnecessary burdens on the economy, on individuals, on public or private organizations, or on State and local governments."[38]

Although the business community had lobbied exhaustively against the CPA, corporate leaders hailed Carter's executive order as a positive alternative. As the self-appointed leader of the campaign for regulatory reform, the Business Roundtable took a particular interest. Frank Cary, CEO of IBM, chaired the Roundtable's task force on regulation (having succeeded Irving Shapiro, who became the group's chairman in 1976) and expressed his organization's approval in a letter to Carter. The fifty-seven-year-old Californian who had earned an MBA at Stanford before joining IBM thirty years earlier praised the executive order for requiring that new regulatory analyses "include an evaluation of the potential *economic impact of the alternative approaches* and final regulation proposed [italics added]." Business leaders agreed, said Cary, that sensible regulatory analysis should not presume that all regulations were beneficial or cost-effective; they should start from the premise that other, cheaper paths to similar results existed. "I expect [this clause] was the subject of much criticism by other groups and individuals," he concluded. "You obviously persevered in this case, and we applaud you for it."[39]

Yet Roundtable executives, while encouraged by what they called Carter's "open, orderly, cost-conscious approach to regulation," believed that the president's executive order did not go far enough. First, it applied only to agencies housed within executive departments, such as OSHA, which existed under the aegis of the Department of Labor. Independent agencies, most notably the EPA, did not fall under its purview. Moreover, the order came with a sunset provision; if it were allowed to expire in June 1980, Roundtable members feared, "relatively little of lasting effect would be achieved." To combat the groundswell of regulation—some ninety government agencies that issued, according to the White House, approximately seven thousand distinct rules each year—business leaders urged more comprehensive reform and hoped to use their newfound lobbying clout proactively.[40]

Buoyed by Carter's executive order, the Business Roundtable redoubled its public information and lobbying campaign for regulatory reform. To convince lawmakers to require economic impact statements by all regulators, Roundtable executives believed that they needed concrete, specific proof of the excessive cost of regulations. In 1978 the group commissioned the accounting firm Arthur Andersen to conduct what Frank Cary called "an independent, objective study" that would for the first time "measure by accounting methods the direct, incremental costs of regulation with a methodology applied consistently across agency and industry lines." In the spring of 1979, Arthur Andersen released *Cost of Government Regulation*, which reported that in 1977, forty-eight companies had spent $2.6 billion to comply with regulations from six departments and agencies. Although the report did not analyze all the regulations those companies faced, the cost it calculated represented more than 10 percent of their capital expenses, nearly half of their tax obligations, and 15 percent of their after-tax income. According to Cary, "Measurement of the benefits of regulation was beyond the scope of this study, as was the measurement of total regulatory costs." Even though the study only considered "the tip of the regulatory cost iceberg," Cary hoped that the discovery of "wasteful and non-productive" regulations would strengthen the movement for reform.[41]

For the Roundtable, the Arthur Andersen study presented an opportunity to do more than simply dramatize the cost of government regulations (although it certainly did that). By measuring with some degree of precision and methodological rigor the exact cost of regulation—even in a limited context—the Roundtable CEOs hoped to buttress their case for mandatory economic impact analysis. Since the group's founding in 1972, Roundtable leaders had deliberately presented themselves as pragmatic, not ideological, defenders of business and economic growth. Rather than devolve into intemperate bromides against the injustice of social regulation, as many conservative politicians, academic economists, and policy institute analysts were prone to do, the chief executives sought to project a measured, reasoned appeal. Cost-benefit analysis, Cary told the Senate, did not represent "an indirect attack on the principle of government regulation." Indeed, he acknowledged, "certain regulations are necessary." Rather, the study merely demonstrated that "some new regulatory programs . . . developed over the past decade . . . have caused excessive and unintended costs." Richard Wood, CEO of Eli Lilly pharmaceuticals, also spoke for the Roundtable and implored the House Judiciary Committee to consider the link between the cost of regulation and the sickly national economy. "Some critics," he explained, "believe that the cost of regulation is irrelevant, but that is a difficult position to maintain publicly in a period of inflation and declining productivity."[42] By positioning themselves as a partner to Carter's calls for less expensive, less wasteful regulation, Roundtable executives hoped to create a political consensus around their conviction that the current regulatory state simply cost too much.

By early 1979, the Roundtable had joined a diverse coalition of business groups, lawmakers from both parties, and public interest activists united by the Carter administration to work on a comprehensive regulatory reform bill. According to the title of an early version, the legislation aimed to "make regulations more cost-effective, to ensure periodic review of old rules, to improve regulatory planning and management, to eliminate needless legal formality and delay, [and] to enhance public participation in the regulatory process."[43] The coalition, which cut across standard alliances in Congress, reflected the populist rhetoric that animated both the consumer movement and conservative groups, including— however ironically—business associations. Indeed, the spirit of the legislation echoed Nader's dedication to Jeffersonian ideals by directly challenging the prerogatives of regulatory decision makers. Moreover, the campaign proceeded from the same beliefs that underlay Carter's embrace of economic deregulation in the aviation, energy, transportation, and telecommunications industries: regulations—whether of markets or "externalities"—generated economic inefficiencies and higher prices. But the push for regulatory reform represented shrewd politics as well as principle, particularly for the president. Carter's domestic policy advisor Stuart Eizenstat, for instance, argued that by taking the initiative on comprehensive reform, the president could set the terms of the debate and provide "a necessary and responsible alternative to reactionary anti-regulatory bills" advocated by congressional conservatives.[44]

Throughout the winter of 1979–80, Carter's regulatory reform bill made steady legislative progress. By the spring of the election year, however, a series of political obstacles began to fracture the once-strong coalition. One important clash concerned a provision known as the Bumpers Amendment. Named after Democratic senator Dale Bumpers of Arkansas, the amendment would have removed the judicial presumption that a regulation was valid until proven otherwise. Its supporters, including the Roundtable, argued that current law inherently favored regulators over firms and sought to level the playing field. Business interests and government regulators should "stand on equal footing," according to a Roundtable report.[45] Backed by the conservative American Bar Association, Roundtable executives lobbied the Carter administration to support the Bumpers Amendment, while labor and consumer groups bristled at the idea. Given business's superior financial resources, liberals argued, a "level playing field" in the courts would actually put regulators—and the public interest—at a disadvantage. In the end, key members of the administration agreed and Carter came out against the amendment.[46]

A second point of contention surrounded a proposal to insert a "regulatory flexibility" clause into the legislation, requiring regulatory agencies to grant smaller firms greater exemptions and leniency. Invoking the same logic he used to explain why pollution standards hit Chrysler harder than General Motors or Ford, NAM president John Fisher argued that smaller manufacturers paid a disproportionate cost to comply with regulations. "[I]t is a myth that regulations protect the 'little guy,'" Fisher opined in an article. "The time and excessive cost required to meet federal regulations favor existing, established companies over new and expanding entrepreneurs." But while the small business community clamored for the flexibility clause, and Jimmy Carter concurred, the big-business interests at the Business Roundtable rejected the claim. "[D]ifferentiated treatment of business based on size," Eli Lilly CEO Richard Wood told the House Judiciary Committee, should not be the guiding force at regulatory agencies. To be sure, he conceded, "certain aspects of regulation . . . can impose disproportionate burdens on small businesses," but the law should not compensate by creating regulations that were "unfairly discriminatory" against *large* firms. Just as administrative distinctions between large and small companies under the Nixon price-control regime had impeded pan-business cooperation in the early 1970s, so too did the issue of regulatory flexibility divide the movement under Carter.[47]

During the summer of 1980, the Business Roundtable CEOs and their staff members worked furiously to promote their plan to comprehensively reform regulatory procedures. The entire Roundtable membership, including paid lobbyists, public information specialists, and CEOs themselves, used their personal connections with members of Congress to urge a floor vote on the existing bill, including the Bumpers Amendment. "[T]ime is short in the 1980 session," Frank Cary wrote to the Roundtable members, "and major obstacles remain. . . . Two years of effort could be lost, and the opportunity might not come again." Although he expressed confidence that the public's antigovernment, antibureaucracy mood begat a political atmosphere that was uniquely conducive to reform, Cary warned that the present bill had to pass quickly to create a "permanent mechanism for bringing economic considerations to bear on the regulatory process and for holding regulators accountable for their actions."[48]

At the White House, however, liberal advisors grew increasingly alarmed at the business community's lobbying offensive and concluded that the bill, in its current form, simply conceded too much to business interests. Labor unions and public interest groups agreed, insisting that the Bumpers Amendment and business's focus on cost-benefit analysis betrayed a philosophical opposition to the very notion of regulation, not a progressive commitment to smarter, more effective regulation. As written, many liberals argued, the bill placed the burden of proof on agencies themselves to show that regulations were "cost-effective" and thus undercut the entire notion of proper social regulation. Facing such opposition from the left, as well as the travails of the reelection campaign that he would ultimately lose to Ronald Reagan in November, Jimmy Carter backed away from regulatory reform in the fall of 1980. In August, Congress passed a more narrowly focused Regulatory Flexibility Act that granted special considerations to smaller firms, despite the Roundtable's reticence. Signing the separate law, Carter managed to simultaneously appease small business groups and provide himself political cover to walk away from the omnibus bill. Despite continued pressure from the Roundtable for comprehensive reform, Congress adjourned without moving on the measure.[49]

The Business Roundtable's leaders regretted their failure to proactively lobby for "meaningful regulatory reform legislation" that institutionalized cost-benefit analysis, but they took solace that the general trajectory of regulatory politics had moved decisively in their direction and away from the public interest vision during the Carter administration. Although liberals in the White House pushed the president back from overtly business-friendly omnibus legislation, Carter signed a second less sweeping, yet quite significant, regulatory reform measure during his lame-duck period. The Paperwork Reduction Act, passed over the objection of many career bureaucrats and regulators, streamlined information gathering, clarified reporting requirements for companies, and reduced bureaucratic bookkeeping in both the federal government and the private sector. More important, the act created the Office of Information and Regulatory Affairs (OIRA) within the OMB and charged it with reviewing proposed regulations to ensure that they corresponded with administration goals. Although little fanfare greeted OIRA upon its arrival, especially from the embittered business lobbyists at the Roundtable, the new government agency marked a clear rejection of Ralph Nader's dream of a truly independent and apolitical arbiter of regulation. Locating the review process squarely in the OMB under the supervision of the president, OIRA provided a check against regulatory excess but one that could easily become dominated by political appointees. Under the incoming Reagan administration, that seminal, if largely overlooked, administrative change helped set the stage for the increased politicization of regulatory policy.[50]

REGULATORY RELIEF

The presidency of Ronald Reagan, long the standard-bearer for arch-conservative critiques of New Deal policies from welfare to regulation, presented both opportunities and challenges for business's regulatory reform campaign. During the Republican primary in 1979 and 1980, many prominent business leaders had looked askance at the former California governor, worried that his social conservatism and radical proposal for deep cuts in personal income taxes were out of step with business's fundamental economic priorities. Indeed, many Republican executives favored Texas oil man John Connally, the Nixon administration veteran with extensive personal contacts among the nation's business elite. When Connally's bid flamed out in early 1980, the pro-business mantle fell to his fellow Texan George Herbert Walker Bush, the former CIA director, UN ambassador, and member of Congress who gave Reagan his most serious challenge and wound up rewarded for his perseverance with the vice presidency.[51] Although the major business associations stayed above the partisan fray during the election, preferring to work with the existing Congress and incumbent Carter administration on issues like regulatory reform, many corporate leaders expressed qualified optimism after Reagan's victory. The chairman of the Business Roundtable, Exxon CEO Clifton Garvin, pledged that the business community would "work closely and cooperatively with the new administration," even as he urged caution among excessive optimists who hoped that "President Reagan will be able to solve the nation's economic problems almost overnight."[52]

Nonetheless, the new president's invective about the debilitating effect of government bureaucracy on private enterprise reinforced the mantra that organized business groups had chanted for years. As a matter of political philosophy, if not coherent policy, Ronald Reagan's famous inaugural decree that "government is not the solution to our problems; government *is* the problem" struck a resonant chord. At the Business Roundtable, Frank Cary handed the reins of the Task Force on Government Regulation to John Opel, his successor as CEO of IBM. Noting that "1981 promises a more favorable environment" for the comprehensive regulatory reform legislation that failed in the waning months of the Carter administration, task force members worked closely with Reagan's transition team during the interregnum and provided what Opel called "detailed recommendations for a 1981 Executive Order on Regulation and a regulatory reform legislative agenda."[53]

In the winter of 1981, the new administration hit the ground running with a vigorous set of policy proposals that aimed to put into practice

Reagan's longstanding admonitions about the foibles of liberal government. In addition to a major proposal to cut taxes and reduce social welfare spending, the president quickly built on his predecessor's regulatory reform initiatives. First, he ordered a moratorium on all regulations that agencies had written but that had not yet gone into effect. Shortly thereafter, he issued the far-reaching Executive Order 12291, which mandated cost-benefit analysis for all rules whose compliance costs totaled more than $100 million per year and required agencies to choose the least expensive regulatory alternative. The order also dismantled the Council on Wage and Price Stability, created by Ford to monitor inflation, and transferred its staff to OIRA. Eliminating COWPS simultaneously ensured that his administration would never entertain a return to wage-price controls and, administratively as well as symbolically, confirmed the Republican's belief that inflation fighting should be explicitly linked to reducing regulatory overreach.

Finally, Reagan created the Presidential Task Force on Regulatory Relief, chaired by Vice President Bush, to monitor and review regulation and make recommendations to the director of OIRA, who would oversee agencies' compliance with the new regime.[54] The task force's very name indicated the new view on regulation that the Reagan administration espoused: no longer was regulation something to be "reformed," as everyone from Gerald Ford to Ralph Nader had urged; instead it was an insidious oppressor from which the free market demanded "relief." In that spirit, Vice President Bush asked Roundtable chairman Clifton Garvin to send him a top-ten list of "specific regulations [that] could be changed in order to increase benefits or decrease costs, thereby generating greater *net* benefits for all."[55] For the next two years, the regulatory relief task force operated as a clearinghouse for complaints, gathering anecdotes and personal testimony from businesspeople across the country who expressed outrage over the regulatory burden they faced. In a typical example, the Texas-based safety director of chemical and aerospace manufacturer Whittaker Corporation claimed that in the aftermath of "an explosion of one of our plants," OSHA inspectors "descended upon us like 'Storm Troopers.'" During the government's investigation into the accident, he continued: "I was in 'Hitler's Germany', 'Stalin's Russia' and 'Hirohito's Japan', and I didn't like one damn thing that I saw from these people."[56]

Reagan's executive order turned the tables on the entire regulatory regime, shining the critical spotlight not on regulated companies but on government regulators. In the same spirit, the administration also worked with Republican leadership in the Senate, as well as several interested Democrats, to revive the push for major regulatory reform legislation. The Senate Judiciary and Government Affairs Committees debated bills that would have made permanent Executive Order 12291's requirement that all regulations, from both executive and independent agencies, provide proof that their benefits clearly and mathematically outweighed their costs. The Judiciary Committee's bill also included the Bumpers Amendment, which would remove the judicial presumption in favor of regulators, as well as a two-house legislative veto of new rules (which White House officials opposed because they worried that it would compromise executive authority). As policy historian James Anderson has noted, "this bill would have been quite objectionable to the Carter Administration."[57]

In the fall of 1981, once the intense negotiations over Reagan's tax cut, discretionary budget reductions, and defense appropriations had concluded, the lobbying effort to pass the regulatory reform bill kicked into high gear. Backed by environmental, consumer, and labor groups, liberal Democrats urged a more moderate bill that exempted many independent agencies from cost-benefit analysis. In a rare instance of overt partisanship, IBM's John Opel, chairman of the Roundtable's task force on regulation, openly chastised the Democrats on the Senate Government Affairs Committee, whom he accused of trying to weaken the bill. The Roundtable coordinated closely with George Bush's Task Force on Regulatory Relief, the NAM, the Chamber of Commerce, and other trade associations, orchestrating an indirect lobbying campaign reminiscent of its successful campaigns against labor and public interest legislation. Chief executives and public relations specialists drafted position papers and talking points, staff members coordinated mail blitzes to local and state-level business organizations, and lobbyists located specific members of Congress whom they hoped to persuade with evidence of popular support for the bill.[58]

In March 1982, the Senate voted 94 to 0 in favor of the omnibus regulatory reform package, and the lobbying turned to the House. In the lower chamber, however, a coalition of public interest and other liberal organizations and their political allies managed to keep the legislation bottled up in the Rules Committee until Congress recessed for the midterm elections.[59] In October, the Roundtable joined eleven other business associations at a rally in Washington to inaugurate a final push for the bill, combatting what the Roundtable described as "intense, well-organized opposition to the legislation by 22 anti-reform interest groups, some labor groups and several Democratic committee chairmen in the House." These twelve groups, the Business Coalition on Regulatory Reform, implored local business leaders, CEOs, trade association lobbyists, and corporate Washington Representatives to "contact members of the Rules Committee and all Members of the House during the recess, *prior to the elections*" and convince them to pass the House's version during Congress's lame-duck session. "A small incremental investment over the next 2 months," John Opel told Roundtable CEOs, "could push the bill through the House, to the Senate, and on to the President's desk, and avoid the need for another 2 or 4-year effort on this legislation."[60]

However, despite earnest support from the conservative, antiregulatory occupant of the White House, the business community's proactive lobbying campaign crashed on the rocky shores of political reality. In November 1982, a disgruntled American electorate registered its disapproval with Ronald Reagan's first half-term in office, delivering 27 additional House seats to the Democrats, who then commanded a 50-vote majority, and emboldening continued liberal resistance to Reagan's economic agenda. Reflecting on the election's consequences for his party, House Speaker Tip O'Neill (D-MA) gloated: "There's no question that we'll have more of a voice than we've had in the last year and a half." Although business lobbyists continued to press for a vote on the comprehensive regulatory reform bill, the House leadership still managed to keep it locked in the Rules Committee until Congress adjourned.[61] A year later, despite a renewed push for the legislation, the Roundtable reluctantly acknowledged that it foresaw "little prospect for early action in Congress on comprehensive regulatory reform" and announced that it would redirect its primary lobbying efforts to other issues. More bluntly, leaders at the NAM chided the Reagan administration for "slowing down" on regulatory reform after going "one-third of the way down the road" by executive order.[62]

While Reagan's commitment to comprehensive procedural reform certainly waned, none could doubt the long-term effect his presidency had on the politics of regulation. In 1983, Vice President Bush's Task Force on Regulatory Relief officially dissolved itself, taking credit for implementing regulatory changes that, it predicted, would save $150 billion over the next ten years. (As the earlier discussion of the Arthur Andersen study indicated, actually calculating the costs or savings of regulation is a deeply fraught task, so it is impossible to know how accurate that prediction was.) The task force left its administrative duties to the OMB, which became during the early 1980s the permanent locus of regulatory review, according to OIRA deputy administrator Jim Tozzi.[63] In addition to procedural changes, the president also achieved lasting results—and notoriety among his critics—through "deregulation by administrative appointment." Over the course of his term, Reagan routinely, and quite deliberately, selected agency and department heads who shared his animus toward the regulatory project in general and thus achieved weaker enforcement, and lower compliance costs, by sheer dint of their inactivity. His selection of conservative mining advocate James Watt as secretary of the interior, anti-environmentalist Ann Gorsuch Burford as EPA administrator, and libertarian economist James Miller as chairman of the Federal Trade Commission (FTC) convinced many critics that the president preferred to "deregulate" simply by posting foxes to guard the henhouse.[64]

By centralizing regulatory review within the powerful OIRA and institutionalizing antiregulatory sentiment through both the Bush task force and his administrative appointments, Ronald Reagan significantly reformed the nation's regulatory system without the omnibus legislation that business groups so fervently lobbied for. As the conservative editorial board of the *Chicago Tribune* reflected, the central pillars of the new social regulation—the EPA, OSHA, the Consumer Product Safety Commission, and the FTC—remained "alive and well," but the administration had reined in the most egregious instances of regulatory excess. (The editorial writers cited, for example, "such insanity as the requirement that two separate individuals count dump trucks at federal highway projects and the proposal that the steps of swimming pool slides be covered with diagrams showing how to climb the steps of swimming pool slides.")[65] Business lobbyists' inability to completely squash social regulations thus formed part of the broader failure of conservative and libertarian activists to "undo" the New Deal by eliminating government agencies. For example, although Candidate Reagan had resolutely vowed to abolish the Department of Energy and the Education Department, both created under Jimmy Carter, President Reagan expended no political capital toward such a rollback. Nevertheless, the tenor of political debate moved decisively toward the rhetoric business conservatives had long employed, even though the institutional apparatus of the new social regulations remained in place during the so-called Reagan Revolution. Taking an uncertain victory, the Business Roundtable in 1983 indefinitely postponed its quest for comprehensive regulatory reform.

REGULATORY POLITICS IN A POST-CRISIS WORLD

The recession of 1981 and 1982, which capped more than a decade of economic upheaval and left the American manufacturing community severely rattled, ultimately yielded to recovery just in time for Ronald Reagan to declare "Morning Again in America" and proceed on his way to overwhelming reelection in 1984. But the economic traumas of the 1970s had marked more than a downturn in the business cycle. As the final two chapters of this book explore, the American economy, even in the bullish 1980s, differed markedly from what had preceded it. New industries and sectors—particularly technology, finance, and retail—came to dominate the business landscape as manufacturers struggled and production moved increasingly offshore. As a political class, American consumers retained their high expectations and their powerful hold on policymakers, even as the ethos of economic conservatism and its faith in unfettered, deregulated markets grew increasingly widespread. As the political and economic terrain shifted decisively under corporate leaders' feet, organized business groups struggled mightily to shift along with it.

In the realm of regulatory politics, the long-awaited recovery from inflation, recession, and energy crisis meant that conservative complaints about the high costs of regulations lost some punch. Perhaps nowhere was this change more evident than in the realm of environmental protection, both in the United States and around the world. From its origins in the late 1960s, the environmental movement had always been a global phenomenon, and by the 1980s "Green Party" politicians began to gain seats in municipal and national legislatures throughout the industrialized world. In response, the leaders of large corporations—particularly those that increasingly operated across national boundaries—took note, modifying their policy positions and operations. In Japan, for example, the heads of major industrial conglomerates and international traders recognized that their success in foreign markets would require greater sensitivity to the regulatory regimes as well as the cultural expectations of the countries with which they increasingly did business. In 1991, after a decade of prosperity in which Japanese firms invested heavily abroad, the Keidanren—the Federation of Economic Organizations that represented approximately one thousand large Japanese corporations—adopted a Global Environment Charter to tout its commitment to global environmentalism.[66]

Just as Japan's industrialists invoked the mantra of environmentalism to improve their public appearance and bolster their compliance with global regulations, so too did their American counterpart, the Business Roundtable, strategically shift its position in the 1980s. Although environmentalism had long constituted one of the group's chief focal points, Roundtable executives in the 1980s understood that clean air and water regulations remained politically popular. Dogmatic opposition in the name of profits, particularly in an economic recovery, promised to alienate far more Americans than it attracted. Although business leaders could not defang the EPA, they injected their market-oriented ethos into the debate by promoting the virtues of voluntary, private sector environmental stewardship. In 1984, for example, the Roundtable's Environmental Task Force commissioned dozens of case histories to document steps taken by large industrial companies such as U.S. Steel, whose chairman David Roderick headed the task force, to clean the nation's air and water. Showing off how "U.S. industry has applied expertise and experience to solve environmental problems," the Roundtable reasoned, would mitigate calls for new, stricter, and more costly pollution standards. Indeed, in April 1990, dozens of Roundtable companies publicized their enthusiastic participation in the twentieth anniversary of the first Earth Day. Such a public celebration of environmental stewardship and embrace of the principles of voluntary self-regulation—the mantra of uncountable antiregulatory industrialists since the nineteenth century—masked the group's continued hostility to command-and-control regulation. In the late 1980s, Roderick and the Roundtable lobbied unsuccessfully against another round of Clean Air Act Amendments, this time addressing acid rain and global climate change, two issues on which many Roundtable members remained skeptical. Invoking the successful economic argument from the crisis years of the 1970s, Roderick charged that the legislation "would be the most expensive environmental legislation ever adopted and the least cost effective," potentially leaving "three to four million jobs . . . adversely affected." Despite such protestations, the amendments passed in 1990, and the Roundtable's dire predictions failed to materialize. Business's longstanding vitriol remained, but in a changed economic and political climate, its effectiveness had been muted.[67]

The Roundtable's embrace of environmentalism despite its lingering opposition to strict regulation found an echo in another strategic change over the issue of consumer product regulation. United corporate lobbying in the late 1970s had successfully halted the public interest movement's momentum and the regulatory reform campaign in the early 1980s, while failing to achieve all of business leaders' aims, further limited the reach of regulatory agencies. As consumer and environmental activists felt their influence with state and national lawmakers wane, many turned to the judicial system for redress. As a result, the number of consumer-based mass tort cases rose dramatically in the 1980s. Such lawsuits, in which a large number of people claim harm from a single source, such as a toxic substance released by a private company or a dangerously defective product, posed a new type of threat to business leaders. In response, politically active business leaders shifted the attention they had previously lavished on consumerism to the issues of product liability and tort law. The Business Roundtable, for example, dedicated substantial lobbying energy during the 1980s and 1990s toward a proposal for what its Tort Policy Task Force chairman called a "single, nationwide, uniform product liability law." Just as the failed regulatory reform proposal would have leveled the playing field by removing the presumption of validity from any rule issued by a federal agency, this law would have legally shifted the burden of proof in a tort case away from offending companies, reducing, according to the Roundtable, "litigation, large damage awards, and . . . [un]affordable liability insurance." Jettisoning conservative notions of states' rights, the Roundtable worked tirelessly—and ultimately fruitlessly—to nationalize mass class action lawsuits. However, although the debates surrounding tort law helped perpetuate the growing belief that American society was unusually or unreasonably litigious, the Roundtable and its allies failed to achieve significant reform of class action law.[68]

Despite the Roundtable's failure to win comprehensive regulatory reform and its subsequent struggles over the Clean Air Act Amendments and tort reform, the mobilized business community's decades-long campaign to refashion the American regulatory state achieved important victories as well. Around the world, the concept of regulation underwent substantial changes—procedural, theoretical, and political—in the last third of the twentieth century, and regulatory governance remains contested and contradictory. The United States emerged as an early adopter and clear leader in risk management and safety regulations for consumer products, workers, and the environment in the 1960s. In Western Europe, particularly among the members of the European Economic Community who would form the European Union in 1993, the push for such risk regulation began somewhat later but followed a different trajectory. While European countries lagged the United States in areas like automobile safety and emissions in the 1960s and 1970s, a shift occurred in the 1990s; since then, Europe has generally enacted stricter product regulations, particularly concerning genetically modified organisms and added hormones in food. To an important degree, this contrast exemplifies the success of conservative arguments in American politics and the ability of producers to frame regulatory issues in terms of consumer costs, skills honed during the fierce lobbying battles of the 1970s and early 1980s.[69]

To be sure, the deregulatory market-oriented ideas that shaped American politics constituted a global phenomenon; the logic of "neoliberalism" shaped regulatory, tax, and even criminal justice policy in industrial powerhouses as well as in developing countries. The Thatcher government in Great Britain, for example, took a famously hard line against labor unions and, in the name of promoting competition, liberalized key elements of its economy, especially telecommunications. France, Japan, and Germany also embarked on deregulatory projects in the 1980s, following the British and American examples. Yet, as political scientist Steven Vogel has argued, these experiments in "deregulation" proved incomplete at best; in many cases, they led to a proliferation of rules despite the allegedly "freer" markets. As in the United States, "deregulation" and "regulatory relief" frequently meant quite different things. Moreover, the persistence of corporatist arrangements in Europe and Japan helped ensure that business prerogatives remained balanced against other interests. In the United States, the political debates surrounding regulatory governance remained similarly muddled. The deregulatory impulse—propelled by both left-wing concerns about capture and right-wing arguments about competition and government interference—achieved lasting legacies, such as the liberalization of telecommunications and financial services, including the refusal by Democrats and Republicans alike to regulate high-risk trading practices like derivatives. And while OIRA and the Reagan administration's policies of regulatory neglect certainly reduced the compliance burdens many firms faced, the spirit of environmentalism and consumerism remained powerful. Although American business associations operated in a favorable political climate in the 1980s and did not face the same type of institutional constraints that compelled their counterparts in Europe and Japan to cooperate more with labor and public interest groups, they nonetheless failed to construct a coherent political and intellectual vision of regulatory reform.[70]

The politics of regulatory reform thus marked both a capstone and a turning point for the business coalition. As a matter of political organizing and message shaping, the campaign for comprehensive reform drew on a critique of liberalism and social regulations whose roots reached back to the earliest days of industrial capitalism. But business leaders' failure to achieve all their goals also signaled the limitations of their political power. After their major lobbying victories in the 1970s, the terrain of regulatory reform proved far rockier. As Roundtable executives and other corporate leaders quickly discovered, proactive lobbying in the American political system posed far greater difficulties than reactive lobbying. In the fight to reform regulatory processes, business groups struggled to maintain unity within the ranks, particularly when policy details exposed divergent priorities among small and large firms. Moreover, many members of the conservative intellectual and political establishment did not share the Business Roundtable's legislative priorities, even if they agreed ideologically with its goals. Those divisions allowed liberal opponents, who still retained vital political power, to thwart the business lobby's efforts, particularly through the types of procedures (such as keeping a bill locked in the Rules Committee) that business had used so successfully against public interest legislation only a few years earlier. The result was a mixed legacy for the quest to reform regulatory governance.

But regulatory reform was not the only issue that hampered business's organizational and intellectual unity in the early 1980s. As the next chapter argues, the explosive problems of taxes and the federal budget overran the politics of business during the Reagan administration, leaving a lasting imprint on the fate of the business movement.

CHAPTER 7

A Tale of Two Tax Cuts

> Practical men, who believe themselves to be quite exempt from
> any intellectual influences, are usually the slaves of some defunct
> economist.
> —John Maynard Keynes, *The General Theory of Employment,
> Interest, and Money* (1936)

BY THE END OF THE 1970S, the Chamber of Commerce of the United
States had much to brag about. "Business people are increasingly recognizing the need for both legislative and political action at the grass
roots—and improving their effectiveness at both," the group crowed in
1980. For example, despite predictions that the Congress elected in the
fall of 1974, right after Watergate, would be "overwhelmingly liberal and
anti-business," the Chamber declared victory on two-thirds of the 71 policy issues it tackled in 1975 and 1976. The 95th Congress elected along
with Jimmy Carter in 1976, it continued, "brought no better outlook for
the business sector," but "business people had now proved to themselves
and others what they could do." Out of 107 issues, the Chamber claimed
a win on 65 percent and a loss on only 12 percent. (The rest were split
decisions.) Finally, by 1978, the group boasted that businesspeople had
finally learned to couple "grassroots" lobbying with a major effort "to
elect leaders who will further advance the nation's economic interests."
In that year's midterm election, the group's political action committee,
the National Chamber Alliance for Politics, identified 83 races where it
found "a clear philosophical difference between the candidates and where
business participation [could] make the difference." Fifty of its candidates
won, helping the Republican Party chip away at Democratic majorities
by gaining fifteen seats in the House and three in the Senate. Looking
ahead to the 1980 elections, the country's largest business association
saw a great opportunity to begin "the task of getting our economic house
back in order."[1]

Yet the Chamber's leaders also saw significant challenges ahead. "The
economy is currently moving into a worse-than-average recession, and
the recovery, when it occurs, is likely to be shallow," reported the group's
chief economist in June 1980.[2] Indeed, the economic turmoil the United
States confronted dwarfed any problems of the previous forty years. The
short-term statistics were dizzying enough. Inflation again hit double

digits, propelled by a second oil crisis in the wake of the Iranian Revolution in 1979. Crude petroleum prices shot up 150 percent and the nominal average price of gasoline in the United States topped one dollar per gallon for the first time ever. Making matters worse, economic growth ground to a halt after newly installed Federal Reserve chairman Paul Volcker launched a radical three-year experiment with monetarism in the fall of 1979. By directly limiting the growth of the money supply, Volcker pushed the country into its third official recession in eleven years. Gross domestic product contracted by a record 9.9 percent in the second quarter of 1980, and interest rates fluctuated with maddening volatility. But the cyclical downturn and inflationary crisis marked only the tip of the iceberg. Long-term shifts in global industrial production underlay those difficulties, hastening the decline of U.S. manufacturing and adding new urgency to business leaders' calls for action. During the 1980s, these new economic dynamics would permanently redefine the contours of American capitalism and profoundly shape the organized business community.[3]

As the economic crisis unfolded, the political world turned its attention to the quadrennial tradition of the presidential election as Jimmy Carter fought for survival against former California governor Ronald Reagan. Adhering to their longstanding practices, the Chamber, the NAM, the Business Roundtable, and most other business associations remained officially neutral during the campaign. Nonetheless, when Reagan won a landslide electoral victory with slightly more than 50 percent of the popular vote, the men who had spent their careers clamoring for business-oriented fiscal policies appreciated the importance of the Republican triumph. To be sure, Jimmy Carter was a far cry from the labor-coddling, heavy-handed regulator that many conservatives feared he might be, and corporate lobbyists had achieved great success pulling him away from his more liberal advisors. All the same, Reagan's victory symbolized a powerful rebuke to much of the rhetoric and promise of modern liberalism, and most business leaders welcomed the arrival of an avowed conservative who preached an antistatist, antiregulatory gospel.

But the political ascent of conservative Republicans ultimately proved a mixed blessing for organized business leaders. Despite the new tenor of national politics, business conservatives soon found that the task of actually implementing their policy agenda amid the pluralistic contentiousness of the American political system was fraught with difficulty. As self-described political outsiders in the 1960s and 1970s, corporate leaders had united around vague yet passionate calls for "pro-business" policies—a hard line against labor power, tight fiscal policy, and opposition to price controls, social regulation, and national planning. Once conservatives took the reins of power, however, those ideological issues devolved into complex and often divisive policy debates. As this chapter argues, nowhere did those tensions flare more brightly than in conflicts over macroeconomic policy, especially over taxes.

The interlocking problems of taxation and the federal budget set the stage for the contentious politics of business in the 1980s. During the Reagan administration, ideological small-government conservatives clashed openly with the heads of manufacturing and other traditional capital-intensive business firms. In spite of their superficial common opposition to Keynesian demand stimulus and organized labor, these disparate groups of conservatives held sharply divergent priorities. Their struggle produced a tale of two tax cuts. One, supported by industrialists, aimed to revitalize manufacturing by providing incentives for investment and savings. The other, an antistatist quest to lower all taxes, garnered greater populist appeal. Although not mutually exclusive—both found a way into Reagan's tax reduction legislation in the summer of 1981— these competing visions marked an emerging schism within the ranks of conservatism. Although Ronald Reagan has achieved a lasting place in conservative lore as a foe of big government, a champion of entrepreneurs, and a tax-cutter nonpareil in American political history, his fiscal policies in fact engendered substantial conflict among conservative organizations, most notably the organized business lobby.

THE CAPITAL ACCUMULATION MOVEMENT

As business leaders, particularly industrial executives, mobilized politically in the 1970s, they rallied around the belief that liberal federal policies depressed profits and productivity by distorting managerial decisions and imposing undue costs. In earlier decades, as the Business Roundtable's newsletter explained in 1980, "new capital invested by business was spent entirely to finance growth." But during the 1970s, "with business responding to public concerns other than increased production, some of the new capital is channeled into other areas—providing safer, healthier working conditions, for instance, and protecting the environment." Every penny corporations had to spend to comply with social regulations, to pay the inflated price for supplies, to compensate a worker in excess of that worker's productivity, or to fund the federal government through corporate income taxes, business leaders argued, represented money they could not spend to improve their operating capacity and hone their competitiveness. The result was a dearth of capital investment in productive facilities. "To recover growth in productivity," a Chamber of Commerce brochure claimed, "requires a higher rate of personal savings and increased investments in modern and efficient equipment and technology."[4]

As profits continued to stagnate and productivity growth remained low, industrial leaders demanded a policy response. Among the most vocal advocates was Reginald Jones, successor to Fred Borch as chief executive officer at General Electric in 1972, who assumed his predecessor's role as a dominant force at the Business Roundtable and chaired the group's Taxation Task Force. The son of a steel mill foreman, Jones emigrated with his family from England to New Jersey as a boy yet retained his British accent and affected certain stylistic trappings that, according to his contemporaries, gave off a patrician air. After matriculating at the University of Pennsylvania with the hope of becoming a teacher in 1930, Jones transferred to the Wharton School of Business, from which he launched his career at General Electric as an auditor. During the 1950s and 1960s, the erstwhile lightbulb company founded by Thomas Edison reinvented itself as a conglomerate, expanding into such diverse fields as computers, nuclear energy, medical products, and financial services. As Jones rose through the corporate ranks, his acumen for financial accounting and broad-ranging business sense dovetailed perfectly with the corporation's larger objectives. He became vice president of finance in 1968 and president and CEO four years later.[5]

His background in finance and position at the helm of the country's leading conglomerate made Jones a particularly forceful ambassador for tax reform centered on capital accumulation. Addressing the Business Roundtable's 1975 annual meeting in Manhattan, Jones laid out the dire straits that American industry faced. In the previous twenty years, he explained, nonfinancial corporations had acquired enormous levels of debt to fund their operations. The trend had accelerated since the late 1960s, and such firms now owed, on average, "almost two dollars for every dollar of net worth." Over the next few years, GE's economists predicted, the nonfinancial sectors would require a total of more than $300 billion per year to pay for "plant and equipment expenditures and working capital." But given the disastrous state of the industrial economy, Jones continued, "[t]here is no way the industry is going to raise that kind of money under the present tax policies, unless it is to go deeper and deeper into debt—assuming it could find willing lenders."

"Facing these financial dilemmas," Jones told his Roundtable colleagues, "businessmen will simply seek to close the gap by lowering their overall capital requirements. You know this from your own experience. They will reduce their investment in plant and equipment; they will cut back inventory spending; and they will cut back their financial asset holdings. The result in all cases is reduced business activity, more unemployment, slower growth in productivity, and the kind of chronic inflation and stagnation that the American people won't stand for."

Figure 7.1. This four-panel cartoon, which graced the cover of the National Association of Manufacturers' "Tax Impact Report" in the late 1970s, succinctly expressed many business leaders' arguments about taxes. In the top two panels, high taxes force the factory to lay off workers, curtail output, and rely on inefficient and outdated machinery. Any combination of lower personal and corporate taxes, the bottom panels argue, would yield greater consumer spending, more hiring, and transformative reinvestment, ultimately paving the way for a prosperous future. Courtesy of Hagley Museum and Library.

"Therefore," he concluded, "we simply must have changes in the national priorities." First, he insisted, Congress had to reduce the federal budget deficit. By selling government bonds to cover its budget shortfalls, the federal Treasury effectively crowded private companies out of the debt market, Jones argued in the *Harvard Business Review*. Since the U.S. Treasury could always undercut corporate bonds on price, "business will have to go to the end of the line for leftovers in capital." The second key to avoiding the slow death of American industry, Jones told the Roundtable CEOs, lay in corporate tax policy. Only by "reducing the tax burden on industry"—and thus permitting companies to retain more of their profits—could business "generate the funds it need[ed] to restore health to this economy and provide future growth in jobs and income for the American people." Specifically, Jones exhorted his colleagues to promote tax reform that would "direct more of the nation's resources into the modernization and expansion of our productive capacity."[6]

Within a few years, advocacy by men like Reginald Jones spawned a political coalition in Congress dedicated to bolstering capital accumulation and industrial reinvestment by promoting the somewhat technical and dry concept of "accelerated depreciation reform." In the summer of 1979, a bipartisan and multiregional group of legislators led by New York Republican Barber Conable and Oklahoma Democrat Jim Jones introduced legislation in the House to speed up the schedule by which corporations could claim write-offs for capital expenses on their income taxes. "The proposed bill," boasted Theodore Brophy, the CEO of telecommunications giant GTE who had by then taken over the Roundtable's Taxation Task Force, "was arrived at after approximately eight months of discussion and negotiations, with the full participation of the business community."[7] Although the measure failed to become law during the Carter administration, it fast emerged as business's "top tax legislative priority," as NAM president Alexander Trowbridge described it in 1980, until Ronald Reagan incorporated it into his signature tax cut in 1981.[8]

The complex and arcane notion of using asset depreciation to encourage capital formation grew from the peculiar nature of corporate taxation and the role of deductions. Like individuals, corporations can deduct certain expenses from their taxable income. But since the goal of corporate taxation is to target profits, not revenue, the universe of potential deductions is far vaster, including such expenses as labor costs and equipment. To reduce taxable profits, corporate accountants thus seek to write off as many operating and capital expenses as they can. Since 1909, when Congress first passed a corporate income tax (technically an excise tax based on income until the ratification of the Sixteenth Amendment in 1913), policymakers recognized that the buildings and equipment that companies used would gradually wear out, lose value, and need to be replaced. To account for this fact, the first income tax laws permitted firms to set aside a "reasonable allowance" to replace such assets and deduct the cost from their tax burden, even if they did not spend money on the asset during a given tax year.[9] Beginning in 1934, the Treasury Department required accountants to spread out such deductions over what was called the asset's "usable life." Accountants and tax attorneys calculated a piece of equipment's worth and divided by the number of years the company could reap a financial gain from it, creating a system known as the "straight-line deduction."[10]

Since at least the 1940s, however, lawmakers recognized that they could manipulate this aspect of the corporate income tax code to encourage certain behavior by private firms without reducing taxes on corporate profits. During the run-up to America's entry into World War II, for example, the Second Revenue Act of 1940 created "accelerated amortization," which allowed companies to write off the entire cost of constructing factories to produce war materiel, even as the government raised overall corporate taxes on "wartime profits." During the postwar reconversion to a peacetime economy, similar provisions encouraged companies to invest in defense-related research laboratories that became integral to scientific development during the early Cold War. Finally, in 1954, tax reformers established a universal system of accelerated depreciation, which allowed a broader range of corporations to claim larger deductions earlier in the asset's life, thus reducing their taxes in the short term and freeing up funds for reinvestment. As historian Thomas Hanchett has argued, Congress intended the new system to spark capital investment in machinery and buildings among manufacturing firms, but by including commercial property as well, the law prompted a tremendous boom in real-estate development, especially suburban shopping plazas, in the 1950s.[11]

The business community strongly backed the 1954 reforms, as well as subsequent acts in 1962 and 1971 that further sped up depreciation schedules, arguing that Congress should accelerate the write-off schedules even more. Support was particularly strong among large, capital-intensive firms, especially extractive and manufacturing companies, which generally had higher ratios of capital expenses to operational expenses and thus benefited more from the write-offs. Smaller firms tended to prefer the simplicity of straight-line deductions, reasoning that the added administrative expense of paying more accountants to figure out their taxes did not justify the value gained by deferring tax payments. The real problem lay with what the NAM called the "myriad of rules, formulas and regulations" that beset the corporate tax code, including depreciation schedules that varied across more than 130 asset classes, including some but not all types of assets. As a representative for both large and small manufacturers, the NAM argued that if the tax code were simpler, smaller firms would also take advantage of the accelerated depreciation schedules and thus have more capital to reinvest in their enterprises.[12]

The legislation introduced by Barber Conable and Jim Jones in 1979, officially called the Capital Cost Recovery Act, sought to appease both large and small business interests by streamlining and accelerating asset depreciation. Backed by the Business Roundtable, the NAM, the Chamber, and many trade associations, the bill proposed just three classes to encompass all depreciable assets, with three corresponding time frames for write-offs. Companies could depreciate buildings over ten years, vehicles over five years, and equipment over three years. Such simplification earned the proposal its common shorthand: 10-5-3.[13]

10-5-3 inspired optimism among many business leaders because it focused lawmakers' attention on productivity and investment rather than sheer corporate profits. Indeed, Conable later wrote that he supported the bill precisely because it aimed at "improving industrial competitiveness by encouraging more investment in capital goods rather than reducing corporate taxes in ways that would increase profitability." "Profits," as the Chamber of Commerce reminded its members, remained a "four-letter word" for a good number of voters, and many lawmakers worried about appearing too beholden to wealthy business interests. Accelerating the depreciation of capital assets, however, reframed business's campaign for tax relief around productive capabilities and job creation. In a clever cloaking maneuver, the arcane accounting procedure reduced corporations' tax burden while avoiding the public scrutiny that would have accompanied direct reductions in the corporate tax rate. Such political framing, as well as the tremendous lobbying orchestrated by business groups, garnered the 10-5-3 legislation significant support in the summer of 1980, when the Roundtable confidently predicted victory.[14]

Accelerated depreciation was not to be, however, at least not under a Jimmy Carter presidency. After reading a Treasury Department estimate that the bill would reduce tax revenue by $50 billion, the president reversed his earlier support and came out against the measure because he opposed inflating the budget deficit by giving corporations a break on their taxes. In particular, Carter chastised the bill for unfairly privileging heavy industry and manufacturing—which he called "special interests"—at the expense of less capital-intensive industries, despite the bill's support from some small business groups. Without support from the White House or Treasury, the bill languished in the Ways and Means Committee and died. The push for accelerated depreciation, the backbone of the capital accumulation movement within the business community, would have to wait for another political moment.[15]

THE "SUPPLY-SIDE" TAX CUT

The campaign for depreciation reform has faded into the obscure recesses of America's collective political memory perhaps because tax accounting strikes most people as dreadfully boring but also because a far more widespread antitax movement overshadowed policy debates in the late 1970s. Like the business leaders who rallied around capital accumulation, the coalition for massive cuts to personal income taxes believed that lower taxes paved the way for economic stimulus. But the core support for cutting individual taxes lay outside the rarified air of corporate meetings and the *Harvard Business Review*. During the late 1970s, a combination of high inflation, prohibitive interest rates (thirty-year fixed mortgages averaged around 15 percent in 1980), and widespread antigovernment sentiment sparked a nationwide tax revolt. Taking their cue from California's Proposition 13 in 1978, which dramatically reduced property tax rates and slashed funds for government services in the process, tax reform campaigns took shape in more than twenty states. The antistatist populism that underlay this activism drew both intellectual and organizational support from the spread of the "supply-side" movement.[16]

During the late 1970s, a coterie of conservative economists and policy-makers hailed themselves as proponents of "supply-side economics," a theory, they argued, that directly opposed Keynesian demand-side economic management. While Keynesians promoted the use of taxation and government spending to manipulate aggregate demand and steer a path between inflation and unemployment, supply-siders argued that economic policy should instead focus on stimulating *supply*: the companies that produced goods, the workers who put labor into that production, and the investment needed to expand the volume of goods and services generated by the economy. To its ardent defenders, such a shift in policy focus represented a revolutionary break with the politics of welfare, corporate subsidies and bailouts, regulations, and labor unions. According to David Stockman, a young Republican from Michigan who entered the House of Representatives in 1977 and later ran Reagan's Office of Management and Budget, the "supply-side solution . . . required the radical dismantling of state-erected barriers to economic activity."[17]

Despite such revolutionary talk, "supply-side doctrine" was in truth an artful repackaging of conservatives' longstanding critique of demand-oriented fiscal policy and reflected a social vision reminiscent of nineteenth-century producerism. Stockman's complaints about market dislocations and preferential incentives would have resonated sonorously at nearly any business association meeting since the late nineteenth century. Moreover, supply-siders' claim that high taxes discouraged work and investment resurrected the basic economic philosophy of business tycoon Andrew Mellon, the treasury secretary who helped engineer substantial reductions in tax rates under three Republican presidents in the 1920s. Ironically, mainstream commercial Keynesians had long argued that lower taxes generated economic stimulus both by increasing consumption and by encouraging productive investment; liberal Democrats made such arguments forcefully, for example, during the debates that led to the Kennedy/Johnson tax cut in 1964. Nonetheless, while supply-side economics may have been derivative and unoriginal as a policy vision, it gained substantial traction as a polemical and rhetorical tool. Low-tax evangelists like Jude Wanniski, the *Wall Street Journal* editor who did more than anyone else to proselytize the doctrine, successfully aroused public passion and quickly constituted a powerful political coalition.[18]

For all their angst over government spending, subsidies, and welfare, the self-identified supply-sider activists of the late 1970s worked hardest to reduce federal income tax rates. The cornerstone of that policy initiative, which ultimately became the central feature of Ronald Reagan's 1981 tax law, was an economic theory known colloquially as the "Laffer Curve." According to a legend (apparently invented by Jude Wanniski), University of Chicago economist Arthur Laffer illustrated his claim that lower taxes could actually raise tax revenue by drawing his eponymous curve on a dinner napkin. Although Laffer later recalled that the dinner in question had occurred at a nice restaurant that used cloth napkins, the elegant simplicity of his model and Wanniski's folksy propagandizing made for a compelling argument. Placing tax rates on the x-axis and government revenues from those taxes on the y-axis, Laffer claimed that the government would receive no revenue when tax rates were zero, for obvious reasons, but also when tax rates reached 100 percent, since no one would go to work if all his or her income were taxed away. As one followed the curve up from a 0 percent tax rate, revenues would increase, but at some point they would decline again as the curve turned back down and reached zero again when taxes reached 100 percent. The inverse U-shaped Laffer Curve thus predicted that if tax rates had already passed the point of peak revenue, reducing tax rates would actually generate more revenue. No one could say for certain where that magic point lay—that is, at what point did the disincentive to work outweigh the higher tax rate—but conservative supply-siders believed the current tax code had gone beyond it. Cut tax rates, they claimed, and people would work more.[19]

In 1978, Representative Jack Kemp (R-NY) and Senator William Roth (R-DE) gave legislative form to the Laffer Curve with a bill to reduce all fourteen federal income tax brackets by 10 percent per year over a period of three years, which its sponsors erroneously called a 30 percent across-the-board cut in tax rates.[20] Although the supply-siders shared business leaders' devotion to economic growth, savings, productivity, and investment, their proposed tax solution differed from the 10-5-3 plan in both form and function. Accelerated depreciation schedules, industrial executives hoped, would spur capital formation by manipulating the existing tax regime. By hacking tax rates "across the board," the supply-siders believed, the Kemp-Roth bill *upended* the existing regime. Although 10-5-3 focused explicitly on capital investment—that is, the actual "supply side" of the economy—true believers like David Stockman chastised the business bill as a special interest sop, philosophically akin to price controls or the minimum wage, that disrupted "natural" market forces by privileging capital-intensive firms (exactly as Jimmy Carter claimed).[21] Kemp-Roth, on the other hand, promised to remove government impediments to work and prosperity. In the language of its supporters at the conservative Heritage Foundation, the bill would make "leisure, consumption, and tax shelters relatively more expensive" than going to work, creating a robust engine for economic growth.[22]

Supply-siders' rejection of 10-5-3 underscored an important intellectual rift between many business conservatives and the newly hatched supply-side movement. Traditional conservatives, including most business leaders, argued that a tax rate cut of the size Jack Kemp proposed would exacerbate the budget deficit by decreasing tax revenues. Few took comfort in Laffer and Wanniski's claim that cutting taxes could actually generate greater revenues right away. Indeed, Stockman later confessed that the Laffer Curve had been mostly a metaphor for the economic bounty that low tax rates would yield by promoting economic growth and, thus, a larger tax base. In the short run, the tax cuts could never pay for themselves. Stockman himself confronted that harsh arithmetic reality directly when, as Reagan's director of OMB after the 1981 tax cuts passed, he faced the Sisyphean task of reducing federal spending to compensate for lost revenue—and he failed.[23]

During the 1980 Republican primary, Ronald Reagan became an early convert to supply-sider theory and the Kemp-Roth tax cut, which jibed well with his populist politics. His challengers for the nomination, however, bristled at the breach of budgetary orthodoxy. Liberal Republican John Anderson, a congressman from Illinois, declared that Reagan's promise to cut taxes, increase military spending, and still balance the federal budget was only possible using "blue smoke and mirrors." Business leaders largely agreed; while few backed Anderson, most preferred either John Connally, former Texas governor and Nixon's treasury secretary, or Texas oil developer George Herbert Walker Bush. The only "anti-Reagan" candidate who remained standing in the spring of 1980, Bush channeled the collective business community's derision when he dismissed Kemp-Roth as "voodoo economic policy" during a primary debate.[24] Instead, the former congressman whose résumé included stints as ambassador to China and head of the Republican National Committee, proposed relatively modest tax cuts to *both* corporate and personal rates, as well as the 10-5-3 plan and an investment tax credit for businesses. Tax cuts focused on business, the patrician Texan argued, represented the true "supply-side philosophy" because they were "directed at increasing supply—not demand." Indeed, in Bush's more accurate usage of the term

"supply side," protecting the interests of business and promoting investment necessarily entailed rigidly balancing the budget, a goal Kemp-Roth
appeared to undermine.[25]

Bush's intransigence did little to charm the Republican front-runner
Reagan, and it signaled a much deeper schism brewing between business
conservatives and supply-siders over the tax issue. Finishing the primary
season in second place, the Texan managed to maintain enough goodwill
to become Reagan's vice-presidential running mate after former president Gerald Ford declined the spot at the convention in Detroit, and the
political fence-mending that such a ticket required mirrored a similar
rapprochement between the divergent tax-cutting factions. The GOP
platform in 1980 technically endorsed both Kemp-Roth and 10-5-3, but
it made no secret about where the party's priority lay: Republicans put
calls for the individual tax cut front and center, lauding it with glowing
language about "fairness to the individual," while they buried the details
of accelerated depreciation deep in the bowels of the long document.[26]
To the chagrin of fiscal conservatives and the heads of major industrial
corporations, Reagan chose the populist tack, embracing the politics of
"tax revolt" and riding a wave of white middle-class anxiety into the
presidency.

The Short Unhappy Life of Reaganomics: From ERTA to TEFRA

Arriving in Washington with what he interpreted as a powerful mandate
to shake up the nation's tax system, Ronald Reagan worked quickly in
the winter of 1981 to form a political coalition around the two complementary planks of his economic plan: a major tax cut (the Economic
Recovery Tax Act, or ERTA) and significant reductions in government
spending (the Gramm-Latta Omnibus Reconciliation Act). Although congressional Republicans had made great strides in the election, riding
Reagan's coattails to their first Senate majority in twenty-six years and
gaining nearly three dozen seats in the House, the new president faced
a difficult political task. Conservatives and many liberals supported the
idea of reducing the tax burden, but deficit hawks—especially in the business community—cautioned that excessive tax cuts would bust the budget. Moreover, interest groups of all political stripes voiced different ideas
about exactly where to cut the budget, how much to reduce taxes, and
on whom.

"The President has proposed a far-reaching program that calls for a
reduction in Federal government spending, taxation and regulation and
a stable, consistent monetary policy," declared Theodore Brophy, CEO
of GTE and chairman of the Business Roundtable's Taxation Task Force,

and "[t]he business community feels strongly that all four parts of the economic recovery plan are essential."[27] Despite Brophy's presumptuous claim to speak for all businesspeople, he accurately gauged the broad support among top executives, conservative think tanks, and trade and employers' associations for the general tenets of what quickly became known as "Reaganomics." ERTA, the tax cut bill, included both the Kemp-Roth personal income tax rate reductions and 10-5-3, which also went by the acronym ACRS, for Accelerated Cost Recovery System. In the spring of 1981, the Roundtable, the NAM, and the Chamber of Commerce all sprang into action, using their well-tested lobbying techniques to generate grassroots enthusiasm for the plan. Roundtable CEOs, for example, mailed thousands of informational packages to constituent companies and other contacts, bragging to White House staffers that the message had been "very well received" throughout the business community.[28]

No business leader distinguished himself more in the fight for Reaganomics than Chamber of Commerce president Richard Lesher, who told Chamber members that the program marked "a real chance for historic change" and implored them: "Don't let it slip away." The country's largest business organization orchestrated mass mailings to thousands of executives, Washington lobbyists, trade and professional association directors, and heads of local chambers of commerce, urging them to organize mail and phone campaigns, meetings, and personal contacts with members of Congress. In addition, the Chamber distributed editorials by Lesher, issued an "Action Call" to its network of 160,000 members, and sent dozens of leaders and staff members to testify on Capitol Hill. Such efforts won Lesher considerable gratitude from the White House; staffers praised his group as "more active than perhaps any organization" in "fully endorsing every aspect of the President's program."[29]

Lesher's zeal for the tax bill grew from deeply held convictions. A business school Ph.D. who had run many organizations, both government and nonprofit, but never a private company, the Chamber president shared more in common with supply-side ideologues than with many of the executives who rallied around 10-5-3 but fretted about budget deficits. "Balancing the budget is not the primary reason for reducing government spending," one Chamber publication argued. "It is more important to reduce Federal competition with private citizens and businesses for scarce resources." At the White House, advisors saw tremendous strategic possibility in Lesher's unbridled advocacy. Because the Chamber of Commerce had long cultivated an image as the mouthpiece for "Main Street" small businesses and "mom and pop" enterprises, administration officials concluded that its enthusiastic support for Reaganomics would demonstrate "broad-based support" from "workers, consumers, tax-payers and small business." Getting the tax cuts through a Democratic Congress would be difficult enough without the stigma that they appealed only to big, wealthy firms, and the Chamber could help bridge that political gap.[30]

The White House's decision to grant Lesher and the Chamber a privileged position was not lost on the heads of other business associations. Complaining to White House aides James Baker and Edwin Meese, NAM president Alexander "Sandy" Trowbridge warned that unilateral meetings with one organization risked weakening the "cohesive strength of [the business] coalition." "To ignore other parts of that coalition, including NAM, the Business Roundtable, the National Federation of Independent Business, and the American Business Conference, is to deny the President a full spectrum of business views," he opined.[31] Neither the NAM nor the Roundtable placed nearly the same priority on the supply-side cuts as did Lesher and the Chamber. Small business owners, including many manufacturers at the NAM, generally preferred lower tax rates to accelerated depreciation, both because they had relatively lower capital needs than large firms and because many paid taxes on their small businesses according to the individual tax brackets. Although the wealthy industrialists who led large corporations would certainly benefit personally from lower individual tax rates, their political allegiances in the early 1980s still aligned with the long-term interests of their firms. Indeed, many corporate leaders supported the personal tax cut more out of political opportunism than supply-side ideology or personal gain; for them, it represented the price they had to pay to keep their real prize, the 10-5-3 accelerated depreciation plan that would help their companies, in ERTA.[32]

Despite this tension between supply-siders and business-oriented tax cutters, the White House successfully tapped the full lobbying power of organized business groups to help push ERTA over the finish line during the summer of 1981. Mobilizing their deep networks of local business owners, community organizations, and other activists, corporate lobbyists launched what House Speaker Tip O'Neill (D-MA) called "a telephone blitz like this nation has never seen" in favor of the president's economic package.[33] On July 26, Congress passed the Gramm-Latta budget, cutting approximately $140 billion to more than two hundred government bodies, primarily in public aid and job-training programs. (The law also increased military spending by 9 percent for FY 1982 and authorized the Pentagon to expand its budget by 8 percent per year thereafter, dramatically reducing the savings.) Three days later, the House of Representatives passed Reagan's tax cut, defeating a milder proposal by the House Democratic leadership, especially Ways and Means chairman Dan Rostenkowski (D-IL). The final bill, scaled back slightly during negotiations with Republican deficit hawks, reduced tax rates 5 percent in

1981 (starting on October 1), then 10 percent per year in 1982 and 1983. It also lowered the top marginal rate from 70 to 50 percent; reduced the capital gains tax rate to 20 percent; indexed tax brackets to inflation beginning in 1985; reduced the maximum estate tax from 70 to 50 percent and exempted all estates valued below $600,000; and, to the joy of the capital accumulation crowd, accelerated depreciation schedules for corporate income taxes according to the 10-5-3 model.[34]

The ink was hardly dry on Reagan's tax cut, however, before the tumultuous politics of deficits and economic stagnation reconfigured the national debate. Before the first 5 percent cut even took effect on October 1, the economy dipped yet again into recession, and by the winter of 1982 White House economic advisors, and eventually the president, grew convinced that the tax cuts would not provide the economic cure-all that supply-siders had promised. The deteriorating economy severely curtailed tax revenues, and Reagan's campaign promise to cut taxes, expand the military, and balance the budget by 1984 increasingly looked like "voodoo economic policy" after all.[35]

Adding to the political turmoil, growing strife over the budget acquired a bipartisan tone, in fervor if not quite in economic rationale. Liberal Democrats, for their part, argued that the Gramm-Latta budget primarily cut welfare, unemployment benefits, and food stamps, placing the burden of recession unjustly on the shoulders of the poor.[36] Business conservatives, on the other hand, complained that however they fell, the budget cuts were too small to offset the coming tax reductions. The Business Roundtable's Policy Committee predicted that the "large projected budget deficits" for the next three years "create[d] the possibility of continued high interest rates," which would "delay reasonable recovery from the current economic slowdown."[37]

But what could be done to restore balance to the budget? For many conservative business and financial leaders, notably those associated with nondefense industries, military spending appeared a logical first target. In a 1982 fiscal policy statement, Roundtable leaders claimed that the defense budget, like anything else, should be evaluated "on its merits, and directly in relation to its contribution to military capability and the Soviet threat—to reaffirm that it is all essential and will be put in place at minimum cost." The heads of the American Stock Exchange agreed, telling pollsters that they "overwhelmingly favored cuts in defense spending," at least by slowing its growth. Such pleas fell on deaf ears at the White House, however. A staunch Cold Warrior, President Reagan categorically rejected calls to streamline military spending. "Defense . . . is not a budget issue," he famously told his budget team. "You spend what you need."[38]

If defense cuts were out, business leaders reluctantly began to reconsider the severity of the supply-side tax cuts. Again, Roundtable CEOs took the lead. In a declining economy, they reasoned, capital accumulation became more important than ever. In the winter of 1982, Roundtable chairman Clifton Garvin (Exxon), Taxation Task Force chairman Theodore Brophy (GTE), and three other Policy Committee members met the president to pitch a "mid-course correction" to the Reaganomics juggernaut. The troop of executives, which included leaders from the energy, defense, telecommunications, and financial services industries, acknowledged the supply-sider creed that "high marginal tax rates reduce the incentive for capital investment and productive effort." Nevertheless, they insisted, the effect was "a matter of degree" and far outweighed by "the need for a steady and significant reduction in the deficit." While lower taxes as a matter of principle might be nice, the CEOs urged Reagan to consider "a stretchout of the 10% July 1983 individual tax-rate cut as a 'last resort' method of raising additional revenue."[39]

For Reagan, however, the deep cuts in personal tax rates represented a sacred cow, the bedrock on which his entire economic vision rested. Thus with defense cuts and tax rate increases off the table, and with little desire to spend political capital on even harsher budget cuts in the years leading up to a reelection campaign, the president found himself quickly running out of options. Republican senators and White House advisors began to pressure him to at least consider some type of tax increase. At first Reagan resisted, writing in his diary: "Damn it our program will work & it's based on reduced taxes."[40] By the spring of 1982, however, the president's economic advisors finally persuaded him to pursue legislation that raised taxes, but only if he could do so while still retaining his precious cuts to marginal rates. The key, according to chief of staff James Baker, one of the administration's loudest deficit hawks, lay in closing tax loopholes and eliminating exemptions, generating greater revenue without changing tax rates. And as it turned out, the weight of such changes would fall disproportionately on corporations.[41]

Reagan thus agreed to support the Tax Equity and Fiscal Responsibility Act of 1982 (TEFRA), which became the largest peacetime tax increase to that point in American history by generating more than $98 billion in new tax revenue over three years through the skillful manipulation of the tax code's detailed minutiae. In addition to limiting deductions and exemptions, TEFRA also repealed or rescinded many of the gains corporate lobbyists had worked into ERTA as a condition for their support, including the investment tax credit, safe-harbor leasing (designed to reduce corporate taxes by spreading tax credits among companies), and, most galling, about one-third of the accelerated depreciation benefits. According to political scientist Cathie Martin, approximately half of TEFRA's revenue came from changes to the corporate tax code.[42] To be sure, economists debate whether corporations really "pay" corporate income tax or whether they simply pass along those costs through higher prices or lower dividends to shareholders, so to say that business paid half of the cost of TEFRA is potentially misleading. Nonetheless, the law undeniably targeted the corporate tax code and corporate leaders rightly interpreted it as a loss, both as an accounting and a political matter. "Business," GTE chief Theodore Brophy opined the next year, "received a small share of the Economic Recovery Act of 1981 benefits, [but] wound up with a large share of the various tax increases . . . enacted since 1981."[43]

Brophy's lingering bitterness reflected the heated debate that ripped through the once-unified community of organized business groups in the months before TEFRA passed in the summer of 1982. As the possibility of a deficit-fighting tax hike grew increasingly real that spring, the long-simmering tensions between supply-side and capital-accumulation oriented business leaders finally boiled over. Representatives from the Business Roundtable pleaded futilely for Reagan to leave the corporate tax provisions in ERTA alone and instead to delay the final 10 percent personal tax cut. When Reagan demurred, the group in turn refused to endorse TEFRA as a compromise, although its chairman, Clifton Garvin of Exxon, publicly insisted that the Roundtable had not "broken" with the administration and still supported the "basic principles and objectives of the President's program." Leaders at the NAM privately agreed with the Roundtable that deferring the marginal rate cuts served business's interests more than changing the corporate code, but the organization publicly stuck by Reagan on the sanctity of the individual cuts and re-luctantly promised to back the administration's corporate tax hike. The National Small Business Association and several trade associations for realtors and builders, whose small and midsized members gained more from lower marginal rates than preferential provisions in the corporate tax code, also pledged loyalty to Reagan and TEFRA. The National Federation of Independent Business, a more ideologically conservative organization for small companies, withheld its support for several months out of principle, but it eventually backed the administration as well.[44]

Political divisions over raising taxes blossomed not only among but also within business associations. Despite its near-constant remonstrations about the perils of budget deficits, the Roundtable's Policy Committee divided over whether to accept a reduction of 10-5-3 and other capital-forming provisions of ERTA. Some members steadfastly opposed the notion of balancing the budget on the back of heavy industry, while others, like General Electric, provoked the ire of manufacturers by lobbying to repeal ERTA's safe-harbor leasing provisions.[45] In another instance, the CEO of Texaco—a member of the Roundtable but not its powerful Policy Committee—wrote to Treasury Secretary Donald Regan in March to express his disappointment that the group's stated position seemed to contradict the president's priorities. Had he been asked, the executive explained, he would have rejected that position. Regan, former Merrill Lynch CEO and past member of the Roundtable's Policy Committee, understood the complexities of the organization's dynamics. He forwarded the Texaco letter to his boss, hoping President Reagan would "find encouragement in the support Texaco and other businesses are giving to the economic program," even if their representative organizations appeared intransigent.[46]

As TEFRA made its way through Congress in July 1982, the Reagan administration worked to sustain a coalition of most Democrats and a handful of deficit-phobic Republicans to combat the strong antitax forces, particularly within the GOP. Frustrated at the Business Roundtable's unwillingness to lend its clout to the effort, Treasury Secretary Regan lobbied his former colleagues directly, urging them to climb onboard not on TEFRA's merits but rather on the political optics involved. Ronald Reagan, he pointed out, was deeply committed to exactly the type of investment-oriented, antiregulatory, free-market capitalism that the Roundtable had been created to defend. It would "be some time before you will encounter a President who so strongly shares your convictions." To lobby in favor of TEFRA, Regan exhorted, was to work for Reagan himself and show support for "his ability to keep restraints on the irresponsible spending instincts of the Congress."[47]

Despite Regan's efforts, Roundtable CEOs remained conflicted, prompting a less diplomatic approach by Senate Finance Committee chairman Robert Dole (R-KS), a staunch fiscal conservative. Dole headed the drive to recruit enough Senate Republicans, who held a 53–47 majority, to join the Democrats on TEFRA, even as his wife, White House Assistant for Public Liaison Elizabeth Dole, spearheaded the administration's outreach to business groups. In an angry memo to Roundtable chairman Theodore Brophy, Senator Dole declared that "silence on the part of the Business Roundtable means opposition" and could only signify that the group was "primarily concerned about retention of special tax benefits" rather than the public good. Faced with such an affront to its public purpose, the Roundtable begrudgingly yielded; two days after they received Senator Dole's letter, its leaders issued a tepid endorsement of TEFRA, despite what they called "serious reservations."[48]

The war over TEFRA erupted more ferociously at the Chamber of Commerce, where divisions over tax policy nearly ripped the venerable organization apart. President Richard Lesher's ebullient supply-side beliefs led the group to resolutely reject *any* backtracking from the ERTA tax cuts, whether on businesses or individuals. Ideologically, the Chamber pushed the supply-side credo even further, denying the very essence of fiscal conservatism: that budget deficits led to higher interest rates, thus slowing economic growth by limiting borrowing and stifling capital investment. According to a Chamber brochure, interest rates had "never shown any direct connection to either tax increases or the size of the deficit" and thus deficit reduction could not justify tax increases. As the chief source of opposition to TEFRA, Richard Lesher and the Chamber's public affairs department drew on the populist antipathy to government that Ronald Reagan had ridden to power but, ironically, now turned that spirit back against the president. TEFRA's tax increase on business would "only encourage more spending," Lesher said, clearly articulating the conservative mantra later known as "starve-the-beast"—that only lower tax revenue could restrain a spend-happy Congress.[49]

But the Chamber of Commerce of the United States was bigger than one man, and many corporate executives on its governing board dissented from Lesher's purist ideology. Opponents included W. Paul Thayer, the chairman of the Chamber's board in 1982 and chairman of the defense, aeronautics, and heavy industry conglomerate LTV Corporation. Possibly swayed by his own industry's close relationship with the Defense Department, Thayer concurred with his fellow executives and the White House that the problem of deficits outweighed the ideological quest for small government. In August, Thayer announced that he and a slim majority of the board of directors had broken with Lesher and threw their weight behind TEFRA. An embarrassing public turf war immediately broke out, as both Lesher and Thayer claimed to speak for the entire organization. Lesher, backed by prominent conservative CEOs like Donald Kendall of PepsiCo, inveighed against the tax bill, Reagan, and Thayer, insisting to the press that most of the Chamber's thousands of members unilaterally opposed the bill. Thayer, meanwhile, convened a directors' meeting to vote on a new formal position in support of TEFRA, which he telegrammed to Reagan.[50]

Paul Thayer, like the members of the Roundtable's Policy Committee, understood the political value of cooperating with government, especially a conservative one, even if doing so violated the tenets of "free-market capitalism." The aftermath of the Chamber schism proved his point. Lesher enraged the administration, particularly by refusing a direct request by Vice President Bush and White House counselor Edwin Meese to use the Chamber's television studio for pro-TEFRA publicity. In retaliation, the White House announced that it no longer welcomed Lesher's input and would "work with the Chamber but only through Paul Thayer," as one staffer reported. For his loyalty, Thayer later received an appointment as deputy defense secretary, a position he held until an insider-trading scandal prompted his resignation in 1985.[51]

In mid-August, TEFRA faced its final legislative gauntlet. House members and senators met in conference to reconcile their different versions of the bill and lobbyists worked hard to influence the details. Although the Democratic leadership and organized labor backed the effort, many Democrats in both houses of Congress worried that voting for a tax increase would hurt their reelection prospects. Although stridently conservative supply-siders in the Republican caucus, led by Jack Kemp and Georgia representative Newt Gingrich, lobbied hard against the measure, many Republicans straddled the fence and looked to their party's leader for reassurance. President Reagan knew that shepherding the bill to its final form would require discipline in the ranks and that he could not do it alone. To marshal proactive support from business, Elizabeth Dole organized an ad hoc group of thirty-five business leaders called the Deficit Reduction Action Group. Within that body, midsized financial and other fast-growth industries took a pronounced leadership role advocating for deficit reduction, while the representatives of heavy industry, so devoted to capital accumulation, continued to drag their feet.[52]

As the final votes on TEFRA approached, the White House realized that a relatively weak effort by reluctant corporate lobbying groups would prove insufficient to sway the key swing votes. In a reversal of the usual pattern—whereby business associations undertook massive telephone blitzes to pressure politicians—Reagan himself worked the White House phones, exhorting business leaders to ask their senators for a yes vote. Over the course of a week in mid-August, the president personally phoned two dozen executives and association heads, often more than once. He called Roundtable Policy Committee members as well as the presidents of the NAM, the National Federation of Independent Business, and other groups but, as promised, not Richard Lesher. After hearing the president's reassurances that he still believed in "the need for capital formation and investment," the Roundtable's Theodore Brophy affirmed his group's support. Jack Welch, who had succeeded Reginald Jones the previous year as CEO of General Electric—a company Elizabeth Dole described as "the most politically sophisticated firm in town"—also weighed in. "Despite the burdens it does impose on both business and individuals," Welch told Reagan, "the bill is needed and will have our support." On August 19, the reconciled bill cleared the House 226 to 207 and the Senate 52 to 47. Out of 244 House Democrats, 123 voted in favor; of those, 96 had voted against ERTA the year before. Half of House Republicans (89 of 191) sided with Reagan. In the Senate, the results were more lopsided: Only 9 Democrats voted with the majority, as many liberals objected to the spending cuts conservatives had demanded in exchange for their support. Two weeks later, a bruising bipartisan fight behind him, the most famous enemy of taxes to sit in the White House signed the bill to raise them.[53]

"Halt the Deficit": Taxing and Spending in Economic Recovery

The struggle over TEFRA cast a pall over Reagan's relationship with the heads of major employers' associations, who could no longer pretend that their defense of free enterprise remained wholly unified. In the debate's aftermath, the administration recognized the need for damage control and actively solicited input from corporate leaders and associations, even making peace with Richard Lesher by including him in a large meeting of Roundtable CEOs, free-trade lobbyists, and Chamber executives with Reagan early in 1983. For their part, organized business leaders responded favorably, if somewhat hesitantly, to the overtures. According to a spokesman for the NAM, "a great reservoir of support for the President" remained, but businessmen were "obviously . . . less supportive than before the deficit."[54]

Yet for all the ill will it generated, TEFRA ultimately did little to slow the growth of the budget deficit. The difference between the federal government's tax revenue and spending outlays increased, in nominal terms, from $128 billion in 1982 to $208 billion in 1983, rising from 4 percent to 6 percent of gross national product; although it dipped slightly to $185 billion in 1984, the deficit remained above $200 billion and 5 percent of GDP through 1986. Yet despite years of dire predictions by fiscal conservatives that deficits would prompt sky-high interest rates and permanent recession, the economy began to recover in 1983 and roared back to life in time for Reagan's resounding reelection in a forty-nine-state electoral knockout. In a timely decision, Federal Reserve chairman Paul Volcker abandoned strict monetary targets and permitted the money supply to expand just as TEFRA made its way through Congress. The consequent reduction in interest rates spurred consumer borrowing and spending, and, Keynesian economists pointed out, deficit spending further stimulated demand and growth. The recession of 1981 and 1982 finally wrung inflation, which had peaked at 13.5 percent in 1980, out of the economy, and it remained low during the recovery; the inflation rate fell below 4 percent in 1983 and, with rare and fleeting exceptions, has remained below that level ever since.[55]

But while the national economy as a whole recovered, the recession of the early 1980s had proved devastating and, in many cases, permanently debilitating to the nation's industrial manufacturers. As economic historians have argued, private debt and mass consumption—rather than industrial revival—really drove the post-1983 expansion. Low domestic interest rates, a strong dollar, and freer flows of international capital combined to create a massive surge in imports, leading the country's balance of trade deficit to quadruple between 1982 and 1986. This debt-financed boom generated tremendous growth in financial services but did little to rehabilitate traditional manufacturing and export-focused industries. Ironically, however, the internal politics, priorities, and discourses within the organized business community continued to focus on a more restrictive set of domestic policy concerns rather than the large-scale changes in the national economy. Licking their political wounds after the TEFRA fight, corporate leaders trained their sights ever more sharply on the same issues that had guided them since the early 1970s: regulatory reform, investment-oriented corporate tax policy, counterinflationary monetary policy, and, more than ever, the budget deficit.[56]

Early in 1983, the Business Roundtable created a formal task force on the budget, distinct from its Taxation Task Force, and appointed Robert Kilpatrick, CEO of Cigna, to run it. The head of a giant health insurance provider, formed in 1982 when the Insurance Company of North America merged with Connecticut General Life Insurance, Kilpatrick expressed a particular interest in reducing federal spending on entitlements, especially Medicare and Social Security, which he believed competed directly with the private insurance industry.[57] Upping the attack on the budget later that spring, Theodore Brophy announced the Roundtable's "major campaign . . . for restraints on Federal spending of all kinds." The group urged Congress not only to reduce spending on Social Security and defense but also to implement "a 12-months freeze on most non-defense discretionary programs, permanent limitation of cost-of-living adjustments for non-means-tested entitlements, and an effort to find further long-term savings in Medicare." At the same time, Brophy, by then a co-chairman of the Roundtable, denied rumors that his group favored another tax increase. "Nothing could be further from the truth," he insisted. The Roundtable had merely acknowledged "that revenue beyond the budget projection might be required to deal with the deficit," but the number one priority remained "spending reductions."[58]

Industrial executives at the Business Roundtable clamored particularly loudly for deficit reduction because of their conviction that fiscal imbalances lay at the heart of American manufacturing's declining international standing. Even as the economy recovered, domestic manufacturing continued to suffer. To be sure, most of the pain fell on the workers who lost their jobs because managers and executives increasingly moved production to regions with lower labor costs, first in the less unionized southern and western states and then, increasingly, abroad. By the end of 1987, 1.7 million fewer Americans worked in manufacturing than had at the end of the 1970s. Yet while workers bore the brunt of this transition, industrial executives also grew anxious about the competitive pressures they faced in an ever more globalized economy. Overall corporate profits failed to reach their 1960s levels even at the height of the 1980s expansion, and manufacturers felt the strongest pinch. The strong dollar relative to the yen, for example, made Japanese cars far less expensive for Americans. "American companies are losing sales to Japanese firms," railed Lee Morgan, CEO of the heavy industry corporation Caterpillar Tractor, "not because of cost, quality, or service, but because of the unearned price advantage due to the undervalued yen."[59]

Underlying the decline of manufacturing and the country's mounting trade deficit, executives argued, was the federal budget deficit. Public debt, many business leaders charged, "crowded out" private borrowing. "[E]very dollar that the Federal Treasury borrows," Cigna's Robert Kilpatrick claimed, "is a dollar that is not available to put people to work." Moreover, budget deficits created high interest rates, which led to the overvalued dollar. Meeting with Reagan late in 1984, Lee Morgan proclaimed that "the extraordinary strength of the dollar is responsible for over half of the deterioration in the U.S. trade position" and that the "major cause of this currency misalignment is the U.S. budget deficit." Although economists debated the validity of Morgan's argument, his fervent appeal to Reagan typified the angst that beset industrial executives. The panic over the deficit ran deeper than platitudes about fiscal solvency; it reflected far-reaching anxiety over the long-term decline of manufacturing.[60]

Fiscally conservative policymakers sympathized. In 1984, Republican senators Robert Dole (KS) and Pete Dominici (NM) led a contingent of budget hawks to persuade Reagan once again to raise taxes. In the political and lyrical spirit of TEFRA, they proposed "DEFRA," the Deficit Reduction Act of 1984, which further altered loopholes in the corporate and individual tax code to make what they called a "down payment" on the deficit without raising Reagan's cherished marginal tax rates. Partly because of the improved economy and partly because TEFRA had exhausted many conservatives' passions and energy, the public debate over DEFRA was notably more muted. Much to Dole's chagrin, lobbyists from the National Association of Realtors successfully negotiated for preferential tax breaks for the real estate industry, but the traditional big-business lobbying powers remained mostly on the sidelines. Chamber of Commerce economists warned that the recovery was not strong enough to support higher taxes and thus opposed the bill, but they did so with little verve. The NAM, on the other hand, announced support for both DEFRA and a balanced budget amendment to the Constitution, which Reagan had urged but Democrats had blocked during the TEFRA debate. Executives at the Roundtable likewise held back, only inserting themselves late in the process to support a handful of specific details. In particular, they joined the successful push, led by the original 10-5-3 enthusiast Barber Conable in the House, to reduce large corporations' tax liability for profits earned abroad on exported goods. As the next chapter explores in detail, the relative weakness of the traditional voices of organized business reflected changing dynamics within the American business community. Information technology, finance, and other non-manufacturing industries like insurance and pharmaceuticals represented the biggest growth sectors by the mid-1980s, but those industries had not traditionally taken leadership roles in major business associations. Similarly, the growth of multinational corporations in the same years complicated issues of trade and tax policy, creating divisions within groups like the Roundtable.[61]

In addition, the debates over DEFRA strained relations between business associations and more philosophically libertarian political activists—the women and men often called "movement conservatives" who had mobilized through think tanks in the 1970s and who, by the 1980s, populated many corners of the Reagan administration. Rather than uniting business conservatives in a principled defense of free markets, tax and deficit politics exposed businesspeople's parochial interests, to the consternation of true believers. Economist Murray Weidenbaum, chairman of Reagan's Council of Economic Advisors in 1981 and 1982, became an outspoken vehicle for that frustration, chastising business groups for putting their own interests ahead of free enterprise in the tax debates. Known for his wit, Weidenbaum claimed business's self-interest led to "Pogo economics"—like Walt Kelly's cartoon possum, conservatism had "met the enemy, and he is us." Clamoring for preferential tax treatment, he maintained, was just as anticapitalist as regulations, minimum wages, or any other government interference in the market.[62]

For all the teeth-gnashing it inspired, DEFRA—like TEFRA before it—did little to redress the imbalances in the federal budget. According to deficit historian Iwan Morgan, the two laws combined generated less than a third of the revenue lost due to ERTA between 1984 and 1988. To the chagrin of many deficit hawks in both political and business circles, however, surveys suggested that most Americans did not worry nearly so much about the deficit as the political class did. As Congress negotiated its next federal budget in the spring of 1985, Roundtable executives announced their intent to return to grassroots lobbying by coordinating a nationwide letter-writing campaign to generate a groundswell of public concern about the deficit. Under the battle cry "Halt the Deficit—Write Now!" Roundtable executives distributed millions of prewritten post-cards for their employees to mail to Congress. Americans perusing the May issue of *Reader's Digest* found a removable postcard, co-sponsored by the Roundtable and the magazine, to send to Washington, saying: "I want you to reduce federal deficits now. . . . I'm willing to do my share."

According to the Roundtable, nearly one million readers mailed in those cards, and many reported "attaching letters amplifying their views."[63]

Prudential CEO Robert Beck, the Roundtable chairman who spearheaded the effort, claimed that the group had "never undertaken a grassroots campaign of this magnitude" and believed that doing so was essential to "demonstrate to our lawmakers that there's strong public support for doing what must be done to get these deficits under control." Reagan's reelection and the economic recovery seemed to have removed the urgency from the deficit issue, and Congress appeared preoccupied with revenue-neutral reform to the tax code. (That movement led to the Tax Reform Act of 1986, which the next chapter discusses.) In that environment, Beck worried that deficit reduction would get lost in the shuffle. Personal contacts with legislators by CEOs and Washington Representatives helped the cause, he told Roundtable executives, but—as business had learned during its successful mobilizations in the late 1970s—lawmakers responded more to messages from constituents than to direct lobbying. As a grassroots campaign, therefore, Halt the Deficit aimed both to incite public outrage and to provide proof of that fervor. In that spirit, its literature and promotional material dedicated substantial space to shrill and apocalyptic claims about interest rates and trade deficits, keeping the specifics to a minimum. Although Roundtable members and their lobbyists worked hard behind the scenes to promote particular changes to federal appropriations, they remained purposefully nonspecific in public about what to cut. Vaguely calling for a retrenchment of defense, entitlement, and social spending, for example, Beck claimed "hard choices" had to be "shared by all sectors of society except the poor."[64]

Although Robert Beck claimed that Halt the Deficit was "a first" for the Roundtable, its methods in fact mirrored the indirect lobbying efforts that the group had deployed against the Consumer Protection Agency, labor law reform, and other issues. As with those earlier mail barrages and public information campaigns, measuring the exact effect of the effort of such lobbying on the legislative process is impossible. Nonetheless, the contrast between the group's stated goals and the legislative outcomes suggests that the Business Roundtable did not enjoy the same measure of influence in the mid-1980s that it had boasted ten years earlier. Roundtable CEOs devoted substantial, if unquantifiable, resources to the Halt the Deficit campaign, which they genuinely believed would tilt the budget process in their favor. Working closely with Bob Dole and other budget hawks, they lobbied furiously for major reductions in federal spending, including a freeze on cost-of-living adjustments for Social Security and other federal pension payments. In the end, however, Democrats in Congress—backed by a White House that refused to expend political capital on such unpopular provisions—passed a budget in 1985 that, in

the words of a bitter Robert Beck, "failed to genuinely address the problem of unbearable budget deficits."[65] Thereafter, the Roundtable's Halt
the Deficit campaign quietly faded away.

A FRAGMENTED LOBBY

The tangled politics of taxation and budget deficits thus proved a bridge
too far for organized business groups in the 1980s. In the years after
1985, the budget deficit remained a major political issue and business
leaders, most vocally at the Roundtable, joined fiscal conservatives in
Congress in a nearly constant clamor for reductions in spending. A final
resolution to the budget problems of the 1980s, however, would have
to wait for a new president, George H. W. Bush. Despite his campaign
promise of "no new taxes," Bush ultimately agreed to work with, and not
against, congressional Democrats, coupling spending cuts with increases
to marginal tax rates in the Budget Act of 1990. Although the Business
Roundtable did not participate significantly in the deal between Bush
and the Democratic congressional leadership, it embraced the outcome,
which one member called "probably the best one could expect from a
politically divided government." Such a lukewarm endorsement likely
came as cold comfort for President Bush, however, who faced intense
blowback from latter-day supply-siders and other antitax conservatives
in his party. As numerous political observers have suggested, the Budget
Act of 1990 did more than anything else to doom Bush's chances for
reelection, although it, along with tight fiscal policy under President Bill
Clinton, effectively put the country on the road to eliminating its budget
deficit entirely by 1999.[66]

Well before Clinton defeated Bush in the election of 1992, however, the contentious politics of taxes and deficits severely undermined
the claims to unity between mobilized business associations and their
ideological allies within the conservative political establishment. While
America's most significant industrial competitors, Japan and Germany,
largely avoided populist tax revolts or indeed major changes to their tax
regimes in the 1980s, the shifting dynamics of industrial capitalism in
the United States upended traditional alliances as the competing agendas
of small-government conservatives and business-minded fiscal conservatives sparked intense internecine conflict.[67] In that ideological battle, the
powerful tradition that fueled calls for "small government" ran squarely
against the harsh reality of deficit spending. To their chagrin, fiscal conservatives realized over the course of the early 1980s that it would prove
impossible to "starve the beast" if the beast could continue eating simply
by putting its food on a credit card. As a result, many American industrial

leaders eschewed the siren call of "movement conservatism," at least in its most ardent manifestation.

The politics of taxation, particularly the tale of two tax cuts that this chapter has explored, suggest another important division between industrial leaders and other conservative activists, at least through the TEFRA battle of 1982. By casting their lot with accelerated depreciation in opposition to reduced marginal tax rates, executives like Reginald Jones of General Electric aligned themselves politically with their firms' economic interests. Although highly compensated individuals like the men who ran the country's largest corporations certainly had much to gain from lower taxes, the political ethos they embodied reflected the mind-set of professional managers. As the eminent business historian Alfred Chandler argued, the professionalization of management and the rise of a managerial class in the second half of the nineteenth century kept American business focused on the long game. Under earlier models of firm governance, Chandler contended, family ownership encouraged short-term planning and immediate rewards. Professional managers, on the other hand, benefited more from their firms' long-term success, since stability provided a guarantee of their future salary. The debates over tax policy in the late 1970s and early 1980s revealed that the managerial mind-set remained dominant among many politically active executives.[68]

But the shifting plates of global capitalism and the growing instability of American business, particularly the industrial manufacturing sector, would soon render such company fidelity a historic relic. As the American economy recovered from the recession of the early 1980s and confronted more directly the new world of globalized trade and finance capitalism, both the operations of America's large corporations and the nature of the men and women who stood at their helms would change. As we will see in chapter 8, a new generation of executives began to occupy the corner offices; unlike the men who founded the Business Roundtable, most of whom had spent their careers with single companies, the CEOs of the 1980s and 1990s increasingly boasted degrees from business schools, where they learned general and transferable management skills. At the same time, investment portfolios and short-term stock positions came to eclipse long-term production goals, and by the turn of the century the fierce devotion with which industrial leaders clamored for accelerated depreciation would become difficult for most businesspeople to comprehend.

Cultural changes within the upper ranks of American business thus overlapped the tumultuous politics of taxes and deficits in the mid-1980s and played a role in organized business groups' diminished capacity to shape budget policy. In earlier fights against wage-price controls, labor reforms, and social regulations, representatives of different sectors within the business community successfully overcame barriers to collective action by working together against a common enemy—the liberal, labor-oriented Keynesian state. But once conservatives gained control of the federal government and had to make hard choices about exactly *how* to cut spending and allot tax cuts, conflicting priorities within and among business groups, and with other conservatives, weakened their collective influence. Yet even as their organizational unity began to fracture, industrial executives remained fixated on the link between fiscal policy and the state of American manufacturing. Reaganomics, which sought to implement a "business-oriented" policy by freeing markets and minimizing the role of the federal government, thus achieved an ironic legacy by fixating industrialists' attention on the budget while other factors hastened the country's industrial decline. As the final chapter argues, business leaders' inability to respond politically to issues like slackened productivity and foreign competition ultimately marked the passing of their unified movement as new types of industries came to dominate American politics.

CHAPTER 8

Every Man His Own Lobbyist

Congress shall make no law . . . abridging . . . the right of the
people . . . to petition the government for a redress of grievances.
—Amendment I, Constitution of the United States of America
(1791)

FOR CHARLS E. WALKER, by many accounts the most influential corporate lobbyist in the nation's capital, the Tax Reform Act of 1986 was a major failure. For more than a decade, the balding and bejowled economist had flexed his political muscles on behalf of industrial clients that included Ford, U.S. Steel, and Proctor & Gamble. A former deputy secretary of treasury under Nixon, Walker served on the frontlines of industry's campaign for accelerated depreciation, largely through his corporate-funded think tank, the American Council for Capital Formation. In 1978 he helped organize the "Carlton Group," a cohort of corporate lobbyists that met each Tuesday morning in the Sheraton-Carlton hotel in Washington to strategize collectively about ways to attain industry-specific tax breaks. Reginald Jones, then CEO of General Electric and chairman of the Business Roundtable's Tax Reform Task Force, relied on the smooth-talking Texan to ensure that Ronald Reagan's 1981 tax cut included the 10-5-3 plan. Yet in the wake of TEFRA and DEFRA, which reversed many of those gains in 1982 and 1984, a bipartisan movement to completely overhaul the tax code took shape and convinced many business leaders that their hard-won capital-forming tax benefits faced a renewed threat. Rather than work to cut deals on specific provisions, the Roundtable dug in its heels and charged its chief lobbyist with stopping the bill completely. "Tax reform," the group's Policy Committee declared incontrovertibly, "is diverting attention from . . . crucial economic issues" and "should be set aside." Returning to its roots in reactive, rather than proactive, lobbying, the organized business community took a firm stand against the Tax Reform Act.[1]

Yet despite their lobbying clout, industrial giants like General Electric, the Business Roundtable, and Charls Walker, not to mention the NAM, the Chamber of Commerce, and myriad other trade associations, failed to stop the Tax Reform Act of 1986. On a sunny morning in October, President Reagan hosted a lavish ceremony on the White House's South Lawn and signed the sweeping legislation. Designed to simplify the tax code, the law replaced the existing fourteen marginal tax brackets with a two-bracket system that taxed individual income at 15 and 28 percent, beginning in 1988. Moreover, since the bipartisan reform effort hinged on "revenue neutrality"—that is, all tax reductions would be offset by tax increases—the law both reduced taxes on low-income households and broadened the tax base significantly. It increased the personal exemption and standard deductions while expanding and indexing to inflation the Earned Income Tax Credit for low-income families with children, even as it eliminated tax shelters and many deductions, including those for state and local taxes, and imposed taxes on unemployment insurance benefits. To the chagrin of business lobbyists, the reform dramatically scaled back investment and capital accumulation incentives, including the investment tax credit and the accelerated depreciation for equipment. And although the corporate tax *rate* declined from 46 to 34 percent, the law closed approximately $500 billion worth of loopholes and exemptions over its first five years. Although some corporate executives supported the reform, the overwhelming consensus among organized business interests saw the reform as a loss for business, a sentiment especially pronounced among lobbyists like Charls Walker and the leaders of the Business Roundtable.[2]

The Tax Reform Act of 1986, given all the policy and lobbying drama it entailed, has become a standard case study for political scientists who seek to understand how the legislative sausage is made in modern America and how various interest groups succeed and fail to advance their causes. From the beginning, the tax reform movement had placed business leaders on the defensive. In 1984, the public learned that 128 of the country's largest 250 corporations managed to escape paying any federal income tax at all for at least one year between 1981 and 1983. Scrambling, business groups tapped their public relations networks to confront what the Business Roundtable called the "common but incorrect perception that the tax burden on the U.S. business community is unfairly low." Although most business leaders agreed that the proposed reform would cut individual taxes at the expense of corporate taxes, the mind-numbing complexity of the details at play prevented employers' associations from rallying around a simple public message, and strategic divisions beset the business community. Hedging their bets in the hope of retaining specific tax preferences, lobbyists for the NAM and the Chamber endorsed eleventh-hour compromise measures. Even more unsettling for the bill's opponents, General Motors CEO Roger Smith—who became the Roundtable's chairman in mid-1986 in the thick of the fight—publicly dissented from his group's opposition, claiming that lower individual taxes would put more money in his customers' pockets and thus help automobile sales. According to *Wall Street Journal* reporters Jeffrey Birnbaum and

Alan Murray, who tracked the process thoroughly, individual firms and trade associations became bogged down negotiating the details of the bill, but corporate America "never joined forces to defeat it." The legislation passed, and as a result, American corporations contributed approximately the same portion of federal tax revenue—12.5 percent—at the end of the 1980s as they had at the beginning of the decade.[3]

To some tax scholars, the Tax Reform Act of 1986 marked a victory for progressive reformers working in the name of the public good over the parochial demands of well-funded special interests. Such an interpretation directly challenges the tenets of public choice theory, which would predict that a minority set of interests with a great deal at stake would in fact triumph over the public good. According to tax historian Elliot Brownlee, the legislation "advanced a process of restoring to federal taxation the sense of balance sought by the founders of the republic. The Act represented a major step in the elimination of tax-based privilege, while reaffirming the duties of citizenship." Political scientist Eric Patashnik, on the other hand, has compellingly illustrated the law's limitations. Changes to the tax code since 1986, Patashnik argues, "have narrowed the tax base and created new opportunities for sheltering taxable income," belying the bill's promise to distribute the tax burden more equitably. Moreover, lobbyists continued to exercise tremendous power over the arcane details of tax-writing procedures, minimizing the reform's influence in the long term.[4]

Both scholarly assessments of the role of corporate lobbyists in the Tax Reform Act of 1986 are accurate, illustrating the central irony of the politics of business in the 1980s. Although organized business associations saw their collective unity wane, corporate lobbying itself boomed. Indeed, the fracture of the once-unified community of business associations created new opportunities for firm- and industry-specific lobbyists to negotiate for special tax benefits and government appropriations for their clients. Unlike the collective lobbying efforts on broad-based issues like regulatory reform or labor law, these parochial special interest negotiations proved tremendously profitable for corporate lobbyists like Charls Walker, win or lose. "A lot of oxen were being gored" during the fights over corporate taxes in the early 1980s, Walker reflected, "and, well, we just made a lot of money."[5]

Lobbyists like Walker straddled two worlds during the tempestuous political battles of the Reagan administration. On one hand, his clients were old-guard industrial firms struggling to cope with a new political and economic order. As the United States recovered from its long battle with inflation, stagnation, and energy crisis, leaders of its traditional industries—what some observers derisively called "smokestack America"—found the landscape of global capitalism irrevocably altered. At the same time, Walker deftly navigated the treacherous shoals of American politics, moving seamlessly from think tanks to corporate boardrooms to the offices of political power, a member of a new breed of corporate lobbyist—part ideological crusader, part entrepreneur. During the 1988 presidential campaign, for example, he helped the Republican nominee, Vice President George Bush, develop proposals to reduce the capital gains tax for all investors; at the same time, his American Council for Capital Formation, which blurred the line between a think tank and professional lobbying firm, parlayed its access to Washington insiders into lucrative contracts for specific corporate clients. As part of the expanding community of "hired-gun" lobbyists, Walker reflected the changing dynamics of influence peddling as the pan-industry policy campaigns led by employers' associations quickly became relics of a bygone era.[6]

This chapter places the transformation of the politics of business during the 1980s at the intersection of two interrelated trends: the realignment of global capitalism, particularly the rise of finance and the decline of industrial manufacturing in the United States, and the political and cultural changes that spawned a new power structure and the proliferation of professional lobbying firms. As the last two chapters demonstrated, the collective influence of employers' associations began to wane along several important fronts during the Reagan administration, even as their ideological perspective became increasingly integral to political discourse. Neoliberal doctrine about the supremacy of the market and the debilitating effects of government "intervention" in the economy came to dominate policy deliberations not only among conservatives and Republicans but, increasingly, among liberals and Democrats. Nonetheless, by the end of the Reagan administration, practically nothing remained of the coherent and organized "business movement" that so dominated policy debates in the 1970s. Individual corporations certainly achieved both influence and self-serving policy benefits, but on such major issues as taxation, deficits, and international competiveness and trade, the business community found itself disparate and ineffectual. The intellectual and organizational disunion that Daniel Rodgers has recently characterized as an "Age of Fracture" in the late twentieth century manifested among right-leaning business leaders as well as the political left. Business's political mobilization devolved, to riff on historian Carl Becker, to a state of "every man his own lobbyist."[7]

Fracture and Financialization

Business groups' headline policy victories in the late 1970s and the advent of the avowedly pro-business and antiregulatory Reagan administration in 1981 prompted a groundswell of business political activity as corporate executives, Washington Representatives, and industrial associations flocked to the nation's capital. Accompanying this boom in trade association and direct lobbying, approximately a dozen corporate-backed policy institutes, created or expanded in the 1970s during the height of business's crisis of confidence, established themselves as mainstream members of the policy establishment during the 1980s. But this proliferation of political activity brought with it a downside, particularly for the "Big Three" employers' groups that had galvanized business lobbying in the previous decade. "More lobbyists doesn't equal more influence," said economist Jerry Jasinowski, vice president of the NAM. "You get to the point where you trip over each other . . . a point of diminishing returns."[8]

A new generation of leaders at the Business Roundtable likewise recognized the changing landscape of corporate lobbying as they transitioned through the retirement of the powerful and charismatic industrial executives who had spearheaded the Roundtable's rise a decade earlier. In the early 1980s, Irving Shapiro of DuPont, Reginald Jones of GE, Thomas Murphy of GM, and John Harper of Alcoa all stepped aside, leaving a major hole in the group's leadership. "You don't have the same perception now of there being some central figures, and that is because there really aren't," said new Roundtable chairman Ruben Mettler, head of the high-tech conglomerate TRW. Although the Chamber of Commerce did not experience a comparable change in leadership—Richard Lesher remained atop that organization until 1997—its directors likewise faced greater competition for attention and political access, exacerbated by the high-profile schism between Lesher and many members over TEFRA in 1982. That year, in the face of mounting budget deficits, the Chamber laid off approximately 5 percent of its employees, the first staff reduction in years.[9]

The arrival of a new pan-industry employers' association, dedicated to the interests of midsized firms and known as the American Business Conference (ABC), exemplified those shifting dynamics. In 1979, American Stock Exchange (AMEX) chairman Arthur Levitt Jr. detected a desire among executives in the financial services industry to unite their political clout in the same way that manufacturing and construction powerhouses mobilized through the Business Roundtable. The son of a powerful New York City politician, Levitt made his career in investment banking before assuming the helm of the stock exchange company in 1978 (and would later serve as chairman of the Securities and Exchange Commission throughout the Clinton administration). Just weeks after Ronald Reagan took the oath of office in the winter of 1981, Levitt announced the creation of the ABC, a consortium of one hundred CEOs from Wall Street brokerages, investment houses, and banks, as well as other fast-growing industries, particularly high-tech ventures, pharmaceuticals, and expanding service-sector companies. The old-guard corporate behemoths, Levitt believed, were as antiquated in their politics as in their business models. "I decided that if there was going to be a more meaningful government-business dialogue," he explained, "it would have to be with the more risk-oriented, upstart firms."[10]

At first, the ABC made a notably small splash in national politics. The longstanding giants of the organized business community paid the group little mind, and Chamber president Richard Lesher dismissed the effort entirely. "One man, a secretary and an answering service are just not going to make a hell of a lot of difference," he said. Yet in short order, the ABC distinguished itself as a major contact point for the young Reagan administration, mobilizing its small army of CEOs to advocate for lower capital gains taxes and the continued weakening of banking regulations. Unlike the industrial legends of the Business Roundtable—General Motors, DuPont, U.S. Steel, and so on—the ABC's membership included less venerable but nonetheless important companies, ranging from accounting firms like Arthur Andersen, to midsized manufacturers like bicycle maker Huffy, to expanding regional retailers like Massachusetts-based Dunkin' Donuts. Conservatives in the Reagan White House found the group's fixation on growth and innovation particularly appealing. According to business liaison Wayne Vallis, the ABC was "at the heart of the whole Reagan philosophy, the entrepreneurial code."[11]

Under the leadership of its president, former economics professor and Capitol Hill aide John Albertine, the ABC quickly established itself as a major force for business politics in Washington. It bolstered its bona fides with Reagan by supporting both the ERTA tax cuts and the far more controversial increases to corporate taxes that followed. In fact, Albertine's support for TEFRA put him at odds with his fellow corporate lobbyists at the Roundtable and the Chamber, with whom he shared fellowship at Charls Walker's weekly Carlton Group meetings. By joining Reagan's side early and forcefully in the TEFRA fight, however, Albertine's ABC skillfully solidified its place in the lobbying hierarchy. As one journalist noticed, a political scene previously ruled by the Big Three business groups—some added the National Federation of Independent Business as the fourth—had by 1983 expanded into a "Big Five."[12]

As the mouthpiece of midsized, growth- and investment-oriented firms disproportionately from the service sector, the ABC not only contributed to the overcrowding of the lobbying field but also typified the new face of business itself. Although industrial giants like General Motors and Alcoa remained important engines of employment and production, their economic, political, and cultural hegemony over what was increasingly known as "corporate America" declined steadily with each passing year. In

1950, more than 35 percent of the American workforce worked in manu-facturing, while the service sector employed only 15 percent, according to the U.S. Bureau of Economic Analysis. That gap closed steadily over the next thirty years, and by the early 1980s service industries employed more people than manufacturers did; by 2000, their relative shares were the precise inverse of those of 1950. In addition, the share of total prof-its shifted remarkably between manufacturing and services in the last three decades of the twentieth century. Through the 1960s, profits from the financial sector, including investment and commercial banks, insur-ance companies, and real estate investors, represented between 10 and 15 percent of total profits in the American economy. But by the late 1980s, financial profits made up more than 30 percent, and the figure reached 40 percent by 2000.[13]

Even the Business Roundtable, stalwart defender of industrial capital-ism, did not find itself immune from these secular economic changes, as the shifting composition of its leadership structure testified. When the Labor Law Study Group, the Construction Users' Anti-Inflation Round-table, and the March Group combined forces in 1973, the men who or-chestrated the merger selected a Policy Committee to set their agenda, designate heads of the task forces and committees, and determine the group's policy positions. Of the thirty-four original members, two were CEOs of national retailers (Macy's and Sears), one ran a food producer (Campbell's), and one led a technology company (Hewlett-Packard). The rest represented manufacturing and production industries: chemicals and petroleum, automotive, mining, railroads, construction, and utilities. FIRE firms (finance, insurance, and real estate), as well as pharmaceutical companies, were nowhere to be seen. (See appendix 3.2.) As the group matured institutionally, its leaders developed a system of rotating Policy Committee seats among interested members, generating greater diversity that reflected the changes in the corporate landscape. Heavy industry and manufacturing firms remained dominant, but by the late 1970s, the forty-plus member committee also included up to a dozen CEOs from nonmanufacturing firms, usually divided evenly among pharmaceuticals, insurance, and finance. In 1988, the Roundtable's executive board—a chairman and two or three co-chairmen—for the first time drew its mem-bership *exclusively* from "new" industries. In the seats formerly held by DuPont and Alcoa now sat the heads of Pfizer (pharmaceuticals), Aetna (insurance), American Express (banking), and IBM, which, while seventy-five years old, nonetheless represented the vanguard of personal comput-ing.[14] (See appendix 8.1.)

But the rise of financial, insurance, and health care companies to the top rungs of the Roundtable tells only part of the story. In the last half of the twentieth century, the relative share of the American economy controlled by manufacturing, service, and FIRE industries shifted dramatically. After accounting for approximately one-third of GDP, manufacturing declined—most precipitously after 1970—to around 15 percent by century's end. At the same time, FIRE rose from just above 10 percent in 1950 to 23 percent in 2000, and services shot from below 10 percent to more than 25 percent of GDP; in all cases, the most rapid changes occurred during the Reagan administration. Whether measured in terms of employment, profits, or share of GDP, financial companies and service industries notably eclipsed industrial manufacturing by the end of the 1980s.[15]

This process, which scholars describe as the "financialization" of the American economy, entailed not only a power shift among industries but also a fundamental change in corporate strategy and economic activity *within* industries. During the 1980s, many nonfinancial companies diversified substantially into financial services, even as they continued to convey a traditional image to the public. Venerable corporations like General Electric, Ford Motor Company, and General Motors, the pride of the industrial revolution and, in the mid-twentieth century, the most influential corporate voices within organized business groups, drew an ever increasing share of their revenue from investments, securities trading, and personal financing. As early as the 1960s, consultants had advised executives at General Electric that a modern, successful firm "behaved as an investor, not as an operator," and executives like Fred Borch, Reginald Jones, and particularly Jack Welch took that philosophy to great lengths. By 2002, twenty years after Welch succeeded Jones as CEO, 41 percent of the company's revenue came from GE Capital Services, whose businesses included insurance, financing for equipment, and real estate. GE had spent most of its history manufacturing appliances, heavy machinery, and electrical infrastructure, but those business units increasingly came to serve as conduits for its credit services. By the twenty-first century, the company originally founded to make lightbulbs now mostly made loans.[16]

One of the most visible hallmarks of the rise of finance and the decline of industrial manufacturing was the massive wave of merger and acquisition activity. During the 1980s, approximately 28 percent of the country's five hundred largest manufacturing firms received takeover bids, mostly unsolicited, or "hostile," and the majority led to mergers. Indeed, by the end of the decade, one-third of America's largest firms had been absorbed by other entities. According to corporate theorists, this merger wave marked the transition from *managerial capitalism*, in which corporate control was rooted in professional managers, to *shareholder capitalism*, where institutional investors from the financial services community exercised far greater influence over the destinies of firms.[17]

Industrial leaders greeted the rise of forced mergers and the growing power of institutional investors like mutual funds, insurance companies, and private equity partnerships with unchecked alarm. "Hostile takeovers," Roundtable spokesman Andrew Sigler told an open meeting of the Securities and Exchange Commission in 1984, "threaten the well-being of the country by causing corporations to react to intense pressures for short-term results." As chairman of the Roundtable's task force on corporate responsibility and CEO of the diversified paper and packaging corporation Champion International, Sigler offered the perspective of both traditional management and the manufacturing community, which were most at odds with the new world of Wall Street investing. The 1980s, Sigler argued, brought "dramatic change in corporate ownership" away from individuals and toward financial institutions that were "looking for quick gains," not stability. "Today's shareholder," he insisted, "doesn't fit the classic description of someone who has a long-term interest in the development of the company."[18]

Such a fundamental transformation in the structure of American capitalism undermined business unity by straining relations between manufacturing companies and the financial firms that reaped tremendous profits by underwriting corporate mergers and acquisitions. Oil tycoon T. Boone Pickens, who gained national renown through several highly publicized hostile takeover efforts in the mid-1980s, attacked Andrew Sigler and the Business Roundtable for embodying the very worst of business elitism: "regimentation, stifling of the entrepreneurial spirit, disregard for stockholders, and obsessions with perquisites and power." The Roundtable's complaints about "unacceptable abuses" from takeovers "orchestrated by professional raiders" represented, to Pickens, an ideologically disingenuous ploy to look out for their own. "For years, the Business Roundtable wanted Congress to keep hands off all takeovers because the big companies were gobbling up the little ones. . . . But now that some of the big ones have been brought down, the Business Roundtable wants Congress to step in and protect them," Pickens protested. Sounding a populist and anticorporate note that echoed the cries of public interest and labor activists, the billionaire corporate raider declared: "We must reduce the influence of big business in Washington."[19]

These shifts in corporate capitalism also frayed personal and professional relationships at the heart of the organized business movement. In 1987, a subset of Roundtable companies—but not the entire organization—joined the Coalition to Stop the Raid on America, a bipartisan group of state and local politicians and representatives from labor and business groups that urged greater transparency for and stricter regulation of corporate takeovers. At the same time, lobbyists for Wall Street firms worked, with support from the Treasury Department, to prevent

Congress from using provisions of the tax code to limit takeover activity. Such conflicting goals put onetime allies on opposite sides of a philosophical line. In 1987, for example, the Business Roundtable declined to renew its retainer with all-star corporate lobbyist Charls Walker, who had, according to Alcoa CEO Charles Parry, "taken a leadership role on publicly proposing specific tax policies that have not been adopted by the Roundtable." As Roundtable executives like Sigler denounced shareholder activism and hostile takeovers, the group's erstwhile lobbyist Walker declared, to the contrary, that "[m]erger and acquisition strength is part of the market strength, and making that more difficult will weaken the market." The split between Walker and the Roundtable, while not as dramatic as some contemporary media accounts suggested, typified the growing rift between different constituencies in the world of organized corporate lobbying.[20]

A Response to Postindustrialism: The Revitalization Campaigns

The rise of finance and the declining unity among corporate lobbyists brought to fruition a historical process that had begun to shake the foundations of American capitalism as early as the 1960s. Ironically, the same uncertainties that inspired political mobilization by the industrial community ultimately led to its fracture, as the firms and industries most galvanized by inflation, social regulation, and fears of a cultural "attack on free enterprise" in the early 1970s found themselves most unsettled by globalization and financialization. Their ultimate fissure unfolded against the backdrop of major policy debates about the state of the industrial economy and what could, or should, be done about it. Industrial corporations had observed their slipping competitive position for years, as national imports outpaced exports and the profitability of manufacturing firms declined both absolutely and relative to financial services. Representatives of the steel and auto industries, for example, had long railed against unfair foreign competition, including the dumping of European steel onto the American markets and Japanese government subsidies to its automobile makers.[21] Yet the task of constructing and promoting a policy agenda to confront those challenges, given the growing ideological and organizational divisions within the business community, proved especially acute during the short but severe economic recession of 1980.

"The buzz words of Washington are now 'supply side economics', 'reindustrialization,' 'rebuilding America', or our particular favorite, 'revitalization of American industry,' " wrote Alexander "Sandy" Trowbridge to Goldman Sachs partner Henry "Joe" Fowler in the summer of 1980. As the president of the NAM, Trowbridge oversaw his organization's newly launched "Program to Revitalize American Industry," a six-point initiative to shift economic policy, as he put it, "from excessive stimulus of consumption and demand to strong encouragement of investment and savings." He wrote to applaud his former colleague—both men had served on Lyndon Johnson's cabinet, Trowbridge at Commerce and Fowler at Treasury—for helping inaugurate a similar effort through a bipartisan group of political luminaries that called itself the Committee to Fight Inflation. That self-described "committee of private citizens with extensive experience in government" drew on members like former Federal Reserve chairman Arthur Burns, former Democratic Ways and Means chairman Wilbur Mills, and several alumni of the Nixon, Ford, and Carter economic teams to "marshal and maintain broad support for effective anti-inflation policies." From his office at the NAM's headquarters, boasting the patriotic address 1776 F Street, Trowbridge both commended his fellow Democrat's efforts and expressed his hope that the two organizations might work together in common cause.[22]

Just six months into what would be a ten-year stint as head of the NAM, Sandy Trowbridge believed that industrial revival would be the defining issue of his tenure. Writing to his friend Art Nielsen, chairman of market research firm A. C. Nielsen, he hopefully predicted that "NAM will become recognized as an affirmative advocate for legislation and policies which will foster fiscal responsibility, increased productivity, capital formation, regulatory reform, technological innovation and international competiveness." In many ways, Trowbridge was an ideal leader to take the NAM on the final leg of its decade-long journey away from knee-jerk obstructionism and radical antilabor politics and toward a more ecumenical posture as champion of America's suffering manufacturers. More privileged in upbringing than most owners of manufacturing firms or heads of business associations, the Andover- and Princeton-educated retired Marine officer and Korean War veteran straddled universes, equally at home among business leaders and the Washington policy elite. In addition to his time running the Commerce Department in the 1960s, his résumé before taking the helm of the NAM included experience as an oil executive for Esso Standard Oil in Puerto Rico, the presidency of the Conference Board, and the vice chairmanship of Allied Chemical. Ensconced in what he playfully described as "a de-bugged apartment at The Watergate," the fifty-year-old recent divorcé relished his chance to distinguish the NAM as the paramount voice for the revival of American industry.[23]

He was far from alone in that ambition. While few business leaders dared utter the dreaded "D word"—deindustrialization—Trowbridge's correspondence demonstrated the many "R words"—rebuild, revitalize, reindustrialize—that riddled the conversations of executives, association leaders, policymakers, and journalists, reaching a fever pitch in the summer of 1980. In June, a special edition of *Business Week* sounded a clarion call for "The Reindustrialization of America" by drawing its readers' attention to the flatlining productivity and rising foreign competition that spawned increasing numbers of plant closings as American firms moved their facilities abroad. Across town on H Street, Trowbridge's counterparts at the Chamber of Commerce rolled out their public relations strategy, "Let's Rebuild, America." Despite their unity of purpose, the joint appearance of those similar policy programs stoked competitive tensions between the two old employers' associations. Embarrassed to realize that the Chamber articulated its specific policy proposals more clearly than the NAM did, Trowbridge berated his subordinates for what he called the "failure in our organization to really work out our top priority" and "put together the details of the program that has credibility" for "broad usage among average citizenry" and "among sophisticated reviewers" in policy circles.[24]

The NAM and the Chamber poured tremendous energy and resources into their revive/rebuild programs, framing their longstanding goals of tight money, lower government spending, and looser and cheaper regulation in the context of America's declining industrial clout. Hoping to shore up bipartisan support, the groups peddled their talking-point-laden programs to both major parties' nominating conventions in the summer of 1980, stressing the specific policy recommendations they prescribed to revive ailing industries, including the 10-5-3 accelerated depreciation reform plan and an aggressive stance against what the Chamber called "predatory trade financing programs" by foreign governments, especially Japan. The GOP platform endorsed 10-5-3 explicitly, while the Democratic platform only vaguely gestured at tax incentives for capital formation. To the frustration of the employers' associations, neither party took a hard line toward Japanese trade policies.[25]

Although the promotional materials the NAM and the Chamber put together offered a handful of specific proposals, they largely trafficked in tired platitudes about reducing the regulatory hand of the state. Critics seized on that ambiguity, suggesting that "reindustrialization," in the words of a *Washington Post* editorial that especially aroused Sandy Trowbridge's wrath, really represented a desperate call for "turning back the calendar to a happier time" of "factories contentedly belching smoke" that appealed to "those industries whose great days were in the past." Such a critique laid bare the often unspoken rivalry between traditional manufacturers and newer, more innovative industries like telecommunications and information technology. Lambasting the editors for their bias against industry, Trowbridge insisted that his "revitalization" philosophy was neither partisan, dismissive of environmental concerns, nor protectionist. To the contrary, he insisted, employers' groups like the NAM and the Chamber advocated "investment and modernization by American industry" in order for "U.S. jobs [to] be saved and new jobs and, in fact, entire new industries created."[26]

The campaigns by the NAM and the Chamber to publicize the plight of industrial manufacturing coincided with the development of a larger national debate, both within and outside the business community, on whether the United States should join other modern nations in proclaiming a formal "industrial policy." As historian Otis Graham has summarized, the central question of industrial policy concerned whether the government should commit to a "declared, official, total effort to influence sectoral development and, thus, national industrial portfolio." During the 1980s, as popular fears grew that foreign competition, especially from Japan, threatened to dethrone the United States as the world's economic superpower, debates over industrial policy dominated many political and business circles. Despite its critical importance, however, the tremendously complex and technical details involved meant that the issue failed to hold the attention of many voters (and most subsequent political historians). But in addition to being confusing and dry, industrial policy also proved intractable because it cleaved traditional political alliances and ideologies. At its heart, the debate revolved around the fact that the governments of countries like Japan intentionally structured tax, subsidy, regulatory, and tariff policies to promote specific industries, such as automobiles, which greatly improved Japanese firms' position in the international market. The United States likewise favored some industries over others, but not according to any coherent or intentional plan. Rather, American policy emerged through the muddled give-and-take of parochial politics. A clear and deliberate industrial policy, according to its proponents, would rectify this imbalance. But what would such a program look like, and whom would it favor?

On the far left of the spectrum, some labor and public interest groups called for reciprocal tariffs, trade quotas, and other measures frequently demonized by opponents as "protectionist." Moderate left-leaning policy theorists, most prominently the economist Robert Reich, eschewed overt barriers to trade but advocated closer collaboration between the private sector and the public sector to encourage innovations and new technologies where the United States had a clear competitive advantage. Rehearsing arguments that ultimately shaped the approach to economic growth and trade under Bill Clinton, whom he served as secretary of labor, Reich predicted that the future lay in high-technology production, not the "smokestack America" of old.[27]

Politically conservative industrial leaders, including Democrats like Sandy Trowbridge as well as Republicans like Richard Lesher at the

Chamber of Commerce, found themselves in a bind. While they concurred about the need for government programs to promote exports through tax incentives and easier financing, they differed over proposals to create a "national development bank" like the institutions in Japan and Great Britain that established clear national priorities for production, wage rates, export quotas, and tariffs. Some agreed with the labor groups and liberal economists who argued for a new institution along the lines of the Reconstruction Finance Corporation (RFC), created at Herbert Hoover's behest during the Great Depression to provide emergency government loans to struggling businesses. Only through such a program, argued Ford chairman Philip Caldwell, could American carmakers deal with Japanese competition. America needed "a new, sensible national industrial policy" because "in the auto industry, individual U.S. companies are competing against Japan as a country." The chairman of the Roundtable's task force on trade and CEO of construction equipment manufacturer Caterpillar, Lee Morgan, concurred. "Your friends are about to desert you!" he berated Japanese business leaders at the Advisory Council of Japan-U.S. Economic Relations in Hawaii in February 1983, because the Japanese government continued to promote high tariffs, an undervalued currency, and import restrictions on American agricultural products.[28]

Despite such widespread consternation, most business leaders could not bring themselves to support a new government agency designed to promote sector-specific industrial goals. An ad hoc Business Roundtable task force concluded in the fall of 1983 that an industrial development bank along the lines of the old RFC simply reeked of the very type of national economic planning the organization had strenuously opposed since its creation. Moreover, the task force concluded, persistent rumors of America's deindustrialization had been greatly exaggerated, protests by manufacturers like Caldwell and Morgan to the contrary notwithstanding. "America is not and will not be deindustrializing," the Roundtable reported. "Provided that there is growth in the U.S. economy, one can reasonably predict that automation and other sources of productivity growth will generate *more output*, higher living standards and more, not less, overall employment."[29]

Faith in the power of unregulated markets to generate prosperity thus trumped the concerns of struggling industries. Like the NAM and the Chamber, as well as the newer American Business Conference, the Roundtable rejected a transformative industrial policy. Instead organized business groups simply doubled down on their support for the same policy prescriptions they had advocated for decades: capital-forming tax incentives, lower barriers to trade, less costly regulation, and tight fiscal and monetary policy. A cohesive American industrial policy thus foundered on the shoals of ideological partisanship, as labor groups and left-leaning economists failed to reach common ground with those elements of the traditional manufacturing community that might have benefited most from such planning. By the middle of the 1980s, the American economy thus emerged from an acute downturn and into the finance- and consumption-led recovery without ever addressing the concerns that had animated the "reindustrialization" push in 1980.[30]

FREE TRADERS TRIUMPHANT

Although problems of industrial decline did not disappear, as the Business Roundtable optimistically suggested, the end of the industrial policy debate shifted public focus to the far more contested terrain of international trade, where the battle lines between labor-liberals and organized business interests were easier to detect. Since its founding, the Roundtable consistently positioned itself as a strong advocate for "free trade," urging its members—no matter their particular competitive position—to lobby for tariff reductions and lower taxes on companies that earned income through foreign subsidiaries. Many of its original members, for instance, participated in a successful effort in 1972 to defeat legislation known as the Burke-Hartke bill, a labor-backed proposal that would have restricted investment overseas by American multinational corporations and discouraged imports. Yet throughout most of the 1970s, trade policy occupied only a minor place in the Roundtable's hierarchy of important issues. Although imports surpassed exports in all but two years after 1971, battles over social regulation, price controls, and labor law, as we have seen, dominated the group's agenda.[31]

During the 1980s, however, trade reemerged as a dominant policy concern, as well as a major point of tension between organized business groups and the Reagan administration. "Trade is getting more attention," Roundtable task force on trade chairman Lee Morgan proclaimed in 1983. "But I'm sorry to report that the commitment of this government to a 'pro-U.S.' trade policy has not yet been demonstrated." Ronald Reagan, Roundtable members worried, did not feel the immediacy of foreign exchange rate imbalances or the budget deficits that, they insisted, fueled trade deficits. Moreover, many CEOs strongly criticized the president for using trade as an instrument of foreign policy, through both embargoes and preferential trade agreements. "U.S. industry," Morgan maintained, "should not be forced to forego business in the international marketplace—and that often means in the USSR—when our international competitors are free to transact the business." Despite their differences with Reagan, however, most Roundtable members agreed that by far the greatest threat to free trade came not from the militaristic conservative in the White House but the labor-oriented and left-leaning politicians who blamed the decline of low-skilled manufacturing jobs on the global economy. Instead of reinforcing "protectionist sentiments" by imposing restrictions on trade to benefit American manufacturers, Morgan insisted, the United States should negotiate free-trade agreements with partners around the world to promote American exports.[32]

Corporate leaders' renewed ideological commitment to free trade mirrored a growing movement by policy elites around the world to further institutionalize the forces of globalization, particularly through two crucial international developments: the Uruguay Round of negotiations that transformed the General Agreement on Tariffs and Trade (GATT) into the World Trade Organization, and the reduction of trade barriers between the United States, Canada, and Mexico that led to the North American Free Trade Agreement, or NAFTA. In 1987, the Business Roundtable joined with the Round Table of European Industrialists, which represented twenty-five industrial manufacturers from several countries, to lobby the trade ministers and other public officials then engaged in the second year of the renewed GATT talks. "In view of mounting trade tensions among the U.S., Europe, and Japan," said the CEO of Volvo and chairman of the European Round Table, "we believe our combined efforts will encourage concrete trade agreements." The year before, representatives of the Business Roundtable and its Canadian counterpart, the Business Council on National Issues, had jointly supported a bilateral free-trade zone between their two nations. Summarizing the Roundtable's central arguments for the primacy of international free-trade agreements, Edson Spencer, CEO of defense conglomerate Honeywell, argued that an agreement "to expand trade and investment between Canada and the United States would stimulate U.S. industry and would serve as an example of what can be accomplished in the multilateral trade talks that have just gotten under way [in Uruguay]."[33]

Business leaders' call for a free-trade zone with Canada ultimately expanded into the NAFTA treaty, which abolished trade and capital flow restrictions not only with America's northern neighbor but also with Mexico when it took effect in 1994. Negotiations began in the summer of 1990 when Mexican president Carlos Salinas formally proposed a continental free-trade zone to his American counterpart, President George H. W. Bush. For three years, trade representatives from the three countries worked to iron out myriad details amid intense lobbying, particularly by labor and environmental groups who feared that the treaty would encourage American companies to relocate their factories to Mexico in search of cheaper workers and more lax environmental regulations. In the summer of 1993, negotiators concluded their work with a final treaty that largely appeased the environmentalists, but American labor groups remained opposed. In response, the AFL-CIO spearheaded a major lobbying effort to block ratification of the treaty in the U.S. Senate, which American law required before it could take effect.

Although many business leaders, especially from Roundtable firms, had loudly clamored for free trade for years, corporate lobbyists responded more slowly than their labor counterparts during the NAFTA negotiations. In 1988, Congress reauthorized "fast-track" rules for trade negotiations, requiring the Senate to take an up-or-down vote, with no amendments or 60-vote cloture motions, on any trade pact negotiated by the president; such authority would run until 1991 and then automatically renew for two years unless Congress voted to revoke it. In the spring of 1991, when President Bush announced his intent to use fast track to negotiate NAFTA, a coalition of Democrats from agricultural and manufacturing regions defied their party leadership and worked to block the extension. Such was their strength that House Ways and Means chairman Dan Rostenkowski, a member of the Democratic leadership who supported NAFTA, told corporate lobbyists: "If you want to win this thing, move your ass." In response, business leaders created the Coalition for Trade Expansion, which evolved into the USA-NAFTA Coalition during the ratification fight in 1993. Comprising 2,300 firms and business associations, this umbrella group organized a state-by-state public information blitz, designating thirty-five corporations as "captains" to promote the virtues of continental free trade. Most of the active firms, such as General Electric, DuPont, IBM, and AT&T, were prominent Roundtable members who had sent representatives to the original negotiations and thus knew the details of the treaty intimately.[34]

While nearly all prominent business associations joined USA-NAFTA, from the CEOs at the Roundtable to the NAM and the Chamber to the American Business Conference, large manufacturers did the heaviest lifting during the public relations blitz. In fact, some smaller and less powerful business groups even lobbied against the treaty, and media reports suggested that many small and midsized business owners remained as ambivalent about NAFTA as the general public was—on the eve of its ratification, less than 40 percent of Americans supported the agreement. Such reluctance to face the harsh forces of unfettered trade reflected a long tradition, particularly among small manufacturers. Indeed, the NAM had been founded upon exactly that sentiment in the 1890s as local producers sought governmental protection to ensure their viability. Nonetheless, a hundred years later, the NAM's guiding philosophy mirrored the preferences of big industry for whom NAFTA provided the ultimate solution to America's declining industrial competitiveness. A common North American market for goods and services, Roundtable spokesman Walter Elisha told a Senate committee, would yield "products of higher quality," "more jobs," and "a better quality of life." Free trade, he claimed, promised to make "the businesses of all three of these nations more competitive."[35]

Critics of the treaty, however, rejected such optimistic projections and accused large American corporations—particularly textile manufacturers like Elisha's Springs Industries—of more sinister motives. Freed of border tariffs, labor leaders and public interest activists argued, American manufacturers would surely move their factories south. Billionaire Texas businessman Ross Perot, who had achieved tremendous success in the oil and gas industry with minimal connections to pan-industry lobbying associations in Washington, launched a high-profile attack on NAFTA as part of his third-party bid for the presidency in 1992. Famously claiming that the free-trade zone would generate a "giant sucking sound" as well-paying manufacturing jobs fled to Mexico, Perot combined the labor-left's critique of corporate offshoring with culturally conservative isolationist politics. In addition, right-wing opposition to NAFTA coalesced around former Nixon aide Patrick Buchanan, whose surprisingly strong showing in the 1992 New Hampshire Republican primary exposed George Bush's weakness among social and cultural conservatives. Attacking NAFTA as yet another manifestation of the "New World Order" that begat illegal immigration, foreign military entanglements, and "world government," Buchanan's neonativism (not to say neo-McCarthyism) cast into sharp relief the persistent tension between business leaders and their putative allies in conservative politics.[36]

While Buchanan's challenge shined a spotlight on Bush's vulnerability, Perot's populist independent campaign ultimately cost the president his job. Running on a platform that opposed NAFTA, called for a balanced budget at all costs (even tax increases), and condemned both parties for their recalcitrance and self-serving policies, Perot won 19 percent of the popular vote. That tally proved sufficient to swing victory to Arkansas governor Bill Clinton. As a centrist and self-described "New Democrat," Clinton claimed to be unbound by traditional partisan loyalties, but he nonetheless preached skepticism about NAFTA during the primary campaign so as not to alienate organized labor and the left. In the fall of 1992, after winning his party's nomination, Clinton announced his qualified support for the treaty, so long as negotiators concluded several sidebar agreements to protect labor and environmental rights. Once in power, the Clinton administration worked furiously to achieve Senate ratification, angering many allies in the labor, public interest, and environmental movements. And in the end, Clinton's personal lobbying proved far more important than business groups' public information campaigns in convincing fence-sitting members of Congress to support the free-trade agreement. In November 1993, a few weeks before the House voted, Vice

President Al Gore debated Ross Perot on the *Larry King Live* television program, anchoring the administration's case and persuading some thirty members of Congress to vote Clinton's way. Last-minute wheeling and dealing by the new president finished the job; the House voted 234 to 200 in favor on November 17, 1993, and the Senate followed suit three days later, 73 to 26. In the House, two-thirds of Democrats and three-fourths of Republicans supported the treaty, while the "nay" votes among the senators split roughly evenly.[37]

The NAFTA debate thus unfolded at the climax of a powerful political realignment wrought by changes in global commerce and the power structure of American corporations. The populist backlash by right-wingers like Buchanan signaled the limits of the business community's intellectual influence over conservative politics. And yet, although the debate pitted traditional antagonists like General Electric against Ralph Nader and the AFL-CIO, NAFTA's real legacy was to finalize a longstanding schism in the Democratic Party. Organized labor emerged as the clear loser, while the centrist, pro-globalization "New Democrats" of the Clinton administration claimed a policy victory. For the organized business community, however, the Democrats' embrace of free trade produced mixed results. The logic of free-market capitalism had triumphed and secured its hegemony in policy circles, even though business lobbyists had played only a bit role themselves. At the same time, the turn to free trade diverted policymakers' and business leaders' attention away from any real effort to boost the competitive status of American manufacturing through a coherent industrial policy. NAFTA thus joined the ranks of regulatory reform and budget policy as a political hot topic that ultimately distracted the industrial community from its underlying structural problems.

The Changing Face of Lobbying

By the end of the 1980s, much of the luster of business's political mobilization appeared to have worn off. Policy battles over taxes, deficits, trade, and regulation exposed the tensions not only among various business constituencies but also between business interests and other conservatives. "We've entered a period where economic forces are producing tremendous strains on business," tax lobbyist Lawrence O'Brien told a reporter in 1987, so "you can no longer come up with an effective consensus." Looking to the 1988 election and beyond, many business lobbying organizations adopted a defensive position quite at odds with the ebullient optimism for reform they had embraced in the late 1970s.[38] In addition, firm- and industry-specific priorities frequently outweighed pan-business unity, and as multinational firms came to dominate the landscape of big business, a clear sense of American identity within the capitalist class became harder to discern. As intellectual historians and social theorists have commented, the intellectual power of neoliberal notions of free trade and deregulation often trumped parochial loyalties at the highest levels of the corporate world. Changes to corporate capitalism and the shifts in policy debates weakened the overarching unity of the managerial elite, so even when their side triumphed, as in the struggle to ratify NAFTA, employers' associations that claimed to speak for a united business community no longer held the same sway over the policy process as they had a decade earlier.[39]

Ironically, the relative clout of organized business associations like the Roundtable and the Chamber of Commerce declined even as the absolute level of corporate lobbying continued its skyward trajectory. Since the 1970s, a combination of structural, ideological, and political factors had spurred activism by organized interest groups. In Congress, the diminished importance of seniority, the proliferation of subcommittees, and the greater professionalization of congressional staffs increased the number of points of contact for anyone wishing to shape legislation. Rising partisan polarization in the wake of the civil rights struggles and ever-costlier campaigns after the legalization of PACs in the mid-1970s also created new opportunities for coalitions and alliances, particularly when ideologically oriented lobbyists doubled as vehicles for raising campaign cash around issues they or their clients supported. Although all interest groups took advantage of this new environment, corporations and trade associations increased their presence the most in real terms. In 1960, according to the *Congressional Quarterly Almanac*, 83 corporations employed Washington Representatives and 214 trade associations set up shop in the nation's capital. In 1980, 3,000 corporations retained lobbyists and 1,153 trade associations worked for business interests.[40]

During the twenty years that followed the economic crisis of the 1970s, the trend continued. Between 1981 and 1987, the number of *registered* lobbyists increased from 5,500 to 7,200; the number peaked at close to 15,000 in 2007 and declined to 12,389 in 2012. Moreover, the number of attorneys registered with the District of Columbia Bar Association doubled from 16,000 to 32,000 between 1972 and 1984, and reached approximately 80,000 in the 2000s.[41] To be sure, these figures merely suggest a pattern—not all lawyers in Washington, D.C., work in politics, and many lawyers and lobbyists represent noncorporate interests, such as labor unions or environmental groups. Moreover, determining the exact number of "corporate lobbyists" with any precision is impossible. First, many lobbyists represent corporate clients as well as other entities, including unions, colleges, and civic organizations. Second, federal disclosure requirements—both under the Federal Regulation of Lobbying Act of 1946, which governed during the events examined in this book, and the 1995 Lobbying Disclosure Act—have historically been ambiguous. One journalist in 1982, for example, estimated that while 5,500 lobbyists registered with the government, more than 16,000 actually worked the halls of Congress. Counting lobbyists, in the past no less than in the present, is as fraught as determining their direct effect on policymakers.[42]

Nonetheless, corporate lobbyists have always outnumbered those from other interest groups, and that gap grew wider in the years of business's political mobilization. Beginning in 1977, a publishing company called Columbia Books and Information began compiling a comprehensive directory of all individual people who represented either themselves or someone else in national politics, including registered lobbyists as well as other influence peddlers. In addition to documenting the swelling ranks of lobbyists in general, this directory documents the growing importance of independent lobbying firms during the 1980s. In 1979, the editors counted approximately 500 law offices and public relations firms whose primary business could be characterized as lobbying. By 1990, 2,000 public relations consultants and another 2,000 attorneys represented corporate clients.[43]

The rise of independent lobbying firms, particularly as trade associations and national business groups fractured and lost their collective clout, fundamentally reshaped corporate lobbying in the 1980s. Some of these "hired guns," such as Charls Walker's American Council for Capital Formation and its successor, Charls E. Walker Associates, adhered to an ideological agenda, taking on clients whose politics and goals matched those of its founders. Others represented all comers, from oil industry executives to the Girl Scouts. As such lobbying firms proliferated, so too did the "revolving door" through which former government officials either opened political consultancies on their own—as did Nixon/Ford veteran William Timmons and Carter policy advisor Stu Eizenstat—or went to work for others, trading on their years of experience with the personalities and peculiarities of Capitol Hill.[44]

As with lobbyists in general, counting such firms is complicated by the fact that many euphemistically referred to themselves as public relations consultants or law firms, since the business of lobbying carried such a stigma. "My mother has never introduced me to her friends as 'my son, the lobbyist,'" one lobbyist reportedly commented. "I can't say I blame her. Being a lobbyist has long been synonymous in the minds of many Americans with being a glorified pimp." Pimps or no, independent government relations firms embodied the new spirit of corporate lobbying by the end of the 1980s, outnumbering those lobbyists directly employed by specific companies and casting a long shadow over public impressions of lobbying itself.[45]

In part, the rapid rise of professional lobbying outfits grew from structural changes in the operation of Congress, especially campaign financing. Between 1974 and 1982, the total amount of money spent by all candidates running for seats in the House and Senate increased fourfold, from $77 million to $343 million. The increased use of television ads and the growing number of hotly contested races, caused in large part by partisan realignment, explain a portion of the cost hike, but the most important reason was the massive influx of campaign contributions inaugurated by newly legal political action committees. With more money to spend, candidates—both incumbents and challengers—increasingly engaged in a type of arms race, where each election cycle seemed to cost more to win than the previous one. Although most large organizations, particularly pan-industry employers' associations, concentrated on lobbying in lieu of campaign donations, entrepreneurial lobbyists discovered that they could prevail on their clients to increase donations to a variety of candidates, earning legislators' gratitude and, with luck, cooperation in the process. Although social scientists argue about the actual effectiveness of this tactic, its logical appeal certainly encouraged large numbers of influence peddlers to give it a try.[46]

At the same time, the eclipse of business groups by professional lobbyists also reflected the changing policy debates of the 1980s. Although a financial services company like American Express may have supported the Business Roundtable's drive to reduce the national deficit, it hired Washington insider Robert Gray, a Harvard MBA holder and veteran of the Eisenhower administration, to reduce government surcharges on credit cards. The American Tobacco Institute may have agreed with Chamber of Commerce president Richard Lesher about the need to lower personal income tax rates, but it hired a specialist to help keep taxes on cigarettes down.[47] In an anxious world of fractured interests, conflicting policy visions, and high political stakes, looking out for one's own proved a more appealing strategy than working collectively for a broader goal.

LOBBYING AMERICA

The politics of business certainly did not come to an end as Ronald Reagan's presidency drew to a close, but the political terrain on which national employers' groups had mobilized, united, and lobbied collectively during the economic crisis of the 1970s had shifted beyond recognition. The social, intellectual, and cultural dislocations of this "age of fracture" mirrored the anxieties that the new globalized and financialized world of modern capitalism stoked among corporate leaders. Moreover, many of the most galvanizing issues that had rallied the business community in the 1960s and 1970s had been settled. In some cases, the "business view" had triumphed. Full employment planning, price controls, and an active "industrial policy" all moldered in their graves. Meanwhile, organized labor staggered on, a shadow of its past self, and a deregulatory "market ethos" appeared to permeate political discourse. In other cases, the victory was incomplete: the national debt still appeared insurmountable at the end of the Reagan years, and business conservatives had accepted a negotiated peace on regulatory reform and the persistence of social regulations. Win or lose, though, by the early 1990s, such big-ticket ideological issues no longer dominated Washington politics. Instead, corporate lobbyists worked on small details and short-term benefits, finding that their most lucrative path lay in locating obscure tax code provisions and spending appropriations, where a tiny line of legislative text could have enormous repercussions for an individual company's bottom line.

The shifting center of political gravity signaled the limitations of collective action by organized business groups, but their legacy loomed large. The economic travails of the 1970s affected the entire industrialized world, and the mobilization of American business groups provided a model for similar experiments in capitalist-class political action in many other countries. Japan, for example, experienced tremendous economic growth in the 1970s, despite relatively minor hiccups during the 1973 and 1979 oil crises. To the chagrin of Detroit-based automobile makers and other American manufacturers, Japan's trade surplus with the United States widened steadily through the 1980s. Although the strength of Japan's exports reflected the active support of its government, many Japanese business leaders saw the low-tax, antiregulatory policies of the Reagan years as an enviable model. In the 1980s and 1990s, its powerful business associations—especially the Keidanren (Federation of Economic Organizations)—began to supplant government agencies as the essential conduits of economic information between industry and policymakers and embrace a sharply conservative economic position on issues from taxes to regulation to the national budget. As Japanese business historian Miles Fletcher has argued, such rigid and well-organized insistence on that economic vision in fact inhibited a vigorous response to Japan's severe economic recession and "lost decade" of the 1990s.[48]

The mobilization of American corporate leaders also provided a model for European employers' associations, which became increasingly engaged in a market-oriented political project in the 1980s and 1990s and often drew on the rhetorical and organizational strategies that American business leaders and their lobbyists pioneered. First founded in 1965, the

Confederation of British Industry grew to include some 13,000 member companies and 200 trade associations by the mid-1980s—approximately the same size as the NAM—and distinguished itself as the unquestioned "voice of business" in negotiations with British government ministers. In 1983, the CEO of Swedish carmaker Volvo spearheaded the creation of the European Round Table of Industrialists, explicitly modeled on the Business Roundtable, which united European manufacturing executives to lobby various European governments on innovation and pro-competitive policies.[49]

But the most significant legacy of the political mobilization of America's business community played out at home. As the history of this movement illustrates, global responses to economic dislocations are inherently idiosyncratic. How the United States, Europe, and Japan responded to the crisis of the 1970s varied based on individual countries' political traditions, institutions, and often the skills and motivations of leaders from its public, private, and intellectual sectors. In the United States, that response bore the clear stamp of the employers' associations and large corporations whose leaders, often in tense collaboration with other conservative activists, pushed their economic vision on policymakers and the public. This historically unique level of coordination and collective action unfolded at a key juncture in the history of American and international political economy in which traditional alliances, priorities, and social visions all found themselves in a state of flux and the outcome was uncertain. The history of this movement belies the notion that the crisis of capitalistic growth in the late twentieth century would naturally lead to the triumph of market fundamentalism. Indeed, the ultimate fracture of the business coalition and the persistence of liberal institutions and ideas in the United States, however weakened, suggest that the triumph of neoliberalism has been exaggerated. Nonetheless, corporate leaders' sustained campaign to "lobby America" reformulated the way Americans debate economic issues from taxes to workers' rights and significantly reshaped the range of politically feasible policy options. So although their acute moment of coordinated activism has passed, business's persistent political clout testifies to their lasting legacy.

APPENDIX 8.1: LEADERSHIP OF THE BUSINESS ROUNDTABLE, 1988

Source: *Business Roundtable Report*, June 1988.

Executive Committee
    Chairman: Edmund Pratt, Pfizer
    Co-Chairman: John Akers, IBM
    Co-Chairman: James Lynn, Aetna
    Co-Chairman: James Robinson, American Express

Policy Committee
    Edward Addison, Southern Company
    Howard Allen, Southern California Edison
    Robert Allen, AT&T
    Rand Araskog, IT&T
    H. Brewster Atwater, General Mills
    Norman Augustine, Lockheed Martin
    Stephen Bechtel, Bechtel
    William Boeschenstein, Owens-Corning Fiberglass
    Edward Brennan, Sears
    James Burke, Johnson & Johnson
    Wayne Calloway, PepsiCo
    Colby Chandler, Eastman Kodak
    John Clendenin, Bell South
    John Creedon, Met Life
    Robert Daniell, United Technologies
    Richard Gelb, Bristol-Myers
    John Georges, International Paper
    Marshall Hahn, Georgia Pacific
    Robert Hanson, Deere
    Philip Hawley, Hawley Carter Hale
    Richard Heckert, DuPont
    William Howell, J. C. Penney
    Jerry Junkins, Texas Instruments
    David Kearns, Xerox
    Robert Kilpatrick, Cigna
    Drew Lewis, Union Pacific
    Richard Mahoney, Monsanto
    Robert Malott, FMC
    Hamish Maxwell, Philip Morris
    John McGillicuddy, Manufacturers Hanover
    Ruben Mettler, TRW
    Richard Morrow, Amoco
    Allen Murray, Mobil

Paul H. O'Neill, Alcoa
John Ong, BFGoodrich
Donald Petersen, Ford Motor Company
Lewis Preston, JP Morgan
Lawrence G. Rawl, Exxon
John S. Reed, Citi
David M. Roderick, U.S. Steel
Vincent Sarni, PPG
George Schaefer, Caterpillar
Frank Shrontz, Boeing
John Smale, Proctor and Gamble
Roger Smith, General Motors
Roy Vagelos, Merck
William Weiss, Ameritech
Jack Welch, General Electric
Henry Wendt, SmithKline
Walter Williams, Bethlehem Steel
Robert Winters, Prudential
John Young, Hewlett-Packard

American Politics, American Business

ON JANUARY 21, 2010, the U.S. Supreme Court handed down a 5–4 decision in the case of *Citizens United v. Federal Election Commission*, inflaming anew a classic debate over the place of business in American politics. The five justices in the majority, all conservatives appointed by Republican presidents, held that the First Amendment's protection of free speech prohibited Congress from limiting political campaign advertising, or "electioneering communication," by incorporated for-profit or not-for-profit organizations. At a stroke, the ruling appeared to undercut a century's worth of legislation, from the 1907 Tillman Act to the 2002 Bipartisan Campaign Finance (McCain-Feingold) Act, the specific law it addressed. And while the majority's language and logic applied to campaign spending by labor unions as well as by business firms, the partisan nature of the decision and the notably muted role of labor in national politics left no doubt that *Citizens United* paved the way for tremendous campaign spending by powerful, wealthy, and presumably right-leaning corporations. Many conservatives—from elected officials to intellectuals at think tanks and universities to organized activists—hailed the ruling as both a victory for free speech and a clear boon to their political influence. Liberals, on the other hand, howled that the Court had opened what President Barack Obama called "the floodgates for an unlimited amount of special interest money" through "unbridled corporate spending." For many such detractors, *Citizens United* seemed to mark the climax of the very process described in this book: the self-conscious campaign by the leaders of major corporations to seize and wield tremendous, self-interested power over American public life.[1]

The long-term effects of *Citizens United* remain to be seen. (As of this writing, the issues and candidates promoted by self-described "business conservatives" have seen mixed results; they performed quite well in the 2010 midterms and subsequent state-level battles over union rights but came up notably short in the 2012 presidential and congressional elections.) Nonetheless, the vehement reaction by its critics, capped famously when Obama took the unusual step of rebuking the conservative members of the Court directly to their faces during his State of the Union address, illustrates that battles over the role of business in politics have only grown more heated in the years since the story told in this book came to a conclusion. In the aftermath of the 2008 financial disaster, both the right and the left exploded in populist indignation at the excesses of corporate influence. From the Tea Party Movement's rants against government bailouts to Occupy Wall Street's denunciation of the injustices of finance, American politics remained as wrapped up as ever in debates over the power of corporations.

Yet one of this book's principal arguments is that business's influence on politics is historically contingent. It is thus vital to recognize that neither "business" nor "politics" in the second decade of the twenty-first century operates in the same way as it did during the 1970s and 1980s. Indeed, the very notion of the "corporation," both politically and economically, has changed dramatically. For some business theorists, the old concept of the corporation as a social institution is a relic of a bygone era; in an age of high finance, instantaneous communication, just-in-time production, cheap global outsourcing, and overhyped IPOs, the modern corporation often appears as little more than a convenient legal construct. If a corporation merely exists as a "nexus of contracts," any larger sense of identity disappears as atomized individual economic actors seek immediate material gains for themselves. Indeed, much of modern "corporate America" (a term whose use has skyrocketed since the late 1980s) would appear quite unrecognizable to the men who formed the Business Roundtable in 1972. To be sure, large industrial corporations still contribute mightily to the American economy. The ranks of the nation's largest firms still include DuPont, General Electric, and, thanks to a timely bailout from the federal government in 2009 that would have made former CEO Thomas Murphy livid, General Motors. Yet those firms' cultural and political status as "Big Business" has been usurped by newcomers, particularly in the technology, retail, and financial services industries.[2]

Of these new sectors, finance is by far the most historically significant. As millions of Americans—indeed, global citizens the world over—learned during the financial crisis of 2008 and 2009, the financial services industry wields nearly unfathomable economic power in modern capitalism. Infinitely complex systems of lending and borrowing at lightning speeds among massively leveraged institutions shape every aspect of today's world, linking a home mortgage in California to a bond issue in Iceland to a pension plan in Greece. Financial interests, from household names like JPMorgan to anonymous but immensely wealthy hedge funds, have largely replaced the titans of the industrial age, both in political influence and in the popular imagination. Indeed, between 1998 and 2009, financial, insurance, and real estate firms spent close to $4 billion on lobbying, dwarfing the political expenditures of all other sectors.[3]

Consider the following: In 1968, a moderate Republican and governor of a northern industrial state unsuccessfully sought his party's nomination for president on the strength of his private sector experience. A generation later, his son—also a moderate Republican and former governor of a northern state—ran for president on much the same grounds, finally winning the GOP nomination before losing the general election in 2012. The differences between these two "business" candidates tell a powerful story about the changes in the politics of American business. The candidate from the 1960s, George Romney, never earned a college degree, began his career at Alcoa, and eventually became CEO of the American Motors Corporation; his son Mitt, holder of an MBA from Harvard, touted his "business experience" based on the millions of dollars he had made as a founder of and investor with an "alternative asset management firm," Bain Capital.[4]

Yet while the corporate world itself has changed profoundly since the period of business's mobilization in the 1970s, the organizations that proved so influential to that story remain intact, well-funded, and active. In 2012, the U.S. Chamber of Commerce spent more money on lobbying (some $95 million) than any other single entity and continued to promote itself as the voice of the entire business community. Although Richard Lesher stepped down as president in 1997, his successor, Thomas Donohue—like Lesher a veteran of the ideological battles of the 1970s and 1980s—imbued the organization with the same commitment to small-government conservative principles. Similarly, the National Association of Manufacturers continues to lobby on regulatory, trade, and tax policy, combining the interests of small and large manufacturers, though it largely remains overshadowed in size, clout, and renown by the Chamber. Finally, the Business Roundtable also maintains an active voice in domestic and international economic affairs, providing a forum in which big-business executives can engage government officials. Founding corporations like DuPont, Alcoa, and Campbell's (but not U.S. Steel) remain, but the group has expanded to include technology firms like Microsoft, Intel, and Yahoo (not Google), as well as retailers like Wal-Mart and Target.[5] (See appendix at the end of the epilogue.)

The fragmentation and fracture that characterized the once-unified business lobbying community by the early 1990s largely persisted in the twenty years that followed, punctuated by occasional moments of cohesion on particular issues. During the acute crisis of late 2008 and early 2009, most prominent voices within the business community favored massive government economic intervention, including the Troubled Asset Relief Program (TARP), the Obama administration's stimulus plan (the American Recovery and Reinvestment Act of 2009), and bailouts of Chrysler and General Motors. Much as they did during the deficit debates of the Reagan years, major employers' associations put their traditional rhetoric about "free markets" aside in the interest of salvaging the economy, much to the consternation of some of their more ideologically libertarian members. Moreover, the political and economic fallout from the financial crisis placed further strains on these conservative business groups. For example, the Dodd-Frank Wall Street Reform and Consumer Protection Act, which aimed to rectify the regulatory lapses that led to the financial crisis, became law in 2010 despite a fevered conservative opposition that included the most powerful voices within the business community, none more so than financial firms.[6]

Finally, the Patient Protection and Affordable Care Act of 2010—the most bitterly divisive social legislation since the 1960s—exposed organized business's persistent limitations. Although the Chamber of Commerce lobbied hard, and successfully, to kill plans for a government-sponsored insurance program known as the "public option," business as a whole remained ambivalent about health care reform, despite widespread conservative and libertarian opposition. In fact, many pharmaceutical companies and hospitals strongly supported certain reform provisions, and the Business Roundtable endorsed placing "an obligation on all Americans to have health insurance coverage." Although organized conservatives, from the Republican Party leadership to the local and national organizations who financed the Tea Party, screamed themselves red in the face over "Obamacare," the business community largely stayed on the sidelines.[7]

The legacy of business's political mobilization in the 1970s extends beyond the institutional players and their often ambivalent policy positions. Just as important, the struggles chronicled in this book profoundly shaped the political debates that the United States continues to confront in the second decade of the twenty-first century. While the business world itself has evolved mightily, many of today's hottest political issues would feel eerily familiar to the corporate leaders whose stories populate this book. Seminal problems that have shaped the American political economy for hundreds of years acquired their modern dynamics precisely during the period of business's mobilization in the 1970s. The social and economic categories, the political language, and the underlying anxieties that prompted Lewis Powell to pen his famous memorandum and pushed Roger Blough to assemble his Roundtable continue to animate the politics of business. From regulation to taxes, trade to organized labor, our world is their world, and the powerful critique of New Deal–style liberalism that organized business leaders helped promote and perpetuate remains a steadfast part of American political life.

As we have seen, the century-long struggle between management and labor came to a head in the late twentieth century as the triumph of corporate lobbying collided with the rapid decline in union membership and the consequent waning of organized labor's political clout. Although many of the industrial giants who spearheaded the creation of the Business Roundtable represented large, stable firms that had forged relatively functional labor relations in the post–World War II decades, they also absorbed the strident antilabor views common among smaller manufacturers. And in the end, business's coordinated assault on union power during the stagflation crisis of the 1970s, both in Congress and in public debate, proved too powerful for labor-liberalism to rebuff. Antilabor practices played out in the operational decisions of individual firms, including plant relocations and offshoring of production, as well as in local and state politics. At the same time, national business groups' pivotal role at the federal level impeded efforts to expand unionization to new regions or new industries, further weakening the labor movement's ability to confront the swiftly changing landscape of global capitalism. As manufacturing moved abroad, union jobs went with it; as service industries replaced heavy industry, organized labor failed to gain a foothold in those new growth sectors. Indeed, in the late twentieth century, the only area in which union membership increased was in public employment.[8]

In addition to losing members, unions also declined as a cultural and political force, in large part because business lobbyists and other conservatives successfully defined labor in the public discourse as a "special interest." One of the most pivotal moments came in the summer of 1981, when Ronald Reagan angrily confronted 13,000 members of the Professional Air Traffic Controllers Organization (PATCO). Despite laws prohibiting strikes by public employees (they worked for the Federal Aviation Administration), PATCO workers had walked off the job to demand higher pay, a shorter work week, and other reforms. Although public sector strikes had succeeded in years past, Reagan—the only U.S. president to have been the head of a labor union (he ran the Screen Actors Guild in the 1940s)—engaged PATCO in a standoff, ordering the air traffic controllers to return to work or face dismissal and possible arrest. When only 1,300 did so, Reagan summarily fired more than 11,500 and later decertified the union. While historians rightly attribute Reagan's ability to stare down and break PATCO to his particular anti-union resolve and personal popularity, the gambit only succeeded politically because a growing segment of the public had come to accept conservative arguments that unions had grown overly powerful and self-interested. Thirty years after the PATCO incident, labor-liberals remain thwarted at both the state and federal levels. Conservatives in midwestern states like Michigan and Wisconsin have battled to invoke the Taft-Hartley Act and adopt "right-to-work" anti-unionization laws, while congressional Democrats fail to make any headway on significant pro-union issues, particularly the Employee Free Choice, or card-check, legislation that would facilitate the formation of unions. Such struggles, even with an overwhelmingly Democratic Congress during the first two years of Obama's presidency, testify to the long-term legacy of business's antilabor efforts.[9]

In addition to their campaign against organized labor, business conservatives in the 1970s and 1980s also helped change the national conversation on regulation. In both spirit and policy, the antiregulatory mantra of organized business groups gathered steam in the 1980s and 1990s. Although the social regulation regime that galvanized business leaders in the 1960s, particularly consumer, workplace, and environmental protections, remained largely intact, a growing philosophical resistance to new regulations blocked efforts to respond to new economic realities, particularly concerning financial services. In 2007, legal scholar (and future U.S. senator) Elizabeth Warren, riffing on Ralph Nader's career-making book, published an article called "Unsafe at Any Rate," explaining that while consumer products benefited from stringent regulations, financial products left Americans susceptible to fraud, hardship, and injury. On a larger level, antiregulatory policymakers (including many Democrats in the Clinton administration) blocked efforts to subject the financial instruments known as derivatives to regulatory oversight. The disastrous economic crisis of 2008 laid bare the consequences of weak financial regulation, which the Dodd-Frank Act of 2010 sought to redress. Only the future shall tell, however, whether the financial crisis and the ensuing Great Recession will ultimately mark a turn away from the antiregulatory ethos that business leaders in the 1970s did so much to nurture. Yet as skeptics of Dodd-Frank point out, its regulations rely to a significant degree on the participation of financial firms themselves, generating precisely the problem of regulatory capture that contributed to skepticism of the regulatory project a generation ago.[10]

Finally, the debates over taxes and deficits that helped unravel the unity of purpose among national employers' associations in the 1980s remain constant fixtures in national politics. Although negotiations between Congress and the Clinton administration yielded three years of budget surplus in the late 1990s, a series of circumstances—themselves the legacy of the battles fought among organized business groups—conspired to undo that solvency in the first decade of the twentieth century. In 2001 and 2003, a divided and partisan Congress, persuaded by supply-side arguments from the George W. Bush White House, dramatically lowered marginal tax rates, quickly turning budget surpluses into shortfalls. Dramatic increases in military spending due to extended operations in Iraq and Afghanistan further inflated the deficits; Ronald Reagan may have told OMB director David Stockman that "defense is not a budget issue," but it is. Beginning in 2009, the disastrous effects of the economic crisis placed enormous strains on the federal budget, driving up social service spending even as sustained unemployment, which reached 10 percent in 2009, decreased tax revenues. America in the Obama years faces protracted and deeply partisan battles over the future of the nation's tax code, social welfare programs, and long-term fiscal health, with no end in sight. The contentious politics of taxes and budgets prove as divisive, not least to business-minded conservatives, as ever.[11]

These issues and myriad others define the landscape of American politics in an evolving, expanding world. As the global economy changes and as American policymakers wrestle with hard choices about how and where to compete, how to encourage innovation, and how to treat and care for their citizens, the leaders of major business enterprises and their representative organizations will remain a permanent fixture in our politics. Their policy preferences and degree of effectiveness, however, will remain as contingent in the future as they were in the past. Corporations are not people, my friend, but people do run corporations. The decisions made and the goals pursued by the people who make up the nation's business leadership resonate across all levels of society. Tomorrow, like yesterday, the women and men who manage private enterprises hold great promise to lead, innovate, and serve the public. At the same time, history teaches us that they also may follow the path of inaction, bogged down in narrow self-interest and overcome by the weight of ideology. How business leaders choose to navigate the world of politics will have just as tremendous an effect on the rest of us in the new century as it did in the last. The history of the politics of business in America is storied; its future remains to be written.

APPENDIX: List of Member Corporations of the Business Roundtable, 2013

Source: www.businessroundtable.org, accessed February 16, 2013.

A. O. Smith	American Express Company
ABB Inc., USA	Ameriprise Financial
Abbott	Amgen, Inc.
Accenture PLC	Anadarko Petroleum Corporation
ACE Limited	Apache Corporation
AES Corporation	Arch Coal, Inc.
Aetna, Inc.	AT&T, Inc.
AGCO Corporation	Automatic Data Processing, Inc.
AK Steel Corporation	Avery Dennison Corporation
Alcoa, Inc.	Avis Budget Group, Inc.
Altec, Inc.	Ball Corporation
American Electric Power Company, Inc.	Bank of America
	Barclays PLC

Bausch + Lomb
Bayer AG
Bechtel Group, Inc.
BlackRock, Inc.
Blackstone Group
BNSF Railway Company
Boeing Company
BorgWarner, Inc.
Brink's Company
C. V. Starr & Co., Inc.
CA Technologies
Caesars Entertainment Corporation
Campbell Soup Company
Cardinal Health, Inc.
Case New Holland, Inc.
Caterpillar Inc.
CBRE Group, Inc.
CF Industries Holdings Inc.
CH2M HILL, Ltd.
Charles Schwab Corporation
Chesapeake Energy Corporation
Chevron Corporation
Chrysler Group LLC
Cigna Corporation
Cisco Systems, Inc.
Citigroup, Inc.
Coca-Cola Company
Cognizant Technology Solutions Corporation
Comcast Corporation
Computer Sciences Corporation
Conoco Phillips
Convergys Corporation
Corning, Inc.
Covidien PLC
Crane Co.
CSX
Cummins, Inc.
CVS Caremark Corporation
Danaher Corporation
Darden Restaurants, Inc.
DaVita, Inc.
Deere & Company

Dell, Inc.
Deloitte LLP
DIRECTV Group, Inc.
Dominion Resources, Inc.
Dow Chemical Company
Duke Energy Corporation
DuPont
Eastman Chemical Company
Eaton
Edison International
Eli Lilly and Company
EMC Corporation
Ernst & Young
Exelis, Inc.
Express Scripts, Inc.
Exxon Mobil Corporation
FedEx Corporation
Fifth & Pacific Companies, Inc.
First Solar, Inc.
Fluor Corporation
FMC Corporation
Ford Motor Company
Freeport-McMoRan Copper & Gold, Inc.
Frontier Communications Corporation
Gannet Co., Inc.
General Electric Company
General Mills, Inc.
General Motors
Goldman Sachs Group, Inc.
Grant Thornton LLP
Hanes Brands, Inc.
Harman International Industries, Inc.
Harris Corporation
Hartford Financial Services Group
Hasbro, Inc.
Hertz Global Holdings, Inc.
Hess Corporation
Honeywell International, Inc.
Humana, Inc.
Ingersoll-Rand PLC
Intel Corporation

International Business Machines
  Corporation
International Paper Company
Interpublic Group of Companies,
  Inc.
ITC Holdings Corp.
ITT Corporation
Johnson & Johnson
Johnson Controls, Inc.
JPMorgan Chase & Co.
Kelly Services, Inc.
Kindred Healthcare, Inc.
KPMG LLP
Liberty Mutual Group
Macy's, Inc.
Marathon Oil Corporation
MassMutual Financial Group
MasterCard Worldwide
McDermott International, Inc.
McGraw-Hill Companies
McKesson Corporation
Medtronic, Inc.
Meijer, Inc.
Merck & Co., Inc.
Meredith Corporation
Meritor, Inc.
MetLife, Inc.
Microsoft Corporation
Motorola Solutions, Inc.
NASDAQ OMX
National Gypsum Company
Navistar International Corporation
New York Life Insurance Co.
NextEra Energy, Inc.
Norfolk Southern Corporation
Northrop Grumman Corporation
Nucor Corporation
Owens Corning
Peabody Energy Corporation
PepsiCo, Inc.
Peter Kiewit Sons, Inc.
Pfizer Inc.
PG&E Corporation

Phillips 66
PricewaterhouseCoopers LLP
Principal Financial Group, Inc.
Procter & Gamble Company
Prudential Financial, Inc.
Public Service Enterprise Group, Inc.
QUALCOMM, Inc.
R. R. Donnelley & Sons
Realogy Corporation
Rockwell Automation, Inc.
Rockwell Collins, Inc.
Ryder Systems, Inc.
Sanofi-Aventis
SAP AG
SAS Institute, Inc.
Sealed Air Corporation
Shell Oil Company
Siemens Corporation
Simon Property Group, Inc.
Southern Company
Stanley Black & Decker, Inc.
State Farm Insurance Companies
Steelcase, Inc.
Suffolk Construction Company, Inc.
SunGard Data Systems, Inc.
Target Corporation
Telephone and Data Systems, Inc.
Tenet Healthcare Corporation
Tenneco, Inc.
Texas Instruments, Inc.
Textron, Inc.
Thermo Fisher Scientific, Inc.
Time Warner Cable, Inc.
Tishman Speyer Properties, L.P.
TransCanada Corporation
Travelers Companies, Inc.
Tyco International Ltd.
UnitedHealth Group Incorporated
United Parcel Service, Inc.
United Technologies Corporation
Universal Health Services, Inc.
Verizon Communications
Viacom, Inc.

Visa, Inc.
W. W. Grainger, Inc.
Wal-Mart Stores, Inc.
WellPoint, Inc.
WESCO International, Inc.
Western & Southern Financial
  Group
Weyerhaeuser Company

Whirlpool Corporation
Williams Companies
Windstream Corporation
WL Ross & Co. LLC
World Fuel Services Corporation
Wyndham Worldwide Corporation
Xerox Corporation
Yahoo! Inc.

Abbreviations

The following abbreviations indicate the major repositories referenced in this book.

BRA	Business Roundtable Archives, Washington, DC
CB	Conference Board Papers, Hagley Museum and Library, Wilmington, DE
CBM	Charles B. McCoy Papers, Hagley Museum and Library, Wilmington, DE
CCAG	Connecticut Citizens' Action Group, Thomas J. Dodd Research Center, University of Connecticut, Storrs-Mansfield, CT
GHWB	George Bush Presidential Library and Museum, College Station, TX
GRF	Gerald R. Ford Presidential Library and Museum, Ann Arbor, MI
JEC	Jimmy Carter Library and Museum, Atlanta, GA
JFK	John F. Kennedy Presidential Library and Museum, Boston, MA
LBJ	Lyndon Baines Johnson Library and Museum, Austin, TX
NAM	National Association of Manufacturers Archives, Hagley Museum and Library, Wilmington, DE
PR	Philip Reed Papers, Hagley Museum and Library, Wilmington, DE
RMN	Nixon Presidential Library and Museum, Yorba Linda, CA
RWR	Ronald Reagan Presidential Foundation and Library, Simi Valley, CA
SE	Sam Ervin Papers, Southern Historical Collection, Wilson Library, University of North Carolina, Chapel Hill, NC
USCOC	United States Chamber of Commerce Archives, Hagley Museum and Library, Wilmington, DE

Notes

1. Philip Rucker, "Mitt Romney Says 'Corporations Are People' at Iowa State Fair," *Washington Post*, August 11, 2011.

2. On the intellectual history of this dichotomy, see in particular Daniel T. Rodgers, *The Age of Fracture* (Cambridge, MA: Harvard University Press, 2011), 41–47.

3. On the state of the field of the history of American conservatism, see especially Kim Phillips-Fein, "Conservatism: A Round Table," *Journal of American History* 98:3 (December 2011): 723–73 and Julian E. Zelizer, "Reflections: Rethinking the History of American Conservatism," *Reviews in American History* 38:2 (June 2010): 367–92.

4. Historians disagree sharply about the place of race and racism among economic conservatives, particularly business leaders. Jennifer Delton has recently argued that many business leaders voluntarily and cheerfully rejected racially exclusive employment practices and embraced inclusiveness in the second half of the twentieth century. Nancy MacLean, to the contrary, documents the persistence of racism within the business world and many business leaders' ardent opposition to affirmative action policies. Jennifer A. Delton, *Racial Integration in Corporate America, 1940–1990* (Cambridge: Cambridge University Press, 2009); Nancy MacLean, *Freedom Is Not Enough: The Opening of the American Workplace* (Cambridge, MA: Harvard University Press, 2006).

5. Alan Brinkley, *The End of Reform: New Deal Liberalism in Recession and War* (New York: Vintage Books, 1995).

6. On think tanks, see Alice O'Connor, "Financing the Counter-Revolution," in *Rightward Bound: Making America Conservative in the 1970s*, ed. Bruce J. Schulman and Julian E. Zelizer (Cambridge, MA: Harvard University Press, 2008), 148–68. On corporate political representation, see Cathie Martin, *Shifting the Burden: The Struggle over Growth and Corporate Taxation* (Chicago: University of Chicago Press, 1991), 119–20.

7. On business associations, multinational corporations, and international economic policy, see Vernie Oliveiro, "The United States, Multinational Corporations, and the Politics of Globalization in the 1970s" (Ph.D. diss. Harvard University, 2010). On capital mobility, see Jefferson Cowie, *Capital Moves: RCA's Seventy-Year Quest for Cheap Labor* (New York: New Press, 1999) and Elizabeth Tandy Shermer, *Sunbelt Capitalism: Phoenix and the Transformation of American Politics* (Philadelphia: University of Pennsylvania Press, 2013).

8. Jeffrey H. Birnbaum, *The Lobbyists: How Influence Peddlers Get Their Way in Washington* (New York: Random House, 1992); Peter Grier, "The Lobbyist

throughout History: Villainy and Virtue," *Christian Science Monitor*, September 28, 2009.

9. Lewis Anthony Dexter, *How Organizations Are Represented in Washington: Toward a Broader Understanding of the Seeking of Influence and of Patterns of Representation* (1969; Lanham, MD: University Press of America, 1987), 64; John M. de Figueiredo, "Lobbying and Information in Politics," *Business and Politics* 4:2 (2002): 125–29.

10. Clive S. Thomas, "Interest Group Regulation across the United States: Rationale, Development and Consequences," *Parliamentary Affairs* 51:4 (1998): 500–515; Birnbaum, *The Lobbyists*, 13.

11. George Thayer, *Who Shakes the Money Tree? American Campaign Financing Practices from 1789 to the Present* (New York: Simon and Schuster, 1973); Stephen Ansolabehere, John M. de Figueiredo, and James M. Snyder Jr., "Why Is There So Little Money in U.S. Politics?" *Journal of American Economic Perspectives* 17:1 (Winter 2003): 105–30.

12. Stephen Ansolabehere, James M. Snyder, and Micky Tipathi, "Are PAC Contributions and Lobbying Linked? New Evidence from the 1995 Lobby Disclosure Act," *Business and Politics* 4:2 (August 2002): 131–55.

13. Kay Lehman Schlozman and John T. Tierney, *Organized Interests and American Democracy* (New York: Harper and Row, 1986).

14. David B. Yoffie and Sigrid Bergenstein, "Creating Political Advantage: The Rise of the Corporate Political Entrepreneur," *California Management Review* 28:1 (Fall 1985): 124–39.

CHAPTER 1

The chapter epigraph is taken from Joseph Coors, "A Call to Action," National Association of Manufacturers Public Affairs Conference, October 24, 1975, box 119, NAM.

1. Lewis Powell to Eugene Sydnor, "Confidential Memorandum: Attack on American Free Enterprise System," August 23, 1971, series 2, box 28, USCOC.

2. Anonymous executive quoted in Leonard Silk and David Vogel, *Ethics and Profits: The Crisis of Confidence in American Business* (New York: Simon and Schuster, 1976), 71.

3. William J. Baroody Sr., "Industry's Future: The Issue Is Survival," speech at the National Association of Manufacturers Public Affairs Conference, October 22, 1975, box 119, NAM.

4. Senator James L. Buckley, Address to the Business Council, Hot Springs, Virginia, October 11, 1974, enclosed in Wallace Bates to Members of the Policy Committee, January 23, 1975, 1975 Correspondence, BRA.

5. Powell to Sydnor, "Confidential Memorandum."

6. As historian Wendy L. Wall has demonstrated, the term "free enterprise system" only became common in the United States in the 1930s, largely through the deliberate work of anti–New Deal business leaders. See Wall, *Inventing the "American Way": The Politics of Consensus from the New Deal to the Civil*

Rights Movement (Oxford: Oxford University Press, 2008), 48–49. Lacking a rigorous definition, the phrase generally evoked a "liberal market economy," in the phrase of political scientists, to be distinguished from "managed market economies" that, while non-socialist, entailed a stronger regulatory and planning role for the state. For many, the term carried a meaning similar to the old-fashioned term "laissez-faire" without the stigma of heartlessness and law-of-the-jungle economic chaos associated with the late nineteenth century. Readers interested in social science discussions of "liberal" and "managed" market economies should see Peter A. Hall and David Soskice, eds., *Varieties of Capitalism: The Institutional Foundations of Comparative Advantage* (New York: Oxford University Press, 2001). On the intellectual history of "laissez-faire" economics in the twentieth century, see in particular Angus Burgin, *The Great Persuasion: Reinventing Free Markets since the Depression* (Cambridge, MA: Harvard University Press, 2012).

7. "Industry Unites for Good of All: 15,000 Employers Combine in Giant Band for Mutual Aid," *New York Times*, November 16, 1916; "Industrial Board Planned: Will Deal with State and National Law Makers," *Washington Post*, November 16, 1916.

8. Silk and Vogel, *Ethics and Profits*, 105, 126. For similar public opinion polls, see Seymour Martin Lipset and William Schneider, *The Confidence Gap: Business, Labor, and Government in the Public Mind* (Baltimore: Johns Hopkins University Press, 1987) and "Confidence in Leaders of Ten Institutions, 1966–84," Robert M. Teeter Papers, box 132, file Selected Issues: Issues/Confidence in Institutions (1), GRF.

9. H. M. Gitelman, "Management's Crisis of Confidence and the Origin of the National Industrial Conference Board, 1914–1916," *Business History Review* 58:2 (Summer 1984): 153–77.

10. Kim Phillips-Fein, *Invisible Hands: The Making of the Conservative Movement from the New Deal to Reagan* (New York: W. W. Norton, 2009), 5.

11. Alfred D. Chandler Jr., "Government versus Business: An American Phenomenon," in *Business and Public Policy*, ed. John T. Dunlop (Cambridge, MA: Harvard University Press, 1980), 1–11; Sanford M. Jacoby, "American Exceptionalism Revisited: The Importance of Management," in *Masters to Managers: Historical and Comparative Perspectives on American Employers*, ed. Sanford M. Jacoby (New York: Columbia University Press, 1991), 173–200.

12. See, among many, Kim McQuaid, *Big Business and Presidential Power: From FDR to Reagan* (New York: Morrow, 1982); Martin J. Sklar, *The Corporate Reconstruction of American Capitalism, 1890–1916: The Market, the Law, and Politics* (Cambridge: Cambridge University Press, 1988); Richard R. John, *Network Nation: Inventing American Telecommunications* (Cambridge, MA: Harvard University Press, 2010); and Robert M. Collins, *More: The Politics of Economic Growth in Postwar America* (New York: Oxford University Press, 2000).

13. Silk and Vogel, *Ethics and Profits*, 65.

14. See Robert M. Collins, *The Business Response to Keynes, 1929–1964* (New York: Columbia University Press, 1981); McQuaid, *Big Business and*

Presidential Power; Lizabeth Cohen, *A Consumers' Republic: The Politics of Mass Consumption in Postwar America* (New York: Vintage Books, 2003); Brinkley, *The End of Reform*.

15. Elizabeth A. Fones-Wolf, *Selling Free Enterprise: The Business Assault on Labor and Liberalism, 1945–60* (Urbana: University of Illinois Press, 1994).

16. Phillips-Fein, *Invisible Hands*; Meg Jacobs, *Pocketbook Politics: Economic Citizenship in Twentieth-Century America* (Princeton: Princeton University Press, 2005); Cowie, *Capital Moves*.

17. See McQuaid, *Big Business and Presidential Power*; Collins, *More*.

18. Jonathan Soffer, "The National Association of Manufacturers and the Militarization of American Conservatism," *Business History Review* 75:4 (Winter 2001): 775–805.

19. David Vogel, *Fluctuating Fortunes: The Political Power of Business in America* (New York: Basic Books, 1989), 33.

20. Judith Stein, *Pivotal Decade: How the United States Traded Factories for Finance in the Seventies* (New Haven: Yale University Press, 2010).

21. Herman E. Krooss, *Executive Opinion: What Business Leaders Said and Thought on Economic Issues, 1920s–1960s* (New York: Doubleday, 1970), 252; "Business: J. P. Morgan Joins with Guaranty Trust," *Time*, December 29, 1958.

22. Hobart Rowen, *The Free Enterprisers: Kennedy, Johnson, and the Business Establishment* (New York: Putnam, 1964), 28–30. On the campaign motto, see "Politics: Who's Moving Where?" *Time*, September 7, 1962.

23. Rowen, *The Free Enterprisers*, 279.

24. For an interesting psycho-biographical discussion of Nixon's social status anxieties that explains his general antipathy toward the business world, see Rick Perlstein, *Nixonland: The Rise of a President and the Fracturing of America* (New York: Scribner, 2008). See also David Greenberg, *Nixon's Shadow: The History of an Image* (New York: W. W. Norton, 2003).

25. Krooss, *Executive Opinion*, 252.

26. Vogel, *Fluctuating Fortunes*, 17; Rowen, *The Free Enterprisers*, 20–22.

27. Elizabeth Tandy Shermer, "'Take Government Out of Business by Putting Business into Government': Local Boosters, National CEOs, Experts, and the Politics of Mid-Century Capital Mobility," in *What's Good for Business: Business and Politics since World War II*, ed. Kim Phillips-Fein and Julian E. Zelizer (New York: Oxford University Press, 2012), 91–106; Tami Friedman, "Exploiting the North-South Differential: Corporate Power, Southern Politics, and the Decline of Organized Labor after World War II," *Journal of American History* 95:2 (September 2008): 323–48.

28. McQuaid, *Big Business and Presidential Power*, 30, 64. Thirty years after its publication, McQuaid's examination of the BAC remains the most authoritative account of this organization from the New Deal through the 1970s. On the BAC in the 1930s, see also Collins, *The Business Response to Keynes*, 56–62.

29. McQuaid, *Big Business and Presidential Power*, 199–202; Rowen, *The Free Enterprisers*, 61–74; Vogel, *Fluctuating Fortunes*, 18–19.

30. On the steel industry before the New Deal, see David Brody, *Steelworkers in America: The Nonunion Era* (Cambridge, MA: Harvard University Press,

1960). On the 1952 crisis and the importance of corporate public relations, see especially Karen S. Miller, *The Voice of Business: Hill & Knowlton and Postwar Public Relations* (Chapel Hill: University of North Carolina Press, 1999).

31. John F. Kennedy, "The President's News Conference," April 11, 1962, in John Woolley and Gerhard Peters, *The American Presidency Project*.

32. Rowen, *The Free Enterprisers*, 104; McQuaid, *Big Business and Presidential Power*, 205–12.

33. On this campaign and the rightward shift in the Republican Party in the early 1960s, see especially Lisa McGirr, *Suburban Warriors: The Origins of the New American Right* (Princeton: Princeton University Press, 2001).

34. Rowen, *The Free Enterprisers*, 280.

35. Joe Califano to Lyndon Johnson, January 15, 1966, BE 4 2/26/65–7/6/66, LBJ. On Johnson's fiscal policies, see Robert Collins, "The Economic Crisis of 1968 and the Waning of the 'American Century,'" *American Historical Review* 101:2 (April 1996): 396–422, and Martin, *Shifting the Burden*, 52–106.

36. Dominique A. Tobbell, *Pills, Power, and Policy: The Struggle for Drug Reform in Cold War America and Its Consequences* (Berkeley: University of California Press, 2012), 91–94; Jennifer Klein, *For All These Rights: Business, Labor, and the Shaping of America's Public-Private Welfare State* (Princeton: Princeton University Press, 2003), 258–60. Although liberal reformers publicly denied conservative accusations that the Social Security Amendments represented a "trojan horse" paving the way to a larger goal, Johnson's Social Security administrator Robert Ball later admitted that "we confidently expected [the reforms] to be the first step toward national health insurance." Robert M. Ball, "Medicare Recollections," speech delivered July 20, 1995, quoted in Edward Berkowitz, "Medicare: The Great Society's Enduring National Health Insurance Program," in *The Great Society and the High Tide of Liberalism*, ed. Sidney M. Milkis and Jerome M. Mileur (Amherst: University of Massachusetts Press, 2005), 322.

37. Herbert Alexander, *Money in Politics* (Washington, DC: Public Affairs Press, 1972), 33, 166–75.

38. Bernadette Budde, Senior Vice President, BIPAC, interview by the author, April 7, 2011; Julian E. Zelizer, *On Capitol Hill: The Struggle to Reform Congress and Its Consequences, 1948–2000* (Cambridge: Cambridge University Press, 2004), 56–60.

39. Budde interview.

40. Business-Industry Political Action Committee, "Guidelines for the Formation of State Political Committees," box 221, NAM.

41. Zelizer, *On Capitol Hill*, 108–24, 318n6; Patrick J. Akard, "The Return of the Market: Corporate Mobilization and the Transformation of U.S. Economic Policy, 1974–1984" (Ph.D. diss., University of Kansas, 1989), 84–89. Despite the proliferation of corporate PACs, a study in 1982 suggested that businesspeople's traditional fears about crossing vague legal lines still restrained their political activities. See Edward Handler and John Mulkern, *Business in Politics: Campaign Strategies of Corporate Political Action Committees* (Lexington, MA: Lexington Books, 1982). For the FEC's count of official PACs over time, see http://www.fec.gov/press/summaries/2011/2011paccount.shtml.

42. George Reeder to Lyndon Johnson, September 26, 1967, BE 4 5/25/67–12/31/67, LBJ; Cathie J. Martin, "Business and the New Economic Activism: The Growth of Corporate Lobbies in the Sixties," *Polity* 27: 1 (Autumn 1994): 49–76. The Business-Government Relations Council still exists and supports lobbyists to congressional members of both parties.

43. Miller, *The Voice of Business*; Birnbaum, *The Lobbyists*, 13; Yoffie and Bergenstein, "Creating Political Advantage."

44. Rodney Markley to John Harper and Fred Borch, June 2, 1972, BRA; Steven A. Sass, *The Promise of Private Pensions: The First Hundred Years* (Cambridge, MA: Harvard University Press, 1997); Alden Whitman, "Sidney J. Weinberg Dies at 77; 'Mr. Wall Street' of Finance,'" *New York Times*, July 24, 1969.

45. Robert Britt Horwitz, *The Irony of Regulatory Reform: The Deregulation of American Telecommunications* (New York: Oxford University Press, 1989), 9–11. See also Thomas K. McCraw, *Prophets of Regulation: Charles Francis Adams, Louis D. Brandeis, James M. Landis, Alfred E. Kahn* (Cambridge, MA: Belknap Press of Harvard University Press, 1984).

46. On the rise of public interest activism, see Michael W. McCann, *Taking Reform Seriously: Perspectives on Public Interest Liberalism* (Ithaca: Cornell University Press, 1986); Jeffery M. Berry and Clyde Wilcox, *The Interest Group Society* (1984; New York: Pearson Longman, 2007); and Cohen, *A Consumers' Republic*, 357–63.

47. Bruce A. Ackerman and William T. Hassler, *Clean Coal/Dirty Air, or How the Clean Air Act Became a Multibillion-Dollar Bail-Out for High-Sulfur Coal Producers and What Should Be Done About It* (New Haven: Yale University Press, 1981), 4–12; E. Donald Elliott et al., "Toward a Theory of Statutory Evolution: The Federalization of Environmental Law," *Journal of Law, Economics, and Organization* 1:2 (1985): 313–40; Richard A. Harris and Sidney M. Milkis, *The Politics of Regulatory Change: A Tale of Two Agencies* (New York: Oxford University Press, 1996), 7.

48. "Remarks by Elisha Gray II, Chairman of the Board, Council of Better Business Bureaus, Inc., the Business Council Meeting, Hot Springs, Virginia, October 20, 1972," box 15, PR.

49. Erdogan Bakir and Al Campbell, "Neoliberalism, the Rate of Profit, and the Rate of Accumulation," *Science and Society* 74:3 (July 2010): 323–42, especially figure 1, p. 328. Profit rates were approximately 8.5 percent in 1965; they hit 7.5 percent in 1998 and 6.75 percent in 2007.

50. Robert Brenner, *The Economics of Global Turbulence: The Advanced Capitalist Economies from Long Boom to Long Downturn, 1945–2005* (London: Verso, 2006); John W. Kendrick and Elliot S. Grossman, *Productivity in the United States: Trends and Cycles* (Baltimore: Johns Hopkins University Press, 1980), 29; Louis Johnston and Samuel H. Williamson, "What Was the U.S. GDP Then?" 2011, *MeasuringWorth*; Stein, *Pivotal Decade*, 30–32; Claudia Goldin and Robert Margo, "The Great Compression: The Wage Structure in the United States at Mid-Century," *Quarterly Journal of Economics* 107:1 (February 1992): 1–34; Geoffrey Moore, "Recessions," *The Concise Encyclopedia of Economics*, Library of Economics and Liberty (1993), http://www.econlib.org/library/Encl

/Recessions.html; Daniel H. Weinberg, "Current Population Reports: A Brief Look at Postwar U.S. Income Inequality," U.S. Census Bureau, June 1996, http://www.census.gov/prod/1/pop/p60-191.pdf; Wyatt C. Wells, *Economist in an Uncertain World: Arthur F. Burns and the Federal Reserve, 1970–78* (New York: Columbia University Press, 1994).

51. National Association of Manufacturers, "Productivity: Trends to Ponder," box 224, NAM.

52. Carl Madden, "Statement on the Economic Report of the President and the Annual Report of the Council of Economic Advisors for Submission to the Joint Economic Committee for the Chamber of Commerce of the United States," March 13, 1970, series II, box 11, USCOC; personal information on Carl Madden from "World Future Society," http://www.wfs.org/node/266.

53. "Remarks by M. P. Venema, Chairman of the Board, Universal Oil Products Company, Des Plaines, Ill., and Chairman of the National Association of Manufacturers, at 48th Institute on Industrial Relations, March 19, 1972, Newport Beach, California," box 200, NAM; Maynard P. Venema, *The Unique Corporate Life of Universal Oil Products Company* (New York: Newcomen Society in North America, 1961); Illinois Institute of Technology Office of the President, http://www.iit.edu/president/past_presidents.shtml.

54. David Harvey, *A Brief History of Neoliberalism* (New York: Oxford University Press, 2005).

55. "Confidence in Leaders of Ten Institutions, 1966–84," Robert M. Teeter Papers, box 132, file Selected Issues: Issues/Confidence in Institutions (1), GRF.

56. Remarks of Daniel Yankelovich, "The Conference Board Second Annual Public Affairs Outlook Conference: Social and Economic Priorities: Business or Government? Whose Function? Who Decides?" Waldorf Astoria Hotel, New York, March 17, 1976, box 185, CB.

57. "Welcoming Remarks of John D. Harper, Chairman, the Business Roundtable at the Annual Meeting of the Roundtable, New York City, June 16, 1975," and "Remarks by John D. deButts, Co-Chairman, the Business Roundtable at the Annual Meeting of the Roundtable, New York City, June 16, 1975," both in 1975 Correspondence, BRA.

58. On Nader, see Michael Pertschuk, *Revolt against Regulation: The Rise and Pause of the Consumer Movement* (Berkeley: University of California Press, 1982); Matthew Hilton, *Prosperity for All: Consumer Activism in an Era of Globalization* (Ithaca: Cornell University Press, 2009), 161–62; Mark V. Nadel, *The Politics of Consumer Protection* (Indianapolis: Bobbs-Merrill, 1971), 141; and Cohen, *A Consumers' Republic*, 354–55.

59. Timothy J. Wheeler, "Nader against the Consumer," American Conservative Union publication, distributed by Young American for Freedom, Washington, DC, 1972, box 224, NAM; John Post, interview by the author, April 7, 2004.

60. "Confidence in Leaders of Ten Institutions, 1966–84." See also "Robert Teeter to Richard Cheney, 12 November 1975," Robert Teeter Papers, box 63, GRF; Chamber of Commerce of the United States Special Projects Division BEE Clearinghouse, "Public Attitudes toward Business and the Enterprise System," Robert M. Teeter Collection, box 1, GHWB.

61. Tom Wolfe, "The 'Me' Decade and the Third Great Awakening," *New York Magazine*, August 23, 1976; *Network*, 1976, dir. Sidney Lumet.

62. Christopher Lasch, *The Culture of Narcissism: American Life in an Age of Diminishing Expectations* (New York: Norton, 1979). On popular protest, see Phillips-Fein, *Invisible Hands*, 151–52. On the declining faith in liberal government, see Bruce J. Schulman, *The Seventies: The Great Shift in American Culture, Society, and Politics* (New York: Free Press, 2001). On income inequality, see Timothy Noah, *The Great Divergence: America's Growing Inequality Crisis and What We Can Do About It* (New York: Bloomsbury Press, 2012).

63. "Welcoming Remarks of John D. Harper, June 16, 1975"; Burt F. Raynes, "Energy Crisis or Management Crisis?" October 10, 1973, box 200, NAM.

64. "John deButts," in *The North Carolina Awards: 1979* (Raleigh: North Carolina Awards Committee, 1979); Martha Derthick and Paul J. Quirk, *The Politics of Deregulation* (Washington, DC: Brookings Institution, 1985), 188–202; Dan Fenn to John deButts, November 10, 1967, Center for Business-Government Relations—Alpha Subject File, American Telephone and Telegraph Company, Dan H. Fenn Jr. Personal Papers, box 41, series 2.3, JFK.

65. Silk and Vogel, *Ethics and Profits*, 111; "Remarks by John D. deButts, June 16, 1975."

66. Irving Kristol, "Business and 'The New Class,'" *Wall Street Journal*, May 19, 1975.

67. See, for example, Collins, *The Business Response to Keynes* and McQuaid, *Big Business and Presidential Power*.

68. Isidore Cross, "The 'New Class,'" Letter to the Editor, *Wall Street Journal*, June 9, 1975.

69. Clinton Morrison, "The Crystal Ball" (Washington, DC: Chamber of Commerce of the United States, 1975), series II, box 29, USCOC.

70. On the history of social networking and the importance of race, gender, and connections to achieving economic and political power, see Pamela Walker Laird, *Pull: Networking and Success since Benjamin Franklin* (Cambridge, MA: Harvard University Press, 2006).

71. Silk and Vogel, *Ethics and Profits*, 46.

72. Countless historians have examined the cultural origins of modern conservatism as a reaction against the perceived liberal "excesses" of the 1960s, including the civil rights movement, the antiwar movement, and the counterculture. See, among many, Perlstein, *Nixonland* and Dan T. Carter, *The Politics of Rage: George Wallace, the Origins of the New Conservatism, and the Transformation of American Politics* (Baton Rouge: Louisiana State University Press, 2000).

73. R. Heath Larry, "The Changing Business Environment," keynote address at 51st NAM Institute on Industrial Relations, October 2, 1977, box 200, NAM.

74. Allen J. Matusow, *The Unraveling of America: A History of Liberalism in the 1960s* (New York: Harper and Row, 1984).

75. Nelson Lichtenstein, *State of the Union: A Century of American Labor* (Princeton: Princeton University Press, 2002), 170.

76. Quoted in Jeremy Brecher, *Strike!* (San Francisco: Straight Arrow Books, 1972), 264.

77. Joseph McCartin, "'Fire the Hell out of Them': Sanitation Workers' Struggles and the Normalization of the Striker Replacement Strategy in the 1970s," *Labor: Studies in Working-Class History of the Americas* 2:3 (2005): 67–92; Jefferson Cowie, *Stayin' Alive: The 1970s and the Last Days of the Working Class* (New York: New Press, 2010).

78. Silk and Vogel, *Ethics and Profits*, 69.

79. Rodgers, *Age of Fracture*; "Address by Leonard Silk (Member of Editorial Board, New York Times) to the Conference Board: The Future Role of Business in Society Morning Session, Waldorf-Astoria Hotel, NYC," September 16, 1976, box 185, CB.

CHAPTER 2

The chapter epigraph is taken from Richard Lesher, "What and Why Is the U.S. Chamber of Commerce?" *Chamber of Commerce Newsletter*, April 1976, series II, box 5, USCOC.

1. "Two Top Business Groups Plan Merger to Combat Growing Antibusiness Bias," *Wall Street Journal*, June 8, 1976; "Business Lobbyists Blend Their Voices," *Business Week*, June 21, 1976; "NAM Vetoes Merger with U.S. Chamber," *Washington Star*, September 22, 1976.

2. Burt Talcott to Douglas Kenna, June 21, 1976, box 179, NAM.

3. "WLL Telephone Conversation with Fred Borch," August 14, 1986, BRA.

4. A. E. Bolin to Douglas Kenna, June 25, 1976, box 179, NAM; "NAM Kills Merger with Chamber of Commerce," *Los Angeles Times*, September 23, 1976; "NAM Vetoes Merger with U.S. Chamber," *Washington Star*, September 22, 1976.

5. Jeffrey M. Berry, *Lobbying for the People: The Political Behavior of Public Interest Groups* (Princeton: Princeton University Press, 1977); Schlozman and Tierney, *Organized Interests and American Democracy*; Zelizer, *On Capitol Hill*.

6. Richard W. Gable, "Birth of an Employers' Association," *Business History Review* 33:4 (Winter 1959): 535–45; Cathie J. Martin, "Sectional Parties, Divided Business," *Studies in American Political Development* 20:2 (October 2006): 160–84.

7. See Martin, "Sectional Parties, Divided Business," 176–77; Collins, *The Business Response to Keynes*, 47.

8. Richard Hume Werking, "Bureaucrats, Businessmen, and Foreign Trade: The Origins of the United States Chamber of Commerce," *Business History Review* 52:3 (Autumn 1978): 321–41.

9. Martin, "Sectional Parties, Divided Business."

10. Richard Tedlow, "The National Association of Manufacturers and Public Relations during the New Deal," *Business History Review* 50:1 (Spring 1976): 25–45; Delton, *Racial Integration*, 195–96. Sales figure adjustment based on relative share of GDP. Samuel H. Williamson, "Seven Ways to Compute the Relative Value of a U.S. Dollar Amount, 1774 to Present," May 2012, *MeasuringWorth*.

11. Quoted in Werking, "Bureaucrats, Businessmen, and Foreign Trade."

12. Coolidge quoted in Collins, *The Business Response to Keynes*, 23.

13. John Edgerton, president of the National Association of Manufacturers, October 1930, quoted in William E. Leuchtenburg, *Franklin D. Roosevelt and the New Deal, 1932–1940* (New York: Harper, 1963), 21.

14. Collins, *The Business Response to Keynes*, 31–42.

15. Sanford M. Jacoby, *Modern Manors: Welfare Capitalism since the New Deal* (Princeton: Princeton University Press, 1997), 214; Ellis Hawley, "The New Deal and Business," in *The New Deal: The National Level*, ed. John Braeman, Robert H. Brenner, and David Brody (Columbus: Ohio State University Press, 1975), 55–78.

16. Philip Burch, "The NAM as an Interest Group," *Politics and Society* 4:1 (September 1973): 97–130; Phillips-Fein, *Invisible Hands*, 13–15; Krooss, *Executive Opinion*, 12, 183.

17. Collins, *The Business Response to Keynes*, 158–59.

18. Leuchtenburg, *Franklin D. Roosevelt and the New Deal*, 282; Lichtenstein, *State of the Union*, 114–18; Jacobs, *Pocketbook Politics*, 222–26, 236–42.

19. William S. White, "Bill Curbing Labor Becomes Law as Senate Overrides Veto, 68–25; Unions to Fight for Quick Repeal," *New York Times*, June 23, 1947; "House Overrides Truman's Labor Bill Veto; Republicans Predict Victory Also in Senate," *Wall Street Journal*, June 21, 1947; Phillips-Fein, *Invisible Hands*, 31–32.

20. Fones-Wolf, *Selling Free Enterprise*; "He Says Only Refusal to Sign 'Monstrous' Measure Will Avert 'Serious Difficulties'—Meany Sees Aim to Weaken Unions," *New York Times*, May 17, 1947, 19; Richard W. Gable, "NAM: Influential Lobby or Kiss of Death?" *Journal of Politics* 15:2 (May 1953): 254–73. Responding to the passage of Taft-Hartley, AFL president William Green called the ultimate merger of the two labor confederations "inevitable." "Anti-Labor Laws to Be AFL-Target," *Baltimore Sun*, May 16, 1947, 2. On the creation of the AFL-CIO, see Paul Buhle, *Taking Care of Business: Samuel Gompers, George Meany, Lane Kirkland, and the Tragedy of American Labor* (New York: Monthly Review Press, 1999), 131–35 and Tracy Roof, *American Labor, Congress, and the Welfare State, 1935–2010* (Baltimore: Johns Hopkins University Press, 2011), 88–90.

21. McQuaid, *Big Business and Presidential Power*, 148; Phillips-Fein, *Invisible Hands*, 33–35.

22. Malcolm Forbes, editorial, *Forbes*, August 25, 1951, 13, cited in Soffer, "The National Association of Manufacturers"; "Management: Fulltime Storekeeper," *Time*, December 14, 1962; Delton, *Racial Integration*, 197; C. W. Borklund, "A New Era: Why the National Association of Manufacturers Moved Its Headquarters to Washington, D.C.," *Government Executive* (July 1973), box 200, NAM. On the John Birch Society, see McGirr, *Suburban Warriors*.

23. Collins, *The Business Response to Keynes*, 122–26, 192; Dexter, *How Organizations Are Represented in Washington*, 21.

24. "Remarks by W. P. Gullander, Staff Meeting, March 12, 1965," box 120, NAM; "Management: Fulltime Storekeeper"; Delton, *Racial Integration*, 199; Leif Sjoberg, ed., *American Swedish '73* (Philadelphia: American Swedish Historical Foundation, 1973), 6. On the purge of the Birchers and NAM's militarization—accepting and embracing a militant foreign policy during the Vietnam War—see Soffer, "The National Association of Manufacturers."

25. Doug Kenna, College Football Hall of Fame, http://www.collegefootball
.org/famer_selected.php?id=40025; "Sport: End of a Perfect Year," *Time*, December 11, 1944; Borklund, "A New Era."

26. Borklund, "A New Era."

27. E. Douglas Kenna, "Industry's Priorities for America's Progress," 79th Congress of American Industry, December 6, 1974, box 200, NAM; William H. Jones, "NAM Plans Move Here," *Washington Post*, February 21, 1973.

28. R. Heath Larry to Hedley Donovan, Editor-in-Chief, Time, Inc., August 2, 1978, box 200, NAM; David B. Meeker, "New Perspectives for Business Leadership," February 4, 1975, box 200, NAM.

29. Donald A. Gaudion, "The Spirit at 1776," December 5, 1974, box 200, NAM.

30. John C. Jeffries Jr., *Justice Lewis F. Powell, Jr.: A Biography* (New York: Charles Scribner's Sons, 1994), 13–43; Phillips-Fein, *Invisible Hands*, 156–65.

31. Jeffries, *Justice Lewis F. Powell, Jr.*, 1–9; Lewis Powell to Eugene Sydnor, "Confidential Memorandum: Attack on American Free Enterprise System," August 23, 1971, series 2, box 28, USCOC.

32. Jack Anderson, "Chief Justice Lobbies against Bill," *Washington Post*, October 5, 1972. On Anderson and Nixon, see Mark Feldstein, *Poisoning the Press: Richard Nixon, Jack Anderson, and the Rise of Washington's Scandal Culture* (New York: Farrar, Straus, and Giroux, 2010).

33. Countless articles, documentaries, and books have perpetuated a conspiratorial interpretation of the Powell Memorandum. In a typical piece, Greenpeace dubbed it "A Corporate Blueprint to Dominate Democracy." See "The Lewis Powell Memo," http://www.greenpeace.org/usa/en/campaigns/global-warming -and-energy/polluterwatch/The-Lewis-Powell-Memo/. See also Sam Pizzagati, "Remembering the Moment Our CEOs Dug In," August 29, 2011, published on Too Much: A Commentary on Excess and Inequality, toomuchonline.org/remembering -the-powell-memo.

34. Steven M. Teles, *The Rise of the Conservative Legal Movement: The Battle for Control of the Law* (Princeton: Princeton University Press, 2008), 61–62. For other scholarly accounts of the Powell Memorandum, see Phillips-Fein, *Invisible Hands*, 156–65 and Jacob S. Hacker and Paul Pierson, *Winner-Take-All Politics: How Washington Made the Rich Richer—and Turned Its Back on the Middle Class* (New York: Simon and Schuster, 2010), 117–19. For a critique of the tendency to overstate the Powell Memorandum's importance, see Mark Schmitt, "The Legend of the Powell Memo," *The American Prospect*, April 27, 2005.

35. Chamber of Commerce Board of Directors Meeting, June 23, 1972, series I, box 1c, USCOC.

36. U.S. Chamber of Commerce, "Seventy-Five Years of Achievement, 1912–1987," series II, box 9, USCOC; "Changing of the Business Guard," *Nation's Business*, August 1, 1997, 62–63.

37. "Report to the Board of Directors on: Contribution to Business-Industry Political Action Committee (BIPAC)," November 6–7, 1975, series I, box 1d, USCOC.

38. Thomas J. Donohue, "Chamber Development," Presentation to the Board of Directors of the Chamber of Commerce of the United States, June 23, 1978,

series I, box 1d, USCOC; "Seventy-Five Years of Achievement." On the role of the NCLC as a mobilizing force against the hegemony of legal liberalism, see Teles, *The Rise of the Conservative Legal Movement*. On links between the NCLC and the Roberts Court, especially related to the *Citizens United* decision in 2010, see Adam Liptak, "Justices Offer Receptive Ear to Business Interests," *New York Times*, December 18, 2010.

39. David Bird, "Waste Disposal Tied to Markets," *New York Times*, October 8, 1972; George C. Wilson, "Recycling of Trash Considered Profitable," *Washington Post*, March 8, 1973; "Lesher to Succeed Booth at Chamber of Commerce, *Washington Post*, March 11, 1975.

40. Dr. Carl Grant, Executive Vice President, U.S. Chamber of Commerce, interview by the author, April 13, 2011.

41. "Seventy-Five Years of Achievement"; Grant interview. The Chamber discontinued its television programs amid the Internet boom of the late 1990s, and *Nation's Business* ceased publication in 1999. "Notebook," *Television Digest*, April 27, 1998; Robert J. Perkins, "The End of a Long Run," *Nation's Business* 87:6 (June 1999): 1.

42. Lesher, "What and Why Is the U.S. Chamber of Commerce?"; Martin, *Shifting the Burden*, 116; Grant interview.

43. Richard Lesher, "Can Capitalism Survive?" (pamphlet published in 1975), series II, box 29, USCOC.

44. John D. Harper, "Private Enterprise's Public Responsibility," *Public Relations Journal* (August 1967): 8–10; Edward J. Balleisen, "Private Cops on the Fraud Beat: The Limits of American Business Self-Regulation, 1895–1932," *Business History Review* 83:1 (Spring 2009): 113–60.

45. Richard Lesher, "Subject: The 'Social Concerns' of Business," July 27, 1976, White House Central Names File: Chamber of Commerce 1.76 to 1.77, box 555, GRF; Johnston and Williamson, "What Was the U.S. GDP Then?"

46. On Friedman's rise, see especially Burgin, *The Great Persuasion*.

47. Milton Friedman, "A Friedman Doctrine—The Social Responsibility of Business Is to Increase Profits," *New York Times*, September 13, 1970.

48. Powell to Sydnor, August 23, 1971.

49. "Americans Do Not Understand Business," *Chamber of Commerce Newsletter*, March 1974, box 3, USCOC; "Public Full of Misconceptions about Business, Chamber Survey Shows," *Chamber of Commerce Newsletter*, July 1973, series II, box 3, USCOC; Silk and Vogel, *Ethics and Profits*, 71.

50. "NAM's Public Affairs Program, 1975–1976," box 119, NAM.

51. Jacoby, *Modern Manors*, 158–66; Fones-Wolf, *Selling Free Enterprise*, 67–107; Phillips-Fein, *Invisible Hands*, 15, 26–27; "Seventy-Five Years of Achievement." On business public relations efforts, see William H. Whyte, *Is Anybody Listening?: How and Why U.S. Business Fumbles When It Talks to Human Beings* (New York: Simon and Schuster, 1952).

52. Bethany Moreton, *To Serve God and Wal-Mart: The Making of Christian Free Enterprise* (Cambridge, MA: Harvard University Press, 2009), 193–221.

53. "NAM's Public Affairs Program, 1975–1976"; "NAM's New Initiatives in Public Relations: A Presentation to NAM's Board of Directors, May 14, 1975,"

box 200, NAM; "Minutes of the Meeting of the Public Affairs Steering Committees," October 22, 1975, box 119, NAM.

54. "Energy: Excess Profits Tax: A Howling Mess," *Time*, February 4, 1974; W. Elliot Brownlee, *Federal Taxation in America: A Short History* (1996; Cambridge: Cambridge University Press, 2004), 193; advertisement for Profits Kit, *Chamber of Commerce Newsletter*, June 1973, series II, box 3, USCOC.

55. Silk and Vogel, *Ethics and Profits*, 110.

56. "Gullander's Travels: A Study in Free Enterprise," *Industry Week*, December 6, 1971, box 147, NAM; "NAM's New Initiatives in Public Relations: A Presentation to NAM's Board of Directors, May 14, 1975," box 200, NAM.

57. "Americans Do Not Understand Business"; "Michigan Tells the Business Story to the Youth of the State," *State Chambers of Commerce in Action* (undated newsletter, late 1975 or early 1976), John C. Vickerman Files 1974–1977, box 6, file Chamber of Commerce of the United States, GRF; Chamber of Commerce of the United States, "Freedom 2000 Teacher's Guide," series II, box 29, USCOC.

58. "How to Promote Constructive Confrontations between the Leaders of Today and the Leaders of Tomorrow," series II, box 27, USCOC; "Teens Trade Myth for Fact in Business Seminar," *Chamber of Commerce Newsletter*, November 1973, series II, box 3, USCOC.

59. "Chamber Expands Education Effort: Public to Learn More about U.S. Business System," series II, box 27, USCOC; "Economic Education on TV: The Competitive Enterprise System," series II, box 28, USCOC. On the history of advertising, both for specific products and for general concepts like "free enterprise," see Roland Marchand, *Advertising the American Dream: Making Way for Modernity, 1920–1940* (Berkeley: University of California Press, 1985).

60. "Confidence in Leaders of Ten Institutions, 1966–84," Robert M. Teeter Papers, box 132, GRF; NBC News/*Wall Street Journal* Poll, December 2000, *iPOLL Databank*, Roper Center for Public Opinion Research, University of Connecticut.

61. Heath Larry, "Economic Education the Other Way Around," August 23, 1977, box 200, NAM; "Changing of the Business Guard," *Nation's Business*, August 1, 1997, 62–63.

62. ORC Public Opinion Index, July 1971, *iPOLL Databank*, Roper Center; "The Study of American Opinion: Public Attitudes toward Emerging Issues, Business, Government, Labor, Professions, Institutions, Sponsored by the Marketing Department of *U.S. News & World Report*, Conducted by Marketing Concepts, Inc., 1978 Report," box 168, NAM.

63. "The Public Image of Business in a Time of Changing Values: A Discussion Paper," NAM Education Department, June 1973, box 219, NAM.

64. "Hopes and Fears," September 1964; CBS News/*New York Times* Poll, April 1981; Council for Excellence in Government Poll, March 1995, all from *iPOLL Databank*, Roper Center.

65. "Confidence in Leaders of Ten Institutions, 1966–84."

66. On the rise of think tanks in the 1970s, see Alice O'Connor, "Bringing the Market Back In: Philanthropic Activism and Conservative Reform," in *Politics and Partnerships: The Role of Voluntary Associations in America's Political Past*

and Present, ed. Elisabeth S. Clemens and Doug Guthrie (Chicago: University of Chicago Press, 2010), 121–50.

67. Baroody, "Industry's Future: The Issue Is Survival."

CHAPTER 3

1. John Sabino, "The Links Club—New York City," *Playing the Top 100 Golf Courses in the World*, February 24, 2007, http://top100golf.blogspot .com/2006/11/links-club.html.

2. On the informal meeting of Blough et al., see Roger Blough to Members of the Policy Committee, April 19, 1973, BRA; Fred Borch to Roger Blough et al., "Memorandum—Washington, DC Meeting—February 14, 1973," box 6, CBM. On the formation of the March Group, see "March Group Washington Reps Memo," Washington Representatives of the Founding Companies to Gentlemen, April 20, 1972, in John Harper to Wallace Bates, July 24, 1973, BRA. On the March Group–Business Roundtable merger, see "The Business Roundtable Policy Committee Meeting April 30, 1973 Minutes," box 6, CBM; "Roundtable and March Group in Affiliation Move," *The Business Roundtable Report*, No. 73-5, May 23, 1973.

3. "Congress: Squaring Off Over 14(b)," *Time*, October 1, 1965; Roof, *American Labor, Congress and the Welfare State*, 100–107; Gilbert J. Gall, *The Politics of Right to Work: The Labor Federations as Special Interests, 1943–1979* (New York: Greenwood, 1988), 168–83.

4. Victor Reisel, "Inside Labor: Management Movement," *Indiana Evening Gazette*, February 7, 1968; Haynes Johnson and Nick Kotz, "Business Takes Aim at Labor's Power: Business Organizes—in Vain—to Combat Organized Labor," *Washington Post*, April 14, 1972.

5. Membership list for "The Business Roundtable—For Responsible Labor-Management Relations," October 13, 1972, BRA.

6. Haynes and Kotz, "Business Takes Aim"; "WLL Telephone Conversation with Fred Borch—August 14, 1986," BRA; William R. Bradt, "Beginnings of the Business Roundtable (The Formative Years: 1972–1973)," unpublished internal history, April 30, 1986, BRA; William Beverly Murphy, interview by Archie K. Davis, July 21, 1977, Interview Number B-0046, the Southern Oral History Program Collection, Number 4007, Southern Historical Collection, Wilson Library, University of North Carolina, Chapel Hill.

7. Williamson, "Seven Ways to Compute the Relative Value of a U.S. Dollar Amount."

8. Wells, *Economist in an Uncertain World*, 23–25.

9. John Maynard Keynes, *The General Theory of Employment, Interest, and Money* (1936; Basingstoke, Hampshire: Palgrave McMillan, 2007); Iwan W. Morgan, *Deficit Government: Taxing and Spending in Modern America* (Chicago: Ivan R. Dee, 1995), 110. On Johnson's feeble efforts to raise taxes to pay for the war and the Great Society, see Martin, *Shifting the Burden*, 81–106. Williamson, "Seven Ways to Compute the Relative Value of a U.S. Dollar Amount";

Office of Management and Budget, *Fiscal Year 2012: Mid-Session Review, Budget of the U.S. Government*, http://www.whitehouse.gov/sites/default/files/omb/budget/fy2012/assets/12msr.pdf.

10. Haliburton Fales 2d, *Trying Cases: A Life in the Law* (New York: New York University Press, 1997), 181.

11. "Suggested Public Education Program for Labor Law Study Group," November 8, 1971, BRA.

12. Ibid.; "Memorandum for Mr. Funston, Re: Labor Law Study Group—Public Education and Other Objectives," December 22, 1971, BRA.

13. See Jacobs, *Pocketbook Politics*.

14. Gilbert Burck, "A Time of Reckoning for the Building Unions," *Fortune*, June 4, 1979, 82–96.

15. For a comprehensive explanation of the debate over wage inflation in the construction industry, see Marc Linder, *Wars of Attrition: Vietnam, the Business Roundtable, and the Decline of the Construction Unions* (Iowa City: Fanpihua Press, 1999), 59–94.

16. Carl Madden, "Construction Wages: The Great Consumer Robbery," remarks before the Annual Meeting of the Association of Builders and Contractors, March 10, 1971, series II, box 11, USCOC.

17. Linder, *Wars of Attrition*, 183.

18. Winton M. Blount, "The Construction Industry Today—A Question of Survival," in Winton Blount to Roger Blough, July 10, 1978, BRA; Winton M. Blount, *Doing It My Way*, with Richard Blodgett (Lyme, CT: Greenwich Publishing Group, 1996).

19. "Construction Users Anti-Inflation Roundtable," in Blount to Blough, July 10, 1978, BRA.

20. Linder, *Wars of Attrition*, 190; Fales, *Trying Cases*, 180.

21. "Business: Roger Blough," *Time*, June 8, 1959.

22. *Construction Users Anti-Inflation Roundtable Report*, December 7, 1970.

23. "WLL Telephone Conversation with Fred Borch—August 14, 1986."

24. Cathie J. Martin, "Business and the New Economic Activism: The Growth of Corporate Lobbies in the Sixties," *Polity* 27:1 (Autumn 1994): 49–76.

25. *Construction Users Anti-Inflation Roundtable Report*, February 17, 1971; *Construction Users Anti-Inflation Roundtable Report*, May 28, 1971; Allen J. Matusow, *Nixon's Economy: Booms, Busts, Dollars, and Votes* (Lawrence: University Press of Kansas, 1998), 94.

26. "The Business Roundtable Links Club Meeting Minutes, October 16, 1972," BRA; "The Business Roundtable—For Responsible Labor-Management Relations, October 13, 1972," BRA.

27. Roger Blough, "Memorandum Re: Labor Law Study Group and Construction Users Anti-Inflation Roundtable, August 30, 1972," box 5, CBM.

28. *The Business Roundtable for Responsible Labor-Management Relations Report*, No. 72-13, December 20, 1972.

29. Lichtenstein, *State of the Union*, 147; Buhle, *Taking Care of Business*, 134.

30. John Oliver to C. B. McCoy, October 11, 1972, box 7, CBM.

31. "WLL Telephone Conversation with Fred Borch—August 14, 1986." On the number of members, see Roger Blough to Members of the Policy Committee of the Business Roundtable, April 19, 1973, BRA.

32. "Past Leaders: Ralph J. Cordiner," www.ge.com/company/history/bios /ralph_cordiner.html.

33. Bernard Nossiter, "GE Chairman's Advisory Role Causes Worry," *Washington Post*, February 15, 1961; McQuaid, *Big Business and Presidential Power*, 200–201.

34. On General Electric, Cordiner, and Boulwarism, see Phillips-Fein, *Invisible Hands*, 90–105.

35. "WLL Telephone Conversation with Fred Borch—August 14, 1986."

36. Ibid.

37. John W. Burke to Charles B. McCoy, April 1, 1969, box 3, CBM.

38. "Notes for John D. Harper, Business Roundtable Meeting, July 20, 1973," BRA.

39. John Holusha, "Fred J. Borch, 84, Chairman of General Electric in 1960's," *New York Times*, March 3, 1995.

40. "John D. Harper, Retired Chairman of ALCOA," *Chicago Tribune*, July 28, 1985. Currency conversion based on relative changes in wages for skilled production workers. Comparing purchasing power based on the constant bundle of products in the Consumer Price Index, which is less accurate for comparing wages, Harper's weekly pay as a freshman in high school totaled around $150. See Williamson, "Seven Ways to Compute the Relative Value of a U.S. Dollar Amount."

41. "Notes for John D. Harper, Business Roundtable Meeting, July 20, 1973."

42. "WLL Telephone Conversation with Fred Borch—August 14, 1986"; Kim McQuaid, *Uneasy Partners: Big Business in American Politics, 1945–1990* (Baltimore: Johns Hopkins University Press, 1994), 145–46; Arthur Schlesinger Jr., *The Imperial Presidency* (Boston: Houghton Mifflin, 1973).

43. "March Group Washington Reps Memo," April 20, 1972.

44. McQuaid, *Big Business and Presidential Power*, 284; "WLL Telephone Conversation with Fred Borch—August 14, 1986."

45. "WLL Telephone Conversation with Fred Borch—August 14, 1986"; "March Group Washington Reps Memo," April 20, 1972.

46. "Roundtable and March Group in Affiliation Move," *The Business Roundtable Report*, No. 73-5, May 23, 1973.

47. "Notes for John D. Harper, Business Roundtable Meeting, July 20, 1973"; Charles B. McCoy, "Remarks at Annual Meeting of the Business Roundtable," June 11, 1973, box 5 CBM.

48. "March Group Washington Reps Memo," April 20, 1972.

49. "Notes for John D. Harper, Business Roundtable Meeting, July 20, 1973"; "WLL Telephone Conversation with Fred Borch—August 14, 1986"; Fred J. Borch to Roger M. Blough et al., "Memorandum—Washington, DC Meeting—February 14, 1973," box 6, CBM.

50. "Roger Blough's Presentation to the Construction Users Group Conference, Dearborn, Michigan, April 3, 1973," quoted in Bradt, "Beginnings of the Business Roundtable."

51. Cook Nelson Tuthill, Inc., "Study for the Business Roundtable," February 12, 1973, BRA; John Post to G. Wallace Bates, August 24, 1973, BRA.

52. "The Public Information Committee: A Capsule History" (undated internal history, likely written in 1984), BRA; John Harper to Members of the Business Roundtable, April 22, 1974, box 6, CBM; Bradt, "Beginnings of the Business Roundtable"; *Reader's Digest*, February 1975, 42–44 (on inflation); *Reader's Digest*, July 1975, 160–62 (on profits and growth); *Reader's Digest*, October 1975, 212–14 (on safety regulations). Cost conversion using inflation-adjusted percentage of GDP. Williamson, "Seven Ways to Compute the Relative Value of a U.S. Dollar Amount."

53. *Roundtable Report*, No. 75-6, August 1975; "The Public Information Committee: A Capsule History."

54. "*Meet the Press* Transcript," April 20, 1975, Ronald H. Nessen Files, box 69, GRF.

55. Cowie, *Capital Moves*.

56. Brenner, *The Economics of Global Turbulence*, 99–117.

57. *Roundtable Report*, No. 75-5, July 1975; *Roundtable Report*, No. 76-4, July 1976.

CHAPTER 4

The chapter epigraphs are taken from Matusow, *Nixon's Economy*, 17; Jimmy Carter, "Anti-Inflation Program Remarks Announcing the Administration's Program," March 14, 1980, in Woolley and Peters, *The American Presidency Project*.

1. U.S. Chamber of Commerce, "Building History," http://www.uschamber.com/about/history/building-history.

2. "ANAC Gets 'Rave Notices' from 1,200 Top Association and Corporate Leaders," *Association Letter* (Washington, DC: Chamber of Commerce of the United States), February 1972, series II, box 5, USCOC.

3. Herbert Stein, *Presidential Economics: The Making of Economic Policy from Roosevelt to Reagan and Beyond* (New York: Simon and Schuster, 1984); Wells, *Economist in an Uncertain World*; Matusow, *Nixon's Economy*.

4. C. Jackson Grayson, *Confessions of a Price Controller* (Homewood, IL: Dow Jones-Irwin, 1974); "ANAC Gets 'Rave Notices.'"

5. Schulman, *The Seventies*, 37–38.

6. "ANAC Gets 'Rave Notices.'"

7. Ibid.

8. Collins, *More*; Jacobs, *Pocketbook Politics*.

9. On the role of consumers as an interest group in postwar politics, see especially Cohen, *A Consumers' Republic*.

10. On the history of conservative opposition to organized labor in the twentieth century, see especially Nelson Lichtenstein and Elizabeth Tandy Shermer, eds., *The Right and Labor in America: Politics, Ideology, and Imagination* (Philadelphia: University of Pennsylvania Press, 2012).

11. "Statement of the Monetary and Fiscal Policy Subcommittee of the Money/Credit/Capital Formation Committee on Inflation Control," National Association of Manufacturers, November 6, 1969, box 188, NAM.

12. Matusow, *Nixon's Economy*, 67; Stein, *Presidential Economics*, 161.

13. Richard S. Landry, "Statement on Title II of H.R.17880, the Economic Stabilization Act of 1970 before the House Banking and Currency Committee for the Chamber of Commerce of the United States," June 18, 1970, series II, box 11, USCOC.

14. Alan Blinder and William J. Newton, "The 1971–1974 Controls Program and the Price Level: An Econometric Post-Mortem," *Journal of Monetary Economics* 8:1 (1981): 1–23.

15. Perlstein, *Nixonland*; Matusow, *Nixon's Economy*.

16. Kevin Phillips, *The Emerging Republican Majority* (New Rochelle, NY: Arlington House, 1969); Jefferson Cowie, "Nixon's Class Struggle: Romancing the New-Right Worker, 1969–1973," *Labor History* 43:3 (Summer 2002): 257–83.

17. "Putting on the Freeze," *Time*, August 30, 1971.

18. Public Affairs Office, Department of the Treasury, "Public Reaction to the President's Program," August 25, 1971, BE box 8, EX BE 3 Economic Controls and N. E. Halaby to Richard Nixon, September 7, 1971, BE box 9, EX BE 3 Economic Controls, both in RMN.

19. Gilbert W. Fitzhugh to Richard Nixon, August 18, 1971, BE box 8, EX BE 3 Economic Controls, RMN.

20. "Associations Act Quickly to Inform Members on Wage-Price Freeze," *Association Letter*, Chamber of Commerce of the United States, September 1971, series II, box 5, USCOC; "News from NAM" Press Release, October 7, 1971, box 188, NAM.

21. Chamber of Commerce of the United States, "Your Commitment to America," series II, box 28, USCOC.

22. Ibid.; "'Freeze Government' Brings Favorable Response from Public," *Association Letter*, December 1971, Chamber of Commerce of the United States, series II, box 5, USCOC.

23. William R. Risher to Richard Nixon, September 2, 1971, BE box 9, EX BE 3 Economic Controls, RMN; Damon Stetson, "Harm to Workers Feared," *New York Times*, August 17, 1971.

24. Blinder and Newton, "The 1971–1974 Controls Program and the Price Level."

25. "Public Reaction to the President's Program"; Nigel Bowles, *Nixon's Business: Authority and Power in Presidential Politics* (College Station: Texas A&M University Press, 2005), 117–32.

26. Donald Kendall to Richard Nixon, September 17, 1971, BE box 11, EX BE Economic Controls, RMN.

27. John J. Abele, "Businessmen Applaud and Criticize Nixon Speech," *New York Times*, June 18, 1970; Grayson, *Confessions of a Price Controller*.

28. Frank C. Porter, "President Names Pay, Price Boards," *Washington Post*, October 23, 1971; "What Made Meany Walk," *Time*, April 3, 1972; Matusow, *Nixon's Economy*, 161.

29. The president of NAM, Werner Gullander, encouraged the Pay Board to fix wage increases "firmly to productivity growth" and was pleased that the board did so (after accounting for inflation). "News from NAM" Press Release, October 7, 1971, box 188, NAM.

30. Marvin H. Kosters and J. Dawson Ahalt, *Controls and Inflation: The Economic Stabilization Program in Retrospect* (Washington, DC: American Enterprise Institute for Public Policy Research, 1975), 16; "Is Phase 2 Soft on Prices? Hearings Find Varied Views," *Industry Week*, April 10, 1972, box 147, NAM; "What Made Meany Walk."

31. "Report to the Board of Directors," June 12, 1972, series I, box 1c, USCOC; Carl Madden, "Statement on Wage-Price Controls before the Joint Economic Committee for the Chamber of Commerce of the United States," November 14, 1972, series II, box 11, USCOC.

32. George Hagedorn to Members of the NAM Ad Hoc Committee on Phase II, November 13, 1972, box 171, NAM.

33. Burt F. Raynes to NAM Board of Directors, December 27, 1972, box 171, NAM; "Nixon Will Seek to Extend Curb on Wages, Prices," *Wall Street Journal*, December 12, 1972.

34. W. B. Murphy to Executive Committee and Policy Committee Members, December 1, 1972, 1972 Correspondence, BRA.

35. Richard Nixon, "Special Message to Congress Announcing Phase III of the Economic Stabilization Program and Requesting Extension of Authorizing Legislation," January 11, 1973, in Woolley and Peters, *The American Presidency Project*; Bowles, *Nixon's Business*, 119; Kosters and Ahalt, *Controls and Inflation*, 22–23.

36. Kosters and Ahalt, *Controls and Inflation*, 23; Wells, *Economist in an Uncertain World*, 110–12. Economists hotly debated the specific causes of this batch of inflation, which included world grain shortages, a global economic growth spurt, supply chain disruptions as factories tried to maximize output, and the devaluation of the dollar.

37. Stein, *Presidential Economics*, 185.

38. "The Meat Furor," *Newsweek*, April 9, 1973.

39. "Nixon Reapplies Prenotification Rule to Some Price Boosts by Big Firms," *Wall Street Journal*, May 3, 1973; Kosters and Ahalt, *Controls and Inflation*, 24–25.

40. Richard Nixon, "Address to the Nation Announcing Price Control Measures," June 13, 1973, in Woolley and Peters, *The American Presidency Project*.

41. Survey results reported in George Shultz to Richard Nixon, October 15, 1973, BE box 15, EX BE 3 Economic Controls, RMN. On the gasoline shortage, see Meg Jacobs, "The Conservative Struggle and the Energy Crisis," in *Rightward Bound: Making America Conservative in the 1970s*, ed. Bruce J. Schulman and Julian E. Zelizer (Cambridge, MA: Harvard University Press, 2008), 193–209 and Richard H. K. Vietor, *Energy Policy in America since 1945: A Study of Business-Government Relations* (Cambridge: Cambridge University Press), 194–202.

42. Frank Fitzsimmons, "International Brotherhood of Teamsters News Service," June 14, 1973, in Charles Colson to Rose Mary Woods, June 15, 1973, BE box 15, EX BE 3 Economic Controls, RMN.

43. Walter Wriston to Richard Nixon, undated, BE box 15, EX BE 3 Economic Controls, RMN.

44. Burt Raynes, "Why NAM Is against Wage and Price Controls," undated, box 218, NAM Publications U–Z, NAM.

45. Wallace Bates and John Harper to Labor Management Committee, Construction Committee, and Public Information Committee, October 5, 1973, BRA.

46. Stein, *Presidential Economics*, 186. See also "The Meat Furor," *Newsweek*, April 9, 1973.

47. Stein, *Pivotal Decade*, 74–100.

48. Roper Report 73-9, September 1973, *iPOLL Databank*, Roper Center.

49. Shultz to Nixon, October 15, 1973; Hobart Rowen, "Requiem for Controls," *Washington Post*, April 7, 1974.

50. Douglas Kenna and Charles Smith, "The Future of Wage and Price Controls," Joint Testimony before the Subcommittee on Production and Stabilization, Committee on Banking, Housing and Urban Affairs, United States Senate, February 1, 1974, series II, box 11a, USCOC.

51. *The Business Roundtable Report*, No. 74-2, February 28, 1974.

52. John Harper to Members of the Business Roundtable, March 15, 1974, 1974 Correspondence, BRA.

53. James Rowe, "House Unit Blocks Controls," *Washington Post*, April 6, 1974.

54. Edward Cowan, "Controls Ending in High Inflation," *New York Times*, April 18, 1974.

55. *The Business Roundtable Report*, No. 74-4, April 26, 1974.

56. Cowan, "Controls Ending in High Inflation."

57. "Critical Public Scrutiny to Be New Form of Economic Control: Blough," *Roundtable Report*, April 26, 1974.

58. "Inflation Losers: You, Your Family, Your Country" (1974) and "Wage and Price Controls: A Failure in History, Theory, and Practice" (1975), series II, box 29, USCOC.

59. John Harper to Alan Greenspan, September 24, 1974, BRA.

60. On the Nixon pardon, see Sean Wilentz, *The Age of Reagan: A History, 1974–2008* (New York: Harper Collins, 2008), 28–32.

61. "National Chamber Finds Need for Inflation-Proof Congress," *Association Letter of the Chamber of Commerce of the United States*, August 1974, series II, box 5, USCOC; "Board of Directors Minutes, November 7–8, 1974," series I, box 1c, USCOC.

62. Zelizer, *On Capitol Hill*, 156–76.

63. *Roundtable Report*, No. 75-7, October 1975.

64. Gerald Ford, "Statement Announcing Intention to Veto the Common Situs Picketing Bill," December 22, 1975, in Woolley and Peters, *The American Presidency Project*; James A. Baker III, *"Work Hard, Study . . . and Keep Out of Politics!": Adventures and Lessons from an Unexpected Public Life*, with Steve Fiffer (New York: G. P. Putnam's Sons, 2006), 36–37.

65. National Association of Manufacturers Policy & Program Development Division, "Major National Legislative Issues, May 1975," box 220, NAM.

66. *Roundtable Report*, No. 76-7, December 1976.

67. "House Deals Big Defeat to Labor," *Chicago Tribune*, March 24, 1977.

68. Rudolph A. Pyatt Jr., "Business Profile: A Foe's Views of Pickets Bill," *Washington Star*, March 28, 1977, box 200, NAM.

69. Jimmy Carter, "Labor Law Reform Message to the Congress Transmitting Proposed Legislation," July 18, 1977, in Woolley and Peters, *The American Presidency Project*.

70. "Major Business Issues: Capsule Comments on National Chamber Positions," June 1978, series III, box 4, USCOC.

71. Cited in Quinn Mills, "Flawed Victory in Labor Law Reform," *Harvard Business Review* (May–June 1979): 92–102.

72. Robert Merry and Albert Hunt, "The Company Line: Business Lobby Gains More Power as It Rides Antigovernment Tide," *Wall Street Journal*, May 17, 1978.

73. "The New Chill in Labor Relations," *Business Week*, October 24, 1977; Stein, *Pivotal Decade*, 187; Mills, "Flawed Victory in Labor Law Reform."

74. "A Potent New Business Lobby," *Business Week*, May 22, 1978; Thomas Ferguson and Joel Rogers, "Labor Law Reform and Its Enemies," *The Nation*, January 6–13, 1979; Jefferson Cowie, "Notes and Documents: 'A One-Sided Class War': Rethinking Doug Fraser's 1978 Resignation from the Labor-Management Group," *Labor History* 44:3 (August 2003): 307–14; Charles Mohr, "Business Using Grass-Roots Lobby," *New York Times*, April 17, 1978.

75. G. J. Santoni, "The Employment Act of 1946: Some History Notes," *Federal Reserve Bank of St. Louis Review*, November 1986.

76. Humphrey's original bill would have "establish[ed] a national policy and nationwide machinery for guaranteeing to all adult Americans able and willing to work the availability of equal opportunities for useful and rewarding employment." "Summary of S.50," introduced January 15, 1975, thomas.loc.gov.

77. Ross Wilhelm, "Inside Business: Employment Bill: Prod to Inflation" (unpublished proof slated for distribution week of June 28, 1976), BRA.

78. Lewis Foy to Members of the Business Roundtable, May 22, 1978, 1978 Correspondence, BRA; R. A. Riley to Members of the Business Roundtable, March 9, 1978, 1978 Correspondence, BRA; *Roundtable Report*, No. 78-2, March 1978.

79. "Full Employment and Balanced Growth Act of 1978," Public Law 95-523, October 27, 1978; David Vogel, *Fluctuating Fortunes: The Political Power of Business in America* (New York: Basic Books, 1989), 156.

80. On the unemployment rate, see Paul O. Flaim, "Population Changes, the Baby Boom, and the Unemployment Rate," *Monthly Labor Review*, August 1990, Bureau of Labor Statistics, www.bls.gov.

81. Jimmy Carter, "State of Union Address Delivered before a Joint Session of the Congress," January 19, 1978, in Woolley and Peters, *The American Presidency Project*.

82. Barry Bosworth to Charlie Schultze, "Current Status of the Anti-Inflation Program, April 22, 1978," Chief of Staff Selig Papers, box 167, JEC.

83. Irving Shapiro, "Du Pont Corporate News," January 20, 1978, Domestic Policy Staff—Eizenstat Papers, box 157, JEC. On Shapiro and Carter, see Phillips-Fein, *Invisible Hands*, 198.

84. "Inflation Is Everybody's Business, Anti-Inflation Brochure," August 3, 1978, Strauss Files, box 8, JEC; "President Carter's Anti-Inflation Program, COWPS/NAAP Anti-Inflation Briefing," December 13, 1978, Chief of Staff Selig Papers, box 167, JEC; Julian E. Zelizer, *Jimmy Carter* (New York: Times Books, 2010), 89.

85. McCraw, *Prophets of Regulation*, 261–96.

86. "All You Ever Wanted to Ask about the Wage-Price Guidelines: An Interview with Alfred E. Kahn, Who Explains in Simple Terms How the Standards Work," *Nation's Business*, July 1979.

87. Richard J. Levine and Urban C. Lehner, "Carter's New Inflation Attack," *Wall Street Journal*, October 25, 1978; "President's Anti-Inflation White Paper," October 24, 1978, Chief of Staff Selig Papers, box 167, JEC.

88. "Remarks of the President at the Dinner Meeting of the Business Council, Washington DC," December 13, 1978, box 15, File Business Council 1978–79, PR.

89. Herbert Markley to NAM Membership, December 4, 1978, box 200, NAM.

90. "Industry's Focus on Inflation" conference brochure, March 28–30, 1979, box 222, NAM.

91. Sheraton Harris to Jimmy Carter, December 13, 1978, Special Advisor—Inflation Kahn Papers, box 8, JEC.

92. "Memorandum for Steve Selig and Richard Reiman Re: Anti-inflation Plan for the Group of Nine," March 12, 1979, Chief of Staff Selig Files, box 167, JEC.

93. "Notes of meeting held December 14, 1978 in the Offices of the Business Roundtable concerning Anti-Inflation," December 14, 1978, Chief of Staff Selig Papers, box 169, JEC.

94. Harris to Carter, December 13, 1978.

95. "Notes of meeting held on December 14, 1978 in the Offices of the Business Roundtable concerning Anti-Inflation."

96. "Memorandum for Steve Selig and Richard Reiman," March 12, 1979.

97. Jack Carlson to Alfred E. Kahn, September 5, 1979, Chief of Staff Selig Papers, box 167, JEC.

98. Missy Mandell and Susan Irving to Anne Wexler and Richie Reiman, September 29, 1979, Special Advisor—Inflation Kahn Papers, box 5, JEC.

99. "Statement of Thomas A. Murphy, Chairman, Business Roundtable," September 28, 1979, Special Advisor—Inflation Kahn Papers, box 5, JEC.

100. "Recommendation to the President: Wage-Price Guidelines Should Be Ended: They Distort Real Inflation Issues," *Roundtable Report*, No. 80-6, July 1980.

101. Market Research Corporation, "Voters' Evaluation of the Candidates on Seven Selected Presidential Qualities," Robert Teeter Papers, series "1980 George Bush Presidential Campaign Data (1979–1980)," box 1, GHWB.

102. "'Inflation Czar' Will Take Apart His Title," *Cornell Chronicle* 14:35 (July 14, 1983); William Greider, *Secrets of the Temple: How the Federal Reserve Runs the Country* (New York: Simon and Schuster, 1987); Greta R. Krippner, *Capitalizing on Crisis: The Political Origins of the Rise of Finance* (Cambridge, MA: Harvard University Press, 2011).

103. See Leon N. Lindberg and Charles S. Maier, eds., *The Politics of Inflation and Economic Stagnation: Theoretical Approaches and International Case Studies* (Washington, DC: Brookings Institution, 1985) and Niall Ferguson et al., eds., *The Shock of the Global: The 1970s in Perspective* (Cambridge, MA: Belknap Press of Harvard University Press, 2010).

104. Werner Abelshauser, *Deutsche Wirtschaftsgeschichte. Von 1945 bis zur Gegenwart* [German Economic History: From 1945 to Present] 2nd ed. (Munich: C. H. Beck, 2011), 28–32, 372–83; Konrad H. Jarausch, *After Hitler: Recivilizing Germans, 1945–1995* (Oxford: Oxford University Press, 2006), 92. On the social and economic effects of stagflation on West German political culture, see also Anselm Doering-Manteuffel and Raphael Lutz, eds., *Nach dem Boom: Perspektiven auf die Zeitgeschichte seit 1970* [After the Boom: Perspectives on Contemporary History since 1970], 2nd ed. (Göttingen: Vandenhoeck and Ruprecht, 2010).

CHAPTER 5

The chapter epigraph is taken from "The Mood Turns Mean" (undated brochure), box 217, NAM.

1. "Consumer Probe" transcript, December 11, 1976, *Saturday Night Live* episode 10, season 2, http://snltranscripts.jt.org/76/76jconsumerprobe.phtml. The video is available at http://www.hulu.com/watch/115713.

2. Virginia Slims American Women's Poll 1974, April 1974, and Harris Survey, May 1975, *iPOLL Databank*, Roper Center.

3. Nuclear Power Development, July 1976 and Cambridge Reports National Omnibus Survey, January 1979, *iPOLL Databank*, Roper Center.

4. Harris Survey, February 1971, and General Electric Survey, October 1980, *iPOLL Databank*, Roper Center.

5. David Skeel, *The New Financial Deal: Understanding the Dodd-Frank Act and Its (Unintended) Consequences* (Hoboken, NJ: Wiley, 2011).

6. Mark Green, "Why the Consumer Bill Went Down," *The Nation*, February 25, 1978, 198.

7. Gerald Ford, "Remarks at the Annual Meeting of the Chamber of Commerce of the United States," April 28, 1975, in Woolley and Peters, *The American Presidency Project*.

8. Lawrence B. Glickman, *Buying Power: A History of Consumer Activism in America* (Chicago: University of Chicago Press, 2009), 155–87.

9. Nadel, *The Politics of Consumer Protection*.

10. Marchand, *Advertising the American Dream*; Richard Tedlow, "From Competitor to Consumer: The Changing Focus of Federal Regulation of Advertising, 1914–1938," *Business History Review* 55:1 (1981): 35–58; Harris and Milkis, *The Politics of Regulatory Change*, 148.

11. On postwar consumerism, see especially Cohen, *A Consumers' Republic* and Jacobs, *Pocketbook Politics*. See also Glickman, *Buying Power* and Hilton, *Prosperity for All*.

12. Newspaper count conducted by author. Newspapers surveyed were the *New York Times, Washington Post, Wall Street Journal, Chicago Tribune*, and

Los Angeles Times. Periodical data from Nadel, *The Politics of Consumer Protection*, 35.

13. Cohen, *A Consumers' Republic*, 14–15.

14. Gary T. Ford, "State Characteristics Affecting the Passage of Consumer Legislation," *Journal of Consumer Affairs* 11:1 (Summer 1977): 177–82; Sharon Oster, "An Analysis of Some Causes of Interstate Differences in Consumer Regulations," *Economic Inquiry* 18:1 (January 1980): 39–54; Kenneth Meier, "The Political Economy of Consumer Protection: An Examination of State Legislation," *Western Political Quarterly* 40:2 (June 1987): 343–59.

15. William A. Lovett, "State Deceptive Trade Practice Legislation," *Tulane Law Review* 46 (1971–72): 724–60; Cohen, *A Consumers' Republic*, 345–63.

16. Daniel P. Carpenter, *Reputation and Power: Organizational Image and Pharmaceutical Regulation at the FDA* (Princeton: Princeton University Press, 2010); Tobbell, *Pills, Power, and Policy*; Cohen, *A Consumers' Republic*, 353, 360.

17. Derthick and Quirk, *The Politics of Deregulation*; Horwitz, *The Irony of Regulatory Reform*, 77–79; Cohen, *A Consumers' Republic*, 22, 25, 353, 365.

18. "Hill Group Charges Nixon Neglects the Consumer," *Washington Post*, August 11, 1969; Morton Mintz, "Nixon Offers Program to Protect Consumers," *Washington Post*, October 31, 1969.

19. Edward Grimes, "Virginia Knauer, Consumer Advocate, Dies at 96," *New York Times*, October 27, 2011; Richard Nixon, "Executive Order 11583—Office of Consumer Affairs," February 24, 1971, in Woolley and Peters, *The American Presidency Project*. Knauer occupied that position under Nixon, Ford, and Reagan, interrupted only during the Carter administration when Esther Peterson, whom Johnson had made the first Special Assistant for Consumer Affairs, replaced her. The Office on Consumer Affairs was eliminated during budget cuts negotiated between Democrat Bill Clinton and the Republican-controlled House of Representatives in the late 1990s. See Bill McAllister, "No Protection in Sight: Consumer Affairs Agency Marked for Death by Congress," *Washington Post*, December 21, 1995.

20. "Republican Party Platform of 1972," in Woolley and Peters, *The American Presidency Project*; "Roy Ash to Richard Nixon, May 23, 1973," Jeffery Eves File, box 1, GRF; "Virginia Knauer to Richard Nixon, May 31, 1973," Melvin Laird Papers, box A144, GRF.

21. Jay Brenneman to Board of Directors [of the Federal Reserve], August 5, 1975, box B20, Federal Reserve Subject File Consumer Confidence, GRF.

22. "The Crisis in Credibility: Theme of a Marketing Conference to Which You Are Invited," April 9, 1970, box 222, NAM.

23. "The Consumer Revolution," May 1970, series II, box 27, USCOC.

24. "Business-Consumer Relations Code," *Chamber of Commerce Newsletter*, April 1970, series II, box 3, USCOC; "Consumer Role for Associations," *Association Letter* (Washington, DC: Association Department, Chamber of Commerce of the United States), November 1970, series II, box 5, USCOC.

25. "Summary of Remarks of Samuel C. Johnson, The Business Council Meeting, Hot Springs, Virginia, October 10, 1975," box 15, PR.

26. "Consumer Role for Associations," November 1970; Ritter F. Shumway, "The Consumer Imperative," address to the Durham, North Carolina, Chamber of Commerce, February 18, 1971, series II, box 27, USCOC.

27. See, for example, Sanford Jacoby's history of welfare capitalism. Jacoby, *Modern Manors*.

28. Friedman, "A Friedman Doctrine."

29. "Third Chamber TV Spot Tells Why Consumer Is Boss," *Chamber of Commerce Newsletter*, May 1972, series II, box 3, USCOC.

30. Malcolm D. MacArthur, "Associations and the Law: The Consumer Product Safety Act," *Association Letter* (Washington, DC: Association Department, Chamber of Commerce of the United States), October 1973, series II, box 5, USCOC.

31. George Koch to William Baroody Jr., September 6, 1973, Melvin Laird Papers, box A133, GRF.

32. Morton Mintz, "Nader Writes off Nixon Administration on Aid to Consumers," *Washington Post*, March 21, 1969.

33. *Trustees of Dartmouth College v. Woodward*, 17 U.S. 518 (1819).

34. Ralph Nader, Mark Green, and Joel Seligman, *Taming the Giant Corporation* (New York: W. W. Norton, 1976); Jules Bernstein et al., "Conceptual Draft of the Corporate Democracy Act," in *The Big Business Reader: On Corporate America*, ed. Mark Green et al. (New York: Pilgrim Press, 1991), 500–511.

35. Michael W. McCann, "Public Interest Liberalism and the Modern Regulatory State," *Polity* 21:2 (Winter 1988): 373–400; David Vogel, "The Public-Interest Movement and the American Reform Tradition," *Political Science Quarterly* 95:4 (Winter 1980–81): 607–27.

36. Samuel Huntington, "The Marasmus of the ICC: The Commission, the Railroads, and the Public Interest," *Yale Law Journal* 61 (April 1952): 467–509; Marver H. Bernstein, *Regulating Business by Independent Commission* (Princeton: Princeton University Press, 1955). For a thorough analysis of the origins and uses of capture theory, see Horwitz, *The Irony of Regulatory Reform*, 27–38.

37. "Summary of S. 1160 as Introduced March 8, 1973," box 346, SE.

38. Joan Claybrook to Public Citizen membership, July 17, 1975, series 1, box 2, CCAG; Congress Watch, "Why We Need a Consumer Protection Agency," series 1, box 2, CCAG; "Summary and Explanation of the Consumer Protection Act of 1977," April 1977, series 14, box 110, CCAG.

39. D. E. Marable, "ABCDEFG Nears Final Verdict," *NAM Reports* 9:30 (August 5, 1974), box 213, NAM; "Dallace E. Marable," *Daily Press* (Hampton, VA), August 16, 2000.

40. Jack Anderson, "An Anti-Consumer Filibuster," *Washington Post*, July 28, 1974; George Schwartz, "The Successful Fight against a Federal Consumer Protection Agency," *MSU Business Topics* 27:3 (Summer 1979): 45–57; Mark Green and Andrew Buchsbaum, *The Corporate Lobbies: Political Profiles of the Business Roundtable and the Chamber of Commerce* (Washington, DC: Public Citizen, 1980).

41. Schwartz, "The Successful Fight," 46–47.

42. John A. Stuart to all members of the NAM Marketing Committee, March 27, 1972, box 171, NAM.

43. "Consumer Protection Organization Act of 1970: Roll Vote No. 407," *Congressional Record* 116 (December 1, 1970): 39320.

44. Jerome R. Gulan to John Young, December 3, 1970, Charles W. Colson Files, box 90, National Federation of Independent Business, RMN.

45. John D. Morris, "House Unit Votes Consumer Panel," *New York Times*, June 12, 1970; David Vienna, "Consumer Agency Gets Approval of Senate Unit," *Washington Post*, July 1, 1970; Morton Mintz, "Senate Passes Bill to Protect Consumers," *Washington Post*, December 2, 1970. The tie-breaking vote belonged to Richard Bolling (D-MO), who was on vacation at the time. Observers disagreed on how Bolling would have voted if he had been present. While he supported the bill in principle, he later told a marketing professor that he felt the bill as presented was poorly structured and likely would have voted against it. See Schwartz, "The Successful Fight" and Green and Buchsbaum, *The Corporate Lobbies*.

46. John D. Morris, "House Approves a Federal Agency to Aid Consumers," *New York Times*, October 15, 1971.

47. Sam Ervin to G. Everett Suddreth Jr., December 9, 1970, box 213, SE.

48. U.S. Chamber of Commerce to Business Leader, July 30, 1970, enclosed with Sam Ervin to James Williams, August 6, 1970, box 210, SE.

49. H. C. Roemer to Sam Ervin, August 3, 1970, box 213, SE.

50. James Allen to Sam Ervin, February 26, 1973, box 299, SE.

51. George Koch to Sam Ervin, October 4, 1972, box 346, SE; George Koch to Sam Ervin, October 4, 1972, box 268, SE; Sam Ervin, "Statement in Opposition to the Consumer Protection Agency Bill," fall 1972, box 346, SE; Anderson, "An Anti-Consumer Filibuster"; Schwartz, "The Successful Fight"; Spencer Rich, "Senate Rejects Cloture Bid on Consumer Bill," *Washington Post*, October 4, 1972. Ervin claimed that one of his staff members, not he, had requested prepackaged speeches from lobbyists, while Allen denied making any request for written materials.

52. All letters enclosed with Paul Rhyne Jr., to Sam Ervin, September 20, 1972, box 268, SE.

53. "Consumer Protection Organization Act of 1972: Roll Vote No. 522," *Congressional Record* 118 (October 5, 1972): 33865.

54. Frederick Williford to Sam Ervin, July 24, 1974, box 330, SE.

55. Consumer Federation of America, "Consumer Federation of America Ranks Senators on Consumer Protection Agency Voting Records," July 14, 1974, box 346, SE.

56. "Consumer Protection—Agency for Consumer Advocacy Act of 1974: Roll Vote No. 415," *Congressional Record* 120 (September 19, 1974): 31904.

57. Anderson, "An Anti-Consumer Filibuster"; Ralph Nader, "Ralph Nader on the Agency for Conusmer [sic] Advocacy," *Washington Post*, September 19, 1974.

58. "Memorandum for: WB, From WV, Subject: Consumer Protection Agency," June 27, 1973, Melvin Laird Papers, box A144, GRF.

59. Roper Report 74-5, May 1974 and Roper Report 75-5, *iPOLL Databank*, Roper Center.

60. Virginia Knauer to Gerald Ford, September 20, 1974, William Timmons File, box 2, GRF.

61. Elizabeth Shelton, "Virginia Knauer: The First Year," *Washington Post*, May 10, 1970; "Consumer Aide Hails Vote on Protection Plan," *Washington Post*, September 29, 1971.

62. "Consumer Protection Agency: You Think You Don't Have a Stake in It? Well, Read On," *Association Letter* (Washington, DC: Association Department, Chamber of Commerce of the United States) March 1972, series II, box 5, USCOC.

63. "An Analysis of the Results of the Business Roundtable Poll on the Consumer Advocacy Agency," Daniel Melnick to Senate Government Operations Committee, May 5, 1975, Max Friedersdorf Files, box 11, GRF.

64. Opinion Research Corporation, "Government and the Consumer," March 1975, Max Friedersdorf Files, box 11, GRF. The $60 million figure came from the Senate bill under consideration in 1975, S. 200, which allocated for the CPA a budget of $15 million for the first year, $20 million for the second year, and $25 million for the third year. The House bill requested less. For reference, $60 million in 1975, as a percentage of the size of the economy, would exceed $500 million in 2013.

65. "Newspapers which have carried editorials opposing independent consumer protection agency (as of June 23, 1975)," L. William Seidman Files, box 291, GRF.

66. Ronald Reagan, "Wanted: Protection from Consumerists," *Globe Democrat* (St. Louis, Missouri), May 30, 1975, John Marsh Files, box 10, GRF.

67. George W. Koch to Max Friedersdorf, May 30, 1975, Max Friedersdorf Files, box 11, GRF.

68. "An Analysis of the Results of the Business Roundtable Poll on the Consumer Advocacy Agency." For data on other polls, see, for example, Marian Burros, "Consumer Unrest Staggering," *Washington Post*, May 17, 1977; *Public Citizen Congress Watch Newsletter*, May 31, 1977, series 14, box 10, CCAG.

69. Charles Percy to Frank Horton, June 6, 1975, Max Friedersdorf Files, box 11, GRF.

70. *Reader's Digest*, May 1975, 192–94.

71. *Richmond Times Dispatch*, May 3, 1975, in Max Friedersdorf Files, box 11, GRF.

72. Pertschuk, *Revolt against Regulation*, 69–71.

73. Sam Ervin to George Meany, June 6, 1974, Jeffrey Eves Files, box 1, GRF.

74. *Public Citizen Newsletter*, July 24, 1974, series I, box 2, file 60, CCAG. See also *NAM Guidelines for Action*, March 27, 1975, Max Friedersdorf Files, box 11, GRF.

75. Forrest Rettgers to NAM Members, April 3, 1975, Max Friedersdorf Files, box 11, GRF.

76. Robert Teeter to Richard Cheney, November 12, 1975, Robert Teeter Papers, box 63, GRF.

77. Bob Wolthius to Max Friedersdorf, January 27, 1975, William Kendall Files, box 1, GRF.

78. Bill Baroody to Gerald Ford, [March 1975], William Baroody Files, box 1, GRF.

79. "Statement by the President, November 4, 1975," William Baroody Files, box 16, GRF.

80. O. Pendleton Thomas to Members, September 15, 1975, BRA.

81. Summary of H.R. 7575 as introduced June 4, 1975, thomas.loc.gov.

82. Morton Mintz, "Senate Passes Bill to Protect Consumers," *Washington Post*, December 2, 1970; Burt Schorr, "Consumer Protection Fadeout," *Wall Street Journal*, November 4, 1975.

83. National Association of Manufacturers, "Major National Legislative Issues," May 1975, box 220, NAM.

84. National Association of Manufacturers, "NAM: A Reflection, We the Representatives of American Industry," 1975, Jeffrey Eves Files, box 3, GRF. See also *Association Letter* (Association Department, Washington, DC), October 1974 and December 1974, series II, box 5, USCOC.

85. *Public Citizen Congress Watch Newsletter*, April 7, 1977, series 14, box 110, CCAG.

86. During the CPA filibusters of 1972 and 1974, Senate rules stipulated that the votes of two-thirds of voting members were required for cloture to end a filibuster. In 1975, the Senate changed the rule to allow debate to cease with the votes of three-fifths of sworn members, or 60 in most cases. See "Filibuster and Cloture," United States Senate, http://www.senate.gov/artandhistory/history /common/briefing/Filibuster_ Cloture.htm.

87. Ralph Nader to Marc Caplan, June 21, 1977, series 14, box 10, CCAG.

88. James L. Ferguson to Members, May 17, 1977, 1977 Correspondence, BRA.

89. Green and Buchsbaum, *Corporate Lobbies*, 109–15; Patrick J. Akard, "Corporate Mobilization and Political Power: The Transformation of U.S. Economic Policy in the 1970s," *American Sociological Review* 57:5 (October 1992): 597–615; Schwartz, "The Successful Fight," 51–52.

90. "Watch out for the Watchdog," *Washington Star*, March 22, 1975.

91. *Public Citizen Congress Watch Newsletter*, November 7, 1975, series 1, box 2, CCAG; "Support the Office of Consumer Representation," in "Marc Caplan to Citizen Lobby Members, January 31, 1978," series 14, box 110, CCAG; *Public Citizen Congress Watch Newsletter*, July 17, 1975, series 14, box 110, CCAG.

92. Esther Peterson, White House exit interview, JEC.

93. Remarks by Jimmy Carter to the Public Citizen Forum, Washington, DC, August 9, 1976, series 14, box 113, CCAG.

94. Public Citizen Congress Watch to District Organizers, June 23, 1977, series 14, box 10, CCAG; Public Citizen Letter, July 17, 1975, series 14, box 110, CCAG.

95. Esther Peterson, White House exit interview; "Carter Dealt Major Defeat on Consumer Bill," *Congressional Quarterly* (February 11, 1978): 323–25.

96. "A Winning Streak for Business," *Business Week*, February 27, 1978.

97. "Carter Dealt Major Defeat."

98. On Southern antibusiness populism, particularly regarding the anti–chain store movement of the early twentieth century, see Marc Levinson, *The Great A&P and the Struggle for Small Business in America* (New York: Hill and Wang, 2011). On regional support for social regulation, see Peter Pashigian, "Environmental Regulation: Whose Self-Interests Are Being Protected?" *Economic Inquiry* 23:4 (October 1985): 551–84.

99. Glickman, *Buying Power*, 295.

100. See Marc Allen Eisner, *Antitrust and the Triumph of Economics: Institutions, Expertise, and Policy Change* (Chapel Hill: University of North Carolina Press, 1991).

CHAPTER 6

1. *Roundtable Report*, June 1993; David W. Dunlap, "Final Pan Am Departure," *New York Times*, September 4, 1992.

2. Stein, *Pivotal Decade*, 254.

3. Dimitry Anastakis, "The Last Automotive Entrepreneur? Lee Iacocca Saves Chrysler, 1978–1986," Business and Economic History On-Line (Business History Conference) 5 (2007), http://www.thebhc.org/publications/BEHonline/2007/anastakis.pdf; James M. Bickley, "Chrysler Corporation Loan Guarantee Act of 1979: Background, Provisions, and Cost," Congressional Research Service, February 8, 2008, http://digitalcommons.ilr.cornell.edu/cgi/viewcontent.cgi?article=1575&context=key_workplace; Robert Sobel, *Car Wars: The Untold Story* (New York: E. P. Dutton, 1984), 286–87.

4. Robert B. Reich and John D. Donahue, *New Deals: The Chrysler Revival and the American System* (New York: Times Books, 1985), 10–46; Joe Kohn, "Courage in the Family: Father, Son to Share Discipleship Message," *The Michigan Catholic*, March 9, 2007.

5. Lee Iacocca, *Iacocca: An Autobiography*, with William Novak (New York: Bantam, 1984); *Roundtable Report*, No. 81-5, June 1981.

6. Jeremy Peters, "Thomas Murphy, 90, Leader of G.M. in 1970's Prosperity, Dies," *New York Times*, January 19, 2006; Marylin Bender, "Murphy Decries Proposals for Planning the Economy," *New York Times*, June 24, 1975.

7. Milliken quoted in Anastakis, "The Last Automotive Entrepreneur." See also Walter Adams and James W. Brock, "Corporate Size and the Bailout Factor," *Journal of Economic Issues* 21:1 (March 1987): 61–85.

8. David R. Henderson, "A Step toward Feudalism: The Chrysler Bailout," *Cato Institute Policy Analysis No. A*, January 15, 1980. For contemporary government reports recapitulating the argument that smaller firms disproportionately bore regulatory costs, see "Corporate Strategies of Automotive Manufacturers, Harbridge House, Inc., Commissioned by the U.S. Department of Transportation, June 1978" and "The Impact of Federal Regulation on the Financial Structure and Performance of Domestic Motor Vehicle Manufacturers, Mark Anderson

and Joseph Blair, U.S. Department of Transportation, National Highway Traffic and Safety Administration, May 31, 1978," Special Advisor Inflation—Lewis, box 68, JEC.

9. "Draft of John Fisher Statement to House Banking & Currency Committee," in Robert G. Wingerter to John W. Fisher, October 11, 1979, box 200, NAM.

10. Reich and Donohue, *New Deals*, 61–66; Anastakis, "The Last Automotive Entrepreneur."

11. "Council for a Competitive Economy," promotional brochure, undated (probably 1978), box 200, NAM; Jerry Knight, "Federal Aid for Chrysler Big Mistake, Lobby Says," *Washington Post*, September 13, 1979.

12. Peters, "Thomas Murphy."

13. "Draft of John Fisher Statement."

14. "Ball Company: Our History," www.ball.com/history/; John W. Fisher obituary, *Leelanau Enterprise*, www.leelanaunews.com/news/OldArchive/Obituaries/John_W_Fisher.html.

15. "Draft of John Fisher Statement." See also David Vogel, "A Case Study of Clean Air Legislation, 1967–1981," in *The Impact of the Modern Corporation: Size and Impacts*, ed. Betty Bock et al. (New York: Columbia University Press, 1984), 309–86 and Michael P. Walsh, "Automobile Emissions," in *The Reality of Precaution: Comparing Risk Regulation in the United States and Europe*, ed. Jonathan Wiener et al. (Washington, DC: RFF Press, 2011), 142–58.

16. Preston H. Haskell to Lee A. Iacocca, October 16, 1979, box 200, NAM.

17. Jimmy Carter, "Inaugural Address," January 20, 1977, in Woolley and Peters, *The American Presidency Project*.

18. Stein, *Pivotal Decade*, 155, 30–39; "U.S. Trade in Goods and Services—Balance of Payments (BOP) Basis Value in Millions of Dollars, 1960 thru 2011," U.S. Census Bureau, Foreign Trade Division, June 8, 2012, www.census.gov.

19. Wells, *Economist in an Uncertain World*, 259.

20. Brenner, *The Economics of Global Turbulence*, 169; Krippner, *Capitalizing on Crisis*.

21. Sam Pickard to William Baroody, November 25, 1974, William J. Baroody Files, box 3, GRF.

22. Gerald Ford, "Remarks Concluding the Summit Conference on Inflation," September 28, 1974, in Woolley and Peters, *The American Presidency Project*.

23. Gerald R. Ford, "Address to a Joint Session of the Congress on the Economy," October 8, 1974, in Woolley and Peters, *The American Presidency Project*; Gerald R. Ford, "Executive Order 11821—Inflation Impact Statements," November 27, 1974, in Woolley and Peters, *The American Presidency Project*.

24. Gerald Ford, "Remarks at the Annual Meeting of the Chamber of Commerce of the United States," April 28, 1975, in Woolley and Peters, *The American Presidency Project*.

25. Center for the Study of American Business, "Ford Administration's Efforts to Reform Government Regulation of Business: Proceedings of a Seminar, Washington University, September 1975," Publication No. 6, October 1975, L. William Seidman Files, 1974–77, box 290, GRF; Harris and Milkis, *The Politics of Regulatory Change*, 102; James E. Anderson, "The Struggle to Reform Regu-

latory Procedures, 1978–1998," *Policy Studies Journal* 26:3 (September 1998): 482–98.

26. Jim Tozzi, "OIRA's Formative Years: The Historical Record of Centralized Regulatory Review Preceding OIRA's Founding," *Administrative Law Review* 63 (Special Edition 2011): 37–69.

27. Marshall Loeb, "The Corporate Chiefs' New Class," *Time*, April 14, 1980.

28. *Roundtable Report*, No. 74-12, December 1974; *Roundtable Report*, No. 75-6, August 1975.

29. Harris and Milkis, *The Politics of Regulatory Change*, 80. See also Vogel, *Fluctuating Fortunes* and McQuaid, *Uneasy Partners*.

30. The classic assessment of industrialists' influence over economic regulations in the first two decades of the twentieth century is Gabriel Kolko, *The Triumph of Conservatism: A Re-Interpretation of American History, 1900–1916* (New York: Free Press, 1963). On broadcast regulation, see Ronald H. Coase, "The Federal Communications Commission," *Journal of Law & Economics* 2 (October 1959): 1–40 and David A. Moss and Michael R. Fein, "Radio Regulation Revisited: Coase, the FCC, and the Public Interest," *Journal of Policy History* 15:4 (2003): 389–416.

31. Robert L. Bradley Jr., *Capitalism at Work: Business, Government, and Energy* (Salem, MA: M&M Scrivener Press, 2009), 178; Horwitz, *The Irony of Regulatory Reform*, 46–89.

32. Derthick and Quirk, *The Politics of Deregulation*, 1–28. On the economic arguments for deregulation, see McCraw, *Prophets of Regulation* and Thomas Romer and Howard Rosenthal, "Modern Political Economy and the Study of Regulation," in *Public Regulation: New Perspectives on Institutions and Policies*, ed. Elizabeth E. Bailey (Cambridge, MA: MIT Press, 1987), 73–116. On the politics of trucking deregulation, see Shane Hamilton, *Trucking Country: The Road to America's Wal-Mart Economy* (Princeton: Princeton University Press, 2008).

33. Derthick and Quirk, *The Politics of Deregulation*, 154.

34. *Roundtable Report*, No. 80-5, June 1980; "Position Statements and Other Documents of the Business Roundtable, 1973–2003," December 2003, BRA.

35. See Akard, "Corporate Mobilization and Political Power."

36. Ford, "Remarks at the Annual Meeting of the Chamber of Commerce."

37. For brief yet thorough accounts of the 1976 campaign, see Zelizer, *Jimmy Carter*, 31–52 and Wilentz, *Age of Reagan*, 64–78.

38. Jimmy Carter, "Executive Order 12044: Improving Government Regulations," March 23, 1978, in Woolley and Peters, *The American Presidency Project*.

39. Barnaby Feder, "Frank Cary, Past Chairman of I.B.M., Is Dead at 85," *New York Times*, January 6, 2006; *Roundtable Report*, No. 78-3, April 1978.

40. *Roundtable Report*, No. 79-11, December 1979.

41. The agencies studied were: the Environmental Protection Agency, the Equal Employment Opportunity Commission, the Occupational Safety and Health Administration, the Department of Energy, the Employee Retirement Income Security Act, and the Federal Trade Commission. *Roundtable Report*, No. 78-5, June 1978; *Roundtable Report*, No. 79-3, March 1979; Arthur Andersen & Co., *Cost of Government Regulation Study for the Business Roundtable* (Chicago: A. Andersen, 1979). In 1976, conservative economist Murray Weidenbaum,

working for the American Enterprise Institute, attempted to calculate the overall economic burden imposed by all government regulations. With dubious methodologies, he estimated the cost at $100 billion. For a critique of that estimate, see Harris and Milkis, *The Politics of Regulatory Change*, 9.

42. "Testimony of Frank T. Cary, Chairman of the Board, International Business Machines Corporation, on behalf of the Business Roundtable before the Senate Governmental Affairs Committee at Hearing on Regulatory Reform, March 20, 1979," in James Keogh to Members of the Business Roundtable, March 27, 1979, 1979 Correspondence, BRA; "Testimony of Richard D. Wood, Chairman and Chief Executive Officer, Eli Lilly & Co., on behalf of the Business Roundtable before the Subcommittee on Administrative Law and Governmental Relations, House Judiciary Committee, February 1, 1980," 1980 Correspondence, BRA.

43. "Summary of H.R. 3263," as introduced March 27, 1979, thomas.loc.gov.

44. Eizenstat quoted in Anderson, "The Struggle to Reform Regulatory Procedures."

45. "Regulatory Reform Should Give the Regulated and Regulators Equal Status," *Roundtable Report*, No. 80-2, March 1980.

46. Anderson, "The Struggle to Reform Regulatory Procedures."

47. John W. Fisher, "Regulation: Like Income Tax," 1979, box 200, NAM; "Regulatory Reform Legislation, Recommendations of the Business Roundtable," in Wood Testimony, February 1, 1980.

48. Frank Cary to Business Roundtable Members, June 10, 1980, 1980 Correspondence, BRA.

49. "No Regulatory Reform Bill Passed; Roundtable Effort Will Continue," *Roundtable Report*, No. 80-8, September 1980.

50. *Paperwork Reduction Act (44 U.S.C. 3501 et seq.)*; Tozzi, "OIRA's Formative Years," 62; Harris and Milkis, *The Politics of Regulatory Change*, 101. See also Philip J. Cooper, *The War against Regulation: From Jimmy Carter to George W. Bush* (Lawrence: University Press of Kansas, 2009).

51. On Connally, see James Reston, *The Lone Star: The Life of John Connally* (New York: Harper and Row, 1989). On Bush, see Baker, *Work Hard*, 73–97.

52. *Roundtable Report*, No. 80-9, November 1980; "Energy's Role in the Economy: The Long and Short of It, Remarks by C. C. Garvin, Jr., Chairman of the Board, Exxon Corporation, at the Economic Outlook Conference, Clemson and Furman Universities and the Greater Greenville Chamber of Commerce, Greenville, South Carolina, December 12, 1980," in Wallace Bates to Members of the Business Roundtable, December 23, 1980, 1980 Correspondence, BRA.

53. *Roundtable Report*, No. 80-10, December 1980.

54. Ronald Reagan, "Executive Order 12291—Federal Regulation," February 17, 1981, in Woolley and Peters, *The American Presidency Project*.

55. George Bush to Clifton Garvin, March 25, 1981, 1981 Correspondence, BRA.

56. Al Simmons to Senator John Tower, March 8, 1981, Task Force on Regulatory Relief: C. Boyden Gray Files, GHWB.

57. Anderson, "The Struggle to Reform Regulatory Procedures," 493.

58. *Roundtable Report*, No. 81-5, June 1981; John Opel to Members, September 4, 1981, 1981 Correspondence, BRA.

59. John Opel to Members, March 31, 1982, 1982 Correspondence, BRA.

60. *Roundtable Report*, No. 82-9, October 1982; "Business Coalition on Regulatory Reform Strategy for Across-the Board Regulatory Reform Legislation (H.R. 746)," October 19, 1982, BRA; John Opel to Members of the Business Roundtable, October 18, 1982, BRA.

61. Steven Roberts, "Democrats Regain Control in House," November 4, 1982; "Reforming Regulation," *Baltimore Sun*, December 22, 1982.

62. *Roundtable Report*, No. 83-8, September 1983; Stuart Auerbach, "NAM: White House Lags on Regulatory Reform," *Washington Post*, September 2, 1983.

63. Felicity Barringer, "Bush's Deregulators Going Out of Business," *Washington Post*, August 11, 1983.

64. Wilentz, *Age of Reagan*, 170; Harris and Milkis, *The Politics of Regulatory Change*, 251–54.

65. "Regulatory Reform's Success," *Chicago Tribune*, August 17, 1983.

66. Anny Wong, *The Roots of Japan's International Environmental Policies* (New York: Garland, 2001), 65–66.

67. *Roundtable Report*, March 1984; *Roundtable Report*, April 1987; *Roundtable Report*, August 1984; *Roundtable Report*, October 1985; *Roundtable Report*, March 1990. On the success of environmental regulation in spite of opposition by business, see Meg Jacobs, "The Politics of Environmental Regulation: Business-Government Relations in the 1970s and Beyond," in *What's Good for Business: Business and American Politics since World War II*, ed. Kim Phillips-Fein and Julian E. Zelizer (Oxford: Oxford University Press, 2012), 212–32.

68. *Roundtable Report*, March 1991; Deborah R. Hensler et al., *Class Action Dilemmas: Pursuing Public Goals for Private Gain* (Santa Monica, CA: RAND, 2000), 15–25.

69. For a comparative analysis of risk regulation between Europe and the United States, see David Vogel, *The Politics of Precaution: Regulating Health, Safety, and Environmental Risks in Europe and the United States* (Princeton: Princeton University Press, 2012).

70. Steven K. Vogel, *Freer Markets, More Rules: Regulatory Reform in Advanced Industrial Countries* (Ithaca: Cornell University Press, 1996); Jonathan Wiener et al., eds., *The Reality of Precaution: Comparing Risk Regulation in the United States and Europe* (Washington, DC: RFF Press, 2011). On neoliberalism, see, among many, Harvey, *A Brief History of Neoliberalism*. On the persistence of corporatism in West Germany, despite the influence of American economic policy ideas, see Paul Erker, "'Amerikanisierung' der westdeutschen Wirtschaft? Stand und Perspektiven der Forschung" [Americanization of West German Economy? State and Perspective of Research], in *Amerikanisierung und Sowjetisierung in Deutschland, 1945–1970* [Americanization and Sovietization in Germany, 1945–1970], ed. Konrad Jarausch and Hannes Sigrist (Frankfurt/Main: Campus-Verlag, 1997), 137–45.

CHAPTER 7

1. Chamber of Commerce of the United States, "Let's Rebuild, America: Summary," in William Verity to John Fisher, July 9, 1980, box 200, NAM.

2. Richard W. Rahn, "A Perspective on the U.S. Economic Outlook and Policy for 1980–81, Substance of a Report to the Board of Directors of the Chamber of Commerce of the United States," June 19, 1980, series 1, box 1e, USCOC.

3. *Economic Report of the President 1981* (Washington, DC: GPO, 1981); Stein, *Pivotal Decade*, 211–15; Krippner, *Capitalizing on Crisis*, 118–19.

4. "The Real Business Agenda: Fight Inflation, Improve Products and Jobs, Enhance Economy and Society," *Roundtable Report*, No. 80-3, April 1980; "Let's Rebuild America's Economic Base," in Verity to Fisher, July 9, 1980.

5. William E. Rothschild, *The Secret to GE's Success* (New York: McGraw-Hill, 2007), 127–43; Robert Slater, *The New GE: How Jack Welch Revived an American Institution* (Homewood, IL: Business One Irvin, 1993), 17–22.

6. Reginald H. Jones, "Capital Requirements of Industry and Government," speech to the Annual Meeting of the Business Roundtable, New York City, June 16, 1975, 1975 Correspondence, BRA; Reginald Jones, "Why Business Must Seek Tax Reform," *Harvard Business Review* (September–October 1975): 49–55.

7. *Roundtable Report*, No. 79-6, July 1979.

8. Alexander Trowbridge to NAM Board Member, August 11, 1980, box 201, NAM.

9. Steven A. Bank, *From Sword to Shield: The Transformation of the Income Tax, 1861 to Present* (Oxford: Oxford University Press, 2010), 66–67.

10. Alan J. Auerbach, "The New Economics of Accelerated Depreciation," National Bureau of Economic Research Working Paper Series, January 1982.

11. Mark Wilson, "The Advantages of Obscurity: World War II Tax Carryback Provisions and the Normalization of Corporate Welfare," in *What's Good for Business: Business and Politics since World War II*, ed. Kim Phillips-Fein and Julian E. Zelizer (Oxford: Oxford University Press, 2012), 16–44; Glenn Asner, "The Cold War and American Industrial Research" (Ph.D. diss., Carnegie Mellon University, 2006); Thomas Hanchett, "U.S. Tax Policy and the Shopping-Center Boom of the 1950s and 1960s," *American Historical Review* 101:4 (October 1996): 1082–1110.

12. National Association of Manufacturers, "Capital Recovery Allowances: Depreciation Reform for 1980," box 217, NAM.

13. Caroline Atkinson, "Senate Unit Votes $33 Billion Cut in Taxes for 1981," *Washington Post*, August 21, 1980.

14. Barber B. Conable Jr., *Congress and the Income Tax* (Norman: University of Oklahoma Press, 1989), 54; "A Call for Moderation of Tax Growth to Halt Industry's 'Decapitalization,'" *Roundtable Report*, No. 80-7, August 1980.

15. Christopher Conte, "A Look at '10-5-3' Depreciation Proposal, Focus of Attention in Tax-Cut Climate," *Wall Street Journal*, July 24, 1980.

16. Schulman, *The Seventies*, 193–217.

17. Stockman's cynical memoir is a scathing indictment of the failed budget policies of the Reagan administration and provides excellent insight into the clash

between ideology and governance. At the same time, the tell-all book success-fully articulates the central arguments and inherent contradictions of supply-side economics. See David A. Stockman, *The Triumph of Politics: How the Reagan Revolution Failed* (New York: Harper and Row, 1986).

18. Brownlee, *Federal Taxation*, 73–81. Mellon, who paid the third-highest amount of taxes in the country after John D. Rockefeller and Henry Ford, claimed that high tax rates encouraged wealthy people to cheat on their taxes and that lowering rates would increase compliance. In the mid-1970s, economist Arthur Laffer merely modified the theory to suggest that lower taxes would encour-age people to work more. See also David Cannadine, *Mellon: An American Life* (New York: Knopf, 2006). On the Kennedy/Johnson tax cut, see Elizabeth Popp Berman and Nicholas Pagnucco, "Economic Ideas and the Political Process: De-bating Tax Cuts in the U.S. House of Representatives, 1962–1981," *Politics and Society* 38:3 (September 2010): 347–72. On supply-side doctrine in general, see Jude Wanniski, *The Way the World Works: How Economies Fail . . . and Succeed* (New York: Basic Books, 1978).

19. See "The Laffer Curve," http://www.laffercenter.com/arthur-laffer/the-laffer -curve/.

20. Jack Kemp originally proposed a one-time 30 percent cut, but upon team-ing up with William Roth, he agreed to cutting 10 percent per year from three years. Politicians, journalists, and, unfortunately, historians are not often known for their arithmetic skills, and few have pointed out that these plans are not the same. Reducing the top rate of 70 percent, imposed on income in excess of $700,000 in 1978, by 30 percent outright would yield a new top rate of 49 per-cent [70 − (0.3 × 70) = 70 − 21 = 49]. But reducing the rate 10 percent per year for three years would yield a different result. The first year reduction would be 7, bringing the rate to 63 percent. The next would be a 10 percent cut to that new rate, or 63 − 6.3, or 56.7. The final cut would be 10 percent from that new rate, or 56.7 − 5.67, or 51.03: two points—and more than 4 percent—higher than in the original plan. See Brownlee, *Federal Taxation*, 136.

21. Stockman, *Triumph of Politics*, 61.

22. "Tax Cuts: A Remedy for Inflation," *The Heritage Foundation: Back-grounder*, no. 143, May 19, 1981, Elizabeth Dole Records, box 15, RWR.

23. In 1981, Stockman caused a great stir when he disclosed to journalist Wil-liam Greider his belief that the Laffer Curve was a convenient political fiction, a "trojan horse" to sneak in cuts to the top marginal tax rates. Stockman, *Triumph of Politics*, 56; William Greider, "The Education of David Stockman," *Atlantic Monthly* (December 1981): 46.

24. "Executives Sign Up to Aid John Anderson," *Business Week*, July 7, 1980; Robert Shogan, "Bush Accuses Reagan of 'Economic Madness,'" *Los Angeles Times*, April 11, 1980.

25. George Bush, "An Economic Policy for the '80s," *George Bush for Presi-dent*, Hoffman Papers, box 1, GHWB; Baker, *Work Hard*, 172–73.

26. Republican Party Platform of 1980, in Woolley and Peters, *The American Presidency Project*.

27. *Roundtable Report*, No. 81-4, May 1981.

28. Radio broadcaster Paul Harvey is credited with coining the term "Reaganomics." See Rupert Cornwell, "Paul Harvey: Radio Broadcaster Who Became the Voice of Middle America," *The Independent*, March 5, 2009. On the Roundtable's indirect lobbying, see Philip F. Jehle to Wayne Valis, April 2, 1981, Elizabeth Dole Records, box OA6385, RWR.

29. "Business Help Asked in Budget Test," *Washington Report* (Chamber of Commerce of the United States), April 20, 1981, Elizabeth Dole Records, box OA6385, RWR; "U.S. Chamber of Commerce Activities in Support of President Reagan Following His February 18 Speech on the Economy," U.S. Chamber of Commerce, Elizabeth Dole Records, box OA6385, RWR; Wayne Valis to Elizabeth Dole, Subject: U.S. Chamber of Commerce, April 3, 1981, Elizabeth Dole Records, box OA6385, RWR.

30. "Economic Recovery Program Calls for Less Federal Spending" and "Cutting Taxes Is the Key to Stimulating Economic Growth," *Mandate for Economic Recovery: A Special Report on President Reagan's Economic Recovery Plan Prepared by the U.S. Chamber of Commerce*, 1981, Jack Burgess Files, box 5, RWR; Elizabeth Dole to Red Cavaney, Subject: Meeting with Ed Meese and Dick Lesher, April 6, 1981, Elizabeth Dole Records, box OA6385, RWR.

31. Alexander Trowbridge to Edwin Meese, January 25, 1982, and Alexander Trowbridge to James Baker, January 25, 1982, both in Elizabeth Dole Records, box 14, RWR.

32. *Business and Public Affairs Fortnightly* 3:6 (May 15, 1981), enclosed in "NAM Field Flash," May 21, 1981, box 122A, NAM; *Roundtable Report*, No. 81-5, June 1981; Martin, *Shifting the Burden*, 116–20.

33. Lisa Myers, "President Basks in Tax Victory; GOP Rides Telephone 'Tidal Wave,'" *Washington Star*, July 30, 1981. For a detailed account of the corporate lobbying for ERTA, see Akard, "Corporate Mobilization and Political Power."

34. Iwan W. Morgan, *The Age of Deficits: Presidents and Unbalanced Budgets from Jimmy Carter to George W. Bush* (Lawrence: University Press of Kansas, 2009), 84–90; Conable, *Congress and the Income Tax*, 60; C. Eugene Steuerle, *Contemporary U.S. Tax Policy* (Washington, DC: Urban Institute Press, 2004); Brownlee, *Federal Taxation*, 150; Stockman, *Triumph of Politics*, 267. The notion of 5-10-10 cuts to personal taxes (replacing Kemp-Roth's original call for 10 percent cuts per year for three years, or 10-10-10) was a political simplification, complicated by the fact that the first cut was pushed back to October 1, 1981; a 5 percent reduction in taxes paid on income earned *after* October 1, 1981, changed the *average* tax rate for the entire year, so tax filers in April 1982 saw an actual rate decrease from 1980 to 1981 of only 1.25 percent. (That is, the rate reduction only applied to three months of tax year 1981, so the total effect on the year was ¼ of 5 percent, or 1.25 percent.) The lowest rate remained 0 percent for the first $3,000 (for married couples filing jointly), as enacted by the Carter-era Revenue Act of 1978. But the second-lowest bracket, on income between $3,000 and $5,000, fell from 14 percent to 13.83 percent.

35. Baker, *Work Hard*, 187.

36. Gil Troy, *Morning in America: How Ronald Reagan Invented the 1980s* (Princeton: Princeton University Press, 2005), 106.

37. *Roundtable Report*, No. 82-2, March 1982; Business Roundtable, "Statement on Federal Budget Policy," May 5, 1982, Elizabeth Dole Records, box 15, RWR.

38. Business Roundtable, "Statement on Federal Budget Policy"; American Stock Exchange Press Release, March 17, 1982, Elizabeth Dole Records, box 14, RWR; Stockman, *Triumph of Politics*, 303.

39. Theodore Brophy to Members, March 12, 1982, 1982 Correspondence, BRA; *Roundtable Report*, 82-2, March 1982.

40. "Friday, December 18, 1982" and "Tuesday, December 22, 1982," in Ronald Reagan, *The Reagan Diaries*, ed. Douglas Brinkley (New York: Harper Collins, 2007), 56–57.

41. In his memoir, James Baker describes Reagan's acceptance of the tax hike, noting the president's colorful language when he finally agreed: "'All right, goddammit,' he said. 'I'm gonna do it, but it's wrong.' . . . The president later said he regretted capitulating." Baker, *Work Hard*, 187–88.

42. Martin, *Shifting the Burden*, 135–38; Alvin C. Warren Jr. and Alan J. Auerbach, "Transferability of Tax Incentives and the Fiction of Safe Harbor Leasing," *Harvard Law Review* 95:8 (June 1982): 1752–86; C. Eugene Steuerle, *The Tax Decade: How Taxes Came to Dominate the Public Agenda* (Washington, DC: Urban Institute Press, 1992), 60.

43. *Roundtable Report*, No. 83-6, July 1983.

44. *Roundtable Report*, No. 82-3, April 1982; Martin, *Shifting the Burden*, 139–41.

45. Thomas Edsall, "Business Divided Over Tax Leasing," *Los Angeles Times*, April 13, 1982.

46. Donald Regan to Ronald Reagan, Subject: Business Roundtable's Budget Recommendation, March 24, 1982, Elizabeth Dole Records, box 15, RWR.

47. Elizabeth Dole to Edwin Meese, July 13, 1982, Elizabeth Dole Records, box 15, RWR.

48. Robert Dole to Theodore Brophy, July 16, 1982, Elizabeth Dole Records, box 15, RWR; Ruben F. Mettler to Members of the Business Roundtable, July 18, 1982, Elizabeth Dole Records, box 15, RWR.

49. Chamber of Commerce of the United States of America, "Reasons to Oppose the Tax Bill," undated position paper, summer 1982, Wendell Gunn Files, box 1, RWR; Chamber of Commerce of the United States of America, "Tax Increase Will Delay Recovery and Widen Deficit," Morton Blackwell Files, box 5, RWR; Chamber of Commerce of the United States, "Q and A on the U.S. Chamber of Commerce Position on the Tax Bill," undated position paper, summer 1982, Wendell Gunn Files, box 1, RWR.

50. "New Deputy for Defense, William Paul Thayer," *New York Times*, December 7, 1982; Timothy Schellhardt, "Chamber of Commerce Showdown Looms after Split on Tax Increase," *Wall Street Journal*, August 30, 1982.

51. Kenneth B. Noble, "Washington Watch: Chamber's Bid to End Split," *New York Times*, August 30, 1982; Schellhardt, "Chamber of Commerce Showdown Looms"; "New Deputy for Defense, Paul Thayer"; William F. Buckley, "What to Do with Thayer?" *National Review*, June 28, 1985.

52. Janice Farrell to Red Cavaney, "Unions That Supported 1982 Tax Bill," August 20, 1982, Ron Bonatati Files, box 1, RWR; Elizabeth Dole, "Meeting with Deficit Reduction Action Group," August 17, 1982, Elizabeth Dole Records, box OA5459, RWR; Lou Cannon and Thomas Edsall, "Big Tax Bill Gains Bipartisan Support as Key Vote Nears," *Washington Post*, August 19, 1982.

53. "Presidential Telephone Calls Re Tax Bill," undated list of phone calls, August 1982, Elizabeth Dole Records, box OA5459, RWR; Theodore Brophy to Ronald Reagan, August 17, 1982, Ronald Reagan to Theodore Brophy, August 26, 1982, Elizabeth Dole to Donald T. Regan, August 24, 1982, and John F. Welch to Ronald Reagan, August 17, 1982, all in Elizabeth Dole Records, box OA5459, RWR; Martin, *Shifting the Burden*, 153; Dorothy Collin, "Congress Passes Tax-Hike Bill," *Chicago Tribune*, August 20, 1982.

54. Red Cavaney, "Meeting with Business Chief Executive Officers," February 9, 1983, BE Business-Economics, box 2, RWR; Leslie Wayne, "Business Talks Back to Reagan," *New York Times*, January 30, 1983.

55. Figures from Morgan, *Age of Deficits*, appendix C, 271. On the Fed and the recovery, see Benjamin M. Friedman, *Day of Reckoning: The Consequences of American Economic Policy Under Reagan and After* (New York: Random House, 1988), 148–49.

56. Krippner, *Capitalizing on Crisis*, 102–5. The difference between imports and exports in goods in 1982, according to the census, was $36.485 billion; in 1987, it reached $159.557 billion. The deficit then decreased somewhat but rose again to a new record of $165.831 billion in 1994, after which time it hardly looked back. The trade deficit in goods reached its all-time high in 2006 at $835.689 billion and stood at $735.313 billion in 2012. Figures are nominal, not inflation adjusted. "U.S. Trade in Goods—Balance of Payments (BOP) Basis vs. Census Basis," March 7, 2013, *U.S. Census Bureau, Foreign Trade Division*.

57. *Roundtable Report*, No. 83-3, March 1983.

58. *Roundtable Report*, No. 82-5, May 1983.

59. Friedman, *Day of Reckoning*, 159; Brenner, *The Economics of Global Turbulence*, 196–97; *Roundtable Report*, No. 82-10, December 1982.

60. *Roundtable Report*, No. 82-10, December 1982; *Roundtable Report*, January 1985; Gerald P. Dwyer Jr., "Federal Deficits, Interest Rates and Monetary Policy," *Journal of Money, Credit and Banking* 17:4 (November 1985): 655–81; Paul Evans, "Do Large Deficits Produce High Interest Rates?" *American Economic Review* 75:1 (March 1985): 68–87.

61. Jeffrey H. Birnbaum and Alan S. Murray, *Showdown at Gucci Gulch: Lawmakers, Lobbyists, and the Unlikely Triumph of Tax Reform* (New York: Vintage Books, 1987), 32–33; "Recovery 'Firmly Under Way,' Chamber Economists State, But Express Caution about Public Policies' Impact over Long Term," U.S. Chamber of Commerce, June 1, 1983, BE Business Economics, box 2, RWR; Morgan, *Age of Deficits*, 96; Conable, *Congress and the Income Tax*, 70–72; *Roundtable Report*, May 1984.

62. Murray Weidenbaum, "I'm All for Free Enterprise, But . . . ," Whittenmore House Series 7, Washington University, St. Louis, MO, September 15, 1982, Elizabeth Dole Records, box 15, RWR.

63. Morgan, *Age of Deficits*, 105; *Roundtable Report*, March 1985; *Round-table Report*, April 1985.

64. Robert Beck to Members, January 24, 1985, 1985 Correspondence, BRA; *Roundtable Report*, May 1985; *Roundtable Report*, June 1985.

65. *Roundtable Report*, August 1985; Morgan, *Age of Deficits*, 109.

66. *Roundtable Report*, November 1990; Morgan, *Age of Deficits*, 158–205.

67. The Japanese government, for example, maintained a favorable tax and subsidy policy toward both the industrial and small business communities and did not wade into tax reform politics until its economy collapsed in the 1990s. T. J. Pempel, *Regime Shift: Comparative Dynamics of the Japanese Political Economy* (Ithaca: Cornell University Press, 1998), 62, 197; Abelshauser, *Deutsch Wirtschaftsgeschichte*, 286.

68. Alfred D. Chandler Jr., *The Visible Hand: The Managerial Revolution in American Business* (Cambridge, MA: Belknap Press, 1977).

CHAPTER 8

1. *Roundtable Report*, November 1985. On Walker, see Jeff Gerth, "A Power Broker's Many Roles," *New York Times*, October 29, 1980; McQuaid, *Uneasy Partners*, 168; and Birnbaum and Murray, *Showdown at Gucci Gulch*, 16–17, 48–50. On the Carlton Group, see Edward Cowan, "Carlton Group Spurns Lobbying Limelight," *New York Times*, March 18, 1982, and Martin, *Shifting the Burden*, 116–20.

2. Steuerle, *Contemporary U.S. Tax Policy*, 129–38; Martin, *Shifting the Burden*, 159.

3. "The Facts about Corporate Taxation," in Edward Jefferson to Members of the Business Roundtable Policy Committee, April 3, 1985, BRA; Birnbaum and Murray, *Showdown at Gucci Gulch*, 11–13, 287; Martin, *Shifting the Burden*, 11.

4. Brownlee quoted in Steuerle, *The Tax Decade*, 122; Eric M. Patashnik, *Reforms at Risk: What Happens after Major Policy Changes Are Enacted* (Princeton: Princeton University Press, 2008), 35–54.

5. Paul Taylor, "Lobbyists Lose the Game, Not the Guccis," *Washington Post*, July 31, 1983.

6. Richard Stevenson, "Quiet on the Lobbying Front," *New York Times*, February 23, 2001; Birnbaum, *The Lobbyists*, 18–20, 44–46.

7. Rodgers, *Age of Fracture*.

8. Taylor, "Lobbyists Lose the Game."

9. Leslie Wayne, "In Washington, Corporate Power Now Rests in the Hands of Many, Not a Few," *New York Times*, May 22, 1983; Linda Grant, "Still Strong: Business Lobbies Find Resistance," *Los Angeles Times*, December 19, 1982.

10. Suzanne Garment, "Hope and Hoopla: Levitt's Lobbyists Go to Washington," *Wall Street Journal*, February 13, 1981; William Miller, "Jim Jones Comes Full Circle," *Industry Week*, June 3, 1991.

11. David Treadwell, "New Lobbying Group Quickly Gains Influence," *Los Angeles Times*, September 19, 1983.

12. Cowan, "Carlton Group Spurns Lobbying Limelight"; Martin, *Shifting the Burden*, 154; Treadwell, "New Lobbying Group."

13. Krippner, *Capitalizing on Crisis*, 28–31; U.S. Bureau of Economic Analysis, *National Income and Product Accounts of the United States, 1929–1994*, vol. 1 (Washington, DC: Bureau of Economic Analysis, April 1998), 25–30 (Tables 6.5A–C). Financial sector profits as a percent of the total dipped precipitously (to –10 percent) during the financial crisis of 2008–9, during which the sector as a whole lost huge sums of money. By 2011, financial profits once again accounted for a third of all profits. Kathleen Madigan, "Like the Phoenix, U.S. Finance Profits Soar," *Wall Street Journal*, March 25, 2011.

14. *Roundtable Report*, No. 72-12, November 28, 1972; *Roundtable Report*, June 1988.

15. Krippner, *Capitalizing on Crisis*, 32.

16. Ibid., 4–5; Louis Hyman, "Rethinking the Postwar Corporation: Management, Monopolies, and Markets," in *What's Good for Business: American Business and Politics since World War II*, ed. Kim Phillips-Fein and Julian Zelizer (Oxford: Oxford University Press, 2012), 195–211; "GE 2002 Annual Report," http://www.ge.com/files/usa/en/ar2002/ge_ar2002_editorial.pdf.

17. Gerald F. Davis, *Managed by the Markets: How Finance Reshaped America* (Oxford: Oxford University Press, 2009), 21–22.

18. *Roundtable Report*, October 1984.

19. T. Boone Pickens, "Two Titans Square Off: How Big Business Stacks the Deck," *New York Times*, March 1, 1987; *Roundtable Report*, May 1985.

20. *Roundtable Report*, September 1987; Alan Murray, "Conflicting Signals: Lobbyists for Business Are Deeply Divided, Reducing Their Clout," *Wall Street Journal*, March 25, 1987; Charles W. Parry, "Letter to the Editor: Charls Walker," *Wall Street Journal*, April 7, 1987.

21. Judith Stein, *Running Steel, Running America: Race, Economic Policy, and the Decline of Liberalism* (Chapel Hill: University of North Carolina Press, 1998), 229–52; Sobel, *Car Wars*, 219–38.

22. Alexander B. Trowbridge to Henry H. Fowler, June 25, 1980, box 201, NAM; "Text of Policy Statement by Panel to Fight Inflation," *New York Times*, June 22, 1980; "Members of Committee to Fight Inflation," June 22, 1980. On the Committee to Fight Inflation, see also Wells, *Economist in an Uncertain World*, 231.

23. Alexander Trowbridge to A. C. Nielsen Jr., June 18, 1980, box 201, NAM; Wolfgang Saxon, "Alexander Trowbridge, 76, Ex-Secretary of Commerce, Dies," *New York Times*, April 28, 2006.

24. "The Decline of U.S. Industry: Stunted Growth of Productivity" and "Revitalizing the U.S. Economy," *Business Week*, June 30, 1980; William Verity to John Fisher, July 9, 1980, box 200, NAM; Sandy Trowbridge to Gene Hardy, "Revitalization Program—Documentation," July 29, 1980, box 201, NAM. On deindustrialization, plant closings, and labor dislocation, see Michael A. Bernstein, "Understanding American Economic Decline: The Contours of the Late-Twentieth-Century Experience," in *Understanding American Economic Decline*, ed. Michael A. Bernstein and David Adler (Cambridge: Cambridge University

Press, 1994), 3–33; Barry Bluestone and Bennett Harrison, *The Deindustrialization of America: Plant Closings, Community Abandonment, and the Dismantling of Basic Industry* (New York: Basic Books, 1982); and Jefferson Cowie, *Capital Moves: RCA's Seventy-Year Quest for Cheap Labor* (New York: New Press, 1999).

25. Verity to Fisher, July 9, 1980; Alexander Trowbridge to John O'Hara, June 12, 1980, box 201, NAM; "Issue: A 1980 Tax Reduction Bill," August 11, 1980, box 201, NAM; "Republican Party Platform of 1980, July 15, 1980" and "Democratic Party Platform of 1980, August 11, 1980," in Woolley and Peters, *The American Presidency Project*.

26. "Forward into the Past," *Washington Post*, July 8, 1980; Alexander Trowbridge to The Editor, *Washington Post*, July 17, 1980, box 201, NAM.

27. Otis L. Graham Jr., *Losing Time: The Industrial Policy Debate* (Cambridge, MA: Harvard University Press, 1992), 1–3, 50–65. See also Stein, *Pivotal Decade*, 205–44, 252–59, 267–70. On Reich's influence on Clinton, see Bob Woodward, *The Agenda: Inside the Clinton White House* (New York: Simon and Schuster, 1984).

28. Graham, *Losing Time*, 48, 53; *Roundtable Report*, No. 83-2, February 1983.

29. Business Roundtable, *Analysis of the Issues in the National Industrial Policy Debate: Working Papers: Staff Working Papers Prepared for the Business Roundtable Ad Hoc Task Force* (New York: Business Roundtable, 1984), 1–26.

30. National Association of Manufacturers, *NAM's Agenda for Regaining America's Industrial Initiative*, 1983, box 217, NAM; Graham, *Losing Time*, 142, 165–79.

31. *Roundtable Report*, No. 74-12, December 1974; *Roundtable Report*, No. 75-3, April 1975. On Burke-Hartke, see Oliveiro, "The United States, Multinational Corporations, and the Politics of Globalization in the 1970s."

32. *Roundtable Report*, No. 82-5, May 1983; *Roundtable Report*, No. 82-6, June 1983; *Roundtable Report*, February 1985; *Roundtable Report*, May 1986.

33. *Roundtable Report*, April 1987; *Roundtable Report*, November 1986.

34. Maxwell A. Cameron and Brian Tomlin, *The Making of NAFTA: How the Deal Was Done* (Ithaca: Cornell University Press, 2000), 74, 201; Hermann von Bertrab, *Negotiating NAFTA: A Mexican Envoy's Account* (Westport, CT: Praeger, 1997), 1–7, 116; Todd Tucker and Lori Wallach, *The Rise and Fall of Fast Track Trade Authority* (Washington, DC: Public Citizen, 2009).

35. Charles Lewis, "The Treaty No One Could Read: How Lobbyists and Business Quietly Forged NAFTA," *Washington Post*, June 27, 1993; "Gallup Poll Finds 46% Opposed; 38% in Favor of NAFTA," *Los Angeles Times*, November 9, 1993; "Effects of the North American Free Trade Agreement: Hearing before the Committee on Commerce, Science, and Transportation, United States Senate, One Hundred Third Congress, first session, May 6, 1993," Senate Hearing, 103–917. Elisha's testimony was also reprinted in *Roundtable Report*, May 1993. On the NAM's early history, see chapter 2.

36. See H. Ross Perot, with Pat Choate, *Save Your Job, Save Our Country: Why NAFTA Must Be Stopped—Now!* (New York: Hyperion, 1993); Patrick

Buchanan, "America First, NAFTA Never: It's Not about Free Trade—It's about Our Way of Life," *Washington Post*, November 7, 1993.

37. Cameron and Tomlin, *The Making of NAFTA*, 202–4; Clerk of the House of Representatives of the United States, "Final Vote Results for Roll Call Vote 575," November 17, 1993; U.S. Senate Roll Call Vote 103rd Cong., 1st Sess., November 20, 1993.

38. Murray, "Conflicting Signals"; Paul Blustein, "What Industry Wants from the Next President: Business Likely to Respond with Defensive Tactics," *Washington Post*, October 30, 1988.

39. On the internationalization of the business elite, see Justin Greenwood and Henry Jacek, eds., *Organized Business and the New Global Order* (New York: St. Martin's Press, 2000). On neoliberal economic ideas in a global context, see in particular Eric Hobsbawm, *The Age of Extremes: A History of the World, 1914–1991* (New York: Vintage Books, 1994). For a comparative view of right-wing policymaking in Britain and the United States in the late twentieth century, see Ravi K. Roy and Arthur T. Denzau, *Fiscal Policy Convergence from Reagan to Blair: The Left Veers Right* (London: Routledge, 2004).

40. Schlozman and Tierney, *Organized Interests and American Democracy*, 77, 301–3.

41. Robert Reich, *Supercapitalism: The Transformation of Business, Democracy, and Everyday Life* (New York: Knopf, 2007), 134–35; Center for Responsive Politics, www.opensecrets.org.

42. David Shribman, "Lobbyists Proliferate: So Do the Headaches," *New York Times*, July 25, 1982.

43. Craig Colgate, ed., *Directory of Washington Representatives of American Associations and Industry, 1977* (Washington, DC: Columbia Books, 1977); Arthur Close, ed., *Washington Representatives, 1979* (Washington, DC: Columbia Books, 1979); Arthur Close and Jody Curtis, eds., *Washington Representatives, 1985* (Washington, DC: Columbia Books, 1985); Arthur Close, Gregory Bologna, and Curtis McCormick, eds., *Washington Representatives, 1990* (Washington, DC: Columbia Books, 1990).

44. Robert G. Kaiser, *So Damned Much Money: The Triumph of Lobbying and the Corrosion of American Government* (New York: Knopf, 2009).

45. Birnbaum, *The Lobbyists*, 7.

46. Zelizer, *On Capitol Hill*, 177–232; Kaiser, *So Damned Much Money*, 115–17; Ansolabehere, Snyder, and Tripathi, "Are PAC Contributions and Lobbying Linked?"

47. Robert Rosenblatt and Ronald Ostrow, "Robert Gray—Capital's King of Clout," *Los Angeles Times*, May 13, 1984.

48. Ulrike Schaede, *Cooperative Capitalism: Self-Regulation, Trade Associations, and the Antimonopoly Law in Japan* (Oxford: Oxford University Press, 2000), 4, 16; W. Miles Fletcher, "Dreams of Economic Transformation and the Reality of Economic Crisis in Japan: Keidanren in the Era of the 'Bubble' and the Onset of the 'Lost Decade,' from the Mid-1980s to the Mid-1990s," *Asia Pacific Business Review* 18:2 (April 2012): 149–65.

49. Michael Useem, *The Inner Circle: Large Corporations and the Rise of Business Political Activity in the U.S. and U.K.* (New York: Oxford University Press, 1984), 71; European Round Table, Origins, www.ert.eu/about#Origins.

EPILOGUE

1. *Citizens United v. Federal Election Commission*, 558 U.S. 310 (2010); Barack Obama, "The President's Weekly Address," January 23, 2010, in Woolley and Peters, *The American Presidency Project*.

2. Gerald Davis, "The Twilight of the Berle and Means Corporation," *Seattle University Law Review* 34 (2011): 1121–38.

3. Nouriel Roubini and Stephen Mihm, *Crisis Economics: A Crash Course in the Future of Finance* (New York: Penguin, 2010); Suzanne Mettler, "Reconstituting the Submerged State: The Challenges of Social Policy Reform in the Obama Era," *Perspectives on Politics* 8:3 (September 2010): 803–24.

4. David Kirkpatrick, "For Romney, a Course Set Long Ago," *New York Times*, December 18, 2007.

5. For recent lobbying figures, see Center for Responsive Politics, opensecrets .org. See also www.uschamber.com, www.nam.org, and www.businessroundtable .org.

6. U.S. Chamber of Commerce, "Letter Calling for Passage of H.R. 1, the 'American Recovery and Reinvestment Act of 2009,' " February 6, 2009, http://www.uschamber.com/issues/letters/2009/letter-calling-passage-hr-1-american -recovery-and-reinvestment-act-2009.

7. Robert Pear, "Health Care Industry in Talks to Shape Policy," *New York Times*, February 20, 2009; Jacob S. Hacker, "The Road to Somewhere: Why Health Reform Happened, or Why Political Scientists Who Write about Public Policy Shouldn't Assume They Know How to Shape It," *Perspectives on Politics* 8:3 (September 2010): 861–76.

8. Lichtenstein, *State of the Union*, 181–85.

9. On PATCO, see Joseph A. McCartin, *Collision Course: Ronald Reagan, the Air Traffic Controllers, and the Strike That Changed America* (Oxford: Oxford University Press, 2011). On divisions over labor among liberals, see Stein, *Pivotal Decade*, 262–300.

10. Elizabeth Warren, "Unsafe at Any Rate," *Democracy: A Journal of Ideas* 5 (Summer 2007): 8–19; Skeel, *The New Financial Deal*.

11. Morgan, *The Age of Deficits*, 206–65.

Bibliography

PERIODICALS

American Prospect
Association Letter (Chamber of Commerce of the United States)
Atlantic Monthly
Baltimore Sun
Business and Public Affairs Fortnightly
Business Roundtable for Responsible Labor-Management Relations Report
Business Roundtable Report
Business Week
Chamber of Commerce Newsletter
Chicago Tribune
Christian Science Monitor
Congressional Quarterly
Congressional Record
Congressional Research Service
Construction Users Anti-Inflation Roundtable Report
Cornell Chronicle
Daily Press (Hampton, VA)
Forbes
Fortune
Globe Democrat (St. Louis, Missouri)
Harvard Business Review
The Heritage Foundation: Backgrounder
The Independent
Indiana Evening Gazette
Industry Week
Los Angeles Times
Michigan Catholic
Monthly Labor Review
The Nation
National Review
Nation's Business
New York Magazine
New York Times
Newsweek
Public Citizen Congress Watch Newsletter
Reader's Digest
Richmond Times Dispatch
Roundtable Report

Television Digest
Time
Wall Street Journal
Washington Post
Washington Report (Chamber of Commerce of the United States)
Washington Star

INTERVIEWS

Bernadette Budde, Business-Industry Political Action Committee
Carl Grant, United States Chamber of Commerce
John Post, Business Roundtable

BOOKS

Abelshauser, Werner. *Deutsche Wirtschaftsgeschichte. Von 1945 bis zur Gegen-wart* [German Economic History: From 1945 to Present]. 2nd ed. Munich: C. H. Beck, 2011.
Ackerman, Bruce A., and William T. Hassler. *Clean Coal/Dirty Air, or How the Clean Air Act Became a Multibillion-Dollar Bail-Out for High-Sulfur Coal Producers and What Should Be Done About It.* New Haven: Yale University Press, 1981.
Alexander, Herbert. *Money in Politics.* Washington, DC: Public Affairs Press, 1972.
Arthur Andersen & Co. *Cost of Government Regulation Study for the Business Roundtable.* Chicago: A. Andersen, 1979.
Baker, James A. III. *"Work Hard, Study . . . and Keep Out of Politics!": Adventures and Lessons from an Unexpected Public Life.* With Steve Fiffer. New York: G. P. Putnam's Sons, 2006.
Bank, Steven A. *From Sword to Shield: The Transformation of the Income Tax, 1861 to Present.* Oxford: Oxford University Press, 2010.
Berkowitz, Edward. "Medicare: The Great Society's Enduring National Health Insurance Program." In *The Great Society and the High Tide of Liberalism,* ed. Sidney M. Milkis and Jerome M. Mileur, 320–50. Amherst: University of Massachusetts Press, 2005.
Bernstein, Jules, et al. "Conceptual Draft of the Corporate Democracy Act." In *The Big Business Reader: On Corporate America,* ed. Mark Green et al., 500–511. New York: Pilgrim Press, 1991.
Bernstein, Marver H. *Regulating Business by Independent Commission.* Princeton: Princeton University Press, 1955.
Bernstein, Michael A. "Understanding American Economic Decline: The Contours of the Late-Twentieth-Century Experience." In *Understanding American Economic Decline,* ed. Michael A. Bernstein and David E. Adler, 3–33. Cambridge: Cambridge University Press, 1994.

Berry, Jeffrey M. *Lobbying for the People: The Political Behavior of Public Interest Groups*. Princeton: Princeton University Press, 1977.

Berry, Jeffrey M., and Clyde Wilcox. *The Interest Group Society*. 1984. New York: Pearson Longman, 2007.

Bertrab, Hermann von. *Negotiating NAFTA: A Mexican Envoy's Account*. Westport, CT: Praeger, 1997.

Birnbaum, Jeffrey H. *The Lobbyists: How Influence Peddlers Get Their Way in Washington*. New York: Random House, 1992.

Birnbaum, Jeffrey H., and Alan S. Murray. *Showdown at Gucci Gulch: Lawmakers, Lobbyists, and the Unlikely Triumph of Tax Reform*. New York: Vintage Books, 1987.

Blount, Winton M. *Doing It My Way*. With Richard Blodgett. Lyme, CT: Greenwich Publishing Group, 1996.

Bluestone, Barry, and Bennett Harrison. *The Deindustrialization of America: Plant Closings, Community Abandonment, and the Dismantling of Basic Industry*. New York: Basic Books, 1982.

Bowles, Nigel. *Nixon's Business: Authority and Power in Presidential Politics*. College Station: Texas A&M University Press, 2005.

Bradley, Robert L., Jr. *Capitalism at Work: Business, Government, and Energy*. Salem, MA: M&M Scrivener Press, 2009.

Brecher, Jeremy. *Strike!* San Francisco: Straight Arrow Books, 1972.

Brenner, Robert. *The Economics of Global Turbulence: The Advanced Capitalist Economies from Long Boom to Long Downturn, 1945–2005*. London: Verso, 2006.

Brinkley, Alan. *The End of Reform: New Deal Liberalism in Recession and War*. New York: Vintage Books, 1995.

Brody, David. *Steelworkers in America: The Nonunion Era*. Cambridge, MA: Harvard University Press, 1960.

Brownlee, W. Elliot. *Federal Taxation in America: A Short History*. 1996. Cambridge: Cambridge University Press, 2004.

Buhle, Paul. *Taking Care of Business: Samuel Gompers, George Meany, Lane Kirkland, and the Tragedy of American Labor*. New York: Monthly Review Press, 1999.

Burgin, Angus. *The Great Persuasion: Reinventing Free Markets since the Depression*. Cambridge, MA: Harvard University Press, 2012.

Business Roundtable. *Analysis of the Issues in the National Industrial Policy Debate: Working Papers: Staff Working Papers Prepared for the Business Roundtable Ad Hoc Task Force*. New York: Business Roundtable, 1984.

Cameron, Maxwell A., and Brian W. Tomlin. *The Making of NAFTA: How the Deal Was Done*. Ithaca: Cornell University Press, 2000.

Cannadine, David. *Mellon: An American Life*. New York: Knopf, 2006.

Carpenter, Daniel P. *Reputation and Power: Organizational Image and Pharmaceutical Regulation at the FDA*. Princeton: Princeton University Press, 2010.

Carter, Dan T. *The Politics of Rage: George Wallace, the Origins of the New Conservatism, and the Transformation of American Politics*. Baton Rouge: Louisiana State University Press, 2000.

Chandler, Alfred D., Jr. "Government versus Business: An American Phenomenon." In *Business and Public Policy*, ed. John T. Dunlop, 1–11. Cambridge, MA: Harvard University Press, 1980.

———. *The Visible Hand: The Managerial Revolution in American Business*. Cambridge, MA: Belknap Press, 1977.

Close, Arthur, ed. *Washington Representatives, 1979*. Washington, DC: Columbia Books, 1979.

Close, Arthur, and Jody Curtis, eds. *Washington Representatives, 1985*. Washington, DC: Columbia Books, 1985.

Close, Arthur, Gregory Bologna, and Curtis McCormick, eds. *Washington Representatives, 1990*. Washington, DC: Columbia Books, 1990.

Cohen, Lizabeth. *A Consumers' Republic: The Politics of Mass Consumption in Postwar America*. New York: Vintage Books, 2003.

Colgate, Craig, ed. *Directory of Washington Representatives of American Associations and Industry, 1977*. Washington, DC: Columbia Books, 1977.

Collins, Robert M. *The Business Response to Keynes, 1929–1964*. New York: Columbia University Press, 1981.

———. *More: The Politics of Economic Growth in Postwar America*. New York: Oxford University Press, 2000.

Conable, Barber B., Jr. *Congress and the Income Tax*. Norman: University of Oklahoma Press, 1989.

Cooper, Philip J. *The War against Regulation: From Jimmy Carter to George W. Bush*. Lawrence: University Press of Kansas, 2009.

Cowie, Jefferson. *Capital Moves: RCA's Seventy-Year Quest for Cheap Labor*. New York: New Press, 1999.

———. *Stayin' Alive: The 1970s and the Last Days of the Working Class*. New York: New Press, 2010.

Davis, Gerald F. *Managed by the Markets: How Finance Reshaped America*. Oxford: Oxford University Press, 2009.

Delton, Jennifer A. *Racial Integration in Corporate America, 1940–1990*. Cambridge: Cambridge University Press, 2009.

Derthick, Martha, and Paul J. Quirk. *The Politics of Deregulation*. Washington, DC: Brookings Institution, 1985.

Dexter, Lewis Anthony. *How Organizations Are Represented in Washington: Toward a Broader Understanding of the Seeking of Influence and of Patterns of Representation*. Lanham, MD: University Press of America, 1987.

Doering-Manteuffel, Anselm, and Raphael Lutz, eds. *Nach dem Boom: Perspektiven auf die Zeitgeschichte seit 1970* [After the Boom: Perspectives on Contemporary History since 1970]. 2nd ed. Göttingen: Vandenhoeck & Ruprecht, 2010.

Eisner, Marc Allen. *Antitrust and the Triumph of Economics: Institutions, Expertise, and Policy Change*. Chapel Hill: University of North Carolina Press, 1991.

Erker, Paul. "'Amerikanisierung' der westdeutschen Wirtschaft? Stand und Perspektiven der Forschung" [Americanization of West German Economy? State and Perspective of Research]. In *Amerikanisierung und Sowjetisierung in*

Deutschland, 1945–1970 [Americanization and Sovietization in Germany, 1945–1970], ed. Konrad Jarausch and Hannes Sigrist, 137–45. Frankfurt/Main: Campus-Verlag, 1997.

Fales, Haliburton 2d. *Trying Cases: A Life in the Law*. New York: New York University Press, 1997.

Feldstein, Mark. *Poisoning the Press: Richard Nixon, Jack Anderson, and the Rise of Washington's Scandal Culture*. New York: Farrar, Straus, and Giroux, 2010.

Ferguson, Niall, et al., eds. *The Shock of the Global: The 1970s in Perspective*. Cambridge, MA: Belknap Press of Harvard University Press, 2010.

Fones-Wolf, Elizabeth A. *Selling Free Enterprise: The Business Assault on Labor and Liberalism, 1945–60*. Urbana: University of Illinois Press, 1994.

Friedman, Benjamin M. *Day of Reckoning: The Consequences of American Economic Policy Under Reagan and After*. New York: Random House, 1988.

Gall, Gilbert J. *The Politics of Right to Work: The Labor Federations as Special Interests, 1943–1979*. New York: Greenwood, 1988.

Glickman, Lawrence B. *Buying Power: A History of Consumer Activism in America*. Chicago: University of Chicago Press, 2009.

Graham, Otis L., Jr. *Losing Time: The Industrial Policy Debate*. Cambridge, MA: Harvard University Press, 1992.

Grayson, C. Jackson. *Confessions of a Price Controller*. Homewood, IL: Dow Jones-Irwin, 1974.

Green, Mark, and Andrew Buchsbaum. *The Corporate Lobbies: Political Profiles of the Business Roundtable and the Chamber of Commerce*. Washington, DC: Public Citizen, 1980.

Greenberg, David. *Nixon's Shadow: The History of an Image*. New York: W. W. Norton, 2003.

Greenwood, Justin, and Henry Jacek, eds. *Organized Business and the New Global Order*. New York: St. Martin's Press, 2000.

Greider, William. *Secrets of the Temple: How the Federal Reserve Runs the Country*. New York: Simon and Schuster, 1987.

Hacker, Jacob S., and Paul Pierson. *Winner-Take-All Politics: How Washington Made the Rich Richer—and Turned Its Back on the Middle Class*. New York: Simon and Schuster, 2010.

Hall, Peter A., and David Soskice, eds. *Varieties of Capitalism: The Institutional Foundations of Comparative Advantage*. New York: Oxford University Press, 2001.

Hamilton, Shane. *Trucking Country: The Road to America's Wal-Mart Economy*. Princeton: Princeton University Press, 2008.

Handler, Edward, and John Mulkern. *Business in Politics: Campaign Strategies of Corporate Political Action Committees*. Lexington, MA: Lexington Books, 1982.

Harris, Richard A., and Sidney M. Milkis. *The Politics of Regulatory Change: A Tale of Two Agencies*. New York: Oxford University Press, 1996.

Harvey, David. *A Brief History of Neoliberalism*. New York: Oxford University Press, 2005.

Hawley, Ellis. "The New Deal and Business." In *The New Deal: The National Level*, ed. John Braeman, Robert H. Brenner, and David Brody, 55–78. Columbus: Ohio State University Press, 1975.

Hensler, Deborah R., et al. *Class Action Dilemmas: Pursuing Public Goals for Private Gain*. Santa Monica, CA: RAND, 2000.

Hilton, Matthew. *Prosperity for All: Consumer Activism in an Era of Globalization*. Ithaca: Cornell University Press, 2009.

Hobsbawm, Eric. *The Age of Extremes: A History of the World, 1914–1991*. New York: Vintage Books, 1994.

Horwitz, Robert Britt. *The Irony of Regulatory Reform: The Deregulation of American Telecommunications*. New York: Oxford University Press, 1989.

Hyman, Louis. "Rethinking the Postwar Corporation: Management, Monopolies, and Markets." In *What's Good for Business: American Business and Politics since World War II*, ed. Kim Phillips-Fein and Julian E. Zelizer, 195–211. Oxford: Oxford University Press, 2012.

Iacocca, Lee. *Iacocca: An Autobiography*. With William Novak. New York: Bantam Books, 1984.

Jacobs, Meg. "The Conservative Struggle and the Energy Crisis." In *Rightward Bound: Making America Conservative in the 1970s*, ed. Bruce J. Schulman and Julian E. Zelizer, 193–209. Cambridge, MA: Harvard University Press, 2008.

———. *Pocketbook Politics: Economic Citizenship in Twentieth-Century America*. Princeton: Princeton University Press, 2005.

———. "The Politics of Environmental Regulation: Business-Government Relations in the 1970s and Beyond." In *What's Good for Business: Business and American Politics since World War II*, ed. Kim Phillips-Fein and Julian E. Zelizer, 212–32. Oxford: Oxford University Press, 2012.

Jacoby, Sanford M. "American Exceptionalism Revisited: The Importance of Management." In *Masters to Managers: Historical and Comparative Perspectives on American Employers*, ed. Sanford M. Jacoby, 173–200. New York: Columbia University Press, 1991.

———. *Modern Manors: Welfare Capitalism since the New Deal*. Princeton: Princeton University Press, 1997.

Jarausch, Konrad H. *After Hitler: Recivilizing Germans, 1945–1995*. Oxford: Oxford University Press, 2006.

Jeffries, John C., Jr. *Justice Lewis F. Powell, Jr.: A Biography*. New York: Charles Scribner's Sons, 1994.

John, Richard R. *Network Nation: Inventing American Telecommunications*. Cambridge, MA: Belknap Press of Harvard University Press, 2010.

Kaiser, Robert G. *So Damned Much Money: The Triumph of Lobbying and the Corrosion of American Government*. New York: Knopf, 2009.

Kendrick, John W., and Elliot S. Grossman. *Productivity in the United States: Trends and Cycles*. Baltimore: Johns Hopkins University Press, 1980.

Keynes, John Maynard. *The General Theory of Employment, Interest, and Money*. 1936. Basingstoke: Hampshire: Palgrave McMillan, 2007.

Klein, Jennifer. *For All These Rights: Business, Labor, and the Shaping of America's Public-Private Welfare State*. Princeton: Princeton University Press, 2003.

Kolko, Gabriel. *The Triumph of Conservatism: A Re-Interpretation of American History, 1900–1916.* New York: Free Press, 1963.

Kosters, Marvin H., and J. Dawson Ahalt. *Controls and Inflation: The Economic Stabilization Program in Retrospect.* Washington, DC: American Enterprise Institute for Public Policy Research, 1975.

Krippner, Greta R. *Capitalizing on Crisis: The Political Origins of the Rise of Finance.* Cambridge, MA: Harvard University Press, 2011.

Krooss, Herman E. *Executive Opinion: What Business Leaders Said and Thought on Economic Issues, 1920s–1960s.* New York: Doubleday, 1970.

Laird, Pamela Walker. *Pull: Networking and Success since Benjamin Franklin.* Cambridge, MA: Harvard University Press, 2006.

Lasch, Christopher. *The Culture of Narcissism: American Life in an Age of Diminishing Expectations.* New York: Norton, 1979.

Lassiter, Matthew D. *The Silent Majority: Suburban Politics in the Sunbelt South.* Princeton: Princeton University Press, 2006.

Leuchtenburg, William E. *Franklin D. Roosevelt and the New Deal, 1932–1940.* New York: Harper, 1963.

Levinson, Marc. *The Great A&P and the Struggle for Small Business in America.* New York: Hill and Wang, 2011.

Lichtenstein, Nelson. *State of the Union: A Century of American Labor.* Princeton: Princeton University Press, 2002.

Lichtenstein, Nelson, and Elizabeth Tandy Shermer, eds. *The Right and Labor in America: Politics, Ideology, and Imagination.* Philadelphia: University of Pennsylvania Press, 2012.

Lindberg, Leon N., and Charles S. Maier, eds. *The Politics of Inflation and Economic Stagnation: Theoretical Approaches and International Case Studies.* Washington, DC: Brookings Institution, 1985.

Linder, Marc. *Wars of Attrition: Vietnam, the Business Roundtable, and the Decline of the Construction Unions.* Iowa City: Fanpihua Press, 1999.

Lipset, Seymour Martin, and William Schneider. *The Confidence Gap: Business, Labor, and Government in the Public Mind.* Baltimore: Johns Hopkins University Press, 1987.

MacLean, Nancy. *Freedom Is Not Enough: The Opening of the American Workplace.* Cambridge, MA: Harvard University Press, 2006.

Marchand, Roland. *Advertising the American Dream: Making Way for Modernity, 1920–1940.* Berkeley: University of California Press, 1985.

Martin, Cathie J. *Shifting the Burden: The Struggle over Growth and Corporate Taxation.* Chicago: University of Chicago Press, 1991.

Matusow, Allen J. *Nixon's Economy: Booms, Busts, Dollars, and Votes.* Lawrence: University Press of Kansas, 1998.

———. *The Unraveling of America: A History of Liberalism in the 1960s.* New York: Harper and Row, 1984.

McCann, Michael W. *Taking Reform Seriously: Perspectives on Public Interest Liberalism.* Ithaca: Cornell University Press, 1986.

McCartin, Joseph A. *Collision Course: Ronald Reagan, the Air Traffic Controllers, and the Strike That Changed America.* Oxford: Oxford University Press, 2011.

McCraw, Thomas K. *Prophets of Regulation: Charles Francis Adams, Louis D. Brandeis, James M. Landis, Alfred E. Kahn.* Cambridge, MA: Belknap Press of Harvard University Press, 1984.

McGirr, Lisa. *Suburban Warriors: The Origins of the New American Right.* Princeton: Princeton University Press, 2001.

McQuaid, Kim. *Big Business and Presidential Power: From FDR to Reagan.* New York: Morrow, 1982.

———. *Uneasy Partners: Big Business in American Politics, 1945–1990.* Baltimore: Johns Hopkins University Press, 1994.

Miller, Karen S. *The Voice of Business: Hill & Knowlton and Postwar Public Relations.* Chapel Hill: University of North Carolina Press, 1999.

Moreton, Bethany. *To Serve God and Wal-Mart: The Making of Christian Free Enterprise.* Cambridge, MA: Harvard University Press, 2009.

Morgan, Iwan W. *The Age of Deficits: Presidents and Unbalanced Budgets from Jimmy Carter to George W. Bush.* Lawrence: University Press of Kansas, 2009.

———. *Deficit Government: Taxing and Spending in Modern America.* Chicago: Ivan R. Dee, 1995.

Nadel, Mark V. *The Politics of Consumer Protection.* Indianapolis: Bobbs-Merrill, 1971.

Nader, Ralph, Mark Green, and Joel Seligman. *Taming the Giant Corporation.* New York: W. W. Norton, 1976.

Noah, Timothy. *The Great Divergence: America's Growing Inequality Crisis and What We Can Do About It.* New York: Bloomsbury Press, 2012.

North Carolina Awards Committee. *The North Carolina Awards: 1979.* Raleigh: North Carolina Awards Committee, 1979.

O'Connor, Alice. "Bringing the Market Back In: Philanthropic Activism and Conservative Reform." In *Politics and Partnerships: The Role of Voluntary Associations in America's Political Past and Present,* ed. Elisabeth S. Clemens and Doug Guthrie, 121–50. Chicago: University of Chicago Press, 2010.

———. "Financing the Counter-Revolution." In *Rightward Bound: Making America Conservative in the 1970s,* ed. Bruce J. Schulman and Julian E. Zelizer, 148–68. Cambridge, MA: Harvard University Press, 2008.

Patashnik, Eric M. *Reforms at Risk: What Happens after Major Policy Changes Are Enacted.* Princeton: Princeton University Press, 2008.

Pempel, T. J. *Regime Shift: Comparative Dynamics of the Japanese Political Economy.* Ithaca: Cornell University Press, 1998.

Perlstein, Rick. *Nixonland: The Rise of a President and the Fracturing of America.* New York: Scribner, 2008.

Perot, H. Ross. *Save Your Job, Save Our Country: Why NAFTA Must Be Stopped—Now!* With Pat Choate. New York: Hyperion, 1993.

Pertschuk, Michael. *Revolt against Regulation: The Rise and Pause of the Consumer Movement.* Berkeley: University of California Press, 1982.

Phillips, Kevin. *The Emerging Republican Majority.* New Rochelle, NY: Arlington House, 1969.

Phillips-Fein, Kim. *Invisible Hands: The Making of the Conservative Movement from the New Deal to Reagan.* New York: W. W. Norton, 2009.

Reagan, Ronald. *The Reagan Diaries*. Ed. Douglas Brinkley. New York: Harper-Collins, 2007.

Reich, Robert B. *Supercapitalism: The Transformation of Business, Democracy, and Everyday Life*. New York: Knopf, 2007.

Reich, Robert B., and John D. Donahue. *New Deals: The Chrysler Revival and the American System*. New York: Times Books, 1985.

Reston, James. *The Lone Star: The Life of John Connally*. New York: Harper and Row, 1989.

Rodgers, Daniel T. *The Age of Fracture*. Cambridge, MA: Harvard University Press, 2011.

Romer, Thomas, and Howard Rosenthal. "Modern Political Economy and the Study of Regulation." In *Public Regulation: New Perspectives on Institutions and Policies*, ed. Elizabeth E. Bailey, 73–116. Cambridge, MA: MIT Press, 1987.

Roof, Tracy. *American Labor, Congress, and the Welfare State, 1935–2010*. Baltimore: Johns Hopkins University Press, 2011.

Rothschild, William E. *The Secret to GE's Success*. New York: McGraw-Hill, 2007.

Roubini, Nouriel, and Stephen Mihm. *Crisis Economics: A Crash Course in the Future of Finance*. New York: Penguin, 2010.

Rowen, Hobart. *The Free Enterprisers: Kennedy, Johnson, and the Business Establishment*. New York: Putnam, 1964.

Roy, Ravi K., and Arthur T. Denzau. *Fiscal Policy Convergence from Reagan to Blair: The Left Veers Right*. London: Routledge, 2004.

Sass, Steven A. *The Promise of Private Pensions: The First Hundred Years*. Cambridge, MA: Harvard University Press, 1997.

Schaede, Ulrike. *Cooperative Capitalism: Self-Regulation, Trade Associations, and the Antimonopoly Law in Japan*. Oxford: Oxford University Press, 2000.

Schlesinger, Arthur M., Jr. *The Imperial Presidency*. Boston: Houghton Mifflin, 1973.

Schlozman, Kay Lehman, and John T. Tierney. *Organized Interests and American Democracy*. New York: Harper and Row, 1986.

Schulman, Bruce J. *The Seventies: The Great Shift in American Culture, Society, and Politics*. New York: Free Press, 2001.

Shermer, Elizabeth Tandy. *Sunbelt Capitalism: Phoenix and the Transformation of American Politics*. Philadelphia: University of Pennsylvania Press, 2013.

———. "'Take Government out of Business by Putting Business into Government': Local Boosters, National CEOs, Experts, and the Politics of Mid-Century Capital Mobility." In *What's Good for Business: Business and Politics since World War II*, ed. Kim Phillips-Fein and Julian E. Zelizer, 91–106. New York: Oxford University Press, 2012.

Silk, Leonard, and David Vogel. *Ethics and Profits: The Crisis of Confidence in American Business*. New York: Simon and Schuster, 1976.

Sjoberg, Leif, ed. *American Swedish '73*. Philadelphia: American Swedish Historical Foundation, 1973.

Skeel, David. *The New Financial Deal: Understanding the Dodd-Frank Act and Its (Unintended) Consequences*. Hoboken, NJ: Wiley, 2011.

Sklar, Martin J. *The Corporate Reconstruction of American Capitalism, 1890–1916: The Market, the Law, and Politics*. Cambridge: Cambridge University Press, 1988.

Slater, Robert. *The New GE: How Jack Welch Revived an American Institution*. Homewood, IL: Business One Irwin, 1993.

Sobel, Robert. *Car Wars: The Untold Story*. New York: E. P. Dutton, 1984.

Stein, Herbert. *Presidential Economics: The Making of Economic Policy from Roosevelt to Reagan and Beyond*. New York: Simon and Schuster, 1984.

Stein, Judith. *Pivotal Decade: How the United States Traded Factories for Finance in the Seventies*. New Haven: Yale University Press, 2010.

———. *Running Steel, Running America: Race, Economic Policy, and the Decline of Liberalism*. Chapel Hill: University of North Carolina Press, 1998.

Steuerle, C. Eugene. *Contemporary U.S. Tax Policy*. Washington, DC: Urban Institute Press, 2004.

———. *The Tax Decade: How Taxes Came to Dominate the Public Agenda*. Washington, DC: Urban Institute Press, 1992.

Stockman, David A. *The Triumph of Politics: How the Reagan Revolution Failed*. New York: Harper and Row, 1986.

Teles, Steven M. *The Rise of the Conservative Legal Movement: The Battle for Control of the Law*. Princeton: Princeton University Press, 2008.

Thayer, George. *Who Shakes the Money Tree? American Campaign Financing Practices from 1789 to the Present*. New York: Simon and Schuster, 1973.

Tobbell, Dominique A. *Pills, Power, and Policy: The Struggle for Drug Reform in Cold War America and Its Consequences*. Berkeley: University of California Press, 2012.

Troy, Gil. *Morning in America: How Ronald Reagan Invented the 1980s*. Princeton: Princeton University Press, 2005.

Tucker, Todd, and Lori Wallach. *The Rise and Fall of Fast Track Trade Authority*. Washington, DC: Public Citizen, 2009.

Useem, Michael. *The Inner Circle: Large Corporations and the Rise of Business Political Activity in the U.S. and U.K.* New York: Oxford University Press, 1984.

Venema, Maynard P. *The Unique Corporate Life of Universal Oil Products Company*. New York: Newcomen Society in North America, 1961.

Vietor, Richard H. K. *Energy Policy in America since 1945: A Study of Business-Government Relations*. Cambridge: Cambridge University Press.

Vogel, David. "A Case Study of Clean Air Legislation, 1967–1981." In *The Impact of the Modern Corporation: Size and Impacts*, ed. Betty Bock et al., 309–86. New York: Columbia University Press, 1984.

———. *Fluctuating Fortunes: The Political Power of Business in America*. New York: Basic Books, 1989.

———. *The Politics of Precaution: Regulating Health, Safety, and Environmental Risks in Europe and the United States*. Princeton: Princeton University Press, 2012.

Vogel, Steven K. *Freer Markets, More Rules: Regulatory Reform in Advanced Industrial Countries*. Ithaca: Cornell University Press, 1996.

Wall, Wendy L. *Inventing the "American Way": The Politics of Consensus from the New Deal to the Civil Rights Movement*. Oxford: Oxford University Press, 2008.

Walsh, Michael P. "Automobile Emissions." In *The Reality of Precaution: Comparing Risk Regulation in the United States and Europe*, ed. Jonathan Wiener et al., 142–58. Washington, DC: RFF Press, 2011.

Wanniski, Jude. *The Way the World Works: How Economies Fail . . . and Succeed*. New York: Basic Books, 1978.

Wells, Wyatt C. *Economist in an Uncertain World: Arthur F. Burns and the Federal Reserve, 1970–78*. New York: Columbia University Press, 1994.

Whyte, William H. *Is Anybody Listening?: How and Why U.S. Business Fumbles When It Talks to Human Beings*. New York: Simon and Schuster, 1952.

Wiener, Jonathan, et al., eds. *The Reality of Precaution: Comparing Risk Regulation in the United States and Europe*. Washington, DC: RFF Press, 2011.

Wilentz, Sean. *The Age of Reagan: A History, 1974–2008*. New York: Harper Collins, 2008.

Wilson, Mark. "The Advantages of Obscurity: World War II Tax Carryback Provisions and the Normalization of Corporate Welfare." In *What's Good for Business: Business and Politics since World War II*, ed. Kim Phillips-Fein and Julian E. Zelizer, 16–44. Oxford: Oxford University Press, 2012.

Wong, Anny. *The Roots of Japan's International Environmental Policies*. New York: Garland, 2001.

Woodward, Bob. *The Agenda: Inside the Clinton White House*. New York: Simon and Schuster, 1984.

Zelizer, Julian E. *On Capitol Hill: The Struggle to Reform Congress and Its Consequences, 1948–2000*. Cambridge: Cambridge University Press, 2004.

———. *Jimmy Carter*. New York: Times Books, 2010.

Journal Articles

Adams, Walter, and James W. Brock. "Corporate Size and the Bailout Factor." *Journal of Economic Issues* 21:1 (March 1987): 61–85.

Akard, Patrick J. "Corporate Mobilization and Political Power: The Transformation of U.S. Economic Policy in 1970s." *American Sociological Review* 57:5 (October 1992): 597–615.

Anastakis, Dimitry. "The Last Automotive Entrepreneur? Lee Iacocca Saves Chrysler, 1978–1986." *Business and Economic History On-Line* (Business History Conference) 5 (2007).

Anderson, James E. "The Struggle to Reform Regulatory Procedures, 1978–1998." *Policy Studies Journal* 26:3 (September 1998): 482–98.

Ansolabehere, Stephen, John M. de Figueiredo, and James M. Snyder Jr. "Why Is There So Little Money in U.S. Politics?" *Journal of American Economic Perspectives* 17:1 (Winter 2003): 105–30.

Ansolabehere, Stephen, James M. Snyder, and Micky Tipathi. "Are PAC Contributions and Lobbying Linked? New Evidence from the 1995 Lobby Disclosure Act." *Business and Politics* 4:2 (August 2002): 131–55.

Bakir, Erdogan, and Al Campbell. "Neoliberalism, the Rate of Profit, and the Rate of Accumulation." *Science and Society* 74:3 (July 2010): 323–42.

Balleisen, Edward J. "Private Cops on the Fraud Beat: The Limits of American Business Self-Regulation, 1895–1932." *Business History Review* 83:1 (Spring 2009): 113–60.

Berman, Elizabeth Popp, and Nicholas Pagnucco. "Economic Ideas and the Political Process: Debating Tax Cuts in the U.S. House of Representatives, 1962–1981." *Politics and Society* 38:3 (September 2010): 347–72.

Blinder, Alan, and William J. Newton. "The 1971–1974 Controls Program and the Price Level: An Econometric Post-Mortem." *Journal of Monetary Economics* 8:1 (1981): 1–23.

Burch, Philip. "The NAM as an Interest Group." *Politics and Society* 4:1 (September 1973): 97–130.

Coase, Ronald H. "The Federal Communications Commission." *Journal of Law & Economics* 2 (October 1959): 1–40.

Collins, Robert. "The Economic Crisis of 1968 and the Waning of the 'American Century.' " *American Historical Review* 101:2 (April 1996): 396–422.

Cowie, Jefferson. "Nixon's Class Struggle: Romancing the New-Right Worker, 1969–1973." *Labor History* 43:3 (Summer 2002): 257–83.

———. "Notes and Documents: 'A One-Sided Class War': Rethinking Doug Fraser's 1978 Resignation from the Labor-Management Group." *Labor History* 44:3 (August 2003): 307–14.

Davis, Gerald. "The Twilight of the Berle and Means Corporation." *Seattle University Law Review* 34 (2011): 1121–38.

de Figueiredo, John M. "Lobbying and Information in Politics." *Business and Politics* 4:2 (2002): 125–29.

Dwyer, Gerald P., Jr. "Federal Deficits, Interest Rates and Monetary Policy." *Journal of Money, Credit and Banking* 17:4 (November 1985): 655–81.

Elliott, E. Donald, et al. "Toward a Theory of Statutory Evolution: The Federalization of Environmental Law." *Journal of Law, Economics, and Organization* 1:2 (1985): 313–40.

Evans, Paul. "Do Large Deficits Produce High Interest Rates?" *American Economic Review* 75:1 (March 1985): 68–87.

Fletcher, W. Miles. "Dreams of Economic Transformation and the Reality of Economic Crisis in Japan: Keidanren in the Era of the 'Bubble' and the Onset of the 'Lost Decade,' from the Mid-1980s to the Mid-1990s." *Asia Pacific Business Review* 18:2 (April 2012): 149–65.

Ford, Gary T. "State Characteristics Affecting the Passage of Consumer Legislation." *Journal of Consumer Affairs* 11:1 (Summer 1977): 177–82.

Friedman, Tami. "Exploiting the North-South Differential: Corporate Power, Southern Politics, and the Decline of Organized Labor after World War II." *Journal of American History* 95:2 (September 2008): 323–48.

Gable, Richard W. "Birth of an Employers' Association." *Business History Review* 33:4 (Winter 1959): 535–45.

———. "NAM: Influential Lobby or Kiss of Death?" *Journal of Politics* 15:2 (May 1953): 254–73.

Gitelman, H. M. "Management's Crisis of Confidence and the Origin of the National Industrial Conference Board, 1914–1916." *Business History Review* 58:2 (Summer 1984): 153–77.

Goldin, Claudia, and Robert Margo. "The Great Compression: The Wage Structure in the United States at Mid-Century." *Quarterly Journal of Economics* 107:1 (February 1992): 1–34.

Hacker, Jacob S. "The Road to Somewhere: Why Health Reform Happened, or Why Political Scientists Who Write about Public Policy Shouldn't Assume They Know How to Shape It." *Perspectives on Politics* 8:3 (September 2010): 861–76.

Hanchett, Thomas. "U.S. Tax Policy and the Shopping-Center Boom of the 1950s and 1960s." *American Historical Review* 101:4 (October 1996): 1082–1110.

Harper, John D. "Private Enterprise's Public Responsibility." *Public Relations Journal* (August 1967): 8–10.

Huntington, Samuel. "The Marasmus of the ICC: The Commission, the Railroads, and the Public Interest." *Yale Law Journal* 61 (April 1952): 467–509.

Lovett, William A. "State Deceptive Trade Practice Legislation." *Tulane Law Review* 46 (1971–72): 724–60.

Martin, Cathie J. "Business and the New Economic Activism: The Growth of Corporate Lobbies in the Sixties." *Polity* 27:1 (Autumn 1994): 49–76.

———. "Sectional Parties, Divided Business." *Studies in American Political Development* 20:2 (October 2006): 160–84.

McCann, Michael. "Public Interest Liberalism and the Modern Regulatory State." *Polity* 21:2 (Winter 1988): 373–400.

McCartin, Joseph. "'Fire the Hell out of Them': Sanitation Workers' Struggles and the Normalization of the Striker Replacement Strategy in the 1970s." *Labor: Studies in Working-Class History of the Americas* 2:3 (2005): 67–92.

Meier, Kenneth. "The Political Economy of Consumer Protection: An Examination of State Legislation." *Western Political Quarterly* 40:2 (June 1987): 343–59.

Mettler, Suzanne. "Reconstituting the Submerged State: The Challenges of Social Policy Reform in the Obama Era." *Perspectives on Politics* 8:3 (September 2010): 803–24.

Moss, David A., and Michael R. Fein. "Radio Regulation Revisited: Coase, the FCC, and the Public Interest." *Journal of Policy History* 15:4 (2003): 389–416.

Oster, Sharon. "An Analysis of Some Causes of Interstate Differences in Consumer Regulations." *Economic Inquiry* 18:1 (January 1980): 39–54.

Pashigian, Peter. "Environmental Regulation: Whose Self-Interests Are Being Protected?" *Economic Inquiry* 23:4 (October 1985): 551–84.

Phillips-Fein, Kim. "Conservatism: A Round Table." *Journal of American History* 98:3 (December 2011): 723–73.

Schwartz, George. "The Successful Fight against a Federal Consumer Protection Agency." *MSU Business Topics* 27:3 (Summer 1979): 45–57.

Soffer, Jonathan. "The National Association of Manufacturers and the Militarization of American Conservatism." *Business History Review* 75:4 (Winter 2001): 775–805.

Tedlow, Richard. "From Competitor to Consumer: The Changing Focus of Federal Regulation of Advertising, 1914–1938." *Business History Review* 55:1 (March 1981): 35–58.

———. "The National Association of Manufacturers and Public Relations during the New Deal." *Business History Review* 50:1 (Spring 1976): 25–45.

Thomas, Clive S. "Interest Group Regulation across the United States: Rationale, Development and Consequences." *Parliamentary Affairs* 51:4 (1998): 500–515.

Tozzi, Jim. "OIRA's Formative Years: The Historical Record of Centralized Regulatory Review Preceding OIRA's Founding." *Administrative Law Review* 63 (Special Edition 2011): 37–69.

Vogel, David. "The Public-Interest Movement and the American Reform Tradition." *Political Science Quarterly* 95:4 (Winter 1980–81): 607–27.

Warren, Alvin C., Jr., and Alan J. Auerbach. "Transferability of Tax Incentives and the Fiction of Safe Harbor Leasing." *Harvard Law Review* 95:8 (June 1982): 1752–86.

Warren, Elizabeth. "Unsafe at Any Rate." *Democracy: A Journal of Ideas* 5 (Summer 2007): 8–19.

Werking, Richard Hume. "Bureaucrats, Businessmen, and Foreign Trade: The Origins of the United States Chamber of Commerce." *Business History Review* 52:3 (Autumn 1978): 321–41.

Yoffie, David B., and Sigrid Bergenstein. "Creating Political Advantage: The Rise of the Corporate Political Entrepreneur." *California Management Review* 28:1 (Fall 1985): 124–39.

Zelizer, Julian E. "Reflections: Rethinking the History of American Conservatism." *Reviews in American History* 38:2 (June 2012): 367–92.

DISSERTATIONS

Akard, Patrick J. "The Return of the Market: Corporate Mobilization and the Transformation of U.S. Economic Policy, 1974–1984." Ph.D. diss., University of Kansas, 1989.

Asner, Glenn. "The Cold War and American Industrial Research." Ph.D. diss., Carnegie Mellon University, 2006.

Oliveiro, Vernie. "The United States, Multinational Corporations, and the Politics of Globalization in the 1970s." Ph.D. diss., Harvard University, 2010.

WEB

The American Presidency Project. John Woolley and Gerhard Peters. www.presidency.ucsb.edu.

iPOLL Databank. The Roper Center for Public Opinion Research, University of Connecticut. http://www.ropercenter.uconn.edu/data_access/ipoll/ipoll.html.

MeasuringWorth. Lawrence H. Officer and Samuel H. Williamson. www.measuring worth.com.

Index

Page numbers in *italics* indicate figures.

POLITICS AND SOCIETY IN TWENTIETH-CENTURY AMERICA

SERIES EDITORS

William Chafe, Gary Gerstle, Linda Gordon, and Julian Zelizer